Planning Democracy

The Indian planning project was one of the postcolonial world's most ambitious experiments. *Planning Democracy* explores how India fused Soviet-inspired economic management and Western-style liberal democracy at a time when they were widely considered fundamentally contradictory. After nearly two centuries of colonial rule, planning was meant to be independent India's route to prosperity. In this engaging and innovative account, Nikhil Menon traces how planning built India's knowledge infrastructure and data capacities, while also shaping the nature of its democracy. He analyses the challenges inherent in harmonizing technocratic methods with democratic mandates and shows how planning was the language through which the government's aspirations for democratic state-building were expressed. Situating India within international debates about economic policy and Cold War ideology, Menon reveals how India walked a tightrope between capitalism and communism which heightened the drama of its development on the global stage.

Nikhil Menon is Assistant Professor of History at the University of Notre Dame.

D1521934

AWARDED THE

Joseph W. Elder Prize
in the Indian Social Sciences
by the American Institute of Indian Studies
and published with their generous support

Planning Democracy

Modern India's Quest for Development

Nikhil Menon

University of Notre Dame

CAMBRIDGE
UNIVERSITY PRESS

CAMBRIDGE
UNIVERSITY PRESS

University Printing House, Cambridge CB2 8BS, United Kingdom

One Liberty Plaza, 20th Floor, New York, NY 10006, USA

477 Williamstown Road, Port Melbourne, VIC 3207, Australia

314–321, 3rd Floor, Plot 3, Splendor Forum, Jasola District Centre,
New Delhi – 110025, India

103 Penang Road, #05–06/07, Visioncrest Commercial, Singapore 238467

Cambridge University Press is part of the University of Cambridge.

It furthers the University's mission by disseminating knowledge in the pursuit of
education, learning, and research at the highest international levels of excellence.

www.cambridge.org
Information on this title: www.cambridge.org/9781316517338
DOI: 10.1017/9781009043892

© Nikhil Menon 2022

First published 2022

A catalogue record for this publication is available from the British Library.

Library of Congress Cataloging-in-Publication Data
Names: Menon, Nikhil, author.
Title: Planning democracy : modern India's quest for development / Nikhil
Menon, University of Notre Dame, Indiana.
Description: First Edition. | New York : Cambridge University Press, 2022. |
Includes bibliographical references and index.
Identifiers: LCCN 2021039316 (print) | LCCN 2021039317 (ebook) | ISBN
9781316517338 (Hardback) | ISBN 9781009043892 (eBook)
Subjects: LCSH: Political planning – India. | Democratization – India. | BISAC:
HISTORY / Asia / India & South Asia
Classification: LCC JQ229.P64 M46 2022 (print) | LCC JQ229.P64 (ebook) |
DDC 320.60954–dc23/eng/20211202
LC record available at https://lccn.loc.gov/2021039316
LC ebook record available at https://lccn.loc.gov/2021039317

ISBN 978-1-316-51733-8 Hardback
ISBN 978-1-009-04458-5 Paperback

For Amma, Achan, and Nitya

Contents

Figures

Acknowledgements

This book owes more to others than the conventions of sole authorship convey.

My first brush with terms like 'the Indian economy' and 'Planning Commission' was in books at The School – Krishnamurti Foundation India (KFI), Chennai. In the shade and amid the blooms of that beautiful campus, I had a wonderful education. Of the many *Akkas* and *Annas*, I am especially grateful to my history teachers, Akhila Seshadri, Jayashree Nambiar, V. Geetha, and M. V. Kumar.

The seven years I spent studying in Delhi, beginning as a teenager, were a revelation. I was the beneficiary of a string of inspiring teachers and formidable scholars, including Mukul Mangalik, Hari Sen, Pankaj Jha, Shahid Amin, Dilip Menon, Prabhu Mohapatra, and Sunil Kumar at Delhi University, and Janaki Nair, Neeladri Bhattacharya, Tanika Sarkar, Radhika Singha, and M. S. S. Pandian at Jawaharlal Nehru University. They modelled committed teaching and rigorous scholarship, demonstrating what it can and should do for our public sphere.

This research owes most to the place where it sprouted. Princeton, quaint and picturesque, was exciting because of its contrast to what I knew. Working there was a feast that I partook of immoderately. Gyan Prakash's interest in, and scholarship on, postcolonial India was part of the inspiration for this project. He channelled unformed ideas into research, offering insight and steadfast support. His acuity helped clear intellectual hurdles, and his levity eased what might otherwise have felt like a slog: I owe much to his generosity. Bhavani Raman's brilliance shone a light on insights that were not apparent to me. Despite my inability to keep pace, she always led me to draw from a deeper well. Jeremy Adelman pushed me to ask broader questions, geographically and analytically. While this work may fall short of the scale he envisioned, he supported it throughout and contributed to widening its scope. I requested Michael Gordin to formally join my committee when I realized that the insights he casually dispensed at seminars were too good to be left to chance. Partha Chatterjee – whose writings on this book's progress and provided reassurance through setbacks. Nitya offered both diversion from the writing and enthusiasm for it, all while keeping up our childhood banter. I dedicate this to them.

Katlyn Marie Carter has endured this book from its inception several years ago when we were in graduate school. She inspires me as a researcher and teacher, wearing her brilliance lightly and without pretension. She has been a co-conspirator, critic, and editor – my partner in rowing this boat. Every page bears her mark. As we wrote our books alongside one another, we have moved cities, got married, began our careers, and had a child. This book, as with so much in my life, would not exist if it were not for her. Our daughter Anjali came into our life recently but has transformed it thoroughly. She is an indescribable joy who puts all else, including this book, in perspective.

Endeavours like this would not have been possible without libraries, archives, and the essential but unheralded work of their staff. I am deeply thankful to librarians and archivists spread across three continents – Firestone Library, Prasanta Chandra Mahalanobis Memorial Museum and Library, Nehru Memorial Museum and Library, National Archives of India, Central Secretariat Library, Yojana Bhavan Library, Films Division of India, Rockefeller Archive Center, The British Library, The Hindu Archives, The Cambridge South Asian Archive, and Hesburgh Library. Yamuna Shankar graciously allowed me to use cartoons by her father K. Shankara Pillai. The former director of the Indian Statistical Institute (Kolkata), Bimal Roy, facilitated my research in Baranagore and accommodated me in a campus dorm. Sanghamitra Bandyopadhyay and Kishor Satpathy granted me permission to use images from the Prasanta Chandra Mahalanobis Memorial Museum and Library.

This research has been the beneficiary of generous funding from Princeton University's Graduate School, the Department of History, the Fellowship of Woodrow Wilson Scholars, and the Princeton Institute for International and Regional Studies. It has also been supported by the History Project at Cambridge University, the Rockefeller Archive Center, the Mellon Foundation, the American Council of Learned Societies, the University of Notre Dame's Department of History, and the Kellogg Institute for International Studies. The book's publication was made possible in part by support from the Institute for Scholarship in the Liberal Arts, College of Arts and Letters, University of Notre Dame, and also from the American Institute for Indian Studies.

At Cambridge University Press, the superb Lucy Rhymer saw potential in my research and has been a wonderful steward throughout. Rachel Blaifeder took the reins briefly and ably nudged the book along. The Press' anonymous readers offered very helpful feedback that sharpened my arguments and pointed me to oversights. Emily McKnight, an independent copy editor, helped scrub the manuscript of infelicities before submission to the Press.

It is a sadness that my grandparents are not alive for me to present this. They would undoubtedly have welcomed it with pride, regardless of merit, as they did for every ordinary step throughout childhood. Their appreciation for learning – captured in the clickety-clack of my grandfather's noisy typewriter – has stayed with me. I owe my parents, Bina Shivram and K. Shivram, and my sister Nitya Menon, more than I can express. They have watched this book take form and accepted it as background noise in our relationship. Amma, an inspiring educator, insisted her children aspire to qualities of mind rather than shallow credentials. Achan affectionately indulged me with interest in the director of the Nehru Memorial Museum and Library, he facilitated my applications for access to the Jawaharlal Nehru papers.

During spells of research in New Delhi, Sowmiya Ashok was a friend and flatmate, enduring frequent and undoubtedly boring updates from the archive with cheeriness and enthusiasm. Our meandering conversations were welcome and necessary. Vishwajoy Mukherjee also hosted me and was subjected to similar punishment for his kindness. He toggled between interest in my project and incredulity that anyone would be fooled into thinking me a scholar. My brilliant and gentle friend, Harsh Malhotra, passed away while I was working on this. A budding economist, I am sure he would have improved my book and even said kind things about it – the latter only because he was unfailingly kind. My time in the city was enlivened by the company of friends, including Maanav Kumar, Tara Narula, Pradyumna Jairam, and Garima Sahai. New Delhi would not feel like a home away from home if it were not for Indira Chandrasekhar and C. P. Chandrasekhar, my Veliamma and Mama. Their house has been a refuge since I first moved to the city. I am deeply thankful for their years of care and intellectual inspiration.

I am very fortunate to be working with such supportive colleagues in the Department of History at the University of Notre Dame. As department chairs, Patrick Griffin, Jon Coleman, and Elisabeth Koll have been helpful and encouraging, as have Alexander Martin and Darren Dochuk in their role as mentors. I have also had the benefit of advice and advocacy from Gail Bederman, Karen Graubart, Jaime Pensado, Brad Gregory, Robert Sullivan, Julia Thomas, John McGreevy, Thomas Tweed, John Deak, Richard Pierce, and Mariana Candido. Ted Beatty has been a sounding board and helpful commenter on this book, taking the time to read two drafts. The department helped put together a manuscript workshop, which enabled me to invite David C. Engerman and Neeti Nair to offer critical feedback. I am grateful to them for agreeing to do so, for their close reading, and for their excellent suggestions. The book is considerably better for it.

Life in the shadow of the university's golden dome or in South Bend would not be the same without the camaraderie of friends like Paul Ocobock, Sarah Shortall, Emily Remus, Rebecca McKenna, Abi Ocobock, James Lundberg, Katie Jarvis, Randy Goldstein, Ian Johnson, Korey Garibaldi, Francisco Robles, Pedro Aguilera-Mellado, and Kate Uitti. Joshua Specht went far beyond the call of friendly duty to read the manuscript and other bits and pieces to offer comments. My colleagues in the nascent South Asia Group – Julia Kowalski, Susan Osterman, and Amitava Dutt – have been forceful allies in our quest to broaden the study of India and South Asia on campus.

subject (as with several others) have been so generative – kindly agreed to read my work and offer his thoughts.

Being embedded in a community of scholars studying South Asia at Princeton was a pleasure. Rohit Lamba was a sunny bridge between university life in North Campus and New Jersey and a welcome source of joviality and conversations on Indian politics. Rohit De and Radha Kumar are friends who helped navigate the path to the PhD and beyond. Sharing a professional interest in independent India, Rohit De has been remarkably helpful – exchanging ideas and commenting on the entire manuscript, whilst also sharing laughs. Aside from enjoying their companionship, I also learned so much from discussions with Rahul Sagar, Rotem Geva, Ninad Pandit, Nabaparna Ghosh, Christina Welsch, Anthony Acciavatti, Ritwik Bhattacharya, Vinay Sitapati, Dinsha Mistree, Rohan Mukherjee, Joppan George, Devika Shankar, Kalyani Ramnath, Sarah Carson, Amna Qayyum, Shoumitro Chaterrjee, Saumyashree Ghosh, Niharika Yadav, and Manav Kapur.

I would not have made it through graduate school without Patrick De Oliveira, Sean Vanatta, Olivier Burtin, Morgan Robinson, Dan Barish, and Fidel Tavarez – all of whom have been wonderful friends and academic allies, reading and commenting on drafts of several chapters. I was lucky to earn the friendship of Saarah Jappie, Christian Flow, Richard Anderson, Joel Suarez, Matthew Chan, Diana Andrade, Meg Leja, and Alex Chase-Levenson. Outside department and discipline, I counted on the company of Sudhir Raskutti, Clementine van Effenterre, Sara Vanatta, Elise Wang, Jasmin Mujanovic, and Veronica Valentin.

Since our undergraduate years, Devika Shankar, Meghna Chaudhuri, and Shatam Ray have been friends and fellow travellers, alongside whom I learned to be a historian. Abhijeet Singh, Vinayak Uppal, and Vimal Balasubramaniam all read my manuscript entirely out of friendship, providing astute advice and ensuring the book did not fall afoul of elementary economics. Vimsa has been the dearest friend, a reliable source of wisdom, intellectual provocation, and mirth since we were very young. Conversation and correspondence with Benjamin Siegel, Aditya Balasubramanian, Mircea Raianu, Eleanor Newbigin, Jahnavi Phalkey, Arunabh Ghosh, and Taylor C. Sherman have improved my work considerably: their scholarship has enriched mine. Ramachandra Guha, C. P. Chandrasekhar, and Srinath Raghavan were all generous in responding to my requests for lessons on finer aspects of the Nehru years, Plan models, and democratic planning. Montek Singh Ahluwalia spared time to discuss his memories of Mahalanobis and the Planning Commission. Mahesh Rangarajan was enormously helpful when, as

Introduction

The recently elected prime minister of India addressed the nation from the sandstone ramparts of the Red Fort in Delhi, his turban's long trail flapping in a dry dusty summer breeze. It was Independence Day 2014, and Narendra Modi's debut on this storied stage. With the Mughal fort's soaring minarets as a backdrop, Jama Masjid's giant white marble dome looming to his left, and the Indian flag fluttering overhead, he put to rest months of rumour. The leader of the Bharatiya Janata Party (BJP) confirmed what the public had suspected. The end was near for India's long experiment with economic planning. The curtain was coming down on the Planning Commission, an institution that had once been the beating heart of the country's economy.

Born the same year, Modi and the Planning Commission shared another milestone together. In his first Independence Day address as India's leader, Modi declared that the Planning Commission had once merited its place and made significant contributions. Now, however, he believed it had decayed beyond repair. 'Sometimes it costs a lot to repair an old house', he said, 'but it gives us no satisfaction'. Afterwards, we realize 'that we might as well build a new house', Modi explained with a smile.[1] *He* would build it by bulldozing a decrepit structure and raising a shiny new one, the NITI Aayog (National Institution for Transforming India).

Sixty-four years earlier, days after the inauguration of the Republic, President Rajendra Prasad delivered a speech in Parliament. The thickly moustached veteran of the Congress Party declared on 31 January 1950 that the primary objective of his government would be to raise standards of living. In order to do so, he announced, 'It is my Government's intention to establish a Planning Commission so that the best use can be made of such resources as we possess for the development of the nation.'[2] The Planning Commission was born.

The Indian planning project was one of the postcolonial world's most ambitious experiments. It was an arranged marriage between Soviet-inspired economic planning and Western-style liberal democracy, at

1

a time when the Cold War portrayed them as ideologically contradictory and institutionally incompatible. With each Five-Year Plan, the Planning Commission set the course for the nation's economy. The ambit ranged from matters broad (free trade or protectionism?) to narrow (how much fish should fisheries produce to ensure protein in the national diet?). The commission's pronouncements set the gears of government in motion. Shaping entire sectors of the economy through incentives, disincentives, and decree, the Planning Commission's views rippled across the land to every farm and factory. Despite this awesome power, economic planning in India was considerably different from the kind experienced in communist regimes. The Planning Commission was reined in by democratic procedure that necessitated consultation with ministries in an elected government, with people's representatives in Parliament, and ultimately with the popular will, through citizens voting every five years.

During the formative decades of the republic, planning was an idea that governed the nation. It was the vehicle chosen for rapid economic transformation after nearly two centuries of colonial rule, and it also became the language through which the government's aspirations for democratic state-building were expressed. It was a staple of national conversation. Five-Year Plans marked the calendar of governance. Politicians seldom tired of invoking the Plans, the media dutifully reported on their progress, they were debated in civil society, and ordinary citizens found themselves called to work ever more energetically towards the Plan's success.

As India emerged from generations of colonial rule in 1947, it faced the following questions: Would life be any better for three hundred and fifty million Indians? And how would independent India define itself? Dr Bhimrao Ambedkar – arch critic of caste and architect of the constitution – articulated the fear that was on the minds of many. In his last speech to the Constituent Assembly in late 1949, Ambedkar warned that India was about to enter a 'life of contradictions'. 'In politics we will have equality', he said, 'and in social and economic life we will have inequality'. These conflicts demanded attention: fail to do so, and those denied 'will blow up the structure of political democracy'.[3] The Indian government seemingly agreed, at least about the economy. The First Five-Year Plan noted that the international context made 'planning not only compatible with democracy, but essential for its very survival'.[4]

The Indian drama had the world watching. Files from the British Foreign Office and the American State Department revealed that they, too, shared Ambedkar's fear. The fledgling nation was widely believed to be doomed. The extraordinary challenges posed by India's diversity and poverty appeared insurmountable. The ugly orgy of ethnic violence and sectarian nationalism that erupted during Partition seemed a dark omen. Predictions ranged from India splintering into smaller nations, to believing it was on the brink of going 'Red' under the malevolent influence of Mao's China or Stalin's Soviet Union, to speculation that it was ripe for authoritarian takeover. Seen from Washington, D.C., and the capitals of Western Europe, the peril was not just to democracy in India but to the success of democracy globally. If breathless columns in the *New York Times* were to be believed, the fate of democracy in Asia hung in the balance. India was a 'Bastion Against Communism' and the 'Best Hope of Democracy in the Far East'. Mao's China and Nehru's India were locked in a battle of 'Communist Dictatorship versus Democratic Freedom'.[5] From Chicago, reflecting on his visit to India, Martin Luther King Jr wrote that it would be a 'boon to democracy if one of the great nations of the world' could provide for its people 'without surrendering to a dictatorship of either the "right" or "left"'.[6] In New Delhi, the influential director of the Ford Foundation in India, Douglas Ensminger, noted in a confidential staff document: 'the world has anxiously watched India's experiences in planning and executing its plans through democratic means'.[7] Writing for *The Observer* in Britain, Thomas Balogh – an Oxford economist who later entered the House of Lords and became a Baron – described 'India's Experiment' in stark terms. His prediction was that it 'may become crucial for the future of the free world'. The Indian government was trying to modernize a vast, materially backward country through consent – to achieve democratically that which had 'hitherto been undertaken, on a comparable scale, only by Communist dictatorships'.[8] Confronting similar afflictions, the eyes of decolonizing Asia and Africa anxiously tracked India's moves.

By planning through what they deemed as democratic means, the inaugural Indian government was trying to bridge the stark and historic misalignment between its political and economic realms. Planning was meant to resolve what Ambedkar had called a 'life of contradictions' by providing Indians parity in their political and economic freedoms and capabilities. Jawaharlal Nehru – anticolonial leader and independent India's inaugural prime minister – recognized the tension between the two but believed they could be eased through planning. 'Planning, though inevitably bringing about a great deal of control and coordination and interfering in some measure with individual freedom, would, as a matter of fact, in the context of India today, lead to a vast increase of freedom'.[9] Nehru was implicitly suggesting that the existence of civil liberties on paper would matter little if citizens lacked the material capabilities to enjoy them.[10] The stakes could not be higher. As Ambedkar warned, and the international press recognized, failure to act could put liberal democracy itself in peril.

This book uses planning as a lens through which to understand the Indian state and the nature of Indian democracy after independence. It interprets planning as a mode of nation-building, state formation, and legitimation in the aftermath of empire. The history of planning, here, is a history of the state – its capacities and posture towards citizens. What follows is a history of the Nehruvian state told through the prism of planning, rather than an economic history of planning or an account of the Five-Year Plans per se.

The first half argues that planning triggered the development of knowledge infrastructures that dramatically expanded the state's footprint, particularly its ability to discern and govern the economy. This new knowledge infrastructure – an elaborate national statistical system and pioneering computer programme – made the economy more legible to the state and has ever since been central to the country's development ambitions. The legacy of this process endures in institutions like the Central Statistical Organization (CSO) and National Sample Survey (NSS), which remain essential to policymaking to this day. It was this context, of a planning-induced explosion in the state's quantitative capacities, that pried open the space for a statistician like P. C. Mahalanobis to sway economic policy. More broadly, this section offers insights into how centralized planning contributed to the technocratic and high-modernist features of the Indian state.[11] Scholars have observed how the colonial origin of India's constitution helps to explain the extraordinary powers the state wields.[12] The choice of economic system – central planning – dovetailed with that legal concentration of might, contributing to a centralized state that ultimately placed expertise ahead of deliberative processes.

While the first part of the book analyses how the drive for data accelerated a drift towards technocracy, the latter reveals the contortions necessary to square that with democracy. Interrogating the government's claim of 'democratic planning', I explore the lengths to which the state went to make the public 'Plan-conscious' and highlight the failings and paradox of these efforts. Democratic planning was meant to be different from communist planning; persuasion and informed consent were its mantras. Significantly, on a practical level, the government was aware that enthusiastic popular participation in the Plans would be necessary for them to succeed. The Indian state simply lacked the ability to fulfil them otherwise. India's democratic planning was an ideology that claimed to nurture Plan-conscious citizens and produce a new kind of state that would walk the tightrope between capitalism and communism during the Cold War. It was the domestic equivalent of what came to be a non-aligned foreign policy. In this democratic avatar, planning functioned as a grand narrative for the nation – diagnosing the country's ills, charting the course to development, and inviting civic partnership. It was a political vision in which the tension between technocratic decision-making and representative democracy could, in theory, be harmonized. Travelling troupes of musical performers, documentary films, college planning forums, and even enigmatic organizations like the Bharat Sadhu Samaj (Indian Society of Ascetics), all promoted planning. These chapters underline how democratic planning was simultaneously a project that many officials believed in, a realist response to weak state capacity, and a language of state legitimation that deployed the rhetoric of democracy despite being almost entirely top-down.

This book is an exploration of how the story of planning became so central to the story of independent India. It does not pass judgment on the economic effectiveness of the Five-Year Plans or seek to explain monumental oversights in spheres such as public health and primary education. Instead, it analyses planning as a technology of governance and means of legitimation. Indian planning was an historic experiment that sought to fuse democracy and centralized economic planning precisely when the rhetoric of the Cold War pitted them as fundamentally antithetical to each other. It is a history of Third World development in an ex-colony, charting how an underdeveloped nation navigated the global Cold War while unaligned with either superpower bloc. More specifically, it demonstrates how planning was made technically feasible and politically viable in a poor, populous, and overwhelmingly illiterate country. These were questions relevant not only to India but to an entire cohort of nations in the Global South during the mid-twentieth century.

***

Development was long fundamental to arguments for why India needed to be free. An economic critique of colonialism was foundational for the Indian National Congress, dating back to early salvos launched by Dadabhai Naoroji, Mahadev Ranade, Gopal Krishna Gokhale, and Romesh Dutt in the late nineteenth and early twentieth centuries. Belief in the empire's material exploitation and wilful mismanagement of the Indian economy were mainstays of nationalist rhetoric.[13] By the 1940s, this had become the primary argument against the British. The nationalists' call for independence was not solely based on the claim that Indians – rather than white Britons – should take the reins of state. Colonial rule was illegitimate because it was exploitative.[14] Self-government was thus justified not simply on the political grounds of self-representation but also because it was the necessary condition for economic advancement.

In the decades leading up to independence, planning emerged as the language through which Indian aspirations were expressed. Japan's economic acceleration after the Meiji Restoration of 1868 turned heads, offering a glimpse of what a modernizing central authority could accomplish. News of rapid industrial advances in the Soviet Union through its first Five-Year Plan (1928–1932) inspired many in India to nurture similar hopes. President Franklin Roosevelt's New Deal policies of coordinated government spending and regulation, drastically expanding the state's economic reach in 1930s America, struck Indian observers as proof that planning was necessary even in capitalist economies. Contemporary free-market economist Lionel Robbins observed, presumably with dismay, that planning had become 'the grand panacea of our age'.[15] The onward march of planning during the interwar period led to an inflated belief in the capacities of governments, producing what one scholar calls 'an intoxicating, and even delusional, sense of "doability"'.[16] To many in India's nationalist mainstream, especially the charismatic leaders of a younger generation like Subhas Chandra Bose and Nehru, the lesson drawn from communist Russia and New Deal America was that planning could either avert or address capitalist crises like the Great Depression.[17]

The rising trust in planning was not limited to those inclined to socialism. It was a language spoken across the Indian political spectrum because it was seen to offer legitimacy and identity to the future Indian state.[18] In 1934, an engineer and former administrator of princely Mysore penned a book titled *Planned Economy for India*. Mokshagundam Visvesvaraya, on whose birthday India marks Engineer's Day, believed India should follow 'every progressive country' in establishing centralized economic planning. He envisioned enlisting the nation's 'shrewdest brains' in enacting a Ten-Year Plan aimed at industrial advancement.[19] 'Sir MV' – the knighted, punctilious, white-and-gold turbaned progenitor of Indian plans – was then on the board of Tata Iron and Steel. That same year, the Marwari industrial tycoon Ghanshyamdas Birla also made a plea for planning. In an address to the Federation of Indian Chambers of Commerce and Industry, a body he co-founded, Birla criticized the colonial state's response to the Depression as 'drifting without a Plan'. Noting that the word planning had 'become popular on account of its good associations', he made a case for 'National Economic Planning' to this gathering of businessmen. Arguing for massive public works programme to inject life into the economy, Birla observed that this 'secret had been realized by most of the countries that have planned'. He was referring to contexts as diverse as Britain under the influence of economist John Maynard Keynes, the New Deal in the United States, and even Germany under Hitler.

To capitalists like Birla, such arguments for planning and economic self-sufficiency expressed an aspiration for a modern economy in which domestic enterprises could prosper while being protected from foreign competition. The direction this businessman motioned towards in the early 1930s was remarkably similar to the import-substitution-industrialization model that characterized independent India from mid-century until the market reforms of the 1990s, with momentous consequences for the country. 'We do not aspire', Birla wrote, 'to build industries artificially on the strength of our export trade. Whatever industrial development there will be, will have to depend entirely on the home market.' Another reason to back planning, for Birla, was that it helped to stave off the possibility of a communist revolution. Indian planners should guard against runaway wealth inequalities, he argued. The reason New Deal policies of redistribution were not resented in America was because even the rich knew that it was ultimately in their interest. There was 'no surer method of inviting Bolshevism, communism, and anarchism than to create an unhealthy disparity' in society. Planning was desirable even if it entailed new and seemingly onerous taxes because it was in the interest of the masses as well as of businessmen. 'No one', he added, 'can grumble at this'.[20]

In February 1938, Bose, the newly elected Congress president – bespectacled, clad in kurta, dhoti, embroidered shawl, and Gandhi cap – addressed a crowd, also in white khadi caps, from a stage in Haripura. Set in Gujarat's countryside, the meeting's public art projected rural themes. On display were hundreds of vividly painted village scenes designed by an artist handpicked by Gandhi.[21] Even the nationalist flag that had been ceremonially hoisted displayed a charkha (spinning wheel) at the tricolour's heart. But during the speech, Bose expressed some decidedly un-rustic ideas. He spoke of the need for a 'socialistic' solution to India's problems through a 'planning commission' that would begin a 'comprehensive scheme of industrial development under state ownerships and state control'. A return to the pre-industrial era was no longer possible. It was a motif in several of his talks that year.

Occupied by these concerns, Bose established a National Planning Committee to generate momentum in advance of freedom's arrival. He offered the top job over telegram to Nehru, a colleague and comrade who was then in London. Following up, he wrote a tender letter addressed to 'My dear Jawahar', while aboard a train from Bombay to Calcutta. It concluded with a plea: 'I hope you will accept the Chairmanship of the Planning Committee. You must if it is to be a success. Love, Yours affectionately Subhas.'[22]

Although led by Nehru and managed by the London School of
Economics-trained socialist economist K. T. Shah, the fifteen-member
committee was no leftist club. It included four industrialists, five scientists, three economists, a representative of labour, and one sceptical
Gandhian. Gandhi himself looked askance. In a handwritten note to
Nehru, he conveyed that he had 'never been able to understand or
appreciate the labours of the committee'.[23] Rabindranath Tagore, the
Nobel-winning litterateur of flowing beard and robe, was much more
enthusiastic. The distance between these elder statesmen on economic
matters was expected. As Nehru would write when imprisoned years
later, Tagore was 'the aristocratic artist, turned democrat with proletarian
sympathies', and Gandhi was 'a man of the people, almost the embodi-
ment of the Indian peasant' representing 'renunciation and asceticism'.[24]
Tagore reached out to Nehru to say that, after a long discussion with
astrophysicist and committee member Meghnad Saha about planning, he
was now 'convinced about its importance'.[25] His secretary followed up
a few days later; Gurudeva (Tagore) was 'rather captivated' by the idea of
planning and wanted to meet Nehru to emphasize the urgency of the
National Planning Committee's work. Underlining Gurudeva's distance
from the Mahatma, the secretary also revealed that Tagore wanted
a 'modernist' to be elected Congress president the following year.
Tagore believed that 'there are only two genuine modernists in the High
Command – you (Nehru) and Subhasbabu'. The poet sought to get Bose
re-elected as leader of the Congress because avant-garde ideas like planning needed backing so that the committee's recommendations 'would
be warmly accepted by the All India Congress and not just shelved'.[26]

The National Planning Committee's office was housed, often rent-free,
in a succession of Bombay's architectural landmarks. It started out in the
Venetian-Gothic Secretariat building, then shifted to the Neoclassical
Town Hall before departing to the ground floor of the Gothic Bombay
University building. After the war, J. R. D. Tata made room for them in
the Art Deco property of his insurance company, the New India
Assurance Building. The committee survived on grants from Congress
ministries in different states, donations by Indian businessmen, and loans
from K. T. Shah and Tata. In recognition of his contribution, Tata was
even invited to two meetings of the planning committee.[27]

From its very first meeting, the committee's deliberations were marred
by elbowing between industrialists, socialists, and Gandhians on questions such as the extent of state control and the relative roles of factories
and cottage industries. In a letter to a friend in 1939, Nehru wrote about
the work he was doing in Bombay with the National Planning Committee,
describing it as 'hard and exhausting business' on account of the sparring

within. He could not leave even for a day, he rued, because in his absence it would descend into dysfunction.[28] Nehru played peacemaker and the creation of myriad subcommittees delayed the inevitable collisions. Barely had the work begun when World War II, the Quit India movement, and the colonial backlash of mass incarceration brought it to a screeching halt. It was hard to make progress when several members, including Nehru, were in prison.

During World War II, the colonial state dramatically expanded in size engaging in wartime controls that most observers recognized as forms of economic planning.[29] The colonial government began to argue that some of these controls would need to be maintained even in the future when transitioning back to a peacetime economy. Besides such considerations, there was the matter of optics. In a volatile political context, where it was increasingly apparent that decolonization of some sort was imminent, colonial administrators were keen to mirror nationalist thinking wherever possible. By this point, colonial policies could only gain traction among the Indian elite if it could appear to 'dress itself in nationalist colours, and in addition to accept socialism'.[30] The resultant Planning and Development Department produced a report that echoed the National Planning Committee in its emphasis on industrialization, interventionism, and protectionism.[31]

The medicine prescribed in the colonies was the same one that war-torn Britain opted for itself. The surprising results of the 1945 elections threw Winston Churchill's Conservative government out of power in London, replacing it with a Labour Party led by Clement Attlee. The Labour manifesto had railed against 'anti-planners' whose 'desire to sweep away public controls' to favour war-profiteers and the wealthy. Planning, it suggested, contrasted with 'the chaos of economic do-as-they-please anarchy'. The programme included public ownership of major sectors of the economy, especially 'basic industries' including iron and steel, inland transportation, fuel, and power. The manifesto did not shy away from its political implications either: 'The Labour Party is a Socialist Party, and proud of it'. The government at the apex of the British Empire was declaring its belief in a planned economy.

As the war drew to a close, planning was the flavour of the season in India as well. Across the ideological gamut, almost everyone seemed to have developed a taste for it and their own unique recipes. Birla was once again a vociferous champion, this time in a pamphlet on planning, which endorsed state monopoly of key industries, continued economic controls, and wide-reaching centralized coordination.[32] In 1944, in particular, plans abounded. Apart from the colonial state's own report on planning, Indians were introduced to the industrialists' Bombay Plan, the communist M. N. Roy's People's Plan, the Muslim League's own Planning Committee, and a Gandhian Plan with a foreword by Gandhi.[33] The best publicized of this crop, the Bombay Plan, was one sponsored by prominent businessmen, including magnates like J. R. D. Tata, Birla, Purshotamdas Thakurdas, and Lala Shri Ram.[34] Many of them were donors to the Congress' National Planning Committee. It germinated in a Tata boardroom and was primarily authored by John Matthai, a Malayali economist and government employee turned Tata adviser. The Bombay Plan or Tata–Birla Plan, as it came to be known, tipped its hat to the National Planning Committee's role as pioneers and frankly stated the need for planning and an extensive role for the government in an independent Indian economy. In its details, and in its backers' interest, the document made sure to highlight the need to shield domestic industries from foreign competition, carefully contoured the state's role in the economy, and nodded in the direction of addressing extreme wealth disparities.

There is debate over how enthusiastic these industrialists really were about economic planning. Some scholars view the Bombay Plan as evidence of industrialists' belief in state-led capitalist development and their support for centralized economic planning (provided it walled off overseas competitors). It was the result of a moment of nationalist optimism and widespread belief in statist economic arrangements – a phase when the interests of businessmen overlapped with that of the party leading the anti-colonial charge. Unconvinced of this, others have argued that it was a defensive rearguard action by capitalists who wanted to push the conversation away from some of the more properly socialist positions within the Indian National Congress. While they certainly appreciated being sheltered from foreign competition, they were not genuinely on board with the state regulation that planning entailed. The point of the Bombay Plan, in this view, was for businessmen to make a public show of their patriotism and commitment to broadly equitable development. This helped ingratiate them with the nationalist leadership and, by using the jargon of plans and state control in limited sectors, erect a bulwark against radical or stridently socialistic policies.[35]

The Indian National Congress, for its part, imagined development as above politics. So defined, it became possible to settle political debates without recourse to politics. By assigning the choice of economic strategy to a planning organization – a body of experts – thorny questions could be ironed out quietly and without referring them to popular opinion. For instance, the debate between Gandhians and socialist modernizers such as Bose and Nehru about the desirability of mechanized industrialization was solved, according to Partha Chatterjee, by 'constituting planning as a domain outside the "squabbles and conflicts of politics"'.[36] More broadly, as Jawaharlal Nehru looked ahead to independence, he saw (or hoped for) a state in which politics itself would be dwarfed by the work of development. Plans were to be the chief priority and politics was to shrink to the role of mere administration. Development would be the narrative of independent India.[37] To India's first prime minister, planning was a refuge: 'something apart from what might be called political ideologies and political conflicts'.[38]

As the British hastily departed from a fractured subcontinent, independent India set out to fulfil a promise it had made through decades of anticolonial struggle – sparking the national economy. To that end, in March 1950, the Planning Commission was created. An official body based in New Delhi, its chairperson was the prime minister and it included cabinet ministers like the Minister of Finance, senior bureaucrats, and invited experts.[39] The mission was to plan the Indian economy and steer it through successive Five-Year Plans. India instituted a mixed economy: a large public sector in which the Planning Commission controlled investment decisions and resource allocation as well as a much larger economy of private enterprise, heavily regulated by controls and licences.

Officially, the commission was an advisory body. In the months leading up to its establishment, some of those involved in the process – like Gandhian labour leader Gulzarilal Nanda and the Congress Working Committee – tried to push for a stronger version, one with more muscle in relation to the ministries and bearing enforcement authority. These proposals were quashed in the cabinet by Deputy Prime Minister Vallabhbhai Patel and other concerned ministers, some of whom feared a reaction from business leaders.[40] While the cabinet's decision limited the Planning Commission's purview, the issue refused to go away. In the summer of 1950, the body's powers became a national controversy when Finance Minister John Matthai resigned, publicly rebuking the government for treating the Commission as a 'parallel cabinet' to which the ministries would have to bend the knee.[41]

The prime minister scrambled to douse the fire. The threat to the Planning Commission's legitimacy, so soon after its birth, worried Nehru enough for him to make it the subject of his public addresses. Soon after another interview in which Matthai aired grievances, Nehru was in the former minister's home state of Kerala (Travancore-Cochin at the time). To a packed, rain-soaked crowd in Trivandrum University's stadium, he downplayed their differences and promised that the Commission did not reflect an authoritarian bent. Either the subject was not enough of a popular issue or the audience was composed of fans because the event concluded with the crowd surging to the rostrum in a 'mighty ovation' and carrying the prime minister on their shoulders to his car.[42] It is an episode that captures how the Planning Commission rode the wave of Nehru's popularity. Despite Nehru's placations, though, the question of relative powers would bubble up repeatedly in the following years.

Even with the rocky start, the body wielded enormous power. Its potency stemmed from its authority to draw up an economic roadmap for the country and back it with all the resources and policy instruments available to the Government of India. The presence of both the prime minister and senior Cabinet officials (like the finance minister) as members meant that its recommendations to ministries or state governments acquired the unofficial stamp of Cabinet approval. For much of the 1950s, there were also other significant overlaps in key personnel between the Union Government and the Planning Commission that shored up the latter's writ. For example, the chief economic advisor at the Ministry of Finance was also the head of the Economics Division at the Commission.[43] The Cabinet Secretary performed the duties of Principal Secretary to the Planning Commission as well.[44]

The language of Plans quickly became pervasive in the lives of Indian citizens. In a *Shankar's Weekly* cartoon from May 1950, a range of plans

Figure 0.1. Planning Commission meeting on 1 June 1952. Nehru is in the centre with C. D. Deshmukh to his right. Gulzarilal Nanda and Tarlok Singh are to Nehru's left. Photo by James Burke, *Life*.

crowd the frame: a Defence Plan in the form of a canon, a Congress Plan and Economic Plan as flying carpets, a Rehabilitation Plan in the shape of a tent sheltering people huddled beneath, and a Transport Plan as a human cannonball. There is even a Plan for Plans, depicted as a potted plant sprouting numerous other plans. Alongside these were less ambitious plans – a Children's Plan, Daughter's Plan, Wife's Plan,

Figure 0.2. Poking fun at the Government's enthusiasm for plans and popular participation. Cartoon by Shankar in *Shankar's Weekly* (7 May 1950).

Shopping Plan, and a Plan for an Evening Out. As the artist dryly concluded, 'there is nobody without a plan'.[45]

Between the atom bomb dropping on Hiroshima and the fall of the Berlin Wall, planning stalked the global policy landscape. Far from an Indian oddity, it drew legitimacy from an international push during World War II, spilling over into a transnational planning moment in the middle decades of the twentieth century. Varying combinations of planning, protectionism, and state-led democratic development were being fused with anti-imperialism and the fight against the perceived threat of neocolonialism.[46] Economist Lionel Robbins recognized the deep historical links between disintegrating empires and planning. To him, as one historian put it, decolonization and planning were both 'formally homologous and structurally reinforcing'.[47] Even outside the command economies of China and the Soviet Union, plans and planning bodies were found in far flung nations – from South Korea, Japan, Vietnam, and Malaysia in East Asia to France, Mexico, and Argentina in the western hemisphere to Ghana, Sudan, and Tanzania in Africa. By 1965, thirty-five African nations had development plans. Observing the 'very ubiquity of development plans', one economist wrote that African states, including those with conservative governments, saw 'economic planning as a logical historical development from the independence effort'.[48] Another remarked that during the 1960s in Africa, '"having a plan" became almost a *sine qua non* of political independence'.[49] A historian of development corroborated that observation, writing of the 1950s and 1960s: 'development concepts, however different their details, shared a faith in the state as an actor and in planning as a method, making it tempting to describe the history of development as a history of planning'.[50] In those mid-century decades, planning represented a spectrum of statist economic arrangements rather than specific policies – seemingly applicable across totalitarian regimes, social democracies, and welfare states. Significantly, though, unlike in communist USSR and China, there were hard limits to the state's power in democratic India. Planning would have to be done differently here.

***

The challenges faced in writing histories of independent India are captured by how difficult it is to access Nehru's unpublished papers during his term as prime minister. When I conducted the research for this book, I had to seek special permission from a legal heir of Nehru. At the time, that was the office of Sonia Gandhi, then the Congress Party president. In late 2014, Sonia Gandhi waived this requirement. However, scholars still have to petition no less than the Prime Minister's Office for permission, where such requests are assessed on a case-by-case basis.[51]

During visits to the National Archives of India, I was surprised to find a fragmentary and insubstantial collection of documents on planning – wholly incommensurate with the influence wielded by the Planning Commission. The shelves of the Planning Commission or Yojana Bhavan Library were also stacked with dusty volumes of books and pamphlets, but none of the departmental files or correspondence that feature prominently in the historian's diet. A high-ranking former member of the Planning Commission had no answer either; on the contrary, it took him by surprise. The likely explanation is grim. As another scholar who pursued this missing cache of documents reluctantly concluded – despite leveraging contacts in ministerial offices and accessing documentary stashes at various ministries – it is probable that 'most old files had simply been thrown away or burned' because 'after a point, clerks decided to simply destroy them'.[52] The path around this gaping absence in the government's own archival records is to triangulate using private papers, correspondence, periodicals, and memoirs available at numerous archives in India, Britain, and the United States.

Despite the knots, historians are untangling the decades following the fateful 'stroke of the midnight hour' on 15 August 1947. Given the cataclysmic nature of Partition, with its unprecedented migrations and frenzied violence, it is natural that this has attracted the most historical attention.[53] The years following this are still mainly the province of political scientists, anthropologists, and economists – with historians recently making more frequent forays.[54] Wide-ranging surveys of the postcolonial period have helped to define the broad contours of the Nehruvian state and consolidated our understanding of it.[55] This was nearly a two-decade phase following independence during which Nehru – the most prominent leader in a Congress party that held power in New Delhi and most state capitals – was prime minister, and that saw the establishment of a constitutional democracy with a powerful centre, a planned economy, and non-aligned Cold War foreign policy. There has now been a new wave of historical scholarship on the Nehruvian state, coinciding with and possibly influenced by, the drastic downturn in the electoral fortunes of the party to which Jawaharlal Nehru belonged.[56]

Studies of planning in India, however, have been dominated by social scientists. Some of these were near contemporary accounts, often technical and dating back decades. A few were by scholars who were involved in the planning process themselves.[57] Since then, works by political scientists and economists have fruitfully explored questions of political economy, state capacity, growth strategy, and outcomes.[58] While undoubtedly valuable, these accounts have their limitations. This literature has little to say about the fundamental tension between Indian planning's technocratic nature and its aspirations for public participation. What they miss are explanations of how planning was used to legitimate the state, how the language of planning infused popular culture, and what the entire project of 'democratic planning' was. We also do not know enough about how planning shaped the Nehruvian state – the knowledge infrastructure undergirding it, debates within the Commission and between it and other ministries, and the relationship with global expertise and the Cold War.

Over the last few decades, historians have begun to address these themes.[59] Medha Kudaisya and Benjamin Zachariah contributed analyses of the ideology, institutional conflicts, and policy choices involved in economic planning from its interwar beginnings.[60] Vivek Chibber and Nasir Tyabji have examined the relationship between capitalists and the state during the Nehruvian era.[61] David Engerman has made a landmark intervention in the study of Cold War development politics, exposing how foreign aid from America and the Soviet Union shaped debates between competing economic visions in India.[62] This book, by contrast, addresses a different set of themes. It steps away from policy content and high politics – the ebb and flow of the Five-Year Plans themselves – first, to reveal how the data infrastructure necessary to mount Plans (through statistics and computers) significantly shaped the development of the state itself; and, second, to uncover how planning functioned as a mode of political legitimation (through the project of democratic planning).

Among more theoretical analyses of Indian development and planning, Partha Chatterjee's is especially noteworthy.[63] In an oft-cited essay, he argued that planning functioned as a mechanism by which experts outside the political sphere could settle political debate and policy disagreements.[64] He also identified a tension between 'rational' planning and the less reason-driven realm of politics, despite which planning needed representative politics to be legitimate, and politicians needed planning to paper over conflicting economic visions. Deeply perceptive, the essay is also predominantly theoretical, given its focus on capital accumulation and the 'passive revolution' of capital.

This book builds on those insights by demonstrating how these dynamics operated in practice, and their effects on the state and its stance towards citizens. I anchor this analysis in a set of specific contexts – national statistics, computers, organizations such as the government's Song and Drama Division, and voluntary bodies such as the Bharat Sadhu Samaj. The initial chapters address the ways in which experts and expertise shaped the contours of state power. The desire for planning to be data-driven quickly led to the installation of new intellectual infrastructures. Hence, those most capable of navigating this domain of data – technocrats and scientific institutions – were further legitimized, embedded, and empowered within the state.

The latter part of this book responds to Chatterjee's brief observation about the opposition between the rational science of planning and the political pressures of representation, and the necessary 'paradox' of their coexistence. It does so through an exploration of the government's democratic planning campaign – an experiment that represented a new political ideology and different path in the Cold War. These chapters explore how the Nehruvian state was conscious of the tension between technocracy and democracy but tried to portray them as essentially compatible. In fact, it sought to creatively resolve this seeming paradox through the ideology and rhetoric of democratic planning. Despite shielding planning from politics as much as it could, the government still wanted to advertise a technocratic process as fundamentally democratic. Focusing on the rhetoric of 'democratic planning' and 'Plan-consciousness' – while remaining sceptical of its claims – I investigate the programmes launched and contortions necessary to make that pitch.

Looking beyond the subcontinent, this story is entangled in the global arc of twentieth-century ideas of development and the Cold War.[65] Instead of tracing the reach of foreign influence, the narrative that follows places a Third World site – India – at the centre and looks outward. Expertise did not just radiate benevolently from western capitals to poorer nations; the sources of new disciplinary knowledge were polycentric and its motivations complex. While India was a recipient of expertise from abroad, several of the most influential individuals and institutions were home- grown. They made their own contributions to the body of knowledge on economic development – for example, in the design of sample surveys, and in demonstrating the utility of extensive household surveys to measuring national living standards and poverty.[66]

* * *

In Part I, I trace the creation of a modern social scientific and technological framework to undergird India's aspirations for development. Planning necessitated state efforts in quantitative description and numerical mastery of the economy, which provoked rapid growth in the government's knowledge infrastructure. The installation of a national statistical grid, and the pursuit of newly invented computer technology, were responses to the need for the legibility that planning required in the economic realm. This apparatus was crucial to governing the economy. Providing the numbers that could stand in for the nation, planning contributed to defining the national economy, making it more visible to the state and more amenable to intervention. As sociologist Michael Mann has argued, modern democratic states operate through 'infrastructural power', which enable them to implement political choices and organize the economic realm.[67] In India, we see the flexing of such power, in the erection of a vast data complex. A thread that runs through the initial chapters is the figure of P. C. Mahalanobis and the Indian Statistical Institute (ISI). Their shared narrative illustrates the argument of Part I – that planning catalysed a hunger for data that led to a swelling of the state's knowledge capacities, with consequences for policymaking at the highest level. Further, they underscored the technocratic mode in which planning operated within the postcolonial state.

Chapter 1 reveals how India's statistical infrastructure was built and establishes its link to planning. I track the early career of Mahalanobis and the institution he founded in Calcutta (the Indian Statistical Institute) to describe the ascent of statistics as an academic discipline in India, and its growing association with applied economics. This was the period that produced organizations such as the Central Statistical Organization and the National Sample Survey, both of which persist and remain significant to policymaking. It was during this phase that India first began periodic assessments of national income (a precursor to Gross Domestic Product (GDP)) and nationwide sample surveys that delivered high-definition snapshots of the economy. The chapter argues that this national statistical framework – pioneering among developing nations and a global trail-blazer in large sample surveys – emerged as a response to the quantitative needs of centralized economic planning.

The next chapter lays out how this planning-induced expansion in the state's capacities led to the formalization of planning's relationship with statistics. Changes at both the Planning Commission and the Indian Statistical Institute bear witness to this. It placed a statistician and a statistical institute in a position where they could, in turn, shape Plans. Chapter 2 traces a boomerang's arc: planning's influence on statistics led to statistics' influence on planning. It explains how the Indian Statistical Institute transitioned from a small scholarly body in the outskirts of Calcutta and on the fringes of mainstream academia in the 1930s, to a nodal agency in Indian economic planning by the mid-1950s. And it describes the way in which Mahalanobis used the close proximity of national statistics and economic planning at this moment to carve a position for himself at the Planning Commission. This culminated in him and the Institute drafting India's pivotal Second Five-Year Plan (1956–1961), the economic blueprint for decades thereafter. The tactics used included courting experts on both sides of the Iron Curtain and developing the Institute as a destination to host a stream of foreign economists, statisticians, and policy experts to burnish its profile. The very possibility that a statistician could transform into an economic planner reveals the wide latitude granted to experts and expertise in a technocratic state.

The burst of information generated by new statistical projects made the question of calculation paramount. The mass of data that the National Sample Survey yielded and the increasing complexity of planning models made the state's data processing needs evident. Chapter 3 reveals the campaign to bring India its first computers. Unlike other parts of the world, computers were not sought for military purposes in India. Instead, India pursued them because they were seen as a solution to central planning's most knotty puzzle, that of big data. The chapter follows the decade-long quest to import computers from the United States, Europe, and the USSR, unearthing the Cold War politics in which it inevitably became embroiled. Overall, Part I demonstrates the building of a technocratic, data-hungry, high-modernist state and its attempts to make the economic realm more legible.[68]

Pivoting from the capacity-building side of India's planning story, the second half of *Planning Democracy* explores the government's unsuccessful efforts at reconciling that technocracy with democracy. The Indian state did this by billing its political project as 'democratic planning'. The project was meant to define Indian nationhood, citizenship, and a path between capitalist democracy and authoritarian command economies. Caught in the crosshairs of a global Cold War, India responded through non-aligned foreign policy and its domestic counterpart – the combination of liberal democratic institutions and centralized economic planning. By expecting citizens to participate in this, the government was not simply asking for their consent on an economic policy; it was also beseeching citizens to step up to the task of building a new kind of state through mass participation (and sharing the blame for failure). During the Nehruvian period, the most expansive social vision for planning was to fashion a productive and informed citizenry and build a movement towards the Plan's fulfilment. Even when deployed as propaganda, the message of democratic planning was significant to the government as a mode of legitimation and a means of Plan fulfilment. After all, given the state's limited capacity during this period, voluntary efforts by citizens were simply necessary if the economy was to grow in accordance to the Plans' timetable.

In Chapter 4, I chart the Indian government's ambition to make planning democratic by convincing its citizenry of the need for planning and securing their participation. The government sought to spur grass-roots enthusiasm by planting it – a campaign that was self-undermining by its very nature. It examines why public participation in planning mattered to the Indian government and uncovers the many channels through which the state sought to spread the gospel of planning. The means employed by government to instil 'Plan-consciousness' included publicity teams on bullock carts and boats, a Khushwant Singh-edited Plan magazine named *Yojana,* plays by leading Hindi playwrights like Ramesh Mehta, musical and drama troupes, and state propaganda films screened for mass audiences through the Films Division. The chapter concludes with a discussion of how this Plan-consciousness even seeped into commercial Hindi cinema or Bollywood.

If democratic planning was to become a mass movement, as the government hoped, it would require the voluntary participation of Indian citizens. In Chapter 5, I examine how, in the absence of spontaneous participation, the state supported voluntary organizations to spread the message of the Five-Year Plans and offered services towards their fulfilment. It analyses the paradox of the state intervening to stimulate voluntary support for its policies. The chapter traces efforts to involve youths through College and University Planning Forums, and other social groups through the Bharat Sewak Samaj (Service to India Society). It also analyses a curious experiment – the enigmatic Bharat Sadhu Samaj (Indian Society of Ascetics). A brainchild of Gulzarilal Nanda, the devout Minister of Planning, its goal was to publicize the Plans using Hinduism as a resource. The attempt revealed how the Nehruvian state propagated Five-Year Plans – the very symbol of secular technocracy and scientific modernity – using saffron-robed Hindu monks and ascetics. The long-term fallout of this project was the Sadhu Samaj's drift towards Hindu nationalism. Ultimately, this religious venture underlines the awkward relationship and largely failed wedding of the technocratic and democratic dimensions of planning.

The book concludes with a discussion of the gradual decline of the Planning Commission's potency from the late 1960s, culminating in its eventual demise in 2014, despite one political party promising to resurrect it from the dead. Through this period, economic planning remained fundamental to how the Indian economy functioned, even as the Planning Commission steadily shed powers it once enjoyed to other arms of government. While the Planning Commission diminished, the knowledge and data infrastructures it had helped to create endured. It remained the basis of policymaking at the highest levels – unless, as is increasingly the case, it revealed governments in an unflattering light. Independent India's search for technocratic solutions to economic problems continues, as does the challenge of fusing technocracy to democracy.

Part I

Data

1   A Nation in Numbers

Summer 1915, England. As bombs rained over Europe, in the relative calm of Cambridge, a slender, sharp-featured, robustly moustachioed Bengali waited to return home. The 21-year-old undergraduate in maths and physics, Prasanta Chandra Mahalanobis, had been forced by the Great War to delay sailing to Calcutta. It was meant to be a short vacation and triumphant homecoming. As a local daily proudly reported, the youth – one of their own – had obtained the sole First Class in his Physics cohort and snagged a scholarship to continue research in Cambridge's Cavendish Laboratory under the direction of Charles Wilson (a future Nobel laureate).[1] In an age when such distinction was rare for a colonial subject of the British Empire, this was newsworthy, and no Indian city was more likely to be pleased.

One morning, his tutor found young Prasanta in the centuries-old King's College Library, near the chapel's stained glass marvels crowned by Gothic spires and the sloping lawn that rolled down to the River Cam. When he drew the student's attention towards bound volumes of *Biometrika*, a journal of statistics, Mahalanobis, although aspiring to be a physicist, was immediately hooked. When he sailed soon after to India, he took with him several issues of the journal to study aboard the steamer. Once in Calcutta, the holiday turned into permanent residence as he accepted an offer to teach physics at his elite alma mater, Presidency College, turning his back on the Cambridge scholarship. But it was not physics at all that would define his professional life. In fact, that branch of science became rather marginal to it. Instead, what Mahalanobis discovered in the pages of that journal would occupy much of his career – founding the Indian Statistical Institute, becoming India's statistician-in-chief, and building a national statistical infrastructure. It was his eminence as a statistician that eventually opened the doors to the Planning Commission in Lutyens' Delhi.

***

Planning transformed the state's knowledge capacities. Stimulated by the needs of a planned economy, the 1950s saw a massive expansion in the fledgling state's data capabilities. It led to the Indian state wielding information on a different order of magnitude and centralizing it in an unprecedented manner, concentrating the state's power to make informed interventions in the economy. During this period, the state introduced new methods and instruments by which to scrutinize the economic life of India's citizens, and in doing so, magnifying it for the planner's gaze. If the economy was to grow and poverty banished, the argument went, governments needed to be able to quantify the obstacles. It was this rapid phase of planning-induced state-building that created a centralized national statistical system for the first time, began periodic calculations of national income, and launched a continuous and pioneering series of sample surveys that generated a wealth of economic knowledge.

The dawn of economic planning led to a burst of statistics. These were years of unprecedented authority for the discipline: national statistics claimed more attention from the government and policymakers than it had ever before and more than it would ever again. The establishment of a national framework of statistics in India was intimately related with the installation of planning during that decade.[2] The explosion in official national statistics was a response to the quantitative requirements of centralized economic planning in a state oriented towards development. Statistics sought to know the economy; the statistical techniques developed and the methods deployed framed the national economy in ways that made it numerically coherent to the Indian government. It made the economy legible to planners and built the quantitative scaffolding necessary for constructing Plans.[3]

At the centre of these developments were Mahalanobis, once described as the 'presiding genius of statistics in India', and the institute of which he was the patriarch, the Indian Statistical Institute (henceforth, the Institute).[4] They were well positioned to respond to the state's needs due to their technical facility in scientific methods and their managerial abilities in institution building. In concert with the Planning Commission and government, they not only generated new parameters by which to quantify the nation but also developed a vast and unprecedented national statistical infrastructure for a freshly minted republic. Over a short period, this partnership produced the office of the Honorary Statistical Adviser to the Government of India, the Central Statistical Organization, National Income Committees, biannual National Sample Surveys and even a new breed of bureaucrat – the Statistical Service cadre – in the Civil Services of India.

Mahalanobis is justly considered integral to the story of planning in India. Not only did he author the crucial Second Five-Year Plan (1956–1961), but the strategy underlying it – of a vast public sector and import substitution industrialization – passed into policy ortho-doxy, defining the Indian economy until the market reforms of 1991. Unsurprisingly, he plays a prominent role in the following pages. But this is not the biography of an individual, shaping history singlehand-edly. His role was only made possible by subterranean historical cur-rents. Centralized economic planning, by its very top-down nature, privileged technocrats like him and cast them in the role of planners-in-waiting. Planning mounted the stage on which figures like Mahalanobis could strut. He served as a vehicle for a larger story: that of planning, the state's resultant data-cravings, and the knowledge apparatus assembled to satiate it.

By the end of the 1930s, it had become increasingly apparent to both the colonial government and sections of the Congress that any future project of comprehensive economic planning in India would require a national statistical apparatus. In the post-war period, after the British departed, it was the needs of centralized planning that led to the explosion in national statistics, thereby creating and polishing the national profile of both Mahalanobis and the Institute. It was this context that enabled them to tie the threads of statistics and computing to planning. The careers of Mahalanobis and the Institute capture this entanglement and its consequences for India.

The role played by Mahalanobis in Indian planning is a fact often stated but rarely explained. The popular view is that it is almost entirely due to an association with Nehru. However, the tale of the charismatic scientist meeting an impressionable prime minister, with a Five-Year Plan emer-ging in the ensuing frisson, is suspiciously neat. We need to reframe the image of an academic parachuting, without warning, into the position of plan-author, carried solely by gusts of prime ministerial favour. To account for Mahalanobis' influence, we cannot rely simply on Nehruvian caprice. It does not explain the context in which this statisti-cian would emerge as a credible candidate for the job of a planner, nor why Nehru held Mahalanobis in such high esteem. To comprehend this, we need to look into the ascent of statistics to the status of a scientific discipline in India in the mid-century, the installation of a national statis-tical infrastructure, and the transformation of the Institute into the pre-mier think tank for planning in the 1950s. To lay all that at the door of a friendship is unconvincing, even if appealing. We need an institutional and structural account to bolster a narrative that has leaned too heavily on chance and personality.[5]

In the mid-twentieth century, several nation states witnessed a spurt in the production of statistics. In India, a country embarking on a new trajectory of development and committing to central planning, the transformation was rapid. As both sides of the 'socialist calculation debate' among early twentieth-century economists like free marketeer Friedrich Hayek and socialist Oskar Lange made plain, planning required quantitative mastery over the economy. By not relying exclusively on the 'invisible hand' of price signals to direct resources, planners had defined the question of organizing the economy as one that was essentially calculable. Statistics, as quantitative descriptions of the economy, were necessary for planners to plan. The simultaneous rise of planning and national statistics in India was, thus not accidental. Centralized planning required data on the economy, and statistics came to be viewed as the discipline that could deliver it. The Institute was instrumental in setting the techniques and parameters by which the economy was made quantitatively intelligible and upon which its performance would be judged. Not only did this generate more information about the economy, but it also helped define the very categories by which the economy would be described and analysed. Creating, sorting, and evaluating this new knowledge made the economy readable.[6] The economy was calibrated and made more tractable for planned intervention. Those processes also produced a climate of opinion in which a statistician and an institute devoted to statistical research could be viewed as both obviously qualified and naturally suited to planning.

The Professor and the Institute

The word 'statistics' originally meant information that was of use to states. In the nineteenth century, many states around the world sought such information. As the spurt in almanacs, gazettes, and censuses indicates, official 'fact-collecting' had become something of an obsession in the United States and Western Europe. As the volume of such data grew, so did the reliance on new specialists and professionals who could interpret its increasing complexity. Over the course of the nineteenth century, statistics played a role in enshrining the technical, scientific expert as a 'truth-teller'.[7]

The colonial state in India was similarly statistically minded.[8] Scholars have variously referred to this as the 'enumerative modality' or 'orientalist empiricism' of an 'ethnographic state'.[9] Its production of statistics was largely decentralized and regional. Collecting information ranging from topography to ethnicity to agricultural arrangements, these exercises were mainly aimed at administration and commerce. In the early nineteenth century, eastern India saw encyclopaedic surveys by Francis Buchanan and Montgomery Martin. In the mid-nineteenth century, Colonel Sykes established a small department of statistics at India House in London and produced statistical papers on the subcontinent. Throughout the nineteenth century, much of the statistical production took the form of detailed district and provincial gazetteers alongside careful annual administrative reports. The doorstopper *Moral and Material Progress Reports* conveyed a wealth of economic detail (even if its title betrayed the tone of its contents). 1862 saw both the presentation of a consolidated single budget for India and the establishment of a Statistical Committee that published a *Statistical Abstract of British India*. 1881 was a watershed, marking the beginning of the first countrywide decennial population census and the release of the nine volumes that composed the *Imperial Gazetteer of India*.[10]

Numerically oriented as the colonial government was, there was sometimes reason to question the veracity of its own statistical output. Conveniently, the British frequently found unreliable natives to blame. Harold Cox, a future Labour parliamentarian, recalled that during his time in Aligarh as a maths tutor he once quoted some statistics to an English judge. The judge responded saying that Cox should not cite Indian statistics with such assurance because, although the colonial government amassed statistics, what 'you must never forget is that every one of those figures comes in the first instance from the *chowty dar* who just puts down what he damn pleases'.[11]

Indian nationalists had different reasons for distrusting the figures published by the colonial state. In some ways, the famed nationalist economic critique of colonial rule was a form of statistical counter-programming. The scholarly polemics of Naoroji, Ranade, and Romesh Dutt questioned the tale that documents like the *Moral and Material Progress Reports* spun. Naoroji, for example, parsed official records and punctured their claims by producing his own studies of national and per capita income. It was this statistical mode of enquiry that led to the theory of the 'drain of wealth' and his magnum opus, *Poverty and Un-British Rule in India*.[12] Works like these represented a strain within Indian nationalism that has been described as 'statistical liberalism', defined as the 'collection of economic data by reformers to refute colonial analysis'.[13] As others have argued, this statistically based economic critique of empire eventually contributed to concepts, such as the Indian economy and even the Indian nation acquiring fixed meaning in the nationalist mind.[14]

By the mid-1920s, calls for establishing a central authority to collate national statistics grew louder and were echoed by several colonial committees.[15] Their recommendations included forming a Central

Statistical Office, conducting national surveys, estimating national income, and centralizing the statistical system.[16] None of this materialized. The transformation of India's statistical infrastructure was to be a postcolonial phenomenon. The statistical exercises of the colonial era – decentralized and oriented towards administration rather than economic policy – were found to be an insufficient baseline for a developmental agenda based on planning. It was after independence that statistics would come to be centrally organized, nationally oriented, and shifted from primarily enumerative methods to large-scale sample surveying. The architects of this makeover were Mahalanobis and the Institute in Calcutta.

Tall, prominently nosed, stern of gaze, vast of brow, with hair severely parted and slicked flat by coconut oil, Mahalanobis looked the part of a serious man. He was born into a family that belonged to Bengal's landed elite, and his early milieu was that of intellectual enquiry and religious reform in turn-of-the-century Calcutta. He grew up to be a prim workaholic, seemingly immune to frivolity and usually found 'day and night, stooping over his calculations'.[17] As a friend of nearly half a century corroborated, he had no time for 'small talk and little capacity to compromise with unreason'. Even his smile – tight-lipped, partial to the right cheek – could seem a grudging concession. Mahalanobis appeared to make a virtue of withholding expressions of affection, believing it was his duty to conceal it, except for to pets, which included dogs, cats, and cows.[18]

An urbane savant, Mahalanobis was once described as 'a physicist by training, statistician by instinct and planner by conviction'.[19] He was also much more – versed in ancient Sanskrit texts, possessed of a discerning ear for Bengali poetry, and a dabbler in architecture. In short, he was a proud polymath, although of uneven talents, despite high estimation of his own abilities.[20] Even an admiring younger colleague conceded: 'He thought he knew best in practically every matter.' Mahalanobis was often referred to in Indian academic and government circles as 'the Professor', and it was a moniker he was not shy about employing while signing correspondence. On the campus of the Institute, it was understood that when someone mentioned 'the Professor', it referred only to him.[21]

When it began, the Professor's statistical work was pursued as a hobby at home. His day job was as a professor of physics at the venerable, century-old Presidency College. His earliest statistical forays were eclectic. A chance encounter in 1920 with the director of the Zoological and Anthropological Survey of India resulted in Mahalanobis' first statistical study, an anthropometric analysis of the stature of Anglo-Indians.[22] Another set of works dealt with meteorology, on the strength of which he was appointed meteorologist at the Alipore Observatory. Disastrous floods in Bengal and Orissa provoked analyses of rainfall patterns with an eye to flood control. A few years later, with the governments of Bihar and Orissa asking him to prepare a report based on his findings, he was compelled to hire more assistants. This meant moving the statistical operations out of his home and into a statistics laboratory – a flattering name bestowed upon a narrow space partitioned by cupboards in the room adjoining his in Presidency's Physics Department.

On the afternoon of 17 December 1931, the Indian Statistical Institute was founded as a learned society, housed where the statistical laboratory had been. Initially, it survived on contracts from governmental bodies and private enterprises. Its earliest patron, the Imperial Council of Agricultural Research, offered funds annually to conduct research into agricultural statistics. The Institute's monetary precarity was further offset in 1935 through an annual 5,000 rupee grant from the government for research and training in statistics. It began offering short training courses in statistics to officers from government departments, scientific institutions, and universities – the only training courses in statistics available in India at the time.[23]

In 1933, the Institute launched *Sankhyā*, a journal of statistics that continues to publish research. Its name was meant to capture the word's varied Sanskrit meanings of number and determinate knowledge, while also referring to an ancient Indian philosophy that found mention in the *Bhagavad Gita*. In an introductory editorial, Mahalanobis wrote that the ideas underlying statistics could be traced back to India's classical past. As evidence, he pointed to the detailed administrative statistics referred to in Kautilya's *Arthashastra*.[24] Tagore offered a paean to the 'magic of mathematics' on its pages, comparing their rhythm to that which animated the atom, 'gold and lead, the rose and the thorn, the sun and the planets, the variety and vicissitudes of man's history'. Although wary of scientific empiricism's ability to reach ultimate truths, the poet conceded that these 'dance steps of numbers' were what produced a 'sense of convincingness' or the 'maya of appearance'.[25] The journal showcased research conducted at the Institute and, through submissions from prominent statisticians abroad, raised its international profile.

Statistics was still a marginal discipline in India. Sobering proof of this came in the form of a blunt refusal by the Indian Science Congress to consider a separate section for statistics at its annual conference. One scientist snidely remarked, 'If statistics is to have a section, you may as well have a section for astrology.'[26] Mahalanobis lamented to a fellow scientist in London, using exaggerated caste analogy: 'Statistics is still an outcaste; in fact an Untouchable among scientific workers in India. With one or two exceptions every responsible scientist in India looks upon

Statistics as that awful stuff with which Economists and Politicians play about and try to prove anything they like.'[27]

The Institute built its reputation on the emerging science of sample surveys. The studies they conducted in the 1930s included sample surveys of consumer preference, rural indebtedness, family budgets, and an extensive survey of the handloom industry. Perhaps the most significant of these surveys were the ones that Mahalanobis supervised for the forecasting of jute yields, one of Bengal's primary cash crops. These were pioneering exercises, among the largest sample surveys ever undertaken until then.[28] Mahalanobis recommended the use of random samples to the Development Commissioner of Bengal, which led to a province-wide sample survey of jute yields in 1935. The Professor noted that it was quite possibly 'the first area sample in the whole world'.[29] Despite unsatisfactory results, a couple of years later, the newly established Indian Central Jute Committee commissioned a five-year sample survey project for jute in Bengal.

The science of random sample surveys – for which the Professor and the Institute were among the earliest crusaders – was yet to gain widespread acceptance anywhere in the world. There were calls to abandon it and return to traditional plot-to-plot enumeration. In 1944, the Bengal government decided to settle this dispute over technique by commissioning both methods in a competition. The idea was to run them simultaneously and then compare their results against the official jute sales figures to determine the more accurate reading. It was to be a moment of sweet vindication for the Institute and the science of sampling. The cumbersome enumeration or counting carried out by the government turned out to be off the mark by 16.6% while the Institute's more sophisticated sample survey erred only by 0.3%. Even more conclusively, the sample survey cost only a tenth of the enumeration.[30] Careful abstraction approximated reality better than painstaking recreations of it.

While the Institute was making a name for itself, nationalists were themselves coming to terms with the statistical requirements of a future independent economy. The Government of India Act of 1935 had belatedly granted provincial governments a substantial degree of autonomy, quintupled the electoral franchise, and enabled elected Indians to form governments in the provinces for the first time. Reflecting the popularity of Gandhi's leadership and years of grass roots mobilization, the Indian National Congress swept the first provincial elections to form governments in eight out of eleven provinces. Half a century after its founding, the party had tasted its first major electoral triumph. Writing in 1937 to their ministers heading provincial governments, the Congress Working Committee adopted a resolution at its Wardha meeting acknowledging that the solution to problems 'necessary to any scheme of national reconstruction and social planning' would require 'extensive survey and the collection of data'.[31]

Within months, the president of the Indian National Congress, Subhas Chandra Bose, called for the formation of a National Planning Committee. When it was time to pick the person to helm it, Bose looked to Jawaharlal Nehru, already a past president of the party and veteran of seven jail terms. Nehru's brush with Fabian socialism during his days training as a lawyer in London, coupled with his admiration for the Soviet Union's rapid economic advances through planning, marked him as a natural candidate. The National Planning Committee's brief was to prepare a series of studies on various sectors of the Indian economy in order to provide a blueprint for the task of planning that would present itself once (for it was no longer a question of 'if') independence was won.

As chairman of the National Planning Committee in 1938, Nehru was confronted with 'the absence of accurate data and statistics'. It became apparent that an overhaul was necessary if the Committee was to progress beyond passing 'pious resolutions'.[32] In June the following year, they decided to create a subcommittee that would draft letters to the Government of India and provincial governments with a recommendation to use the forthcoming census 'to collect additional information of various kinds which would help in drawing up a Plan'. The subcommittee was also requested to consult Mahalanobis and John Matthai, an economist associated with the Tata corporation, regarding what kinds of data the government should gather.[33] As Nehru stated at a later meeting: 'It is clear that adequate data and information is of the essence of planning and therefore the very first step that a planning authority must take is to organise the proper and scientific collection of statistics.'[34]

Nehru had met the Professor socially on several occasions, usually when calling on the poet Rabindranath Tagore. The first Asian winner of the Nobel Prize in Literature was a mentor and friend to the Mahalanobises and a frequent house guest at Gupta Nivas, their lakeside home on the outskirts of Calcutta.[35] It was at Mahalanobis' home where Tagore stayed when he was in Calcutta during the final years of his life. The Professor was present, for example, when Nehru visited the poet in 1939 to ask if his creation, *Jana Gana Mana*, could be used as the national anthem when freedom arrived.[36]

It was not until 1940, however, that they first discussed planning at length. The Professor paid the politician a visit at Anand Bhavan, Allahabad's most sumptuous address. Set in a parkland estate, the two-storey domed mansion was ringed by pillared verandas that had been built by Motilal Nehru, Jawaharlal's father, the physically imposing and spectacularly successful lawyer turned nationalist. In this opulent, high-ceilinged villa that had become a hotbed of nationalist activity, they stayed up past two in the morning discussing India's economic future and the challenges that lay ahead. That year, the Professor had also written to the younger Nehru to offer his cooperation to the National Planning Committee. He attached two detailed notes, explaining that planning would require proper statistical organization and recommended that the National Planning Committee's findings be examined from a 'purely statistical point of view'.[37] In a planning committee meeting on 1 May, 1940, Nehru observed that every subcommittee 'complains of the unsatisfactory nature of statistics and data'.[38] India was fortunate to have a body with the expertise of the Institute, he noted, and welcomed the support Mahalanobis had extended. The Professor's notes were circulated to all committee members, and the subcommittees' reports were all sent to him for expert inspection. Soon after, he was asked to prepare a statistical supplement to the committee's studies. The relevance of statistics to planning was recognized by others as well. In 1942, a University of Lucknow sociologist and economist, Radhakamal Mukherjee, submitted a short note to *Sankhya* titled 'Statistics in Service of Planning'. In it, he stated, 'More significant than the theoretical import of statistical studies is their role in social and economic planning.' It was a theme 'demanding attention from social scientists throughout the world'.[39]

The dramatic years of World War II and the Quit India movement saw changes at the Institute. Swelling in personnel and profile beyond what the cramped, makeshift confines at Presidency College could accommodate, some staff moved in with the Mahalanobises at 204 Barrackpore Trunk Road, their home north of the city in the suburb of Baranagore. Set amidst mango trees and palms, the two-storey colonial bungalow had a large balcony that overlooked a pond. It was named Amrapali by Tagore, after the Jataka tale of the talented and beautiful royal courtesan of ancient Vaishali who donated her mango grove to the Buddha's order that she joined after hearing him preach. Appointed college principal in 1945, Mahalanobis' responsibilities at Presidency had increased. But in the summer of 1948, the Professor committed exclusively to statistics, and resigned from his positions at Presidency. The next year, the Institute acquired a three-acre plot adjacent to Amrapali. Soon this ribbon of dense green skirting Barrackpore Trunk Road would sprawl into a lush thirty-acre estate and become synonymous with the Institute. In time, the bus stop outside the estate came to be known as Statistical, a nickname commuters, bus conductors, and taxi drivers still use.

In the years leading up to independence, the Institute gained a valuable ally in Chintaman Deshmukh, who worked at India's central bank.

Beginning in 1939, when Deshmukh joined the Reserve Bank of India, top bank officials migrated every winter from their Bombay headquarters to Calcutta in order to track the pulse of this eastern financial hub. It was during these seasonal stays that he became familiar with the Institute's work. A diminutive man of chiselled face, Deshmukh was the suave, cerebral product of an elite Bombay and Cambridge education who ranked first in the Indian Civil Service exam. He was a rooted cosmopolitan, combining anglicized sophistication with Brahminical learning – a figure known for reciting Vedic *slokas* for pleasure, translating Kalidasa's *Meghaduta* from Sanskrit and Tagore's poetry into Marathi, and quoting scripture to buttress economic policy. Commitment to the classical ran deep: years later, as a widower, he proposed marriage by scrawling Sanskrit verse on the trunk of a eucalyptus tree.[40]

In Calcutta, Deshmukh renewed a friendship with Mahalanobis that had begun two decades earlier. They spent several leisurely Sundays together at Amrapali.[41] Deshmukh's casual interest in the Institute quickly escalated to membership, and as he rose to the central bank's pinnacle, he used his influence to aid a 'decidedly deserving cause'.[42] In 1944 – the year Deshmukh was knighted, became Governor of the Reserve Bank of India, and was one of India's delegates at the Bretton Woods Conference – he was also named the Institute's president.[43] His fundraising efforts on the Institute's behalf bore fruit in 1945 when, the Ministry of Education began an annual grant of 500,000 rupees, placing it on surer financial footing.

Undisputed in his authority on the Institute's campus, Mahalanobis directed affairs like a benevolent autocrat. He was, as one contemporary described, 'a charming authoritarian', and as another visitor observed, the 'founder, secretary, director and *paterfamilias*'.[44] The adolescent Institute basked in the glow that reflected off Professorial accomplishment. While attracting students from across the country to enrol in the Institute's year-long programme in statistics (the only one of its kind in India), the Professor found little time to teach. This did not, however, soften the harsh glare of an overbearing administrator. Students and staff were expected to record their daily activities in a diary, and an attendance register was used to record entry and egress. The Professor was not exempt from marking attendance, either. The Institute's staff – across hierarchy, and Mahalanobis included – were designated as workers. They were often summoned by the worker-in-chief to his room for discussions. Discussion with the Professor, a staff member recalled, was a regular entry in campus diaries.[45]

Statistics began breaking out of the academy's margins. In 1941, Calcutta University offered the first postgraduate courses in statistics in

India, an MA and MSc in Statistics. The Professor was the Head of the Department, it was staffed entirely by the Institute for the next five years, and its offices were located in the Institute's rooms at Presidency College. In 1946, the Indian Science Congress finally granted statistics a separate section, conferring upon it formal recognition as a distinct scientific discipline.[46] Reflecting this new standing, the Professor also became the Secretary at Indian science's apex body.[47] Another attendee at this Calcutta session of the Indian Science Congress was Jawaharlal Nehru. He was scheduled to spend five days in the city in order to preside over the Indian Science Congress, serve as chief guest at Calcutta University's convocation ceremony, and address rallies in his election campaign. All of this, Nehru wrote to the Professor, left little time for conversation. To pull some time together during his week in Calcutta, Nehru suggested to the Professor that he spend it as a house guest of the Mahalanobises. The insufficiency of national statistics was still a matter of concern to the Congress leader. Only a few months earlier, he had complained that 'Ever since we began the work of the National Planning Committee ... our work has been hampered by the lack of reliable data and statistics and other materials.'[48]

Despite Nehru practically inviting himself over, the welcome at Amrapali was warm. A photograph from that visit shows the Professor and Nehru sharing a sofa in front of a statue of the seated Buddha while they peer over a document, with other files precariously balanced on Mahalanobis' lap. Another finds them eating breakfast on a newspaper-strewn table. The Professor escorted Nehru around the Institute's verdant grounds while explaining projects underway and emphasizing their significance to planned development in independent India. Mahalanobis asked Nehru to assign four promising Congress party workers to the Institute, for them to be trained in statistics and its applications.[49] The next month, Nehru sent his private secretary Pitambar Pant – a former lecturer in physics in Allahabad University and a fellow jail mate from Quit India days – to serve as the Professor's understudy at the Institute. Nehru believed that Pant's time there would help not only with acquiring 'special knowledge', but also in 'developing a wider appreciation of our problems and how to tackle them. Most of us lack this completely'.[50] Amiable and conscientious, Pant would become a close friend to the Professor and another steadfast ally of the Institute. Over the next two decades, while juggling ever-expanding roles at the Planning Commission and the Institute, Pant acted as a bridge between both.[51] Given this position, it was helpful that he possessed a remarkable ability to remember facts and figures regarding the Indian economy. As he was fond of saying, '*Baba, humse pucho*' [Just ask me].[52]

Postwar, the Professor began to receive international recognition. In 1945, he became only the eleventh Indian to be elected as a Fellow of the Royal Society for pioneering contributions to sample survey design and application. He joined an exclusive subcontinental scientific elite that included Meghnad Saha, Homi J. Bhabha, and the Professor's one-time companion on long Sunday morning strolls in Cambridge – the mathematical genius from Kumbakonam, Srinivasa Ramanujan, to whom new vistas were revealed by the goddess Namagiri Thayar in his sleep. Among the many invitations Mahalanobis received during this period was from the United Nations to discuss the terms of reference for a proposed UN Statistical Commission in New York. The ensuing report envisioned a global statistical system.[53]

It recommended the creation of a permanent Statistical Office in the UN, made arrangements for the assumption of the League of Nations' statistical work, and worked out how to coordinate the statistical services within and between various UN agencies and beyond. Based on Mahalanobis' initiative, the report also endorsed the immediate creation of a sub-commission on statistical sampling, a method described in the report as a recent development that had been limited to just a few countries.[54]

As the chairperson and moving spirit of the sub-commission, the Professor was an advocate for the spread of sampling methods and applications worldwide.[55] The body's activities included standardizing international sampling terminology, promoting its use across fields in more countries, formulating syllabuses on sampling methods, and quite literally writing the textbook on the subject in 1950.[56] It laid out the procedures of modern sample surveys for statistical offices across the globe.[57] According to statistician Jelke Bethlehem, the recommendations of this report, along with later additions, hold up today. They 'still provide a useful guide for achieving clarity, comprehensiveness, and international comparability in sample survey reporting'.[58] With his reputation improving, Mahalanobis was being asked to advise and lecture internationally, and over the 1950s the Professor was voted Chairman of the UN Statistical Commission numerous times. As fellow statistician Edwards Deming wrote, 'No statistician ever had more influence on the entire profession and on governmental statistical offices the world over'.[59]

By the mid-twentieth century, the professor of physics was better known as a statistician, and the Institute was among Asia's leading lights in statistical research, training, and application. In the field of sample surveys, the Professor and the Institute were at the cutting edge. As famed British statistician Ronald Fischer put it, the Institute's achievements 'brought India not far from the centre of (the) statistical map of the world'.[60] But that status was a reflection of the Institute's achievements, and not the country's. India had little to boast of by way of national statistics. And to the Professor's mind, statistics could not be justified through advances in research alone: 'Statistics must have a purpose', he often cautioned.[61] And while a part of this could be scientific advance, 'Poverty is the most basic problem of the country; and statistics must help solving this problem.'[62] If the fragmented development of statistics in India at mid-century was attributable to the needs of colonial administration and the lonesome labours of the Professor and the Institute, the drama of its transformation in the decades to follow resulted from a newly independent nation sworn to centrally plan its economy. A new kind of state demanded a new statistical infrastructure.

Numbers for a Nation

Gripped by planning, India erupted into a rash of statistics. In the five years following decolonization, there was a spasm of official statistics. Spurred by a number-hungry nation state and moved by the impulse to plan, India quickly mounted a national statistical infrastructure. India had fallen in love with statistics.[63] National statistics, it was agreed, were an urgent prerequisite for national development. It was, as the Professor would often argue, a 'key technology' for accelerated economic growth in India and the developing world.[64] This faith in numbers was not limited to the subcontinent. India, like several other countries, was swept in a global mid-century wave of what has been described as a 'quantitative positivism'.

Driven by post-war reconstruction and postcolonial material ambition, the heyday of development economics and modernization theory was marked by widespread belief in the boon of data. Both new nations and emerging global institutions, such as the UN and the World Bank, emphasized the importance of data collection.[65] This seemingly ubiquitous belief was also the result of processes that varied across nations. In India, the local context that drove this statistical impulse was economic planning: planning was what contemporaries saw as the cause, and it was what shaped the kind of statistical system India would build. Years later, Mahalanobis was certain that the acceleration in statistical activities following independence was 'mainly in response to the increasing demand for information required for the purposes of planning'.[66] Recalling this phase, Chintaman Deshmukh (who would become Minister of Finance in 1952) similarly observed that the growth in the country's statistical apparatus was due to 'Nehru's awareness of the role of statistics in planned economic development'.[67]

A couple of months before India's independence, the report of the Advisory Planning Board had laid out the need for statistical organization.

'A Central Statistical Office is vitally necessary for planning, but does not exist at present', it stated.[68] As one contemporary bluntly put it, 'We had no facts'.[69] In March 1948, Nehru shared his anxiety when addressing the Constituent Assembly about reorganizing the colonial Planning Department. Despite several ministries possessing statistical wings, he said, 'we are very bad in regard to statistics' even though 'Indian statistics have a very high reputation in the world today'. The dichotomy was due to the advances in statistics being made outside of government. The prime minister ended his address with a plea, one that would suggest the shape of things to come: 'I hope that before very long we shall organise a set-up connecting governmental activities with non-official statistical organisations . . . . That will also be the foundation for the planning activities in the future.'[70] In August 1948, Nehru sent a note to all ministries in which he stated the need for a central organization to coordinate national statistical activities. Given the 'very backward' state of official statistics in the country, he urged, there was a need for more statistics to measure the 'temperature of the nation's economic and other life'.[71] A few months later, the Cabinet constituted Standing Committees of Departmental Economists and Departmental Statisticians. They also decided that a small statistical unit should be formed within the Cabinet Secretariat.[72] Development policy, as it was emerging, was to be data driven, reliant on expertise, and predicated on ramping up intellectual capacity.

The prime minister reiterated the case for adopting modern statistics nationally and in as many fields as possible at a meeting of the Cabinet in early 1949. As other countries had shown, he argued, this would not only aid in tracking the effectiveness of policies, but would also help in formulating them. He recommended that Mahalanobis be appointed Honorary Statistical Adviser to the Cabinet to make recommendations on the course that this statistical overhaul should take.[73] The Professor was also made Chairman of the Committee of Central Statisticians. Within a week, the government resolved to create a Central Statistical Unit that would be attached to the Cabinet Secretariat and headed by the Professor.[74] It was conceived of as the point of coordination for all ministerial and departmental statistical activity: its function would be to advise government agencies on statistical matters, ensure quality control in all official statistics, and produce its own publications, such as the *Annual Statistical Abstract*, the *Monthly Abstract of Statistics*, and the *Weekly Bulletin of Statistics*. Meanwhile, Pitambar Pant and N. T. Mathew (an Institute employee) prepared a report on the organization of statistics in India – nationally and by state – with the help of Institute staff. Soon after, Mathew travelled to Delhi to set up the

Central Statistical Unit and a small outpost of the Institute. For the next two years, the Unit was staffed entirely by personnel from the Institute.[75]

India began measuring national income – a forerunner of GDP – in August 1949. Modern measuring of national wealth dates back to Colin Clark's estimates for Great Britain in the 1920s. Over the next two decades, economists Simon Kuznets and Richard Stone advanced the field with their own calculations for the United States and the United Kingdom, respectively, culminating in 1940 with the publication of Colin Clark's study of comparative national incomes across the world. A scholarly sensation, the study supplied sobering statistical proof of what most people already knew – that 'the world is a wretchedly poor place'.[76] That same year, a young scholar from the southern city of Kanchipuram, V. K. R. V. Rao, published his doctoral thesis (among the first three in economics from Cambridge). The research set a fresh foundation for estimating India's national income using novel methods.[77] Nine years later, to address the 'inadequacy of the factual data available for the formulation of economic policies', a newly appointed National Income Committee once again attempted to distil the economic activities of hundreds of millions of Indians into a common denominator.[78] Mahalanobis chaired the Committee, which included Rao, economist Dhananjay Gadgil, and an advisory board that featured both Kuznets and Stone.[79] Another member of the Institute served as the Committee's Secretary and also led the National Income Unit within the Ministry of Finance.[80]

Statistics, in its avatar as handmaiden to planners, was enjoying unprecedented national attention. At the start of 1950, the Professor addressed the Indian Science Congress, now as its president. He spoke of the role that statisticians must play in the task of economic advance. What was ultimately necessary, he asserted, was a 'comprehensive system of social accounting for the whole nation' because statistics had a part to play at every stage of the planning process. The *Amrita Bazaar Patrika* also reported him on elucidating the crucial role of statistics in economic planning. He explained that during the initial preparation of sectoral plans statistics were indispensable for understanding basic information. Next, while the plan was being integrated at a national level, statistics served as the 'common denominator and supplies the common binding of medium for the whole'. Finally, while the plan was being implemented, statistics would help in the continuous tracking and assessment of results.[81]

The Professor was not deluding himself or fellow statisticians about their importance. Just three days later, when answering a reporter's query about the proposal to establish some planning machinery at the Centre, the prime minister stated: 'Planning can only take place with a(n) organization. That is the first requisite. You cannot just plan in the air. You must have facts . . . . So we are going ahead with the organisation of the statistical organisation.'[82] Nehru recognized that central planning and national statistics were inseparable; institutionalizing national planning required national statistical institutions.[83] On the last day of January 1950 – within days of India pronouncing herself a Republic – the president introduced the Planning Commission to Parliament. Immediately following the introduction, he added, 'Such planning will need the fullest help of statistical information. It is proposed therefore to establish a Central Statistical Organisation [CSO]'.[84] Emerging from the nucleus of the Central Statistical Unit, the CSO took over the reins of statistical responsibility for the country. Following close on the heels of the president's remarks to parliamentarians, the prime minister also presented the idea of the Planning Commission to Chief Ministers in his fortnightly letter to them. Reminding them that planning relied 'very much on proper statistical information', he stressed 'the necessity for improving our statistics'.[85]

The Planning Commission and CSO were born within months of each other, and it was understood that they were joined at the hip.[86] At one of the earliest meetings of the Commission, Nehru suggested that two academics – economist Gyan Chand and statistician Mahalanobis – be regularly invited to its meetings. The first meeting attended by the Professor was shortly thereafter and its notes reveal the quick knotting of statistics and planning. The second item on the meeting's agenda was a 'Paper by Professor Mahalanobis on Statistical Requirements for National Planning', and the topics of discussions that immediately followed were 'Central Statistical Organisation' and 'Indian Statistical Institute, Calcutta'. The next morning, at a meeting in the Deputy Chairman's room, the Commission 'discussed with Professor Mahalanobis general problems bearing on statistical work in relation to the requirements of planning'.[87] When the Planning Commission got its own building four years later on Parliament Street – a wide six-storey structure with a grid of square windows protruding from its façade – it surprised no one that the CSO occupied Yojana Bhavan's upper floors.[88]

It was apparent that the Institute would have a role to play in the work of planning. In April 1950, Nehru wrote to Abul Kalam Azad, the Minister for Education, requesting that the Institute be transferred to the Finance Ministry. Offering an explanation, he wrote: 'The work of the Statistical Institute is obviously connected with the organisations here dealing with economic affairs. Now that we are thinking more and more of planning, statistics plays an ever-increasing part.'[89] Later that year, the prime minister once again underlined this connection: 'If this Five - Year Plan is to proceed, statistics becomes an essential basis for it. We cannot proceed without adequate data'.[90]

Technocrats in Nehruvian India were granted broad licence. As Nehru once acidly remarked, he preferred one technocrat to four bureaucrats.[91] Given the emerging nexus between planning and statistics, the work of the Planning Commission began to manifest in the Professor's behaviour in initially minor but ultimately significant ways. He thrust himself into situations that were properly the domain of diplomats. In 1951, he discussed the possibility of Soviet aid for capital goods to India with Georgy Aleksandrov, the head of their cultural delegation to Delhi. He reprised the subject when he visited Moscow the following spring for an economic conference. These were not isolated infractions of diplomatic etiquette. Throughout the next decade and a half, Mahalanobis would not think twice about personally approaching officials of foreign governments in his attempt to secure technical aid, equipment, or foreign investment for India. Never one to be constrained by official niceties or protocol, the Professor did not have a high opinion of India's diplomatic community either. His letters reveal a 'boiling resentment' towards diplomats, describing the majority of them as 'pompous', 'inefficient', 'rigidly hierarchical', and sometimes just 'basically stupid'.[92] Predictably, he incensed actual diplomats who did not take kindly to such presumption. Choosing neither to upbraid nor to endorse this flagrant toe-stepping, the prime minister only made sure to remind Mahalanobis that he did not speak on the government's behalf.

In 1950, a year of manifold statistical developments in Delhi, Calcutta also catapulted itself into an international landmark for advanced training in the subject. For a couple of years, the UN Statistical Commission, the International Statistical Institute, and UNESCO had been concerned about the paucity of statisticians in parts of the world that needed them most. Offering the Institute's services, Mahalanobis proposed a solution – to create an International Statistical Education Centre on an adjacent campus in Calcutta. It opened in October 1950, offering courses at various levels in theoretical and applied statistics to participants from the Middle East, Southeast Asia, South Asia, and East Asia. The Institute made facilities and faculty available, the International Statistical Institute provided visiting international faculty, and UNESCO pitched in with funds.[93] To the Professor, developing these statistical services was vital to the development of South and Southeast Asia.[94] Meanwhile, the Institute had itself continued to expand its educational offerings in its Research and Training School. Mahalanobis also managed to bring the premier international conference of statisticians to New Delhi in 1951, a gathering that attracted 300 statisticians from twenty-eight countries.[95] Apart from having alighted once in Japan, this was the first time the conference was held in Asia or Africa. The following year, in 1950, the Union Cabinet deemed the Institute a focal centre for the advanced study and training in statistics, enabling the possibility of joint programmes with the CSO.[96]

Within India, during the 1950s, statistical training spread from Calcutta to many other campuses. Visiting Chinese statisticians noted that fifteen of India's thirty-three national universities housed either a Department of Statistics or offered statistical training, with over 2,000 students enrolled.[97] By the middle of the decade, students from fourteen countries were receiving training at the International Statistical Education Centre and returning home with knowledge about sample design and large-scale sample surveys that were being pioneered in Calcutta. The Institute was contributing to the spread of cutting-edge statistical techniques throughout the developing world – an instance of under-recognized South-South knowledge and transfer of skills in the mid-twentieth century.[98] By the end of the decade, the Government of India was advertising the availability of jobs for these new cohorts of statisticians. 'Plan Activities Need More Statisticians', one of them pleaded. It described the profession enticingly, detailing the qualities statisticians needed to possess, and the stable, upwardly mobile careers on offer.[99]

Installing a grid of official statistics required unfurling sample surveys across the country. It had to be executed nationally, with regularity, and track a wide spectrum of activities. The success of the Institute's colonial-era sample surveys in eastern India, coupled with the lack of accurate food statistics during the calamitous Bengal Famine that had claimed three million lives, had convinced the independent government of its necessity and urgency. Despite this, the collection of statistics on food had progressed little by independence.[100] As Nehru ruefully noted, the insufficiency of sample surveys across India meant that it was hard even to know whether the government's Grow More Food campaign was a success or a failure. 'We have no data', he admitted, and as a result, 'we function largely in the dark'.[101] A week before Christmas in 1949, the prime minister made it known that he wished to see a series of sample surveys that could statistically summarize the nation's economic life. The Professor laid out the broad strokes of a National Sample Survey (henceforth NSS) within a week and presented it on Christmas to Chintaman Deshmukh, now Financial Adviser to the Government of India.

The NSS was approved in January 1950. Its brief was to conduct continuous biannual urban and rural surveys that would shed light on socio-economic, agricultural, and industrial trends. A newspaper report defined its purpose as filling 'the lacuna in the statistical information, so that planning and formulation of policies can be done in an intelligent manner'.[102] The NSS described its mission and method in the following manner: it was not physically possible to collect statistics from each of the 60 million households across the country, so investigators would have to collect information from a smaller number of households (a sample) such that 'it would be possible to estimate, on the basis of the sample, the required information for the country as a whole'. Determining the sample, then, was critical. Data would be distorted if the investigators selected all the households from the same state, or only from weaving or agricultural families, or exclusively from poor or rich households. They had to make sure that the sample households were chosen in a properly random manner.[103] Once the samples were determined, investigators extracted data from them through interviews (for households or shops), physical observation (in crop surveys), or measurement (by actually harvesting and weighing, to estimate yield).[104]

An NSS Committee, composed of Mahalanobis, economist Dhananjay Gadgil, and bureaucrat P. C. Bhattacharya, had been established to play a supervisory role. Cracks soon appeared in this body, with Gadgil and Mahalanobis finding themselves at war with each other over the design and methods of the sample survey. It was as much a clash of personalities as a professional disagreement between an economist and a statistician.[105] The solution was to carve up the work of designing the survey between the fractious parties. Given its greater experience with large-scale sample surveys, the Institute was asked to take the lead with regard to designing the sample surveys and scrutinizing its results – with the Gadgil-directed Gokhale Institute of Politics and Economics in Pune playing junior partner.

The survey was an extraordinarily complex operation. The Professor closely monitored its establishment in the summer of 1950, involving himself in 'all sorts of details about forms and schedules, maps, tehsil or village lists, computation forms, and accommodation and staff problems'.[106] Designing the survey was an intricate task. The workers at the Institute were confronted with a lack of detailed maps for some parts of the country, and scarce official records for even village populations and locations. For nearly 16% of India's landmass neither population nor area figures were available – only village names were known – and for approximately 6% of the country, even village names were not available. Once the survey was designed, and a proposal forwarded to the government, the inaugural round of the NSS was allocated 2.5 million rupees in May 1950. Since the field survey would require manpower resources far beyond that available to both the Calcutta and Poona

Institutes, the survey itself was to be conducted by officers and investigators employed by the Directorate of the NSS, a government agency within the Ministry of Finance.[107]

It was, as the *Hindustan Times* reported, 'the biggest and most comprehensive sampling inquiry ever undertaken in any country in the world'.[108] Even to statisticians sympathetic to the Professor, the sheer scale seemed foolhardy. As the American statistician William Edwards Deming recalled: 'We in this country, though accustomed to large scale sample surveys, were aghast at Mahalanobis' plans for the national sample surveys of India. Their complexity and scope seemed beyond the bounds of possibility.'[109] These were, to quote the Nobel Prize-winning economist Angus Deaton, the 'world's first system of household surveys to apply the principles of random sampling'.[110]

After filling scores of new posts through advertisements in newspapers and government employment exchanges, the NSS recruits gathered at the Institute in Calcutta to spend three weeks training at the end of July 1950. From there they fanned out to six regional centres where they instructed the investigators who would go out into the field. Each investigator was armed with a carefully compiled book that provided clear instructions on how to approach respondents in villages, as well as explanations of what each question meant. Out in the field, they collected survey information through interviews. The investigator approached members of the sample households and asked them to answer a schedule of questions, which was then cross-checked with existing information.

The inaugural NSS began in October 1950 and ended in March 1951: the sample consisted of 1,833 villages that had been carefully selected from India's 560,000 villages. The field branch of the survey was carried out with 607 employees in its first round – only 40% of the number they actually required. Out of the sample villages, the majority were given the questionnaire prepared by the Institute in Calcutta, and the rest were to respond to the one provided by the Gokhale Institute in Poona. India was divided into sixteen blocks, with villages assigned to each of them in accordance with their populations as per the 1941 census. These blocks were cut up into smaller areas, and each of the 350 field investigators had to survey a group of six villages. Complications abounded: the exercise involved the use of fifteen languages (all of which had to be translated back to English) and the discovery of a 140 local systems of weight measurement, each of which had to be standardized back to the norm laid out in Calcutta.[111] The first round took longer than expected as many investigators quit due to falling sick when visiting the villages they surveyed, or found the work conditions too difficult. When the

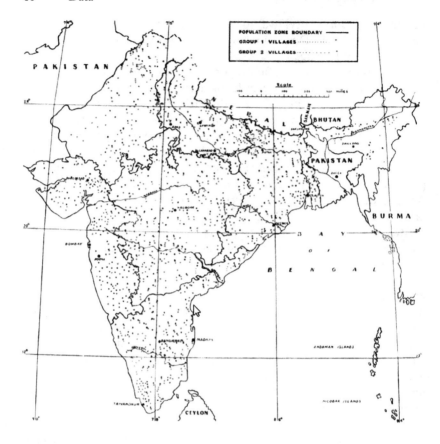

Figure 1.1. Locations of the sample villages in the NSS first round
(October 1950–March 1951).

schedules came back from the field to Calcutta, they were first checked
by computing clerks, after which the information was transmitted onto
punched cards. These were then sent to the tabulation section, where
IBM machine tabulators sorted and compiled the data.[112]

An inkling of the daunting scale of the survey's panorama is provided in
a diary entry by Mahalanobis. He wrote of the difficulty in accessing some
of the sample villages, scattered as they were all across the country. There
were, for instance, villages in the 'wild areas' of Orissa where investigators
had to make their way through twenty miles of forests accompanied by
armed guards. To get to another sample village, the investigator had to
wait for the snow to melt over high Himalayan passes.[113] Another

description from the report of the inaugural round attests to the peculiar difficulties faced. In the north eastern state of Assam, the field staff met both 'the most civilized people reputed for their arts and crafts, their rich language and literature' and also 'uncivilized naked tribes, who speak a dialect known to none but themselves, who even to this day know not what money means'. Travelling from one sample village to another sometimes took up to six days due to the trek through dense hill forests. Of the twenty-five tribes that were selected, many spoke dialects unknown to the staff. To add affront, 'they laugh at the word economic development'. There were 'unlawful elements' as well, leading to reports of 'mishandling of National Sample Survey staff'. In summary, the 'dense impregnable forests with wild animals and epidemic tropical diseases, hills, and climbs, contribute to the difficulties of the survey'. Braving the jungle appears to have been part of the surveyors' job description: investigators working in Odisha complained about having to make their way through 'deep jungles infested with wild-beasts and man eaters'.[114]

The surveys delivered remarkably textured detail about the life of ordinary citizens. They covered agriculture, industry, household enterprises, animal husbandry, transportation, trade, employment, and the cost of living in urban and rural India, to mention a few. The level of granularity is startling. For example, the second round of the NSS focused on rural India and covered 10,870 households in 1,142 villages. Each of those families was visited by an investigator who conducted an interview, and in the case of crops and certain other items, made direct observations. For instance, we know that in June 1951, investigators S. R. David and N. Harigovinda Menon visited the family of thirty-five-year-old farmer Chidambaram Mudaly in the village of Erisinampatti in Coimbatore district. The schedule filled out by the investigators was a detailed sketch of this family's economic life. It recorded how much Mudaly, his wife, three daughters, and mother-in-law consumed and how they spent their money. Under food, for example, this included the outlay on rice, wheat, millets, ghee, *paan* (betel leaf), turmeric, chilies, *kothamalli* (coriander), tea, coffee, and sea salt, among many provisions. The richness of detail extended to clothing, entertainment, intoxicants, furniture, land, and other assets. Unfortunately, we know little about how those surveyed, such as Chidambaram Mudaly's family, responded to this new and direct interface with the government. This level of intrusive official interest in the particulars of their daily lives was likely to have been greeted with surprise and some degree of suspicion.

The informational bounty harvested was not relevant – for the purposes of planning – for what it said about just this one family. But when agglomerated and calculated alongside more than 10,000 other data

Figure 1.2. Investigators from the Institute estimating rice yields (undated).

points about employment, income, and consumption in rural India, the results transformed the planner's abilities and constituted a massive leap in the state's knowledge capacities.[115] These investigators were among the many standard-bearers of the government of independent India, in effect, making the governed more governable. In a profusion of tables and charts, the material lives of hundreds of millions of Indians were presented to the state's gaze, with greater magnification and legibility than ever before.[116] The surveys made the citizenry the object of the state's scientific scrutiny, while taming the wild complexity of people's lives into utilitarian tabulation. Knowing the people en masse, rather than individually, abetted the function of a centralized state engaged in planning the economy.

***

Planning kindled the generation of a complex, yet concentrated, national statistical system. It marked a new stage in the data capacities of the state and the centralization of power within it. David Ludden succinctly described the continuities in development discourse across the colonial and postcolonial periods in this way: 'Better data means more state power.'[117] India was not unique in its attempt to order, classify, and count society. In some ways, this was typical of other twentieth-century, high-modernist states that were, in James Scott's description, excessively 'optimistic about the possibilities for the comprehensive planning of human settlement and production'.[118] Ranging across the political spectrum – from the Tennessee Valley Authority in the United States, to Soviet collectivization, to villagization programmes in postcolonial Tanzania – they were all engaged in schemes to simplify and order society from above and to draw meaning from it. Certain kinds of abstraction yielded knowledge and the resultant ability to intervene and control. Arunabh Ghosh, the historian of Chinese statistics, notes that the period after World War II, which saw widespread decolonization and international organization, was a 'globalized epoch of statistics-driven numerical positivism', in which statistics came to represent a crucial ingredient in development and cooperation.[119] Faith in data entered the era's *zeitgeist*.[120]

A statistical lens made the economy more visible to the government, and more tractable for planned economic intervention. Adam Tooze observes that our understanding of the economy as a distinct sphere is itself the product of an imaginative leap. Gathering statistics was an important part of the process by which the idea of a national economy turned from an 'abstract conception' into an 'objective reality'.[121] India in the early 1950s was engaged in just such a process; one that had started with the statistical critiques of the colonial economy back in the late nineteenth century. The postcolonial data surge was not only significant for what it enabled the state to perceive, but it could also play a part in the consolidation of the 'national economy' in the public mind.[122] As Tooze suggests, the 'flood of statistics carries a national message. Citizens are invited to relate their individual and local economic experience, whether as employees or employers, as consumers or taxpayers, to a wider narrative, that of the national economy'.[123] We might even think of this as a step in the journey towards what Michelle Murphy has termed the 'economization of life'; the thirst for quantification and the downpour of statistics as part of the story of how the economy came to be the ultimate measure of value in society from the mid-twentieth century onwards.[124]

The NSS, which continues to this day, was one of the lasting successes of this period of national statistical expansion. Twenty years after it began, statistician Edwards Deming, a one-time sceptic was convinced: 'No country, developed, under-developed or over-developed, has such a wealth of information about its people as India in respect of expenditures, savings, time lost through sickness, employment, unemployment, agricultural and industrial production'.[125] Drawing lessons for China, You Poh Seng noted that 'in India, the conditions approximate more nearly ... to the conditions of those countries, which like China, have no genuine statistics, and where such statistics, if they are to be obtained at all have to be obtained mainly by surveys, for which the experience of India will serve as a guidance and an example worth imitating'.[126] Frank Yates, a statistical luminary, remarked that the survey produced information that was 'at all times desirable' but was of 'very special importance to India in the present phase of its active planned development'.[127]

Sample surveys had even entered popular vocabulary in India. As Vidura would joke in the pages of *Shankar's Weekly*, 'Some people are for the Plan, and others are against it. It is rather difficult, in the absence of a sample survey, to know which is which'.[128] Addressing a gathering of the states' chief ministers at Hyderabad House in 1954, Nehru remarked that India had for a while been 'groping in the direction of planning'. The nation had been stumbling forward, like a person blindfolded, because until recently it did not 'have all the information, data, statistics which are essential for planning'. Earlier they 'just did not have enough data', but now, 'we have got much more ... we are at a stage, a definite stage'.[129] With the blindfold loosening, the problem and its solution were shifting into focus.

Beginning in 1962, the Planning Commission used information generated by the sample surveys to first craft India's primary index of deprivation – the poverty line. India was a front runner in doing so: the United States developed its own poverty line only three years later.[130] Through their impact on the UN Statistical Commission, the UN Sub-Commission on Sample Surveys, and the International Statistical Education Centre, the Professor, the Institute, and the NSS continue to play a role in estimating poverty across the developing world. The methods they pioneered became the norm for household surveys everywhere. The World Bank's flagship household survey programme, conducted in numerous countries since 1980 – the Living Standards Measurement Study – can trace its lineage back to India's NSS.[131] At the beginning of the new millennium, the UN World Development Report noted that '85 per cent of the developing world's population lives in countries with at least two household income or expenditure surveys'.[132] As economists Pranab Bardhan, Rohini Somanathan, T. N. Srinivasan, and Nobel winner Abhijit Banerjee write, 'There is no other instance of an entirely homegrown institution in a developing country becoming a world leader in a large field of general interest'.[133]

Catalysed by the requirements of a planned economy, the 1950s witnessed a transformation in the Indian state's informational capacities and quantitative sophistication, alongside a concentration of its power in unelected bodies of technocrats, whether the Planning Commission itself or the Institute. The decision to centrally plan the Indian economy unfurled an unprecedented national statistical infrastructure in the decade after independence. Even present-day critics of planning recognize its thirst for data. As the subtitle of an opinion piece in the *Wall Street Journal* announced in 2019, 'Without statistics, you can't prepare a five-year plan'.[134] It was this period of accelerated state-building that generated a centralized coordinating agency for national statistics, instituted the regular calculation of national income, and set into motion the periodic assessment of the economy's health through a vast NSS. Together, they constituted a sizeable achievement for postcolonial India. Their legacy accounts for India possessing – until recently – among the most reliable, fine-grained, and well-established series of national statistics in the developing world. At the time, however, what mattered most was that together they generated the 'information required for planning'.[135] Planning was the context in which Mahalanobis would transform from a college professor who published research in a once-marginal science to one of the most influential Indians of his generation. Planning paved the way for Calcutta to conquer New Delhi.

2   Calcutta Conquers Delhi

How did an academic institute in the quiet outskirts of a city far away from the capital come to determine the path of a country of 400 million? It is a question that has been asked from the mid-twentieth century because it marked a turning point for India's economy. Mahalanobis and the Indian Statistical Institute played a crucial role in crafting independent India's economic strategy. The era-defining Second Five-Year Plan (1956–1961), which they authored, stamped its imprint on subsequent decades. In some ways, Mahalanobis and the Institute were responsible for the country's economic trajectory right up to the period of market reforms in the early 1990s. Less clear is how they came by such influence. What took them from academy to policy, from the dense foliage of a lakeside campus in Calcutta's suburbs to the bland, yet consequential, offices of the Planning Commission in New Delhi?

The impact of planning on statistics led to a statistician shaping the Plan. A planning-induced expansion in the state's intellectual infrastructure had formalized the relationship between planning and statistics. It was this process that placed the Professor and the Institute in a position where they could, in turn, shape policy. It was as much planning's affinity for statistics in the decade after independence as association with Nehru that explains Mahalanobis' fingerprints all over the Second Five-Year Plan. The explanation I offer here is structural rather than personal. While I trace how Mahalanobis and Institute came to formulate economic policy, this is not meant to be an account of the Second Plan or its fate. Instead, I convey how a context in which planning privileged statistics led to an institutional nexus between them, opening the door for the Professor and the Institute to enter, and then dominate, the Planning Commission. Further, my account shows how – institutional turf wars notwithstanding – planning not only privileged technocrats by its very nature but also led to the installation of data capacities that further legitimized experts and entrenched their role in the state.

Soon after India became independent, the interweaving of planning and statistics produced a context in which the Professor and the Institute were drawn ever deeper into the corridors of the Yojana Bhavan. They would play starring roles in the country's development saga. During the decade and a half after independence, the Institute became a national think tank, second only to the Planning Commission itself in its influence over planning. Capitalizing on a context in which national statistics were viewed as integral to economic planning, the Professor embarked on a campaign to court foreign experts to bolster his claim to writing economic policy. This involved long tours abroad and hosting hundreds of experts in Baranagore, during which he wooed like-minded social scientists and credentialed foreign economists. The Institute broadened its ambitions and opened an entire wing dedicated to studying Plan strategies and inaugurated an outpost in New Delhi. Their rising reputations combined with auspicious circumstances to create a space for them that transcended statistics and academia.

When confronting rivals in government and the professoriate during the Second Five-Year Plan debates, Mahalanobis was able to weaponize the credibility he had acquired from years of brushing shoulders with a curated army of foreign experts. Global expertise was employed to outmanoeuvre powerful critics within the Planning Commission. In order to jostle their way to a seat at the policymaking table, the Professor and the Institute leveraged a variety of resources: their centrality to national statistical organizations (which had become critical to planning), proximity to the prime minister and finance minister, and support cultivated from actors and institutions on both sides of the Cold War. The Planning Commission did not roll out the red carpet for the Professor. It was a coup whose swiftness took Delhi by surprise.

Lessons of Travel

Mahalanobis' jet-setting drew attention. As academics go, he was no ordinary conference-hopper. As an awed and perhaps slightly bewildered Edwards Deming later recalled, 'Probably no statistician ever attended so many meetings the world over.'[1] The travels earned a separate section in the Institute's Annual Reports and were later published in *Sankhya*. Titled 'Tours Abroad by Professor Mahalanobis' or some variation on this, it was a diary of lectures delivered, commissions chaired, conferences pit-stopped, memoranda signed, academic exchanges facilitated, technical aid secured, and intellectual eminences met. What resulted was a meticulous and immodest paper trail of international academic schmooze. The extent of these travels raised some eyebrows at the

Figure 2.1. P. C. Mahalanobis aboard a steam ship (December 1956).

Institute. British-born Indian geneticist J. B. S. Haldane complained about the Institute suffering from the Professor's frequent absence. Of Mahalanobis' seasonal migrations, he wrote: 'The journeyings of our Director, define a novel random vector.'[2]

The Professor left India in order to be relevant in India. As one of India's pre-eminent scientists and her foremost statistician, Mahalanobis was invited to universities and academic institutes around the world. He revelled in them because, apart from satiating his varied intellectual urges, they magnified his reputation at home. For while his scientific bona fides were above reproach, as an economist he had no credentials. If he aspired to be a planner, he would need backers.

Committing a few months to travel almost every year, Mahalanobis criss-crossed continents in his role as unofficial scientific ambassador and public intellectual, most often visiting Europe, the United States, and the Soviet Union. The Professor networked with a vengeance. The combination of academic renown, involvement in every aspect of Indian statistics, a seeming lack of political affiliation, and access to the Indian finance minister and prime minister opened doors on both sides of the Iron Curtain. These included the offices of statisticians, planners, and economists from Washington to Moscow, Tokyo to Puerto Rico.

Tracking the Professor's travels in 1954 alone offers a glimpse of the hats he wore and the manner in which he styled himself as a planner. We join him in Switzerland in April where he chaired the UN Statistical Commission (his name having been proposed by the United States, seconded by the USSR, and carried unanimously). He was mulling travel to Austria, where he had been invited to the Committee for the Promotion of International Trade at the suggestion of the Polish economist and diplomat Oskar Lange. Vienna was a temptation due to Lange; Mahalanobis was devising a way to bring the socialist planner to India. Lange's 'intimate knowledge of capitalist and planned economies', he believed, would be of help to India's mixed economy.[3]

In Geneva, he dined with Swedish economist and future Nobel laureate Gunnar Myrdal, who had recently been in India. To his satisfaction, Mahalanobis found Myrdal's views 'a good deal in agreement with mine'. On their way from Europe to the United States, the Mahalanobises alighted in Paris, where he spent time in discussion with economist Charles Bettelheim at the Commissariat Général du Plan (France's planning body). Following that stop, they crossed the English Channel and spent a week visiting statistical pioneers Sir Ronald Fischer in Cambridge and Frank Yates at Rothamsted. Among conversations in England, the one that the Professor judged to be most significant was with economist Richard Stone, another future Nobel winner. The Professor explained his ideas and was pleased to hear Stone's approval. It was a fortifying tonic for him, imparting 'a good deal of confidence'.[4]

After crossing the Atlantic, the Professor spent most of his American sojourn in New York, squeezing in time for North Carolina, Washington, Berkeley, and Palo Alto. The topics of discussion included statistical quality control, electronic computers, and technical aid. However, among the matters uppermost on his mind was the need to 'collect technical information on capital coefficients [ratio of the value of capital to the value of output], inter-industry relations etc. and to have discussions on the economics of growth'.[5] He counted himself lucky because he was able to secure copies of American capital coefficients based on an inter-industry relations study. He sent the two volumes to Calcutta, swaddled in a diplomatic bag, and took precautions to keep a microfilmed copy in London in case it got damaged in transit. He was taking such care with this information and was after even more because he believed it would prove useful for physical planning – a technique for devising plans based on physical targets (tons of x, litres of y) instead of financial ones.

Mahalanobis did not see his role in India as confined to statistics. He was anxious to take the next step: 'now I am eager to make a beginning with actual models of physical planning'. In an unusually candid letter, he wrote:

I had only very vague ideas of planning when I first came to Delhi. From 1950, when I first started handling national income data, I began to learn. My first visit to USSR in 1951 was of crucial importance because I got a vivid impression of planning . . . . One reason I have been coming abroad so often is a partly conscious and partly sub-conscious urge to seek contacts, to discuss, to collect information and to equip myself for physical planning. There is practically no literature on this subject. Economists in my own country are great experts on Western text books (about which my own ignorance is profound) and they do not even see the problem as I see it . . . . To be quite frank, I am so ignorant about academic economics and my Indian colleagues have been so cock-sure about their own infallibility that I had a little bit of [a] inferiority complex about economic matters. My frequent visits to the West have given me not only a much greater breadth of vision but have also give my (sic) increasing self confidence.[6]

This was a rare confession of insecurity from someone who otherwise conveyed invulnerability. It was probably this complex that manifested in the contempt Mahalanobis showed for economists, particularly Indian ones. As a junior colleague and future biographer would note, he was 'highly distrustful of professional economists' and openly declared 'total disregard for theoretical economics'.[7] The Professor certainly had ideas about the economy and wanted to play a role in policymaking, but was loathe to consider himself an economist. Unlike them, he claimed, he was not interested in 'politics, philosophy, subjective aspects'. He intended to approach the economy as he did physics, with the expectation of a single value-neutral answer. It was why he often brushed aside questions regarding his own politics or the political ramifications of his prescriptions for the economy. All of that was politics, he said: 'I am interested in physics.'[8]

Through personal discussions with celebrated economists – Ragnar Frisch, Jan Tinbergen, Charles Bettelheim, Oskar Lange, and Gunnar Myrdal in continental Europe; Joan Robinson, Richard Stone, and Richard Goodwin in England; Simon Kuznets, Paul Baran, and Robert Dorfman in the United States – Mahalanobis realized to his relief that he was taken seriously. Many of them, in his mind at least, agreed with him. The irony, lost on the Professor, was that the world's foremost expert on sample design was not perturbed by the possibility of this sample being contaminated by selection bias. The greatest benefit of the tour, he concluded, was that it gave him 'complete confidence to start the detailed work of planning'.

Take the case of Joan Robinson. A major twentieth-century economist who worked in Marxian and Keynesian frames, she was predicted by many to be the first female winner of the Nobel Prize in economics.[9]

Mahalanobis described the formidable Cambridge academic as 'one of the most brilliant economists' of the United Kingdom, 'considered by some to be the most brilliant'. Her student then and later PhD advisee, Amartya Sen, concurred, characterizing Robinson as 'totally brilliant but vigorously intolerant'.[10] As Mahalanobis excitedly recounted, she had come down to London from Cambridge to meet with him. The Professor was gratified to learn that she had recently read two pieces by him, on national income and another on a bisector economic model – and found much to approve of. He felt especially gladdened because, to the best of his knowledge, not a single economist in India had read them, barring those in his immediate circle. Upon hearing about Robinson's plans to travel to India, the Professor convinced her to spend a few months at the Institute later that summer. Quite apart from the benefit to the Institute's workers, Mahalanobis revealed, her 'support may carry conviction that our approach to development planning is not foolish'. Upon hearing this, the Cambridge don smiled and chimed, 'Yes, I think I would be able to knock some sense into the heads of the economists in your country.'[11]

Despite the support abroad, Mahalanobis realized that the problem of India's planned development was not something that Western economists could or would solve themselves. Though they could be of help in providing expertise and technical knowledge, the 'dirty work' had to be done 'with our own hands', by people like him. Nonetheless, these talks were critical to Mahalanobis, straightening his spine as an economic thinker. Through these conversations with 'some of the leading economists of the West' he came to believe, or convinced himself, that they agreed India requiring physical planning. He was also beginning to feel that economic growth in India needed a jump-start. Not only was gradualism unacceptable in a situation where the task was colossal, it also might not work at all. Sounding more physicist than planner, he wondered if there were certain 'fundamental' or 'basic' states of the economy: 'one can only jump from one state to another – or not change at all and stagnate'.[12]

The Professor travelled to the Soviet Union at the end of June. In Moscow, the Professor and two scientists from the Institute (Mani Mukherjee and Samar Mitra) had lengthy discussions on development at the Institute for Economics, the Institute of Oriental Studies, and with high-ranking members of the USSR Academy of Sciences.[13] They were also afforded a sitting room in their hotel where the Indians held talks with Soviet economists. Given the Soviets' seniority in planning, the Professor felt he had much to learn. And the Soviets, as uber planners, were pleased to offer lessons. 'At the back of everything is one single aim', Mahalanobis wrote back to Pant: 'what effective help can we secure in making our own plans and in implementing them?'[14] The discussions traversed a range of themes and concluded that the need of the hour was 'rapid and State-initiated and State-controlled development of the basic industries'.[15] With officials of the Ministry of Foreign Affairs and Foreign Trade Office, they spoke about the possibility of Soviet technical aid to India for planning, visiting experts, statistics, and computers.

Modeste Rubinstein accompanied the guests from Calcutta for the duration of their stay. A stalwart of the Gosplan, he reminisced about how preparation for it had begun under Lenin's direction. Central planning, carried out correctly, was a technocrat's theme park: 'hundreds of technologists, engineers of all kinds, and specialists sat down with economists and finance experts to prepare the earliest plans', he recalled. In fact, many Soviet planners found it hard to comprehend India's seemingly half-hearted commitment to centralized planning. If India were serious about it, the Soviets stressed, they would need 'not scores, but hundreds of technologists and scientists and engineers'.[16] Only Rubinstein understood, after repeated explanation, that the people he was chaperoning were not formally planners (yet) and did not represent India's Planning Commission in any official capacity. It was only an eager, amateur hunting party beginning to take aim.

The Professor's spirits were lifted by the Soviet welcome. He realized that his hosts evinced a desire to strengthen relations with India because it appeared a possible political ally, and Nehru's prestige was at its zenith internationally. He was struck by repeated references to the prime minister and the emotion his homeland evoked. Wherever he went, across class, people spoke with admiration for Nehru. In Leningrad (St Petersburg), he attended a church service one Sunday, and when he emerged 'some of the women were so overcome to speak of India and Nehru that two or three began to cry softly – tears came to their eyes in an upsurge of feeling'.[17] While this sentimentalism might appear an exaggeration, other Indian travellers to the Soviet Union confirmed Nehru's remarkable personal popularity. Touring the Russian countryside a few months later, filmmaker Khwaja Ahmad Abbas wrote to his brother about what transpired when he and his Soviet writer friends stopped in a small town for lunch. One of the Russians proposed a toast: '"to Nehru – the most important man in the world today" – and, lo and behold, a crowd of people from other tables and even waiters and waitresses crowded around to join us in drinking this toast'. It was a good time to be an Indian in Russia. Abbas wrote of the 'universal respect and affection for our P.M.' as well as Russians' enthusiasm for Indian cinema. He was taken aback by the 'unbelievable popularity' of the film *Awara* and its song *Awara Hoon* 'which has swept the whole country'.[18]

Mahalanobis was bowled over by the hospitality. He was invited by Minister Georgy Aleksandrov to spend a day at his riverside cottage on the banks of the Moskva. It was a rare gesture for a ranking member of the Soviet establishment, apparently due to fears of espionage.[19] Located outside the city amidst pines and conifers, Alexandrov's two-storied retreat was among a cluster of *dachas* belonging to the Council of Ministers, a group described by the Professor as the 'highest level of society'. Joined by the Rubinsteins and other members of the Academy of Sciences, they grazed on a 'distressingly lavish' spread, sipped choice wines, and raised their glasses in many toasts.[20] One was to the health of the two nations' prime ministers. Another invoked Newton's laws of gravitation to explain the relationship between China, India, and the USSR. It was convoluted but unsurprising, given the company. 'The whole atmosphere is something wonderful', the Professor proclaimed in rapture.[21]

Occasionally, the thrill was rudely interrupted by doubt. In the midst of relaying the uplifting Muscovite goings-on to Pitambar Pant, he screeched to a halt. 'These people have taken me very seriously – much too seriously, I am afraid – because I do not know if we would be able to do anything real except write background papers'.[22] The news from the Planning Commission and Government of India was often deflating. Just as airborne castles began to take shape, he would receive mail from Delhi and 'drop down to earth'.[23] Matters were coming to a head for the frustrated Professor. He was tired of producing background notes and studies, moving 'furiously like a rocking horse without any progress'.[24]

At half-past midnight in mid-July, 1954 Mahalanobis peered out of his hotel room across Red Square – ringed by Lenin's mausoleum and the fairy-tale domes of Saint Basil's cathedral – at the lights twinkling atop Kremlin's towers. The Professor wished there were closer relations between Delhi, Beijing, and Moscow. He sensed that the moment on which his life would hinge was imminent: there was 'a growing conviction of a kind of crisis'. It was not possible anymore to simply stick to statistics, which had always been 'merely the means to an end'. What really inter-ested him was planning for national development. 'I hope New Delhi will give us a chance.'[25]

Drafts and Frames

Planning began to take root in Baranagore. In a conversation with Chintaman Deshmukh – now finance minister and member of the

Planning Commission – Mahalanobis expressed interest in putting together a small group in Calcutta to undertake policy-oriented studies on the national economy. It was out of this exchange that the Operational Research Unit was formed. Established as a department within the Institute, it addressed econometric problems relating to development in tandem with the CSO, National Income Unit, and the NSS. More specifically, it would focus on problems connected with planning in a mixed economy.[26]

One of the foreign consultants invited was the French Marxist economist Charles Bettelheim.[27] The papers by Bettelheim during his time at the Institute – particularly the Frenchman's endorsement of physical planning – were widely circulated in official circles. After reading them, the scholarly Chief Minister of Madras, C. Rajagopalachari, expressed disquiet. 'Rajaji', a grandee of the Congress Party, instantly recognizable by his round tinted glasses, was once Nehru's first choice to be the country's inaugural President. 'I fear a church is growing round the God of Planning', he warned the prime minister in a 'mood of deep depression'. It was a church in which 'expert priests' were taking centre stage. 'Everyone assumes everyone will act according to order and the only thing to do is to discover the mathematics of it, the utmost allowance to human nature being a percentage discount!'[28] Before the decade was out, Rajagopalachari had founded the Swantantra Party to battle the now-completed cathedral to planning.

In September 1954, at the end of a Planning Commission meeting about the upcoming Second Five-Year Plan, the finance minister asked whether it was possible for India to eliminate unemployment in 10 years while simultaneously boosting national income. The Planning Commission entrusted this question with the new Operational Research Unit. At the same session, it was also decided that the Institute should formally begin studies relating to planning immediately.[29] The government was effectively contracting out some of the work of planning to a private entity. A few days later, the Professor discussed the kernel of his ideas on the Second Five-Year Plan with the prime minister and, encouraged, submitted a short note on the subject. Echoing the substance of the Planning Commission's suggestion, Nehru responded by asking him to begin a series of working papers on planning at the Institute.

Standing at the head of a crammed room in Baranagore the following month, the prime minister inaugurated a Planning Division at the Institute. Like many politicians, Nehru rarely encountered a room that could not benefit from lecturing. It was a characteristically meandering speech, expounding on China, the perils of being doctrinaire, democratic planning, and federalism. Though brevity was not one of his virtues, self-awareness was. As he admitted with humour, 'I am not an expert to talk to experts about their subjects; so I talk vaguely about vague things.'[30]

The Institute took to its role as the Planning Commission's think tank with gusto. Its in-house magazine *Samvadadhvam* (taken from a Vedic text, meaning 'united we speak') carried an article with the zealous rhyme, 'statistics without planning has no fruit, planning without statistics has no root'.[31] Translations of French and Russian works on planning theory and practice were begun. With the Institute becoming a private outpost of the Commission, planning was moving further from the realm of politics. Already an expert body insulated from politics, the Planning Commission was now passing on some of its work to another body of experts who were even more insulated.

Within a month of the Planning Division's ribbon-cutting ceremony, the Professor gave the prime minister a general note with his ideas on the approach to the Second Five-Year Plan. Late morning on 10 November, 1954 the Professor was asked to present this to the National Development Council (comprising the Planning Commission, the Union Cabinet, and the Chief Ministers of all Indian states), assembled at Hyderabad House in New Delhi. Invited to explain the studies on planning that had begun in Calcutta, Mahalanobis used the opportunity to hold forth on his view of what planning was and the form it should take.[32]

Towards the end of the year, Baranagore received a string of high-profile visitors to assess the Planning Division's work and to discuss the new partnership between New Delhi and Calcutta.[33] Both the Ministry of Finance and the Planning Commission became increasingly involved in the Institute's work. Two economists were asked to work closely with the Institute's team and liaise with the government. Those tapped were J. J. Anjaria, chief economic adviser at the Ministry of Finance and head of the Economics Division at the Planning Commission, and his youthful deputy at the ministry, I. G. Patel. The Planning Division also had the help of several other visiting economists that winter: Oskar Lange, Ragnar Frisch, Charles Bettelheim, Richard Goodwin, and Academician D. D. Degtyar of the Gosplan, who headed a team of Soviet experts that included I. Y. Pisarev, Modeste Rubinstein, and P. M. Moskvin.

In late December, the Lok Sabha debated India's economic predicament and the road map to be followed. Flashing a clear signal to planners, the nation's representatives adopted a motion stating that the objective of economic policy should be a 'socialistic pattern of society'. They believed this entailed a full-throttle acceleration of the economy, especially industrial development.[34] Exactly a month later, at a meeting of the Indian National Congress in Avadi near Madras, a 'socialistic pattern of society' was affirmed by the party as the objective of national planning. While the signal may have been clear, the phrasing was anything but. The choice of 'socialistic' was a convenient obfuscation that allowed vague agreement within the party without tying it down to specific commitments. This was because very different points on the political spectrum at the time saw themselves as socialist or socialist-adjacent. The term 'socialistic' was a large umbrella that accommodated many under it. As scholars have argued, mid-century Indian socialist thought was a shape-shifting ideology threading together members of the Congress Party, those of the opposition Praja Socialist Party (of Jayaprakash Narayan, Rammanohar Lohia, and Kamaladevi Chattopadhyay), and even Gandhians like J. C. Kumarappa and Vinobha Bhave.[35] Socialism or radical democracy had acquired what Sudipta Kaviraj called an 'ironic hegemony'. Ironic because even the Hindu nationalist Jan Sangh occasionally claimed some version of socialism as their goal. The result was a 'bewildering variety of socialisms, from Communist to Hindu'. The more significant political consequence was that the indiscriminate usage of the socialist label robbed it of any meaning, effectively 'creating a Socialist night in which all parties are black'.[36]

The next month, growing impatient, Nehru wrote to the deputy chairman of the Planning Commission expressing dissatisfaction about the insufficient coordination between planners in Delhi and Calcutta. Gently chiding a man who was less than thrilled about Calcutta's expanding footprint, Nehru reiterated the extent of the Institute's role in planning. The work being carried out in Calcutta was 'a part of the Planning Commission's work' especially since it was the Commission that had asked the Institute to go down this path at its last meeting. He reminded V. T. Krishnamachari of the many 'very eminent planners and statisticians' from abroad who were working at the Institute because it offered facilities that Delhi did not. It was essential that they cooperate. 'We should give them the fullest help and not treat them as some extraneous element.' The Institute was to be treated 'as part of our planning organization'.[37]

The Planning Commission soon put together an impressive Panel of Economists to produce working papers on planning and to offer learned opinion on the work being done both at the Planning Commission and at Baranagore. Deshmukh chaired it, D. R. Gadgil was its vice-chairman, and the rest included twenty of India's leading economists. The CSO created a Planning Cell, which was located on the premises of the Planning Commission.[38] But within this profusion of bodies, the Institute's influence was becoming unmistakable. It is telling, for example, that at the inaugural meeting of the Panel of Economists, it was

Mahalanobis who addressed the gathering, bringing them up to speed on the work that was being done at the Institute.[39]

At Baranagore, 1955 began in a whirl of activity. Statisticians, economists, visiting foreign experts, and the Professor worked feverishly along with associates from the Institute's Planning Unit in Delhi, the CSO, Ministry of Finance, and Planning Commission, to produce its most consequential document. By this point, Mahalanobis had been accorded de facto membership in the Planning Commission. Membership was meant not just to harness his own expertise, but also to represent those working on 'statistical planning' at the Institute's Planning Division.[40] He had turned down the offer of a formal position as Member of the Planning Commission in favour of a de facto post because he wanted to continue to 'function as a scientist' and retain not only his independence, but also that of the Institute.[41] Planning was being contracted out to the Institute and the Professor, resulting in actors whose primary home remained outside of the state apparatus assuming a core function of the state. Technocracy was straining against democracy.

The person nominated to act as a liaison between Calcutta and New Delhi was the young and urbane Gujarati, I. G. Patel, then a deputy economic adviser at the Finance Ministry. He was sure that the need for this position had arisen due to discomfort with the Professor's growing stature in the corridors of the ministry, not to mention in the Planning Commission. 'I.G.', as he was known, had just turned thirty. He had scaled academic peaks at the Universities of Bombay, Cambridge, and Harvard and was infected with an idealism that was abundant at this moment of nation-building. He had returned from a stint at the International Monetary Fund to work for his country. The months spent shuttling between Calcutta and Delhi were exhilarating to this youthful policy mandarin who would go on to work under four prime ministers and lead institutions, such as the Indian Institute of Management (Ahmedabad), London School of Economics, and the Reserve Bank of India.[42] To an awestruck Patel, the Institute resembled 'an ancient *gurukul* set in sylvan surroundings'. It was a cocktail of disarming hospitality, famed intellects, and erudite debate amidst a context of national importance.[43]

The Planning Division was ready in March 1955 to submit its views on the shape that the Second Five-Year Plan should take. The Professor travelled to Delhi by rail, making revisions to the draft with Patel and other Institute workers as the train chugged northwest across the Gangetic plain. Once in Delhi, they were based at a bungalow designed by Herbert Baker on 8 King George Avenue (Rajaji Avenue today), immediately south of the Secretariat buildings. Assigned to the Professor when he was named Honorary Statistical Adviser to the Government, the bungalow functioned as the Institute's Delhi office and the Mahalanobis residence in the capital.[44] A report from the Institute described this address as a link between it 'and the Cabinet Secretariat, the Central Statistical Organisation, the Planning Commission, and various other Government departments'.[45] Here, the Professor and I. G. made last-minute changes and added final touches before submitting the *Draft Recommendations for the Formulation of the Second Five Year Plan* on 17 March 1955.[46] The Plan Frame, as it came to be known, made sure to emphasize the role to be played by the Institute in the nation's planning process. It stated that the Institute along with the CSO 'must function as an integral part of the planning machinery at the Centre'.[47] The Plan Frame – which a contemporary column in the *Times of India* described as emerging from a 'statistical sieve' – would later come be recognized as 'the single most significant document on Indian planning'.[48]

Following suit, the Finance Ministry and Planning Commission turned in a *Tentative Framework for the Second Five Year Plan*, which differed little in substance.[49] Invoking the *Ramayana*, a contemporary commentator said that it 'dittoes the Mahalanobis targets and investment allocations almost as monotonously as the faithful Lakshmana following the great Rama'.[50] The two documents were then sent for review to the Panel of Economists chaired by the finance minister. The overwhelming approval of this body of leading experts – with only one dissenting vote out of twenty-one – did much to certify the credibility of the Draft Plan Frame, granting it the imprimatur of economists.

The solitary dissent was by Mangalorean economist B. R. Shenoy, a member of the Mont Pelerin Society, an international organization advocating free markets, co-founded by Friedrich Hayek.[51] Shenoy, along with Bombay University's C. N. Vakil and P. R. Brahmananda, were the most prominent economists critical of the Second Five-Year Plan. While Vakil and Brahmananda were also part of the Panel of Economists, and expressed misgivings, they did not formally register a note of dissent. Together, these economists were critical of the levels of deficit financing in the Plan Frame and advocated for greater focus on consumer goods industries and more investment in agriculture. Brahmananda recalls the 1950s to mid-1960s with bitterness as a 'nightmarish period' for economists critical of the Mahalanobis model. According to him they were deliberately sidelined and left out of planning meetings. Further, anyone attacking the 'Mahalanobis strategy' was branded an 'anti-nationalist or worse, a CIA-agent'.[52]

In early May, the National Development Council approved of the Draft Plan Frame as the strategy for the Second Five-Year Plan, quibbling only with some of the numbers.[53] It was agreed that the document should be released to the public to stir a discussion about the upcoming Plan and solicit feedback. Over the ensuing months, the Draft Plan Frame and its more detailed iterations were presented again before the National Development Council, the central Ministries, State Governments, and an independent cross-party Consultative Committee composed of members of Parliament.[54]

This synopsis of the Plan Frame's onward march papers over the snags it faced behind the scenes. Stalwarts of the Planning Commission like Krishnamachari (deputy chairman) and Tarlok Singh (joint secretary) resented the commission being upstaged by the Institute and Finance Ministry. These were powerful opponents. The prime minister apart, the deputy chairman was the highest-ranking member of the Planning Commission. At the time, it was a position that commanded cabinet-level powers. Born in the rural Tamil south to landed wealth and educated at Madras' Presidency College, the portly Vangal Thiruvenkatachari Krishnamachari had a distinguished record as senior administrator to princes. Respected for his long service as a modernizing Diwan of Baroda and subsequently as prime minister of Jaipur State, he had been recognized by a knighthood. His ally was Tarlok Singh, a Sikh civil servant and economist who was once Harold Laski's favourite pupil at the London School of Economics. Singh was the engine that kept the Planning Commission running. Having overseen the grim work of rehabilitating refugees in Punjab after Partition, his time serving at the Commission was likely less challenging. And, as Nehru's private secretary during the pre-independence interim government, Tarlok Singh also had the prime minister's ear. Such was his grip on its institutional workings that it led to the joke that the Planning Commission might as well be called the 'Tarlok Sabha'.[55]

A letter from Mahalanobis to Pant presents a glimpse of the intrigue roiling backstage. Recounting events in Delhi over the past week, the Professor wrote that Anjaria and I. G. Patel were 'very upset', 'greatly depressed', and 'quite fed up' with the criticism the Plan Frame was receiving from the Planning Commission's leadership. Anjaria complained of the 'bullying' at their hands. Even Finance Minister Deshmukh was apparently 'completely fed up' with the commission. The alleged bullies were Tarlok Singh and V. T. Krishnamachari, who were reportedly 'jubilant' as they made swipes at the Plan Frame. It was in response to this that the Professor wrote a new preface to it. Deshmukh also spoke to Mahalanobis about Krishnamachari whispering about the Professor behind his back. In general, the Professor noted with disgust that 'the whole atmosphere is poisonous' because they 'will not oppose openly but sabotage everything'. The situation had become venomous enough for Mahalanobis and Deshmukh to seriously consider quitting. They even made a resignation pact: if matters continued to sour, they agreed, both would walk out.[56]

Eventually – backed by a formidable coalition of the Institute, the Finance Ministry, and the independent Panel of Economists – the Plan Frame carried the day. The document was published and publicized under Mahalanobis' name, conferring on him national name recognition and the enduring distinction of being the only individual with whom any Indian Five-Year Plan was so directly associated.[57] It also represented a tilt in the scales of a disciplinary dust-up. A statistician had authored the most important national policy directive, side-lining all of Delhi's economists and bureaucrats. The surprise among the cognoscenti was evident and it set the commentariat abuzz. Brahmananda, then a junior lecturer at Bombay University and a critic of the Plan Frame, spoke of the Professor crashing into the Planning Commission's world.[58] *The Economic Weekly*, predecessor to today's *Economic and Political Weekly*, described him as a 'figure emerging from the background'. The Professor, it continued, appeared to have 'thoroughly superseded the whole tribe of economists'.[59]

Over the course of 1955, the pages of *The Economic Weekly* tracked the dizzying ascent of Mahalanobis and the statisticians, and the cold shoulder they presented to economists. In its Republic Day issue, an anonymous article stated that a powerful minister said that hard-working departmental people had done more to devise the First Five-Year Plan than economists, and this time statisticians had been entrusted with the job. Economists, it continued, were hurt that the Government did not properly recognize the role of economists when making economic policy. But there was little economists could do about it. Although Economics had become a prestigious discipline, economists were not popular with politicians because, the author argued, they cramped politicians' style. As the bearer of unpleasant truths economists often got in the way of politicians doing what they wanted. There was a reason why statisticians were more popular in administrative circles. 'Not only do the rather unintelligible mathematical symbols used by the statistician have their value as a "*mantram*" [mantra] with the lay public, the statistician is also only a useful subordinate. Not so the economist; he is a potential competitor in the field of policy-making, and no politician likes a competitor.'[60] But within months, a statistician had, in fact, turned policymaker. The infiltration was complete.

An editorial in April assessed the reaction in New Delhi to the Plan Frame. In government circles, the widely held view was that Mahalanobis had 'emerged as a super-economist', with hand-wringing professional economists realizing that they had 'missed the bus once again and can't afford to hail a taxi!' The reason offered by the editorial once again underlined the official attitude as being decisive. Politicians and bureaucrats could grasp the 'physical magnitudes' of statisticians; in contrast, economists' doctrines appeared as 'mystic nonsense'. 'The economist', it continued, 'is actually a term of abuse among the [civil] services'. The bureaucracy was held responsible for the purge of professional economists from various positions in such governmental agencies as the Ministry of Finance, the Department of Planning, the Commodity Prices Board, the Ministry of External Affairs, and the Cabinet Secretariat. The economists' exodus from their natural habitat meant that the policymaking landscape now resembled 'Vrindaban Without Krishna'. What was no longer in doubt was that the Professor had 'come out on top'.[61]

Another article, published in mid-June, piled scorn on Indian economists as a group, and the government's Panel of Economists in particular, for being so thoroughly outmanoeuvred by statisticians. Referring to the meeting when the Panel had submitted its findings, the author noted that while 'they had prepared about fifty papers. Professor Mahalanobis' "Plan Frame" swamped them all'. Easing on the disparagement, the writer conceded that the Panel was still likely to be called on again to contribute to the Second Five-Year Plan, but, twisting the knife, the author added, only if 'statisticians find the job too lowly'.[62] In another piece in the same issue, a contributor berated the Planning Commission for having failed thus far to adopt a 'sound planning technique' like, for example, Leontief's input-output approach, instead of relying on haphazardly collated figures and platitudinous introductions. That proper technique was being applied to planning in Calcutta and not Delhi was, to the author, telling: 'Should the function of planning be transferred from the Commission to the Institute?' After all, 'it now appears that the real centre for planning is the Institute'.[63]

According to Ashok Mitra, then a young economist in the capital, the Professor had caused a 'convulsion in the national capital'. Granted a foothold in the Planning Commission, he had 'lost little time in taking charge of the country's planning apparatus' and made 'mincemeat of the sitting members in the Planning Commission', by rejecting their 'easygoing, cautious, conservative approach'. And in circles given to seduction by technocrat, Mahalanobis was the cynosure: the Draft Plan Frame had captured the imagination of the nation's intelligentsia. The spell cast was such that 'in the hoopla generated around the Mahalanobis plan, few either noticed or were prepared to question the suitability of such a model ... Herd instinct was at work.'[64] The economist and politician Meghnad Desai – now critical of Nehruvian planning – reminds us that it was 'hard to imagine now how thrilled large sections of the Indian elite were' by the Mahalanobis model. Then a teenager studying economics, he recalls how 'to admire and support Mahalanobis was to be left wing' and opposition to the Professor's plans was 'hopelessly right wing'.[65] Ashok Mitra remembers how swiftly 'PCM' became 'the most towering personality in the Commission, reducing to non-entities the half-senile doddering crowd'. The Professor's confidant, Pitambar Pant, was not far behind. Trained as a physicist, he was also known to be sceptical of economists.[66] Together they were 'truly devastating in that phase, Mahalanobis with his hauteur and contempt for the sheep in sheep's clothing and Pitamber overwhelming the Commission by reeling off endless statistics on facets of the Indian economy'.[67]

A rise this swift, coupled with an economic approach as ambitious as the Plan Frame, was bound to set tongues wagging. In the summer of 1955, dark whispers swirled. A surprisingly common theme was that the Professor and the Plan Frame were edging the country towards totalitarianism. This fear was apparently provoked by a combination of the emphasis on physical planning (a method associated with the Soviet Union), the presence of several Soviet economic experts as advisers, the Professor's known admiration for the USSR's material accomplishments, and, not least, his haughtiness. It was further bandied about, as a column in *The Economic Weekly* put it, in 'kitchen gossip about who had seen whom and who was where'. Some commentators alleged that the Plan Frame smelled 'more of Muscovy than of Mahalanobis'.[68] British economist Thomas Balogh, then in New Delhi, believed it plausible that Mahalanobis had purposely advanced a 'Plan which could not be achieved without the adoption of totalitarian methods.'[69] An anonymous column in the *Times of India* suggested that the 'cloven foot of totalitarianism peeps through' in the Professor's interviews. It ended with the hope that by the time 'Operation Mahalanobis' made its way through state assemblies, inter-party committees, and Parliament, it would be defanged. That it 'might acquire a new look with Marx no longer standing assertively in the foreground but peeping coyly over the shoulders of George Washington – and Mahalanobis'.[70] The President of the Indian Merchant's Chamber, Mr Chinoi, stated that 'the physical approach must logically lead to a vast authoritarian and bureaucratic control'. Even the socialist Jayaprakash Narayan expressed concern over the 'highly centralised totalitarian kind of planning, which Prime Minister Nehru is getting done by experts of Communist countries'.[71]

These expressions of a fear of creeping communism and a drift towards totalitarianism were serious enough that the Professor, the finance minister, and the prime minister had to issue clarifications to allay them. While paranoia of a malevolent Mahalanobis paving the path to totalitarianism was unwarranted, his reputation for being a Soviet sympathizer was well earned. Two years earlier, the Professor had written in a letter about how 'stunned' he felt hearing 'of the passing away of the great Stalin', adding that the Soviet Union and other socialist countries would 'constantly miss his guiding hand'.[72]

Despite these fears, the Professor did his part to inform the public on the Plan Frame and advertise it. The phone rang more than usual; his office was receiving visitors who had read about the Draft Plan Frame in newspapers; and he became the subject of editorials. Cashing in, he set off on a countrywide tour of promotion. During a week-long visit to southern India in August, he addressed crowded halls in universities, institutes, government offices, social clubs, and even factories in Madras, Bangalore, and Mysore. He crammed '10 sessions of group discussions and 7 lectures in one week'. He was a travelling salesman for the Plan Frame, conveying its details in 'clipped sentences, succinct and non-tolerant of any ifs and buts'.[73] Enjoying the attention and touched by popular support, Mahalanobis told Pant that the tour through the south had made him realize that it was possible to arouse 'mass enthusiasm' for the Plan.[74] His personal exertions were only a small part of the government's ongoing campaign to educate the public on the Plans and encourage participation in them under the banner of 'democratic planning' (which we will turn to later). The Professor was an effective messenger for the Planning Commission because he had himself become, as one scholar put it, a 'Five Year Plan Hero' in a popular culture that increasingly valorized experts, scientists, and development itself.[75]

He took to the airwaves on a late Sunday evening, 11 September 1955, to explain the plan strategy to the nation in a fifteen-minute address on All India Radio. In Calcutta, a weekly journal noted the sociological implications of the Mahalanobis effect. To begin with, he had made news agencies and correspondents aware of physical planning. Everyone in Calcutta seemed to know about the Institute in Baranagore, and that 'Prof Mahalanobis is the Institute'. He had made Bengalis so 'conscious of statistics' that 'most of the bright boys in economics or mathematics go in for statistics for the postgraduate studies'. The Institute had become 'the Mecca of statisticians throughout the world'. The Professor was quite simply, 'the person who is most talked about in Calcutta now'.[76]

Foreign tours continued to be a source of rejuvenating affirmation of the Professor's economic beliefs. Mahalanobis wrote to Pant on his way to Geneva in October 1955, after spending nearly four weeks in the United

Kingdom. Meetings in London and Cambridge had given him 'much confidence on the technical side'. He reported that everyone he met agreed that the Draft Plan Frame was sound. This validation came from different quarters: economists in Geneva, London, and Cambridge; engineers such as Charles Goodeve and F. J. Baker; scientists including P. M. S. Blackett, Harry Campion, and Frank Yates; politicians and administrators like John Strachey, Harold Wilson, alongside some Tory Members of Parliament and Treasury officials; journalist Kingsley Martin and staff at *The Times* and *The Economist*. According to the Professor, many described the Draft Plan Frame as 'the most important document about Asia', significant not just for India but for the entire world. He found support for the view that planning in India may be the 'only alternative to explosion' and that if it succeeded, it could point towards a 'truly "middle way"' in the Cold War.[77] The famed British biologist J. B. S. Haldane – soon to permanently leave his position at University College London for the Institute and India – described the Plan Frame's significance in grandiose terms.

Even if one is pessimistic, and allows a 15 per cent chance of failure through interference by the United States (via Pakistan or otherwise), a 10 per cent chance of interference by the Soviet Union and China, a 20 per cent chance of interference by civil service traditionalism and political obstruction, and a 5 per cent chance of interference by Hindu traditionalism, that leaves a 50 per cent chance for a success which will alter the whole history of the world for the better.[78]

The hoopla struck the Professor's ally, Pitambar Pant, as dangerously distracting. He was in no mood for boosterism and not one for fawning. After having set down two newspapers carrying pieces about yet another speech by Mahalanobis about the Plan Frame, the usually amiable understudy lashed out; sarcastically acknowledging his ignorance of the Professor's strategies, he made clear his indignation at Mahalanobis chasing headlines. Bathing in the spotlight also meant being marked as a target: 'it would be resented by many people and not always without justification'. Unable to contain his annoyance, Pant acidly concluded: 'I am sorry to strike this discordant note, when I should like others, be telling you what a Saviour you are!'[79]

On the eve of the Second Five-Year Plan, national statistics and planning were effectively fused. As the prime minister explained to members of the National Development Council, planning required a statistical approach rather than 'vague ideas and vague ideals'. That, he asserted, was the increasing significance of 'statistical data, sample surveys and calculation at every stage'.[80]

The Second Plan

On April Fool's Day 1956, India launched the ambitious and soon to be controversial Second Five-Year Plan. It was submitted to Parliament as a fat blue book, which the prime minister described as a 'horoscope of Mother India', based not on the position of planets but on 'the circumstances of the country and the pulse of the people'.[81] As I. G. Patel recalled, the success of the First Five-Year Plan, propelled as it had been by favourable monsoons, deep sterling reserves, and nationalist aspiration, had emboldened planners. At the time, 'overoptimism was a part of our national vision or patriotic vision', driven by the 'humiliation we all felt for being left so far behind by colonial rule'.[82] There was near unanimity that the Second Plan needed to be bold. In Mahalanobis' mind, while the first one had just been a diffuse 'anthology', this one was to be a 'drama'.[83]

Dealing with the fallout of World War II and Partition, with little time to prepare and projects already underway, the First Plan had been a slapdash consolidation of schemes. Given the dire food situation that had deteriorated during the war and was then made worse by Partition, hunger became the inaugural Plan's top priority. The spiralling prices of grain and the resulting need to import large quantities of it was unsustainable, despite the government's efforts with the 'Grow More Food' campaign. Agriculture had to be the focus.[84] It had been partly drafted by K. N. Raj, a twenty-seven-year-old Malayali economist who had only recently returned from the London School of Economics. He had written its foreword on his own.

Its successor was formulated with greater methodological sophistication and analytical cohesiveness. The Second Five-Year Plan nearly doubled public investment and charted a distinct path for the economy through a rapid advance in heavy industries. In contrast to its predecessor, it reduced the proportion of state investment in agriculture and dramatically cranked up public spending in factories producing steel, machine tools, and chemicals. The Second Plan would cast a long shadow over those that followed and would come to be recognized as pivotal in the economic history of modern India.[85] As a report in the *New York Times* recorded, this was 'one of Asia's most important political and economic adventures'.[86] In the assessment of a leading development economist, Peter Bauer, India's Second Five-Year Plan was one of the two most influential policy documents in the developing world during the 1950s.[87]

The strategy aimed at ratcheting up growth through a reorientation of national investment towards the capital goods industry in the public sector,

Figure 2.2. The Second Five-Year Plan's imbalanced priorities. Astride the public sector are central ministers including Lal Bahadur Shastri, Gulzarilal Nanda, and T. T. Krishnamachari. Cartoon by Shankar in *Shankar's Weekly* (6 May 1956).

that is, machines that would produce machines.[88] As Nehru told those gathered at a meeting of the National Development Council a few months earlier, there was not time anymore to 'potter about with odd little factories producing hair oil and the like'.[89] The disdain for consumer industries rested on the notion that while they broadened the basket of commodities available to consumers, they offered little transformational potential to the broader economy. As the prime minister said in Parliament a few years later, 'you can't build the future on Coca-Cola'.[90] At this stage of the country's development, it was argued, consumer products were a relative luxury. In the long-term interests of the economy, India's citizens were asked to participate as producers rather than consumers. Delaying consumer gratification was cast as a patriotic duty.

In the context of the global Cold War, this was music to Soviet ears but discordant to Americans. The United States backed a consumer goods and agro-centric model for developing nations, especially ones seen as pivotal to the fate of the Cold War. Poverty and empty bellies made a country particularly susceptible to communist revolution, it believed, more so if one's neighbours included the People's Republic of China and the Soviet Union.[91] India could not delay fulfilling the consumer wants of its citizens without risking going red. To the USSR, the path of heavy industrialization was the one best suited to jumping forward technologically and becoming a modern economy. It was also the strategy that best served its belief in a proletarian march towards socialism. To one superpower, the village and peasant were key determinants in the battle against communism; to the other, factories and their workforce paved the path to eventual revolution. These contrasting visions were reflected in the kinds of foreign aid that India received from Washington, D.C. and Moscow in the three decades after independence. American aid was usually in the form of grain or funds for agrarian and rural community programmes and the Soviet Union's was mostly directed towards helping build steel plants and providing technical assistance.[92]

So closely were the Professor and the Institute attached to the Plan's strategy that a satirist mockingly granted them scriptural authority. Punning on the *Panchatantra* – the Sanskrit animal fables – a magazine carried a humorous essay titled *Pancha-Varshiya-Yojana Tantra* ('The Five Year Plan Treatise'). In the piece, described as a fable for planners, a learned man treats the Institute's statistical journal and the Professor's policy pronouncements as ancient Hindu wisdom. He declares: 'It has been stated in the Sankhya Kanda of the Prashantha Chandra Purana that in the beginning shall be built machines to build machines'. As long as one built 'temples to Yantra Bhagwan' [Machine God] the rest would take care of itself.[93]

The Second Plan reflected the popularity of import-substitution industrialization in Indian policy circles. An economic model that favoured production at home over imports, it was prescribed in the mid-twentieth century by Raul Prebisch, Albert Hirschman, Gunnar Myrdal, Arthur Lewis, and Ragnar Nurske, all leading practitioners of the emerging field of development economics.[94] In vogue across the Global South until the 1980s, it was especially popular in countries that for historic reasons of colonialism or unequal trade were uncomfortable with dependence on rich nations. India's experience in the British Empire's economy had made its political elite nervous about capitalism and distrusting of foreign trade. Reducing expensive imports by producing those goods within India appealed to a strain of self-reliance and autonomy that had animated

Indian nationalist thought for decades.[95] State-led industrialization and import substitution was a mainstream choice at this time for a country playing catch up.[96] Swept up in the force of this near-consensus, I. G. Patel believed that its 'overwhelming appeal' lay in its 'essentially patriotic and nationalist flavour'.[97] As Patel clarified, Nehru was not wedded to import substitution or the Russian model; his obsession was industrialization.[98]

The popularity of import substitution at this historical juncture owed something to the context of global decolonization across Asia and Africa, which led to economic self-sufficiency being equated with anti-imperialism. But the justification for its implementation received a shot in the arm through the publication of new research in economics, and specifically in trade theory. In 1949, an economist in the UN Statistical Office published the *UN Report on Relative Prices of Exports and Imports of Underdeveloped Countries*. When the author, Hans Singer, published its findings in the *American Economic Review* the next year, it caused a stir. It demonstrated that when poor countries engaged in international commerce, their terms of trade declined relative to that of richer nations. In his work for the UN Economic Commission for Latin America, Argentine economist Raul Prebisch was simultaneously making a similar argument and drawing out its political ramifications. The 'Prebisch-Singer thesis', as it came to be known, was widely influential, and anchored the case for import-substitution industrialization in cutting-edge scholarship.[99] British economist Peter Bauer, a life-long opponent of state planning and protectionism, remembers how, by the middle of that decade 'Mahalanobis's Draft Plan Frame and the Second Five-Year Plan very largely reflected the then-dominant opinion of development economics in the West'. These ideas were 'then-current orthodoxy' and received endorsement not only from 'prestigious and influential publications in the West' but also from representatives of international aid agencies like the Ford Foundation and US AID.[100]

There were also some structural reasons, according to Vivek Chibber, that made import-substitution attractive throughout the developing world in the 1950s including, for a while, in Korea and Taiwan. The most salient of these was the international trade regime. While the post-war General Agreement on Trade and Tariffs sought to reduce tariff and quota barriers between nations, this mostly applied only to commerce between North America and Europe. Countries outside the charmed circle of the rich Organization for Economic Cooperation and Development (OECD) still ran up against protectionist barriers. It was free trade among relatively affluent countries. Imports from developing nations faced higher tariffs in comparison to goods flowing from fellow

OECD countries. This dynamic induced mid-century export-pessimism in the developing world.[101]

As one of the few critical economists recalls, during the Delhi School of Economics' heyday, V. K. R. V. Rao, K. N. Raj, Sukhamoy Chakravarty, Amartya Sen, and even Jagdish Bhagwati 'were all euphoric about the Mahalanobis plan frame'.[102] According to economist Prabhat Patnaik, some of Sen's earliest contributions were to the theory of planning. And in 'common with much of the radical intelligentsia of the time Sen was an advocate of the Mahalanobis strategy'.[103] Columbia economist Jagdish Bhagwati – who would become a critic of the policy dating from the late 1960s and subsequently a celebrated champion of market reforms – remembers that back then, 'we were all export pessimists'. 'I don't know anyone whom we respected who was against import-substitution in those days.' When on a government-sponsored visit to Japan, Bhagwati even tried to convince an economist there that they should follow suit.[104] His contemporary at Cambridge and another critic-to-be, Manmohan Singh (later a liberalizing finance minister, and eventually two-term prime minister), admitted to groupthink. In the 1950s, 'I subscribed to it, in fact, most of us did ... Everyone who came to India also advocated that policy.'[105] Sen, Bhagwati, and Singh – the triad of India's most celebrated economists – were in broad agreement.[106] Underscoring the influence of contemporary scholarly opinion, Bhagwati noted decades later that the 'central role of the economists, and their responsibility for India's failings, cannot, therefore be lightly dismissed. It is not entirely wrong to agree with the cynical view that India's misfortune was to have brilliant economists'.[107] The business community was not pushing for an export-oriented strategy, either. Protected from foreign competition by a moat of tariffs, Indian firms were satisfied with slicing up the domestic market and looking to foreign shores only to deal with excess capacity during local downturns.[108]

The other thrust behind the Second Plan were ideas that had purchase within development economics in the midcentury – 'poverty traps' and the 'Big Push' necessary to escape its clutches. First proposed by Polish economist Paul Rosenstein-Rodan in 1943, the Big Push model contended that underdeveloped countries required the injection of industrial investment beyond a certain threshold in order for them to break through a low equilibrium. The push had to exceed a critical minimum because of economies of scale and indivisibilities within the economy. The model claimed that a more gradual and piece-meal approach would fail. The economy was likened to an aircraft: 'Launching a country into self-sustaining growth is like getting an airplane off the ground. There is a critical groundspeed which must be passed before the aircraft can become airborne.'[109] To the Professor, the big push was not just of material significance; it was meant to set off a ripple across the nation's social fabric. He believed it was needed to push society forwards as a whole. It would be like a 'flame, or a chain reaction ... the spearhead of a movement' that would attack 'authoritarian structure of institutions giving support to inequalities, social rigidities, superstitions, and ritualistic religious practices devoid of spiritual values'.[110]

There was quite plainly something about a Five-Year Plan – the presumptions undergirding it, the processes of economic and social transformation it invoked, and the machinery of its operation – that matched how the world operated in Mahalanobis' head. The celebrity economist and free-market crusader Milton Freidman had a theory about mathematicians' predisposition to central planning. In his memoirs, he recounted that 'close contact' with Mahalanobis in the summer of 1955 only reinforced it. Mathematicians, he claimed, were prone to economic planning for a reason: those who were mathematically gifted from a young age developed a confidence in their ability to solve problems and derive the correct solution. When they moved to the field of economics, they carried over this belief in the existence of clear-cut solutions and their ability to find them. They viewed society as a chessboard on which the policy maker can govern the movement of pieces. But in the 'great chessboard of humanity', Friedman continued – quoting Adam Smith – 'every single piece has a principle of motions of its own, altogether different from that which the legislature might choose to impress upon it'. As a result, in economics, there is often no clear right or wrong answer.[111] Mahalanobis, however, was not one to tolerate such grey inexactitude.

The Second Five-Year Plan encountered a hail of questions in Parliament. Many of these were about details, sectoral outlays, and scale. The Planning Commission ultimately brushed these objections under the carpet, stating in the Plan document that there was 'always room for differences of emphasis'.[112] The near contemporary scholar, political scientist A. H. Hanson, wrote that the Planning Commission became carried away by the success of the First Plan, giving 'itself the full benefit of every possible doubt'. It had 'convinced itself and tried to convince others that two and two, when added together by an Indian planner, could make considerably more than four'.[113]

There were, however, some disagreements of a more fundamental order. These were differences on the very shape the Indian economy should take, not just the path and pace it should pursue. For example, in the afternoon of 8 September 1956, the spindly 'Acharya' J. B. Kripalani rose to deliver a stinging repudiation. A Congress stalwart during the nationalist movement and its party president at Independence, he had since left to form the Praja Socialist Party. In the Lok Sabha that day, the veteran Gandhian began by asking the country's planners if they had paused to consider forms of industrialization that were not 'centralized, and mechanized big industry'. He reminded those assembled that rapid industrialization – the path followed by Europe in the nineteenth century, and Bolshevik Russia and Nazi Germany in the twentieth – had left a trail of victims. In contrast, he held up another path; the one endorsed by the Father of the Nation, that of decentralized and small-scale manufactures. 'Gandhiji was not a slave to theory', he recalled for old colleagues. Gandhi recognized that centralized industry had some role to play in a modern society, but he knew that disaster would follow if 'big, mechanized, centralized industry were to permeate the whole life of India, in pursuance of merely material aims'. Big centralized industry, Kripalani cautioned, begat big centralized government and that was a far cry from Gandhi's dream of a decentralized state with villages as production hubs. If the Nehru government were serious about promoting local self-government through *panchayats* (village councils), then it would bolster a rural industrial structure.

Kripalani was reminding the Congress of the social vision that its own leadership, during the height of Gandhi's influence, had nodded along to (even if they disagreed). When questioned by a relative newcomer to the Congress, Kripalani shot back: 'our friend has never known what the Congress policies were, what the Congress stood for'. What was the point of the Congressman wearing *khadi* – the symbol of village industries – if his party was burying that vision? The Congress and this Plan had betrayed the Mahatma.[114] The Acharya was not wrong: in its conception of the economy (dominated by large mechanized industries) and its implications for the state (centralized and powerful), the Plan was un-Gandhian.

Believers in the free market issued their own denunciation. Speaking in the Lok Sabha a year later, amidst inflation, food shortages, and choked foreign exchange, another former Congressman made the case for the market. The dapper Parsi Minoo Masani was once an admirer of Soviet planning. He was now a lapsed leftist running in the opposite direction, 'with all the fervour of the apostate'.[115] The independent parliamentarian was a key figure in an advocacy group called the Forum for Free Enterprise and would co-found the Swatantra Party (Freedom Party), a political outfit that was liberal, market-friendly, and explicitly opposed to planning.[116] Masani decried the Second Five-Year Plan for contributing to a paternalist bureaucratic state, a '*ma-baap sarkar*' that throttled 'enterprise, hard work and the capacity to take risks'. If you knew who to listen to, Masani pointed out, you would know that the Plan Frame spelled trouble as was evident, for example, in B. R. Shenoy's note of dissent in the Panel of Economists. But, he said, they had been irresponsibly waved away. Why? Because, he continued in a thinly veiled reference to the Professor and the Institute, 'the voice of false prophets and quack economists were listened to. People who talked of "physical planning" and slogans taken from totalitarian countries ... rather than other economists and trained administrators.'

According to the pro-US Masani, planning in India needed a 'radical rethinking' that would spurn the Mahalanobis model with its excessive investment in heavy industry and instead reorient itself towards agriculture and stocking retailer's shelves.[117] As he would say during another speech in Parliament, the planners had a 'fatal fascination' for steel. It was ordinary citizens, asked to wait ever longer to satisfy basic consumer desires, who paid the price of this obsession. The Plan publicity poster he had seen in Bombay – 'Work today for a better tomorrow' – was misleading, Masani claimed, for the Plan was actually asking Indians to 'Work hard today for a better day after day after day after tomorrow.'[118] India needed the 'real, democratic planning' of countries like Switzerland, Britain, the United States, and West Germany that allowed 'the laws of the market and the enterprise of the people to vent'.[119]

The Second Plan's defence in Parliament was led by the Minister of Planning, the finance minister, deputy chairman of the Planning Commission, and the prime minister. And while the technical objections about the Plan's economic robustness could be thrashed out, the Gandhian and laissez-faire critiques were another matter altogether. They questioned the very basis upon which Indian planning had emerged after independence. Fortunately for the government and the Planning Commission, the Congress Party's strength in Parliament and consistent messaging meant that these more foundational challenges did not require changing course. Furthermore, despite fractious contests within the Communist Party of India about the appropriate attitude towards the Nehru government, the Politburo of the main opposition party extended its support to the Second Plan.

Meanwhile, over latter part of the 1950s, statistical studies came to play a more formal role within government. The Planning Commission's offices now included a new Statistics and Surveys Division. The civil services also sprouted a new arm. Discussions between the Professor, Home Ministry, and the Planning Commission resulted in the creation of an Indian Statistical Service (and an Indian Economic Service) within the bureaucracy.[120] The Plan document itself devoted a chapter to 'Research and Statistics for Planning', acknowledging that they 'have a most important contribution to make'. It referred to the increased requirements of statistical information given the physical planning technique employed in the new Plan. It also repeated the need for statistics to provide feedback in real time on the progress of Plans allowing for course correction, and the greater integration between Central and State statistics.[121] The Professor's own position within the Planning Commission was substantial in practice and amorphous in letter. Occupying a zone somewhere between Statistical Adviser to the Government and Member, Planning Commission, his unofficial portfolio included statistics, surveys, and long-term planning. He transitioned from de facto Member of the Planning Commission to a formal one only in 1960.[122]

Experiments in Time and Gender

The Institute's bungalow at 8 King George Avenue in New Delhi grew from a mere outpost into a research centre in its own right. A new line of inquiry in Calcutta and even more so in Delhi, was perspective planning, the forecasting and planning for the long term. Believing that the First Plan had been short-sighted, despite its success, planners began to think about long-term societal requirements. They asked questions such as: how many tons of steel would be needed in 20 years? What would the demand for fertilizer be? How much electricity is likely to be consumed in a decade and a half? The Institute had begun exploring perspective planning towards the end of 1955 and Pitambar Pant rushed in headfirst.[123] As Pant was more or less in charge of the Institute's Planning Unit in Delhi, perspective planning came to dominate the research carried out there. The Planning Commission also set up its own Perspective Planning Division.[124] As the chief of this division as well, Pant embodied the close collaboration between Delhi and Calcutta. The Institute engaged extensively with the USSR and Japan on the subject of long-term planning, even drawing experts from the former and collaborating with the latter's Economic Planning Agency on joint investigations.[125] According to one contemporary economist, with both Mahalanobis and Pant so closely involved in the Perspective Planning Division, its office perched atop Yojana Bhavan could easily be mistaken for 'a cell' of the Institute.[126]

A stable of brilliant young economists and statisticians worked for Pant in the capital. The roster included some of India's best-known economists: Jagdish Bhagwati, Amartya Sen, Suresh Tendulkar, T. N. Srinivasan, and B. S. Minhas. They were employed as academics at the Institute, but often worked at the Planning Commission.[127] It had only taken a nudge from Mahalanobis to dislodge Bhagwati from a research fellowship at Oxford University. He was happy to answer the call to sign up as 'one of "the

Professor's boys'" and was pleased to have been picked.[128] The Institute's Planning Unit in the capital had quickly emerged as one of the leading research centres for economics in the country. The compound at 8 King George Avenue with its lawn, cats, and fragrant blooms of *rajnigandha* and jasmine was also a guesthouse for academics hosted by the Institute, serving to extend the famed hospitality of Amrapali and Baranagore all the way to the national capital.[129]

Pitambar Pant led ground breaking studies on poverty. One particularly influential paper, published in 1962, not only measured the extent of abject poverty in India, but also laid out the basis for determining a 'minimum level of living', or a poverty line. It argued that the state owed every citizen a bare minimum standard of life. This study would become the foundation and inspiration for a new burst of research into poverty measurement, its causes, and how to address it. According to economist Terence Byres, this was 'truly seminal . . . .It would be difficult to imagine a more influential document.'[130]

The perspective planners were also drawn to the problem of manpower planning, for example, assessing the number of trained educated women and men that India would need and calculating the shortfall to be overcome over the decades to follow. Compared with the time it took to establish factories to produce consumer goods (from 2 to 3 years), or heavy machinery (from 7 to 15 years), a fresh batch of technical and scientific experts was the slowest to gestate, taking the longest to come off the assembly line (from 25 to 30 years).[131] And these were all linked in the Professor's mind as four stages.[132] Apart from working on projects that looked decades ahead, the Institute in Delhi also began the crucial task of outlining and running the numbers for the more imminent Third Five-Year Plan. Pitambar Pant and Mani Mukherjee had been asked to begin rough sketches of the Plan that would commence in 1961.[133]

Baranagore was the site of less abstract experiments as well. In late February 1956, inside a small shed on a corner of its leafy campus, the Institute inaugurated a project by lighting a ceremonial lamp to the sounds of Vedic hymns and songs by Tagore.[134] A production centre that studied the economics of cottage handicrafts, Kalyanashree was inspired and directed by Nirmal Kumari Mahalanobis.[135] Marrying the Professor against the initial wishes of her father, Rani – as she was known to friends – was never likely to play the housewife. She was an admirer of Rabindranath Tagore, who attended her wedding, and would become a companion and expert on the poet's works, authoring a book on the subject. Short, soft-featured, and round-cheeked, she struck a contrast with the rigid angularities of her husband who loomed a foot above. Frequently accompanying the Professor on his travels abroad, she was always dressed in a sari. A picture taken in Turkey shows Rani striding ahead of her plainly dressed husband, pulling off a brocade sari, fur coat, and leather glove ensemble with smiling aplomb. It is a rare moment in the photographic record where she seems to step out from the shadow of her husband, the Professor, or her guru, the Poet.

Running Kalyanashree appears to have been another such instance. According to Nirmal Kumari Mahalanobis, the venture had been inspired by Tagore's efforts at promoting cottage industries in Sriniketan in 1921. Kalyanashree was an experiment in the productivity of village industries and informal labour, launched at the height of the national belief in hulking factories and towering dams.[136] It represented the Institute's outlook on female labour and rural India. The Second Five-Year Plan's ideological focus was on heavy industry, which was identified as the key determinant of growth. But planners recognized that this was not the most labour-intensive path and would not adequately address unemployment. The disproportionate emphasis on the investment goods sector also meant that the needs of consumers would have to take a backseat. This was why the Professor, and consequently the Second Five-Year Plan, looked to villages and cottage industries as a sponge that could mop up idle hands and squeeze out consumer products. Setting hundreds of millions of limbs to work – despite the inefficiencies of cottage industries – would still boost the national product, tackle unemployment, and control inflation. As a severely optimistic Mahalanobis told the National Development Council in May 1955: 'if hand industries could be activated, the fear of unemployment could disappear during a period of five years'.[137] Kalyanashree was an attempt to research the possibility of this 'through partly controlled laboratory-type experimentation and also through field studies'.[138]

Left unstated, but certainly presumed by those involved, was that this sector of the economy was best suited to rural women. Their labours, since often unremunerated, had hitherto contributed little to the economy in the way that category was defined. Implicitly, the cottage industry, by encompassing labour performed from within the home, represented feminine work.[139] Which might be why the Professor was quite happy to leave its operation, one he considered a sideshow to the main event of planning for masculine heavy industry, to Rani Mahalanobis. The feminizing of Kalyanashree and its work was evident from the moment it was named. At the opening ceremony, the Professor explained that the Sanskrit words for 'Kalyana' (welfare) and 'Shree' (beauty, grace) had been fused together because household industries in India had a tradition of 'welfare wedded to beauty'.[140]

Kalyanashree invited the local unemployed, many of them female Partition refugees from East Pakistan, to utilize the space, tools, and raw materials provided to them to produce traditional handicrafts. Beginning with a dozen women trainees, that number rose to fifty workers within months. Nearly all of them were women: nine worked on the Ambar Charkha (a newly designed spinning wheel that promised greater productivity), thirteen wove on semi-automatic flying shuttles and pit looms, six tailored, and eight wove Manipuri-style fabrics and engaged in other crafts.[141] The Institute guaranteed the purchase of all the items they manufactured, and they were paid on a piece-rate basis. The provision of tools and materials extended that summer to households across three villages located a few miles from Calcutta.[142] It began with the Institute conducting surveys of household consumption and domestic industrial production in these villages in order to establish a baseline. Following this, the Institute selected fifteen families who would be given loans to increase production. Indicative of the gender norms at play, Kalyanashree entered into legal contracts and advanced cash loans only to the 'heads' of these households (in all likelihood the patriarch) to put to work 'unutilised domestic labour', presumably that of his wife, daughters, and daughters-in-law. While Kalyanashree's purpose was quite clearly related to assisting women and ascertaining their role in the planned economy, it seemed to have also operated within patriarchal structures that prevented them from participating as independent economic agents.[143]

The industries covered in Kalayanshree's scheme included handloom weaving, yarn-spinning, sewing, footwear, blacksmith, *bidi*, weaving with hogla leaves, pottery, and paper packets. The selected households were assured that all unsold products would be purchased. In return, they promised to step up household production, diligently maintain data on it, and hand it over to the Institute's investigators. In the way Kalyanashree was set up, the economists and statisticians were outside looking in, scrutinizing the effects of this experiment on production, income, purchasing power, and consumption. This data was then analysed to glean insights into market price, living wages, marketing, and the design of cottage industry tools.[144] The investigators also tried to ascertain how long it took to train someone in handicrafts to earn them a modest remuneration, the best methods to improve productivity, and how to assess the viability of extending such units across Indian villages.

Kalyanashree opens a window onto how Rani, the Professor, and the Institute sought to address the debate over the relative merits of capital good industries and consumption-oriented village manufactures, two sectors representing differing conceptions of the Indian economy. The experiment lasted ten years before being shuttered. During that time, it received important political visitors, such as Cuba's Che Guevara, Vietnam's Ho Chi Minh, and China's Chou-En Lai. Tellingly, while the economists John Kenneth Galbraith and Nicholas Kaldor spent a good deal of time at the Institute, contributing to conversations on the Second Five-Year Plan, it was their wives that dropped by at Kalyanashree. A photograph taken inside Kalyanashree during Czechoslovakian Prime Minister Viliam Siroky's visit in January 1958 is revealing. In a sparsely furnished room with unpolished flooring, lit only by white tube lights hanging from a low ceiling, a group of European men in suits, ties, and polished shoes face the Professor, who is addressing them. Gathered around – but ignored by the men – are women mostly dressed in simple cotton saris, two of whom are seated cross-legged as they work at rudimentary handlooms. Rani Mahalanobis looks on as her husband speaks to the distinguished guests. Women and their work were central to Kalyanashree, but what they represented was ultimately marginal to the Plan underway.[145]

Figure 2.3. Prime Minister of Czechoslovakia Viliam Siroky with P. C. Mahalanobis and Nirmal Kumari Mahalanobis at Kalyanashree (14 January 1958).

What was true of Kalyanashree was also true more broadly of independent India's Plans. The Nehruvian government chose to sidestep
economic measures that would undo the unproductive patriarchal systems that inhibited female participation in the economy. Instead, as
scholar Nirmala Banerjee observed, the government (including women
who held important posts) bolstered the 'problematic tradition of
regarding women as targets for household and motherhood-oriented
welfare services'.[146] This was in stark contrast to the radical position
voiced by the pre-independence National Planning Committee's sub-
committee on the role of women in the planned economy. Chaired by
Rani Laxmibai Rajwade, the all-female committee featured a long list of
formidable nationalist figures, including Mridula Sarabhai, Hansa
Mehta, Jahanara Shah Nawaz, Vijayalakshmi Pandit, Sarojini Naidu,
A. V. Kuttimalu Amma, Aruna Asaf Ali, and Shareefa Hamid Ali. Over
ten chapters and 200 pages, the document they produced sketched out
a visionary programme that would recognize women as economic units,
asserted their right to control their earnings, and made a raft of recommendations to equalize pay and render all workplaces accessible to
female labour. Their most far-sighted suggestion, Banerjee pointed
out, was that the state should legally recognize the uncompensated
labour of women in the family's economic activities and within the
household.[147]

After independence, these structural recommendations did little more
than gather dust. Reading India's early Plan documents, one could be
forgiven for thinking that the planned economy had never undergone
a feminist critique. This despite some women holding powerful positions
in the Nehru government, several of whom had been co-authors of the
progressive National Planning Committee document.[148] A number of
reasons could account for the gender-blindness in the early Plans, according to Banerjee. It is likely, she argues, that these women knew what
measures were unpopular with the rest of the male-dominated Congress
Party. Hence, theirs was probably a tactical decision not to push policies
that might be perceived as 'radical', out of fear that the already limited
space for women in government would be endangered by it.[149] Lacking
support on the streets from an organized mass women's movement, they
were entirely dependent on the state for reform.[150] Bearing equal or more
blame for the gender-blindness of the Plans, however, was the
Mahalanobis model itself. Privileging organized heavy industry over agriculture and consumer goods enterprises also meant privileging the sector
that accounted for only a very small fraction of female employment.
These neglected spheres, and therefore, most labouring women,
remained outside the charmed circle.

The career of the very first female member of the Planning Commission is revelatory. Durgabai Deshmukh was a criminal lawyer, social worker, and self-denying satyagrahi who was among the few women in the Constituent Assembly.[151] She was chosen by Nehru to join the early Planning Commission; there she took charge of a social welfare and social services portfolio that was clearly gendered female. She was also instrumental in the creation of the Central Social Welfare Board in 1953.[152] But despite believing in planning enough to name her Pune home 'Yojana' (Plan), she would soon quit Yojana Bhavan to devote her time to social welfare.

You Are the Company You Keep

The Professor's inter-continental zigzagging had a flip side. The Institute was renowned for hosting a procession of international academics, many of considerable stature. Cultivating a cosmopolitan intellectual forum was important because it signalled and contributed to the Institute's esteem. To begin with, there were the sheer numbers. Just as *Sankhya* reported on the Professor's tours abroad, it also annually recorded the stream of visiting experts, which became a flood during the Second Five-Year Plan. During the first three years of the Plan period, more than 400 foreign academics made their way to Baranagore from well over 100 countries.[153] No other Indian research institute or educational body came close to matching this international draw. As economist Hans Singer put it, Mahalanobis had become 'the prophet (or guru) of the development economists ... and Calcutta became their Mecca'.[154]

Just as with the Professor's tours abroad, the collective effect of all these visitors – especially foreign economists – was to polish the reputation of both the Professor and the Institute, bolstering their credibility in economic policy. The list of guests included some of the most prominent names of the generation, including several of the earliest recipients of the Nobel Prize in Economics. But the line-up also featured many who were less distinguished. According to Swedish economist Gunnar Myrdal, 'every second-rate economist from Europe or America was [then in India] advising the Planning Commission'.[155]

Reflecting India's non-aligned stance in the Cold War, the Institute's guests included names from both sides of the Iron Curtain, although most of the invitees harboured some sympathy for the strategy of state-directed development with an accent on heavy industry. The open invitation was the academic analogue of political non-alignment during a period of superpower competition. As John Kenneth Galbraith, who visited twice in the 1950s as a Harvard economist before returning to India as the US Ambassador in 1961, said: 'In no other place in the world at the time was there such easy and intense exchange between peoples of the socialist and the nonsocialist worlds and of the rich countries and the poor.' Galbraith's first visit was the result of a chance encounter with the Professor in Geneva. When Mahalanobis spoke about his successful efforts in bringing scholars from all over the world to Calcutta, he mentioned that the American government had offered to send Milton Friedman. Galbraith and Friedman, American successors to the European Keynes and Hayek, made for an easy contrast. The former was an extraordinarily tall Harvard social democrat, the latter an uncommonly short-statured University of Chicago champion of the market. Amused at the thought of the free market evangelist advising the Planning Commission, Galbraith quipped: 'to ask Friedman to advise on economic planning was like asking the Holy Father to counsel on the operations of a birth control clinic'. The remark tickled Mahalanobis enough to invite Galbraith instead.[156]

Despite being increasingly enamoured of Soviet economic achievement and, by 1958, an Honorary Member of the Soviet Academy of Sciences, Mahalanobis tried to portray himself as unencumbered by political moorings. And, to a certain degree he genuinely believed that disinterested experts could scientifically resolve the issues of development when removed from the lowbrow muddle of politics. Whatever Mahalanobis' politics may have been, however, the Institute was developing into something of a haven for socialists. Sociologist Andre Beteille, who worked as a researcher there in the late 1950s, remembers the Professor as a 'liberal in the tradition of the Bengal Renaissance' who nevertheless treated communists with 'sympathy and some indulgence'. As a result, the campus was a 'stronghold of left intellectuals', some of whom came on the recommendation of P. C. Joshi, the Communist Party's General Secretary, whom the Professor 'liked and trusted'. According to Beteille, the sympathy ran troublingly deep; although Stalin had died in 1953, he was 'still widely venerated in the Institute'.[157]

What attracted foreign academics to Baranagore was a combination of factors: a personal acquaintance with the Professor and respect for his influence in domestic economic policy; the opportunity to play a part in what was considered one of the great global dramas unfolding at the time (decolonized India's attempt at democratic development, right in communist China and Soviet Russia's backyard); and, undoubtedly, the chance to further their Cold War agenda within it. After all, by now, New Delhi had become an important coordinate in the global Cold War

map, and the question of India's allegiances, non-alignment notwithstanding, evoked heated debate and energetic courting in both blocs.[158]

During trips to the Institute that lasted from weeks to months, the
visitors gave lectures, swam in the lakes, picnicked in the grove, and
contributed working papers to the Planning Division's series on planning.
Conversations spilled from long breakfasts at Amrapali, to the mango
grove's shade, to garden tea parties. The Professor and Rani Mahalanobis
were exceptionally gracious hosts who strove to anticipate the needs of
their guests. They personally looked into accommodation, curated itin-
eraries, and organized sightseeing jaunts to the countryside and cities.
These forays could involve a Community Development site or gigantic
hydroelectric undertakings such as those at Bhakra Nangal. The
Professor would find time to discuss the aesthetic merits of the exquisite
bronze figurines at the National Museum, or offer a tour of the Taj Mahal
complete with a learned exposition on the geometry of its floor plan.[159]
For their guests, the Professor and Pant would also line up talks, and fix
appointments in Bombay and Delhi – a lecture here at the Delhi School of
Economics, a meeting there with the Reserve Bank of India, or at the
Planning Commission. If the guest was important enough and schedules
aligned just so, they could even deliver an audience with Nehru, New
Delhi's biggest attraction for credentialed tourists.

Despite going out of his way to play host, Mahalanobis did not always
endear himself to guests. On New Year's Day 1959, Australian economist
Heinz Arndt quickly regretted accepting the Professor's invitation to ride
with him from the stately Rambagh Palace Hotel in Jaipur to Agra.
Mahalanobis was not always the best company for a long drive. He
spent the four-hour car journey on a diatribe against the West and
capitalism. Arndt, the sole recipient of this harangue, was left shaken.
'He [Mahalanobis] must be nearly seventy, immensely vigorous, alert and
intelligent, but also domineering, vain and bigoted, a Bengali aristocrat
who in moving towards a Stalinist-type authoritarianism has completely
by-passed democratic liberal notions, never in any doubt who would plan
and who would be planned for (or against?).'[160] It was not just those
ideologically west of the Iron Curtain who sometimes viewed the
Professor with apprehension. Even an official at the Soviet Academy of
Sciences found reason for concern: 'Mahalanobis gave the impression of
a very intelligent and cunning (*khitrogo*) person, his external frankness
and good nature hiding his true intentions.'[161]

The Professor and the Institute were not without domestic detractors
either. Writing to physicist Homi Bhabha from Poona, the polymathic
D. D. Kosambi did not hide his bitterness towards Mahalanobis. The
mathematician-historian-philologist was conveying a 'bit of sad news'.

Mahalanobis had begun inviting several scholars to India, including ones 'who can't tell one Indian from another'. It was all for the 'personal aggrandizement of PCM's reputation'. Kosambi warned Bhabha that he should make clear that those invited to the Tata Institute of Fundamental Research in Bombay knew that they were entirely separate from Mahalanobis' plans. Otherwise, the letter continued, Mahalanobis would convince their guests to spend time at his institute in Calcutta and take over the negotiations with them. The reason for such suspicion? 'He is that sort of a person.'[162]

What was the impact of throwing open the doors to this assorted caravan of academics and intellectuals? To begin with, the Institute contributed to the training of statisticians from numerous developing nations in Asia and Africa and to the spread of modern statistical techniques on these continents. The stopovers in Baranagore could set off transnational reverberations, as demonstrated by the influence the Institute had on how China organized its massive statistical system. When Chinese premier Zhou Enlai visited on Sunday, 9 December 1956, he was not supposed to spend as long as he did. Throwing his day's carefully prepared itinerary out of sync, Zhou Enlai took time to ask many questions and get involved in extended discussions during his tour of the Institute. As Mahalanobis reported excitedly to Pant: 'No VIP visitor had taken a more intelligent interest in our work or had asked more pertinent questions.' One of the subjects Zhou Enlai engaged, according to the Professor, was 'the distribution of NSS villages and the NSS itself'. After touring other wings of the institute, such as Kalyanashree, planting a mango sapling in the mango grove, and delivering a short speech, Zhou EnLai was taken to the building that housed the NSS Unit. There, once again, 'he started asking detailed questions; and, at one stage sat down on a table and said he would not move until he had got certain things clear'. As he was being led towards the vehicles to be whisked away, he suddenly 'caught hold [of] me by the arm and deliberately side-stepped the waiting car, waved his hand to shake off everyone' so that they could talk in private. He then proceeded to ask the Professor questions about the state of statistics internationally and in India. Zhou Enlai informed Mahalanobis that a group of statisticians could visit Calcutta soon: 'I want them to see everything in detail. We want to learn from you. How long should they stay?'[163]

This remarkable episode has to be understood, as historian Arunabh Ghosh explains, as part of a historic crisis of faith in China's Soviet-inspired statistical system. India's own apparatus, as we have seen, hinged on the National Sample Surveys which were underpinned by probability theory, sampling techniques, and mathematical statistics more generally. These methods, championed by the Professor and the Institute in India, were anathema in the USSR and subsequently in the People's Republic of China. Since Marxist theory, in the determinist interpretation of Moscow and Beijing, did not admit of chance and uncertainty in the economic and social realms, methods like sample surveys were dismissed as bourgeois and capitalist. Instead, these communist states and their planners relied on that which India had spurned, namely complete and painstaking enumeration.[164] However, between 1956 and the Cultural Revolution, it seemed possible that China might abandon its alignment with the USSR on the question of what kinds of statistics were appropriate to a communist state. In these two years, and as a result of a growing crisis in China's statistics and inspired by conversations in Beijing and Calcutta with statisticians from the Institute, the party leadership and the State Statistical Bureau revisited its view on whether sample surveys and mathematical statistics should really be dismissed as bourgeois and inappropriate to communist states. While improved bilateral ties smoothened the way towards greater Sino-Indo interaction in the field of statistics, the turning points had been a spring tour of China by a team from Calcutta (led by Pant) and the visits of Zhou Enlai and a team of Chinese statisticians to Baranagore later in 1956. Over the next two years, further visits were traded, culminating in two members of China's State Statistical Bureau, Wu Hui and Gong Jianyao, spending most of 1958 in Calcutta and travelling across India on a study tour to learn Indian sampling techniques. The possibilities of this brief moment of knowledge transfer, however, were abruptly shut in the convulsion of the Cultural Revolution.[165]

Again, what purpose did these hordes of experts from distant shores serve? Indian planning gained significantly in various technical and methodological dimensions, such as linear programming and input-output tables from this access to foreign expertise and data sharing. But on the question of whether it moved the needle on policy, it is best to be more guarded. Despite all the noise generated by these visits, the impact on policy, according to historian David Engerman, 'was very close to zero'. And this was not a sign of failure either; it was by design. The logic of having these academics pass through was to 'learn specific techniques, from Western economists and East-Bloc planners alike'.[166] Further, the Institute and the policies emanating from there were thrown in an altogether more flattering light by the wattage of their guests' celebrity. It elevated their status within Indian and international academia, made the Institute even more attractive to students and researchers across the country, and fortified their position within domestic policy debates.

As early as the summer of 1955, a contributor to *The Economic Weekly* noted how the Professor's trips abroad and his role as a host in Calcutta had marginalized opponents. Perhaps, the writer mused, Mahalanobis will be in Europe once again in the summer recruiting a fresh batch of economists, 'for striking terror in the hearts of complex-ridden indigenous economists'. Soon it might be proven that local economists are only 'novices, averagely good for writing tutorial essays'. Given this imminent day of reckoning, 'would it not be better if they migrated to, say, sociology?'[167]

* * *

For all its aspirations, the Second Five-Year Plan was consumed by crisis no sooner than it began.[168] By midsummer 1956, just a few months in, it was becoming evident that the economy was bleeding its foreign exchange reserves. India had used up most of the accumulated pound sterling balances during the previous Plan, and it was fast running out. Put simply, imports outpaced exports considerably, and by the middle of the next year, India was in a foreign exchange crunch. The economy was staring at dire scenarios. As a direct consequence of this, the Plan had to be drastically scaled back. The government hastened to slash bold Plan targets, particularly in the public sector, leaving only a rump of core projects relatively unscathed. The Plan, with the Professor on its prow, was in choppy waters, with waves of criticism crashing onto it and the Mahalanobis model. The Minister of Finance, T. T. Krishnamachari, and his ministry took advantage, casting themselves as the responsible and realistic counterpoint to the profligate and overambitious Planning Commission. He adopted this stance despite agreement among contemporary observers and scholars thereafter that some blame for the foreign exchange crisis lay with the Ministry of Commerce and Industry for liberalizing consumer goods imports and indiscriminately granting licenses to private sector projects. The person running that ministry at the time these decisions were taken was none other than the soon-to-be Minister of Finance, T. T. Krishnamachari.[169] Regardless of who was responsible, this financial emergency would have lasting implications for the position of the Planning Commission. It began the gradual diminution of its powers, and a slow drift towards the Finance Ministry's ascendancy in economic policy.

The fate of the Second Five-Year Plan did not, however, delegitimize the role of statistics in planning. The data infrastructure had percolated too deep into planning and processes of state for that to happen. In 1959, the prime minister successfully steered the Indian Statistical Institute Bill through Parliament. Nehru urged everyone to recognize the work being done at the Institute. It was of 'the utmost importance. There can be no planning without statistical work on a big scale'.[170] The resulting Indian Statistical Institute Act declared it to be an autonomous institution of

national importance that could award degrees. In the decade that pre-
ceded this, statistics had gone national, entering the very fabric of central
planning and economic policy. As the prime minister put it during
a meeting of the National Development Council, 'Planning was based
not only on certain political objectives, but on statistical data.'[171]

In the following decade, the Institute would shape the next Five-Year
Plan as well. According to a contemporary scholar, Pant was the principal author of the 'Plan Frame for the Third Plan', which was essentially
'a continuation and intensification of the Second'.[172] The inheritance
from this period – national income accounts, the NSS, the CSO and the
Indian Statistical Service – continue to be regularly called upon as part
of the Government of India's toolkit. If statistics were, as an Institute
scholar put it, the 'bricks out of which plans are made', then the Institute
was the kiln where they were fired.[173] Today, the Professor's profile and
the Institute's outline can be found on a one-rupee postage stamp, and
the NSS Organization's office building in Kolkata is named
Mahalanobis Bhavan. The Professor's birthday, 29 June, is now
National Statistics Day. 'Any story of economic policy in India',
I. G. Patel wrote in his memoir, 'must narrate not only the involvement
of economists and civil servants or ministers; it must also have a chapter
on the contribution of statisticians.'[174]

This chapter has traced one of the most important consequences of
the planning-instigated expansion in the state's data infrastructure:
a formalization of the connection between planning and statistics,
and the subsequent entry of the Professor and the Institute into the
domain of the Planning Commission. More broadly, it demonstrates
the long leash granted to technocrats by both the Nehruvian state and
the logic of planning itself despite the pushback from those whose toes
were trampled on. Not only did the nature of planning privilege
technocrats, but the installation of quantitative capacities elevated
their role even further, and magnified their position in the state. The
rapid ascent of the Institute and the Professor in the realm of national
economic policy was a manifestation of deeper currents. They were
epiphenomena in more tectonic shifts–the decision to centrally plan
the national economy, the hunger for numbers that it excited, and the
creation of new intellectual infrastructures. The Professor and the
Institute had leveraged the post-war ascent of statistics as
a discipline and the importance of national statistics in central economic planning to pull up an outsized seat for themselves at the
Planning Commission table. Their role had been made possible by
the profusion of the Indian state's quantitative capacities, which itself
had been stimulated by the need to plan. Statistics would have been

integral to planning regardless of them. However, understanding the parts they played is crucial to grasping the specific route India took. That route was one in which statistics and planning would become interlocked in an even tighter embrace in ways that profoundly shaped the Indian economy.

3   Chasing Computers

On a cold February morning in 1959, a tall square-jawed American nervously boarded a jet to flee Prague, aware that his escape could be foiled at any moment. Circumstance and opportunity had aligned to pry open this window, and he was anxious it might slam shut. Once airborne, Morton Nadler finally felt safe. He had waited a long time for this.

For the past few years Nadler had been a de facto prisoner of the Czechoslovak government, and until now, disallowed from leaving the country.[1] During a refuelling stop in Greece, he briefly considered striding up to the counter to declare: 'I'm an American. I've just escaped from Prague. Take me to the American Embassy.' The moment passed, as did the flicker of daring, and he swatted the idea away. Nadler was in the delicate situation of being under suspicion by his country of birth, the United States, *and* that of his adopted citizenship, Czechoslovakia. The thought of what might befall those who vouched for him back in Prague, and fear of the American government, gripped his tongue and nudged him aboard the connecting flight to India. Upon landing in Calcutta, he was driven along a dusty road lined with ramshackle huts to the Institute. Calcutta's winter, in contrast to Prague and matching his mood, was 'mild and pleasant'. Amidst the mango grove and ponds that dotted the garden campus, Nadler would spend the next fifteen months working on India's first computers.[2]

* * *

Planning launched India's globetrotting quest for computers. Computers represented a solution to the problem of big data, a problem that arose as a consequence of the decision to pursue centralized economic planning. India entered the computer age as only the second Asian nation to acquire digital computers. These machines represented another expansionary stage in the growing knowledge infrastructures and data capacities of the state. Planning the economy demanded a variety of statistical indicators regarding Indian material life; the National Sample Survey ensured that there was a sudden deluge of such information. The magnitude of data generated was beyond the country's computational abilities, unless computers were harnessed. Apart from fulfilling a need, the computer also had other allures. Once invented, they quickly came to symbolize ultimate technological mastery and numerical omniscience, a swoon-inducing combination for technocrats. For techno-utopians like the Professor, and the rest of India's scientific elite, computers were dizzyingly expensive dream toys.

Those involved in bringing India its first computers were those most closely associated with statistics and planning. The years during which computers made their entry into the subcontinent were those in which Mahalanobis and the Institute acquired unprecedented national influence and gravitated towards the heart of the planning process. Their starring role in the computer's journey to India demonstrates, yet again, not just the degree of autonomy that technocrats could negotiate vis-à-vis the Indian state but, significantly, also how the state's burgeoning data infrastructure entrenched the reliance on those experts.

Mahalanobis was not alone in his faith in the computer's ability to transform economic management. At least two very prominent economists, Oskar Lange and Nobel laureate Tjalling Koopmans, suggested that computers provided a solution to the computational complexities of centralized economic planning. This was part of a major debate among economists, referred to as the economic calculation or socialist calculation debate. In the interwar years, advocates of mostly unregulated capitalism such as Ludwig von Mises, Friedrich Hayek, and Lionel Robbins argued that planned economies were fundamentally incompatible with efficient resource allocation because they spurned the only instrument that guaranteed it – the market's famed invisible hand. The socialist economist Oskar Lange responded that 'rational economic accounting' was certainly possible under socialism since planners only needed to solve a series of simultaneous equations. Hayek retorted that since making thousands of such calculations in any reasonable time frame was impossible, efficient planning was a chimera. But the invention of the computer changed the debate, according to Koopmans and Lange. The latter saw vindication for socialist planning in the computer. As he put it, 'My answer to Hayek and Robbins would be: so what's the trouble? Let us put the simultaneous equations on an electronic computer and we shall obtain the solution in less than a second.'[3] Mahalanobis, it appears, was a silent partisan.

The Professor tried to harness computers towards the creation of an idealized economy in which numerical omniscience allowed optimal outcomes. The computer's liberation from human computational constraints also promised, when yoked to planning, an escape from underdevelopment.

In marked contrast to the global centres of advanced computing, the first use found for computers in India was development, not the military.[4] India's ability to develop a computer programme did not, however, depend solely on domestic factors since it operated in a Cold War context. In the 1950s and 1960s, India was one of the primary theatres of the economic Cold War in which both the United States and the Soviet Union vied to direct the Indian economic trajectory towards their own. As an impoverished buyer of computers on the international market, India's image in the optics of the Cold War mattered a great deal. Transnational transfer of technology involving duelling superpowers and a non-aligned nation was bound to ruffle Cold War feathers. American and Soviet perceptions of India's political slant framed real limitations on computer developments in India.

The history of computers in India is relatively unknown, as is the career of computers outside Europe, the United States, and the Soviet Union.[5] It is rarely recognized that in India economic planning opened the door to the computer age, forever changing the knowledge infrastructures and quantitative capacities available to the state. It was the logical extension of the state's commitment to central planning and its investments in creating a vast statistical infrastructure. The combination of National Income Committees, the CSO, and the NSS produced a flood of data that needed to be processed to be of use to the Planning Commission. Centralized planning was premised on the ability to calculate masses of data, and computers presented a revolutionary means to do so. At a time when these machines were coming to be seen as essential to planning, the Professor and the Institute's association with India's earliest computers only strengthened their claims to policymaking.

Escape to India

Raised in Brooklyn, Morton Nadler had joined the Communist Party of the United States of America in the 1930s. During World War II, the combination of Nadler's political sympathies and his training as a radio engineer drew unwelcome attention at the Federal Bureau of Investigation (FBI).[6] When working at a radio company in Chicago, he became a member of the Communist Party's Hyde Park branch. It soon caught up with him; in 1946, he was fired from his job because of pressure applied by the US Army.[7] Incensed by the dismissal and dreaming of helping in the building of socialism, he decided to seek employment behind the Iron Curtain. Telling his parents and passport authorities that he was headed to Paris for a doctorate at the Sorbonne, Nadler left the United States aboard the SS America. On 6 March 1948, the idealistic 27-year-old boarded a flight from Paris with a one-way ticket to

Prague.[8] He would spend the next decade in the Soviet bloc, in communist Czechoslovakia.

Nadler began his life in Eastern Europe by working on radar systems for a state-owned electronics enterprise. Within a year and a half and unbeknown to him, the US Department of Defense asked the FBI Director, J. Edgar Hoover, to investigate whether 'Nadler may be passing information on radar developments to the Czechoslovakians'.[9] In 1950, when Nadler went to the American Embassy in Prague to renew his passport, it was confiscated on the charge that he was betraying American radar secrets and 'inventing weapons for a potential enemy'.[10] It would be returned only if he bought a one-way ticket back to the United States. Unaware of the gravity of the case being built against him by the FBI and CIA, and also under pressure from the Czechoslovak communist party that suspected him of being an American spy, Nadler renounced his American citizenship.[11]

True to the odious Soviet script, local secret police began to recruit Nadler as an informant. Czech spymasters believed that Nadler's American background and access to the engineering elite made him a useful source. He could 'easily gain the confidence of the class enemy'. Before approaching him, they had him followed, tapped his work phone, monitored his mail, and even infiltrated his friend circle. To their surprise, Nadler was more than cooperative. He was, after all, a 'revolutionary romantic' who felt duty-bound to help the communist state. Code-named 'A', Nadler met diligently with his handlers (insisting they pay for meals) and submitted written reports. Since trust runs in deficit in such circumstances, the spies had their spy tailed by other spies. The file on 'A' had this description: 'The collaborator has a very rough personality, sometimes arrogant, clever to the point of being sly ... for money, which he likes very much, he would work even harder. His weakness is women.'[12] Despite cooperating, Nadler sensed he was under surveillance. He even suspected that a lover – one among many extramarital dalliances – was a 'honey trap' set by the Party.

Nadler was still, however, an ardent communist. When his wife gave birth to their second daughter, they named her Maia – after Mao. In early 1955, following a month of cross-country skiing and winter sports, Nadler began a job at Czechoslovakia's premier computer institute, *Ústav Matematických Strojů* (The Institute of Mathematical Machines). He worked under the mentorship of Antonin Svoboda, a brilliant and pioneering computer scientist who had escaped the Nazi advance through western Europe by fleeing first to Paris, then to the United States where he researched at MIT, before returning after the war.

Although doubts about communism and evidence of official anti-Semitism had been growing for years, it was ultimately news of Soviet tanks rolling into Budapest in 1956 to crush the Hungarian Revolution that left Nadler thoroughly disenchanted. It was a 'sudden emotional shock' to the one-time Stalinist. He had also grown tired of the mindless bureaucracy of Party personnel and the stunning inefficiency of the Plan. The dangers of the regime were also becoming personal. Soon after the Hungarian uprising, he received an anonymous note in his mailbox threatening him with hanging from a lamp post – the fate of Hungarian collaborators. He feared that his telephone line was being tapped. As if he was not terrified enough, a friend lent Nadler a novel that hit too close to home; it was *1984*, George Orwell's template of totalitarian dystopia. The chapter in his memoir dealing with this period is grimly subtitled, 'Can I Get out of this Mess?'[13]

Looking for ways to leave the country, it took Nadler many months to realize that not only was the Czechoslovak government reluctant to grant him passage (delaying his passport), but the American Embassy would also not give him a visa to return.[14] Czechoslovak authorities believed he possessed information too sensitive to allow him to depart. In the United States, the FBI and J. Edgar Hoover suspected Nadler might be part of a sinister ploy to 'assist Czechs or Soviets for intelligence purposes' by 'plant[ing] an industrial spy in the US'. This was despite, or because of, his abilities being judged impressive enough to receive an offer of employment from the University of California, Los Angeles to work on their computer programme. Nadler, still considering himself an American and unaware of how dark the FBI's view of him was, even bought a new suit and shoes to attend a party with his wife at the US embassy to celebrate the Fourth of July.[15]

Tragically for Nadler, the FBI's sprawling network of informants included his own mother. Dorothy Nadler had approached the FBI in Washington, DC, offering to relay information about her communist son based on what her granddaughter confided in her. Returning home, she told her husband and rabbi what she had done. The rabbi approved but the husband did not. As Morton Nadler would later recall, his life had become a 'parody of a John le Carré spy'. Even years later, the betrayed son remembered, 'she never gave me the least inkling about these contacts with the FBI'.[16]

Nadler was forced to choose between leaving the country illegally or, as some friends suggested, get 'invited to some country that the communist government of Czechoslovakia couldn't refuse, such as India'.[17] India appeared an opportune destination because it was non-aligned in the Cold War and was courted by both superpowers. A cable from the

American Embassy in Prague observed that, 'the local [Czech] authorities would be able, on the one hand, to rid themselves of a dissatisfied convert and, on the other hand, to avoid the publicity which would appear in the world press as a result of his turning from the unfilled promises of Communism directly to the bounties of capitalism'. As for Nadler, whose secret ambition was to return to the United States, spending time in India would serve as a necessary 'cooling off period', diluting the stain of communism in the eyes of America and pacifying its authorities that he was not a secret agent.[18]

It was around this time that Nadler made a fortuitous connection with an Indian student who was searching for an English-speaking scientist to help with his postgraduate practical training. Nadler became a mentor to him, and through this student made contact with the Institute. Repeated strolls to the Indian Embassy, located down the street from his workplace, and friendship with the Third Secretary there, yielded information about an imminent visit by the Professor.

When Mahalanobis arrived in Prague, Nadler met him along with the resident Indian Ambassador. The Professor invited Nadler to join the Institute's staff for two years and the Ambassador helped smooth bureaucratic hurdles.[19] But despite obstacles seeming to melt away, Nadler's ordeal had not quite ended. His application for a passport continued to be ignored until he went on a hunger strike and demanded to meet the Minister of Interior to present his case. Having secured the attention of the minister, Nadler convinced him to provide the requisite documentation. Passport in hand, he was now ready to abandon Czech nationality (and another lover). On 21 February 1959, Nadler proceeded to the airport to honour the contract that would take him to Calcutta 'to work on electronic computers and to train graduate students in computer hardware'.[20] The FBI learned of it when Dorothy Nadler telephoned their Newark office to inform them that her son had moved to Calcutta to work at the 'India Statistical Bureau'. The American public would read about the movements of 'one of the most talented of the expatriates', 'an expert in electronic computers' six months later in the pages of the *New York Times*.[21]

Nadler's archival trail runs cold with his departure to India. However, to grasp how a young communist from New York who had renounced both American and Czech citizenships, and who invited the unwelcome interest of intelligence agencies on both sides of the Iron Curtain, wound up on a verdant campus outside Calcutta, we must consider what brought him there. India's nascent computer programme was the magnet. And the tale of computers in India cannot be narrated without economic planning playing the lead.[22]

Machine Dreams

From when he first laid eyes on an electronic computer, Mahalanobis was smitten.[23] Amazed, and convinced of its utility to his country's development, he was soon involved in a lengthy quest to bring these machines to India. The Professor's search for calculating contraptions predated the invention of the electronic computer. His craving was for calculating machines in general. During the war, the Institute had found mechanical calculators hard to acquire. Frustrated, in 1942 Mahalanobis decided to purchase machine tools and workshop equipment to see if it would be possible to manufacture hand-operated calculating machines in India.[24] But they soon found that attempting to manufacture these machines in the manner of a cottage industry would prove uneconomical.[25]

In March 1946, when in the United States, Mahalanobis heard the polymathic genius John von Neumann make a presentation on a computer ('electronic brains' to the American public) under development at the Institute for Advanced Study in Princeton.[26] The Professor broached the possibility of developing a computer in India and von Neumann was open to working on an Indian computer the next winter, but warned that the cost of building it would be steep. However, von Neumann assured Mahalanobis, once the first model had been built, subsequent ones would come with a moderate price tag of 'only 30 or 40 thousand dollars'.[27] The next month in New York, Mahalanobis met statisticians from Columbia University and dropped by the Watson Computation Laboratory. Based on these conversations he concluded that if statistics were to progress in India, it was 'essential to build up at least one first rate computation and calculating laboratory'. It was a matter deserving 'serious attention at an early date'.[28]

Early the following year, with his country's independence still months away, Mahalanobis saw a digital computer in operation for the first time. During a visit to Harvard University, he was given a tour of the Mark I by computer pioneer Howard Aiken with whom he spent much of the day. The reason Mahalanobis had not seen this machine on earlier trips was because it was still a 'Navy secret'. The Professor proceeded to Princeton University, where he renewed discussions about computing with von Neumann. When in Princeton, Mahalanobis also made the pilgrimage to its most famous resident, Albert Einstein, who expressed hope that the transfer of power from British to Indian hands would proceed smoothly.[29]

Increasingly occupied with national income assessment, sample surveys, and planning in India, Mahalanobis believed that computers would prove vital to addressing these questions. Digital computers could perform complex mathematical calculations at hundreds of times the speed of humans and the Professor realized that they would be of tremendous help in tabulating and processing data emanating from the NSS. Feeding this raw information into a computer, planners would be able to generate estimates and parse trends in the Indian economy in a fraction of the time it would otherwise take. Another major application for computers in the realm of planning was modelling the economy through inter-industry input-output tables. These tables, first systematized by economist Wassily Leontief in the 1930s, defined the interrelationship between different sectors of the economy. It was based on the understanding that one industry's output is often the input for another. The input-output table became a widely adopted method of tracking the movement of goods and services between sectors of the economy, providing a structural snapshot of the entire economy. Leontief began using computers in developing these tables: in 1949, he entered data on forty-two sectors of the US economy into Harvard's Mark II and ran it for 56 hours to create an input-output table representing the American economy.[30] Nearly a quarter-century later, Leontief would win the Nobel Prize in Economics, primarily for his work on this technique. The United States continued to conduct input-output research on a regular basis, except for a few years in the 1950s, when the Eisenhower administration had it shuttered due to its perceived proximity to communist planning.

Never burdened by any formal training in economics, Mahalanobis was instinctively predisposed towards this kind of mathematical abstraction. It was the distillation of a technocrat's vision. Quite apart from these applications, the computer was also an object of status and fantasy. It was chased after as much for the fabulous possibilities it evoked as it was for the more modest capabilities it delivered. Rare, notoriously expensive, and seemingly boundless in potential, it promised the future and appeared to belong to it. The Professor salivated at the prospect.

In the decade and a half after independence, the Professor sought ways to manufacture computers in India (a technical challenge) or import them (a political and financial challenge). While the dream of a computer in India would have to wait a few more years to come to fruition, the Institute opened an Electronics Laboratory and Workshop in 1950 whose brief was to deliver an electronic computer.[31] The person in charge of this project was mathematician and engineer Samarendra Kumar Mitra, one of the few Indians with any training in computers. The previous year, Mitra had been offered a year-long UNESCO Fellowship to travel to the United States to study electronic computers. Upon completion, Mitra joined the Institute.[32] By 1953, he and the Electronics

Division had assembled India's first electronic computer. It was a small analogue machine capable of solving simultaneous linear equations of up to ten variables.[33] Lacking the resources to import expensive parts, they built it using materials salvaged from World War II surplus in the scrap markets and disposal depots of Calcutta's Chandni Chowk market.[34] To the Professor and the Institute, it was a matter of pride that they had built it themselves.[35] In December, Prime Minister Nehru dropped by to see the country's first computer in operation. Early the next year, work began on the grander project of building India's first advanced digital computer.

The Professor was after money, equipment, and the technicians necessary to build computers in Calcutta.[36] In the early 1950s, he was involved in several discussions in Washington, DC, regarding America's ability to offer technical aid to India.[37] Despite pursuing this for more than three years, he was left empty-handed. He wondered whether these efforts failed due to uncooperative officials in New Delhi. It was hard to explain to bureaucrats that this was not an isolated item, but instead 'closely integrated with a general plan of development of statistics – which, in turn, is an essential step in national planning'. During the spring and summer of 1954, the Professor travelled with 'Rani' through Europe, the United States, and the Soviet Union. In between meeting economists and statisticians, and attending sessions of the UN Statistical Commission, he tracked down computer equipment and sniffed for avenues through which to bring a digital computer to India.[38] Building an Indian computer or bringing in one from abroad was an urgent matter; there was no time to lose. 'Otherwise', he wrote to Pant, 'we will never be able to cope with the tremendous volume of primary information which is accumulating through the NSS every month. Secondly, for planning ... the help of high speed electronic computers would be simply indispensable.' He was 'desperately anxious' to begin.[39]

When in London, Mahalanobis and Mitra took special interest in a computer sold by the British Tabulating Machine Company. Unlike other computers they had seen or heard of, this one appeared to match both their need and means. The Hollerith Electronic Computer, Model 2 M (or HEC 2M), was noted for its flexibility in the kinds of operations it could perform. Although its computing capabilities were modest, the Professor felt that it would prove adequate for the time being. Mahalanobis inspected the machine and was told that it would cost £18,500 and could be ready by April 1955. It would take nine months to manufacture, three to ship to India, and two more to set up in Calcutta. The manufacturer had made it clear that they would not assume responsibility for its installation or maintenance. The Institute would have to send a couple of workers to spend a few months at their workshop in

Britain to observe its assembly, and to be trained in working the computer.[40] The Professor and his protégé rolled the dice and placed an order.

Computer technology in the United States had progressed impressively in a short span. At the Bureau of the Census in Washington, DC, they saw the new FOSDIC computer in operation. This computer could directly scan or 'read' information from a field schedule or questionnaire without first needing it to be entered onto punched cards. As the Professor noted, 'You will easily realise how this would expedite the processing of NSS data.'[41] The problem for the Indians was the price of these machines. The UNIVAC, for example, cost over a million dollars (and a further $200,000 annually for upkeep).[42] That was an upfront cost of roughly 5 lakh rupees in mid-1950s India. The cheapest computer in America was the University of Illinois-Urbana Champaign's 'Illiac,' but even that was beyond India's budget. Purchasing an electronic computer in America, Mitra and the Professor agreed, was simply not affordable. India was still a poor republic and foreign exchange a scarce resource. To come by a million dollars was not easily done.

The Professor concluded that it made more sense to construct one in India with help from American aid agencies.[43] Talks with government officials in Washington, DC, gave him the impression that an Indian request for aid in computing and statistical equipment would be looked on kindly.[44] The idea was to build a machine that could solve a set of linear equations with fifty variables. Dishearteningly, it was evident that even this would not suffice because physical planning and inter-industry calculations would soon require up to 300 variables.[45] He wrote in a letter to Pant from London later that year: 'I have a great sense of urgency. I know that the NSS [National Sample Survey] would get choked without electronic equipment. I know that real planning would require the use of such computers.'[46]

The Professor's itinerary allowed him to peek behind the Iron Curtain as well. Writing from Prague, he told Pant that his purpose in travelling to the Soviet Union was to 'explore what help we can get in economic planning or in constructing electronic computers'.[47] Apart from streamlining the NSS and the task of economic analysis, developing 'modern high speed electronic computing machines is an essential part of the programme'.[48]

Mahalanobis had laid the groundwork for Moscow months in advance. Earlier that year, in February 1954, he had attended an informal lunch hosted by the prime minister for a Soviet delegation of scientists. Mahalanobis found himself opportunely seated next to the Soviet Ambassador, Mikhail Menshikov, an official who would later become

Ambassador to the United States, where his reputation as 'fashionably attired, faultlessly mannered' earned the sobriquet 'Smiling Mike'.[49] The Professor casually asked Menshikov if the Soviets would be able to help India in building digital computers. The secrecy surrounding Soviet computer research was such that Mahalanobis did not even know if they had begun making such computers.[50] Cold War security concerns and interagency competition in Moscow had plunged their computer programme into an information blackout.[51] Mahalanobis' query was hence speculation based on a hunch. Not above bluntly reminding the diplomat of the Cold War stakes, he provocatively added: 'Surely the USSR can have no objection in giving and teaching us things which are known to the Americans.'[52] Taking the bait, Menshikov responded with a laugh: 'Why don't you ask us?' The Professor gladly complied, and in the ensuing discussion the Ambassador suggested drafting a formal letter and handing it over to the Soviet delegation that was scheduled to fly back to Moscow the next morning.

Spurred by the opportunity that had presented itself, Mahalanobis sprang into action. He made an appointment with the prime minister and met him that night with a draft. Nehru made some changes to the letter and the Professor took it to Palam Airport the following morning to hand it to the departing scientists. A couple of months later when in Berne, Switzerland, to attend the meeting of the UN Statistical Commission, he was spotted by a Soviet embassy official and was handed a document. It was an invitation by their Academy of Sciences to visit Russia to discuss technical aid and computers.[53] Incidentally, this did not go down well with the Indian Ambassador to Switzerland, Y. D. Gundevia, who was indignant that the letter had been handed to Mahalanobis instead of being formally presented to a diplomat. He complained about this breach of protocol in a letter to the External Affairs Ministry in New Delhi, stating that this was not the first time the Professor had conducted negotiations with the Soviets and meddled in matters best left to diplomats.[54]

That summer, the Professor, Mitra, and a delegation of scientists from India spent 5 weeks in the USSR.[55] The visitors from India were offered a tour of the Institute of Precision Mechanics and Computer Engineering in Moscow, where the BESM computer was being built.[56] They were perhaps the first outside scientists to be allowed access.[57] The Indians gathered that the Soviet computer programme was fairly advanced: Mitra pronounced it more sophisticated that anything he had seen in the United Kingdom, though not yet as advanced as recent work in Princeton.[58] They were also alert to the possibility that some aspects of Soviet computer infrastructure, possibly 'connected with guided missiles, or defence generally' had been kept from view, just as had been done in some places in the United States.[59] That their tour might have been blinkered did not irk Mahalanobis. He was categorical that he was not interested in the military applications of computers.

During his stay in the Soviet Union, the Professor also broached the subject of technical aid to help build electronic computers. His timing was propitious because there was 'clearly a great deal of appreciation of what JN [Jawaharlal Nehru] has done at the international level and evidently also the desire to have closer and actively cooperative relations with India at the technical level'.[60] Mahalanobis was buoyed because his conversations led to a promise of computer hardware from the Soviets.[61] While this was initially supposed to be channelled through bilateral aid, arrangements were made at the Professor's suggestion to route it via the UN. Since it was to be used for national development, rather than just independent scientific research, Mahalanobis also recommended that the equipment should formally become the property of the Government of India instead of the Institute's.[62] The Professor had his eye on aid that went beyond the merely monetary. In a letter to Pant, he conveyed his vehemence about it: 'It is not money, not money, NOT MONEY – I am worrying about – for the electronic computer and such things. I want an equipment project ... because through the process ... we get the opportunity of linking on to relevant technical knowledge.'[63]

Later that year, after returning to Calcutta, the Professor closely tracked the progress of the application. Reiterating the stakes involved in securing these machines, he described statistical work as being as essential to planning 'as vitamin is in relation to health'. The aid from Moscow was a start, but not nearly enough. The Professor's ambition was more expansive. 'I shall not be happy', he declared, 'until we become independent of other countries in the matter of calculating machines.'[64] His experience chasing computers all over the world, and coaxing foreign officials and private corporations, had convinced him that India could not continue looking abroad for computers, hat in hand.

Computers in Calcutta

In December 1954, two Bengali engineers made their way from Calcutta to the garden city of Letchworth in England. Mohi Mukherjee and Amaresh Roy were at the British Tabulating Machine Company's workshop to observe the manufacture of the computer bound for India. The machine took 6 months to build and they used the time to familiarize themselves with its processes, learning how to operate it.[65] Once their training ended, they travelled throughout Europe to visit 'computing machine laboratories' and returned home in early 1956.[66] India's first digital computer followed them to Baranagore in two crates.

Ten feet in length, seven in breadth, and six in height, the computer consisted of three vertical metallic cabinets. Given Calcutta's humidity, it was housed in an air-conditioned room on the Institute's campus.[67] The HEC 2M could perform 200 additions or five multiplications per second, and it could only handle a total of nine digits.[68] It took 2 months to install, and as it had arrived from England with no manuals, Roy and Mukherjee had to assemble it based on their notes, sometimes relying just on instinct. When, for example, the chain-smoking Roy realized that he needed a specific clearance between the sixteen tracks constituting the computer's memory, he found that his trusted cigarette paper did the job just fine.[69]

The computer was not easy to use. Roy and Mukherjee arranged sessions to train other engineers at the Institute and soon created their own instruction manuals. Within months of being inaugurated, in March 1956, a dozen workers at the Institute's Electronics Computer Laboratory had learned how to operate it. Over the preceding 2 years the number of engineers working at the laboratory had grown. For example, Dwijesh Majumdar had joined in September 1955 right after taking the exam for his Master's degree. A piece in a Calcutta newspaper about Mahalanobis showing an analogue computer to Nehru had drawn him to the Institute. When they met, the Professor invited Majumdar to join the fledgling electronics laboratory, but not before delivering 'a detailed lecture on the importance of computer[s] for developmental planning in India'.[70] Majumdar was among the first engineers to work on the British computer in Baranagore.

Apart from processing data related to the NSS, and performing calculations for various divisions within the Institute, the HEC 2M received numerous computational requests from scientific institutions across the country.[71] However, the biggest task that the computer was tackling was a mathematical one sent by the Planning Division at the Institute.[72] As the first digital computer in India and one of the very few in Asia, it was also a tourist attraction for ministers and other dignitaries.[73] But, as Mahalanobis had noted before its purchase, this computer was never going to meet the needs of the NSS and economic planning. It functioned ultimately as training wheels.[74]

The Institute had begun inviting computer experts from abroad to help with the considerably more ambitious project of building a digital computer on site.[75] Begun in early 1954, the plan stumbled within months of having been announced. Talks with Soviet computer experts had given the laboratory pause; the Indian engineers realized that designing and constructing a new computer would take years. It made more sense to focus on operationalizing the British computer and simply acquiring another computer from abroad.[76] Meanwhile, the deal that Mahalanobis brokered with the Soviet Union had jumped through bureaucratic hoops and met with approval. The Institute initiated a request to the UN, through New Delhi, for a Soviet machine.[77]

The Ural – named presumably to evoke the mighty Russian mountain range – arrived in Calcutta only in late 1958, two years after it had initially been expected.[78] The Soviet computer was formally handed over after a conference inaugurated by a member of the Planning Commission. The only two digital computers in South Asia were now in Baranagore, on the Institute's campus. The *Times of India* reported that the new computer could work '600 times faster than a single man'.[79] Eight Soviet engineers followed the massive computer and it took them 3 months to install it in yet another air-conditioned room. Unlike the earlier British machine, this one arrived with instruction manuals but, unfortunately, they were all in Russian. With the help of an interpreter, the Soviet engineers held classes on construction, operation, and maintenance of the computer.[80] Indian engineers also learned some Russian in order to follow the manuals.[81] Soon the Ural was running two shifts a day, its printer generating 'ridiculous sounds'.[82] When not involved on tasks relating to the Institute's priorities (sample surveys and planning), its time was contracted out to other universities and scientific institutions.[83] By 1959, the Institute had secured two digital computers and served as the de facto national computation centre. It was apparent, however, that the Institute required more computing power.

The One That Got Away...

If the British and Soviet computers were quests fulfilled, the saga of the American UNIVAC was one of unrequited interest. Mahalanobis had first inquired about this machine as early as 1948, when its manufacture had only just begun. Standing for Universal Automatic Computer, it had been unveiled in 1951 when its manufacturers handed it over to the US Bureau of the Census. It acquired national recognition the next year when it starred, alongside television news anchor Walter Cronkite on CBS. On election night it accurately predicted Dwight D. Eisenhower's surprising landslide victory in the US presidential election over Adlai Stevenson. This had been both the first presidential election that was broadcast on television coast-to-coast and the first time that computers were used to anticipate the result. In the 1950s, the UNIVAC became a byword for computers in the American public. It would later be featured on the cover

Figure 3.1. Nobel Prize-winning physicist Niels Bohr, Margrethe Bohr, Nirmal Kumari Mahalanobis, and P. C. Mahalanobis on the URAL computer floor at the Institute (16 January 1960).

of a Superman comic book and in a Wile E. Coyote cartoon where it helped ensnare Bugs Bunny.[84]

The Professor pursued this machine for years. Its cost, and the shortage of foreign currency in India, made outright purchase impossible (it was valued, three years later, at a million dollars). In an effort to route the UNIVAC through international aid, the Professor directed his efforts at the US Technical Cooperation Mission to India, a part of the US Technical Cooperation Administration. But despite his persistent tugging at the sleeve of aid agencies for more than a decade, he never succeeded.

The Indian government, like the Professor, remained unaware that the person spearheading the mission to bring computers to India was himself an obstacle. India was unable to get a digital computer from the United States throughout the 1950s partly because of Mahalanobis' reputation as a Soviet sympathizer during the Cold War. Between 1950 and 1954, Mahalanobis engaged in numerous informal discussions in Washington,

DC, regarding the provision of technical aid to India, and computers in particular.[85] This was at the height of the Red Scare in the United States, with the fear-mongering Senator Joseph McCarthy leading a crusade against real and imagined communist influence in American society and Soviet infiltration into its government. It was not a context likely to favour the Professor. Files at the State Department painted a menacing picture of him. Allergic to his political slant, they described him as 'extremely sympathetic to communist doctrine'.[86] A dispatch, classified 'Secret Security Information', from the American Embassy in New Delhi to the State Department in the summer of 1953, corroborates the ominous glare in which the Professor was viewed. It indicated that the State Department already possessed files that described him as a 'notorious fellow traveler and sympathizer of the Soviet Union' and the Institute as a 'Communist apparatus'.[87]

The American consulate in Calcutta sent a confidential note to Washington, DC, bolstering this view. It contained the transcript of a 2-hour-long conversation between Mahalanobis and the President of Brooklyn College, Harry Gideonse. The value of this memorandum, the message claimed, lay in the insight it provided into the Professor's political loyalties from a new and independent source. The report began complimentarily, describing Mahalanobis as a person of 'exceptional personal charm and broad cultural background'. After that, however, it was downhill. It pointed out that Mahalanobis, unlike most Americans, was convinced that the Soviet Union had ultimately peaceful objectives. Gideonse even sensed sinister designs afoot. 'To me, Mahalanobis is far more significant than straight communist propaganda. He has personal and moral authority, apparent integrity, and an impressive command of relevant information. His ideas are in my judgment a direct preparation for an authoritative solution to India's economic problems'.[88]

By next winter, the view that Mahalanobis was a closet communist who was distressingly sympathetic to the Soviet Union had congealed in American back channels. Ironically, the Professor himself became a liability in the attempt to convince America to grant India a computer. Another confidential memorandum sent from the US Embassy to the Department of State warned: 'The problem of P.C. Mahalanobis ... is well known to the Department ... It will be noted that the present position of the Embassy and TCM/India is not to give any assistance to the Indian Statistical Institute because of Professor Mahalanobis' reputation of being at least a fellow traveler.'[89] Unsurprisingly, nothing came of the Professor's negotiations with the Technical Cooperation Mission. It also appears he remained in the dark about his own unwitting role in stymying the progress of the proposal.

By early 1957, there had been either a change of heart or strategy, at least among American officials in New Delhi. The icy opinion of him had thawed. The Technical Cooperation Mission office in Delhi forwarded a project worth $1.5 million in favour of the Institute to Washington with $1 million for the computer, and $0.5 million for the cost of training over a period of 2 to 3 years.[90] Much to the Professor's chagrin, the proposal was once again turned down. A letter from Ambassador Bunker during the summer of 1957 suggests that this time even the Embassy in New Delhi was dissatisfied with the outcome. According to the note, the real reason the Director of the International Cooperation Administration, John Hollister, had turned down the request was on the grounds that 'with all the unemployment in India spending a million dollars on a fancy calculating machine cannot be justified'.[91] Hollister was known to be lukewarm about India.[92]

Aggravated, and no doubt puzzled, by Washington's repeated unwillingness to part with a computer, the tireless Professor looked to the Ford Foundation. He communicated with Douglas Ensminger, the Ford representative in India, to inquire about the foundation's willingness to help.[93] That autumn, some of the Professor's friends in America – all of whom had recently spent time at the Institute – wrote to the President of the Ford Foundation. The Institute, they explained, was responsible for 'collecting, tabulating and analyzing much of the social and economic data which provides the basis on which India's plans are prepared and progress is evaluated'. Presenting them with a computer 'not only would aid India in its planning and development, but would contribute greatly toward building a stronger bond between India and our own country'.[94] Four years later – despite the Professor remaining an uncomfortable pebble in the boot of US agencies – nothing budged on the American front.

Mahalanobis maintained pressure on the government. He raised the matter with the prime minister, discussed it with the Planning Commission, and wrote beseeching letters to the Ministry of Finance and Union Cabinet.[95] Broadening the pitch from planning and statistics, he now expanded the list of potential beneficiaries to scientific and industrial research and military calculations. He detailed how the UNIVAC could perform very different types of calculations than the Ural. The Soviet machine was best suited to solving algebraic or differential equations or preparing mathematical tables. The American one was more efficient at scrutinizing large volumes of numerical data, such as that involved in processing information unearthed by the countrywide sample surveys. Further, he stated, the two computers were not interchangeable. Using one instead of the other was just as impracticable as using 'an aeroplane as a substitute for a car in going from one place to another in the same city'.[96]

The Professor and the Institute had sought this contraption for a decade but had nothing to show for their Sisyphean task. Through most of the 1950s, external forces effectively regulated the Indian computer programme. As the world leader in computer technology, America's stance on India's computing aspirations mattered a great deal. In the harsh glare of the Cold War, American agencies turned down Mahalanobis and the Institute due to misgivings about their political loyalties and their perceived vulnerabilities to Soviet encroachment. Their proposals were either smothered behind the scenes or ignored, so they died on the vine. Even when such suspicions receded, the tepid attitude of American aid agencies and the Ford Foundation conspired to deny India this computer. By the end of the decade, Mahalanobis was also confronting the much bigger issue – convincing his own government.

Losing Favour

The Institute lost the distinction of being the only centre for computers in India by 1960. Under the direction of physicist Homi Jehangir Bhabha, the Tata Institute of Fundamental Research in Bombay had stolen a march in the quest for the first domestically built digital computer. Like Mahalanobis, Bhabha had also been inspired by Jon von Neumann's ground breaking computer designs in the late 1940s, when he learned of them while on a visit to Princeton University, returning to India with a report.[97]

The Bombay computer project started in 1955, at the same time the Institute harboured similar designs.[98] But unlike its competitor in Calcutta, and perhaps because it was not able to import computers, the programme in Bombay was not abandoned. It was completed in 1960, although it would acquire a name only 2 years later when Nehru christened it Tata Institute of Fundamental Research Automatic Computer (TIFRAC). By the time it had been named, however, developments in computer technology in the rest of the world had left it, in the words of its principal designer, 'an obsolete first generation machine'.[99] As a result, the Tata Institute was also on the market for the import of another computer. The arrival of a second player on the Indian computing scene led to a tussle between Mahalanobis and Bhabha, ISI and the Tata Institute of Fundamental Research (TIFR).

Bhabha wielded considerable sway with the Government. A cleft-chinned scion of a notable Bombay Parsi family, he had grown up lunching at the plush ancestral mansion of the Tata's, his relatives across the road, absorbing talk of industrial advance and witnessing Gandhi's visits during the civil disobedience movement. Bhabha was a scientist of cultural refinement who was at ease with theoretical physics, watercolours, and Beethoven.[100] Apart from directing TIFR, he was also Chairman of the Atomic Energy Commission, the founder of India's nuclear programme. When Bombay did not have its own computer, the Atomic Energy Commission's secret calculations were sent to Calcutta to be solved on the Institute's computers. As accomplished Cambridge-educated physicists who became institution-building scientific heroes in India, Mahalanobis and Bhabha were too alike not to eventually get in each other's way. Facing off may have felt like looking in a mirror.

In August 1961, Bhabha wrote to Mahalanobis to say that he was aware of the Institute's request to the Government for the purchase a computer and informed him that the Tata Institute had put in a similar request as part of the Third Five-Year Plan. He suggested they make common cause: 'We should jointly press for both computers and I have a feeling that we will succeed in getting two from the Americans under TCM or under some other agency.'[101] Bhabha had obviously not shared the Professor's history of rejection. The response from Calcutta made sure to put the two claims into proper perspective. Mahalanobis pointed out that the proposal to bring a computer to work primarily on sample survey data had been initiated by the Institute years ago. A 'timely flow of economic information would become increasingly of crucial importance for the efficient functioning of the planned economy'. While he was willing to join forces, 'If for any reason, two computers are not available, I should have no hesitation in giving a higher priority to the data processing equipment for the National Sample Survey.'[102]

In the spring 1962, Tarlok Singh, now a Member of the Planning Commission, wrote a short paper acknowledging the need for a digital computer in Delhi, particularly for the calculation of inter-industry relationships. It would soon be necessary, he believed, to establish modern high-speed computational facilities for the Planning Commission and the CSO.[103] At an informal summer meeting at Yojana Bhavan, there was a discussion over this proposal for a new national computing centre. It was decided that a committee would be set up to report soon on the types of computers that would be required and the agencies that should be entrusted with them. Members of this committee belonged to organizations most interested in computers: the Institute, the Tata Institute, the CSO the Department of Atomic Energy, and the Planning Commission. Mahalanobis was named the Chairman of the Committee - no doubt to his great relief.[104] By late monsoon, even newspaper reports were clamouring for a new computer facility to aid in national development. An article in a national daily stated that it would be 'very desirable' for the Government to import 'one or more large scale machines . . . for national use in government, planning and industry'.[105] Ultimately, the Institute was not granted the large data processing computer it was after.[106] They might have been mollified though at being granted a license to import a smaller computer, an IBM (although the Government did not offer any grants for its purchase).[107]

It was clear by this point that the Institute had been displaced from its perch of exclusivity. These were years during which other institutions and corporations in India acquired their own computers. In the early 1960s, Esso Standard Eastern of Bombay installed the country's first commercial computer; the Defence Ministry had set up its computer centre; and the Indian Institute of Technology at Kanpur received an IBM machine. Possibly due to the Tata Institute's atomic energy project, Bhabha managed to persuade the government and within 2 years his institution was in possession of a CDC 600.[108] The addition of the largest computer commercially available propelled it to the status of a national computing centre, like the Institute in Calcutta. Describing computers as a futuristic 'Magic Tool', the *Times of India* pronounced: 'A giant has been installed in Bombay's backyard'. As a national facility, it handled requests from scientific, engineering and educational institutions, and even the Planning Commission said that it would be of 'vital assistance' to their work.[109] By the end of 1964, there were at least fifteen computers in operation in India, and the numbers would grow rapidly over the course of the decade. The Institute was no longer the only computation centre in the country, and it had also lost its exclusive association with the handling of planning data.

If the rise of a computing centre in Bombay overshadowed the Institute's computer programme, the installation of one at Yojana Bhavan effectively marginalized it. It was the realization of the Professor's fears. The Ford Foundation had belatedly come around to the view that awarding India a computer was worthwhile. With the Government of India's ravenous appetite for statistics, a computer would 'aid in planning and in the management of activities designed to implement the plan'.[110] It was assumed that the computer would be located in Delhi and run by the Institute. But despite their cajoling, it did not turn out in their favour; the Institute had slipped out of the frame. In late 1965, computer centres funded by the Ford Foundation were opened in New Delhi. The centres were the result of grants made by the foundation that summer to the Delhi School of Economics, the University of Bombay, the Institute of Agricultural Research Statistics, and the Planning Commission.[111] On 23 September 1965, Asok Mehta, the Deputy Chairman of the Planning Commission, inaugurated a computer centre at Yojana Bhavan, effectively closing the door on the Institute's hopes of remaining the Planning Commission's computational arm.[112]

The Ford Foundation grant to the Planning Commission was worth close to half a million dollars (approximately 23,00,000 rupees at the time). It was used by the Planning Commission to purchase a medium-sized electronic computer, the IBM 1620, and ancillary equipment. The 2,000 square-foot Computer Centre at Yojana Bhavan worked on an open shop basis that permitted outsiders to be charged fees based on cost. The lack of trained staff and teething troubles meant that the computer could be used for only one shift a day until 1968 when improvements allowed for a two-shift operation (an average of 13 hours a day). But demand for the services of the computer centre was twice what was available. By 1971, the computer system at Yojana Bhavan was already outdated and prone to break down. In January that year an Expert Committee was appointed to look into how the system could be replaced. As an official file noted, 'the importance of having a modern computer facility in the Planning Commission ... cannot be overemphasized. Planning and Development admittedly deserves the highest priority, and, therefore, the proposal to install a suitable computer system in the Planning Commission may be accorded high priority'.[113]

Afterlife

'The Big Data Revolution Can Revive the Planned Economy'. It is a headline that could well have been written by Mahalanobis in the early 1950s, during the Cold War. Instead, it is the title of an article published in late 2017 by the *Financial Times*. The author, journalist John Thornhill, sounds much like the Professor when he speculates that 'the explosion of data in our modern world could – at least in theory – inform far better managerial decisions and reduce the information imbalances between a planned and a market economy'.[114] Another article, a month later and this time in the *Wall Street Journal*, referred to how Chinese premier Xi Jinping 'aspires to use big data and artificial intelligence to correct the planning errors of the past and micromanage the Chinese economy'.[115] The previous year Jack Ma, billionaire founder of the mega multinational conglomerate Alibaba, predicted the triumphal return of planned economies. In the next three decades, he declared, 'the planned economy will get bigger and bigger'. The reason? 'Big Data will make the market smarter and make it possible to plan and predict market forces so as to allow us to finally achieve a planned economy ... Properly harnessed, that data could mimic the price mechanism as a means of matching demand and.'[116] Once again, these were words that could have come from the lips of a certain Indian planner in the mid-twentieth century.

The decision to plan the economy brought the problem of big data into prominence. Calculation assumed an unprecedented significance. Planners required ever-improving data processing capabilities in order to put the gushing hose of survey data to use in order to model the economy through input-output tables. The computer's appeal was its promise as a solution. Writing in January 1956, an economics teacher conveyed this idealized vision of planning in which 'electronic machines would calculate input-output co-efficients and an army of statisticians would concentrate on linear programming and the leading economists of the country would carry out complicated exercises in an attempt to allocate relative priorities'.[117]

The story of the computer in India cannot be understood outside the context of planning, national statistics, technocracy, and the state's expanding quantitative capacities. Computers were imported and then developed to bolster the knowledge infrastructure that supported state planning. It complemented the government's new data-gathering methods and national statistical system by arming it with a revolutionary means of data processing. The person principally responsible for its adoption explicitly invoked planning in his justification for why it was worth investing in, and the institution that would host the first computers used them primarily to process and tabulate statistical data essential to planning. Their potential for planning was also why the Government of India sanctioned the purchase of computers in the 1950s, even though such commitments were a considerable strain on a poor country.

In the middle of the twentieth century in India, planning was synonymous with technical and technological advance. It had, in fact, paved the way for a digital modernity in South Asia. The history of India's earliest computers reveals that it was the country's socialistic planned economy that brought these machines to the subcontinent, long before its liberalizing capitalist avatar. Viewed through this lens, the popular view of Prime Minister Rajiv Gandhi as the 'Architect of Digital India' and its 'Computer Man' seem inflated; the product of political branding. While no doubt responsible for deregulating the information technology and telecommunications sectors during his term, the young, technologically savvy prime minister of the late 1980s was not a pioneer in recognizing the importance of digital computers to a modern economy, nor in bringing them to the subcontinent. It is Mahalanobis and the Institute (with their quest to fuse computers to a planned economy), or Bhabha and the TIFR a little later (with their pursuit of nuclear technology), that own a more robust claim to that distinction.

We have, thus far, looked at planning as a form of technocratic state-building. Looking back at the changes it wrought in India's statistical systems and computing abilities, the significance of planning to the Indian state's quantitative capabilities and data capacities is evident. But the exaltation of experts, and the elite nature of Plan debates (between the Institute, Planning Commission, and the Finance Ministry) was discordant with the claims of democratic planning that the government was also simultaneously pushing, and to which we will now turn. To figures like the Professor, the business of persuading citizens about Plans, and the rhetoric of democratic planning, belonged to the messy politics of implementation, a realm that lacked the neat perfectibility of input-output tables, models, and Plan Frames. Planning was an elite, expert-driven enterprise, and the nature of this vision rendered ordinary citizens faceless, with little agency to shape it. As a result, they are also mostly voiceless in these archives. But 'the people' mattered in the context of the Indian state's claims of democratic planning. For reasons of both necessity and ideology, the Plans could not succeed without a willing citizenry. Technocracy sat uncomfortably, but necessarily, beside democracy.

In the next part of this book, I look at the flip side of planning's coin – its ambitious role as a political project of participatory democracy. Where technocratic planning made the Indian people the object of state scrutiny by using a downward gaze onto a population from which information was harvested and then policies applied, democratic planning reveals the state's lateral approaches to this populace by seeking to recruit them as partners and participants. If the natural habitat of technocratic planning was a government office or academic institute, that of democratic planning was the local cinema hall and village fair. In the master narrative that planning ascended to in these years, these two facets – technocratic and democratic – were part of the same whole, their inherent tension seldom explicitly acknowledged but recognized and believed to be resolvable.

Part II

Democracy?

4   Help the Plan – Help Yourself

An anonymous contribution to *The Economic Weekly* captures, with tongue-in-cheek, what Five-Year Plans might have meant to Indians in the 1950s.[1]

If one were asked what the most common obsession of the common man in the sixth year of the Republic is, the answer would be: planning. Planning takes him away from the realities of the present situation; it gives him a sense of importance of being associated in some mysterious way with great undertakings, of being an estimable part of a burgeoning whole; and more than all, it provides food for compensatory reverie and scope for indulging in impressive facts and figures and mouthing learned phrases and abstruse theories ... Planning has a touch of magic about it, and an element of weird ritual too; and what can appeal more to the average Indian mind than magic and ritual?[2]

As a satirical piece in *Shankar's Weekly* noted, visitors to the country may notice, 'India is very plan-minded'.[3] Nehru reported reading in a foreign publication that in India 'you cannot get away from this planning business ... Whatever you talk about somehow they [Indians] lead you to the question of planning as though everything depended on planning everywhere.' He was heartened to know that even an unsympathetic outsider 'felt enveloped by some kind of an atmosphere of planning'. To the prime minister, it simply reflected a rosy reality: 'India is very much planning-conscious and I think it is a great gain.'[4]

In early independent India there was no escaping the Plans. They dominated public discourse. It was even the language through which the government articulated its aspirations for democratic state-building: in the official view, democracy fulfilled its meaning through the Plans. They were a fixture in the national conversation, and the timeline of the Plans effectively denoted an alternate national calendar. The Plans were ceaselessly invoked by politicians, extensively covered by the news media, and debated in civil society. Calls by the government to work towards the Plan's goals became part of the everyday din in the public sphere.

While the Soviet Union's *Gosplan* and its Five-Year Plans were no doubt an important influence, the Indian planning project self-consciously marked its distance and forged its own path. Planning in a democracy was meant to be distinct from communist planning. The Congress Party had committed to 'democratic planning' well before independence (the phrase appears in Nehru's handwritten notes as early as the summer of 1939).[5] After independence, now constitutionally committed to representative politics and universal adult franchise, the Indian government sought to negotiate an unorthodox marriage between parliamentary democracy and centralized economic planning. It was an experiment whose timing drew global attention: this was, after all, precisely when Cold War discourse framed Western liberal democracy and the Soviet planned economy as fundamentally incompatible, both in terms of institutional arrangements and political values. Indeed, during the Cold War, India's combination of parliament and planning served as the domestic reflection of Nehru's foreign policy of resolute non-alignment with either bloc.

In the preceding pages I examined how planning raised state capacities and operated as a technocracy. Those that follow argue that it was also a political project to build a productive citizenry. Both, in combination, were critical to the enterprise when understood in its fullest scope, even though they coexisted uneasily. This chapter, and the next, examine the many ways in which the state sought to inform citizens about Plans, enthuse participation, and build what was called a 'Plan-consciousness'.[6] They emphasize how the idea of democratic planning operated variously as a political vision, a realist response to weak state capacity, and a mode of legitimation that deployed the rhetoric of democracy to mobilize citizens.

As our emphasis shifts from Calcutta and Yojana Bhavan to the more popular terrain of democratic planning, so does our cast of characters. While technocratic planning spotlighted experts like the Professor and Deshmukh, it was government officials and a range of private citizen-volunteers who spearheaded democratic planning. The former were interested in democratic planning only in so far as it counterbalanced poor state capacity. The latter, however, while sharing this concern, expressed broader ideas about what distinguished planning in a democracy and what citizens owed the Plan, and through it, their nation.

The widespread image of the Planning Commission has been that of aging upper-crust men dressed in *khadi* or tailored suits, discussing dams and steel plants in dull Lutyens Delhi offices; in short, technocratic planning. Planning has persuasively been described as using the cover of expertise to hover above the messiness of politics, designed to enable the legitimation of electorally unpalatable measures.[7] While this insight does reflect the Planning Commission's formal status (extra-constitutional) and its method of operation in large measure, it also blinds us to the ways in which the commission sought to engage the populace. It draws a veil over the political ambitions of planning and masks the extent to which the Indian government reached out to citizens, and the lengths to which it went to make Plans popular. In fact, the government even went so far as to routinely refer to Indian planning as democratic – plainly an exaggeration, but a telling one. This view also underestimates the Indian government's investment in the narrative of democratic planning. It was a slogan dear to the government as it formed the basis of the claim that India was engaged in an experiment that represented a different path in the Cold War, one combining democracy and centralized planning in a poor, recently decolonized country while remaining independent of the two superpower blocs.

Planning in India has usually been understood and written about as a technocratic enterprise exclusively concerned with the economy.[8] But India's Five-Year Plans were more than simply an elite instrument of economic policy and resource allocation; the government also conceived of it as an expansive political project and a mass national undertaking. By asking citizens to participate in democratic planning, the government was not simply seeking their consent on an economic policy. It was also beseeching citizens to step up to the political project of building a new kind of state through mass participation. As Sumit Sarkar observed, Nehruvian development represented 'a basically bureaucratic-statist thrust operating alongside with democratic and populist-socialistic impulses'.[9] Christopher Bayly noted this as well, describing the age as one of 'contradiction between elite intellectualism, centralisation and popular democracy'.[10] Unearthing this facet of the history of planning – in which it spilled out of boardrooms and into the realm of the popular – yields a deeper understanding of the role it was designed to, but never quite successfully played, in Nehruvian India.

The project of planning had political ambitions. It was a pedagogical state tutoring its inhabitants on Plan-consciousness, Plan-participation, and productivity as self-help and national duty.[11] The goal was to build a society of informed and productive citizens who would enthusiastically throw their weight behind the nation's Five-Year Plans – rather than remaining bystanders or ignorant participants. As the contemporary Swedish scholar Gunnar Myrdal observed, in India the phrase democratic planning meant 'not only the support of the masses but also their active participation in plan preparation and implementation'. In addition, the phrase conveyed, 'that this popular participation and cooperation should emerge voluntarily'. In Myrdal's view, there was a 'sincere adherence to this ideal', despite its shortcomings in practice.[12] The Plan's proponents would have approved of the spirit animating the popular Hindi song *Mera Joota Hai Japani*, in which a Charlie Chaplin-esque tramp played by Raj Kapoor sings, while astride a camel: "*Nadaan hai jo baithey kinarey, poochey raah vatan ki*" (Foolish are those who sit by the wayside, asking for directions to their own country).[13]

The new nation state was drawing on a specific understanding of citizenship. In independent India, citizenship was based on the view that rights were not gifts; instead they came attached with certain duties. The state had expectations of its citizens.[14] These duties often reflected themes of sacrifice, self-help, and an ethic of work. It could manifest, for example, in the government's call for citizens to change their diets and eating patterns during food crises, or in official slogans such as, 'Help the Plan – Help Yourself' or '*Yojana Ki Siddhi – Aap Ki Samriddhi*' (The Plan's Accomplishment – Your Prosperity). In seeking Plan participation, the state was reminding Indians of their duties as citizens, and specifically underlining their obligation towards economic development. As a plan document put it, 'Development, thus conceived, is a process which calls for effort and sacrifice on the part of the entire body of citizens.'[15] The nature and content of these state campaigns are critical because the Indian government had no other means of ensuring mass participation in planning. Unlike in the Soviet Union or China, the Indian government could not *compel* its citizens to comply.

The rhetoric of planning was the ever-present background noise in people's lives. The following pages walk a path between accepting the government's claims about democratic planning and dismissing them entirely as irrelevant. They recognize that studying these campaigns reveals more about the Nehruvian state – its ideology and methods of self-legitimation – than it does about the views of the citizenry. However, it offers insights into an important question: what were the ways in which Indians would have heard of Five-Year Plans, and why might they have heard of them at all? Answering this reveals the medium and idioms through which ordinary citizens in India's villages, towns, and cities encountered what the Planning Commission pronounced from its lofty perch. The government was endeavouring to create a Plan-consciousness in independent India. This chapter primarily explores the state's campaign of publicity and outreach in pursuit of that. The one that follows examines the episodes when voluntary groups and civil society organizations like University Planning Forums, the Bharat Sewak Samaj, and Bharat Sadhu Samaj stepped up to make the alleged fruits of democratic planning evident and build bridges between the Plans and the people.

Plan-Consciousness

For phrases like democratic planning and economic democracy to retain any meaning beyond the corridors of Yojana Bhavan and Parliament, it was not enough that India held elections and planned the economy. There was broad political consensus within the Congress Party and Planning Commission that they needed to embark on a colossal programme of outreach. As far back as the summer of 1939, the National Planning Committee had resolved to create a publicity arm. The next year, they also decided that all reports produced by them and their subcommittees should be presented to the press.[16] As Nehru told journalists that summer: 'we require of course the fullest intelligent co-operation of the public and the press ... Perhaps one of the most important and desirable consequences of our work is to make people think of planned work and a co-operative society.'[17] Later, as Chairman of the Planning Commission, Nehru explained to members of the Indian Chambers of Commerce and Industry that the Planning Commission's task was not merely technical. It was 'something much more. It is how to get the villager ... to realize that something is not only being done for him but he is doing it and is a part of the machinery doing it ... [It is why] I lay stress on this psychological approach.'[18] In other words, democratic planning required a psychological change in Indians in order for citizens to become Plan-conscious.

What were the government's motivations behind these attempts to popularize the Plan and foment Plan-consciousness? They were to communicate a specific vision of the nation's path and progress, legitimize its own role in that process, and demand citizens' participation in order to ensure the Plan's success. The appeal to voluntary contributions from the populace was an important admission of weak state capacity. The Indian state was not in a position to deliver on the Plans unless its citizens were willing to offer their active support for it. People had to know about the Five-Year Plans in order to labour towards their fulfilment. Success depended not only on citizens working towards plan priorities, but also saving, spending, consuming, and investing in accordance with them.[19]

The degree of enthusiasm could determine the fate of a Five-Year Plan. A Congress Party resolution from April 1950 stated, 'economic planning presupposes a period of austerity on the part of the people'.[20] But even the Planning Commission realized that this demand for self-denial could only be temporary, for 'unrelieved austerity was likely to chill people's enthusiasm for planning'.[21] Later, when discussing whether the Second Plan was too ambitious or just about feasible, Bhimsen Sachar, the Chief Minister of Punjab, told the National Development Council that popular participation could carry the Plan over the last mile. The optimistic

Sachar hoped that 'if sufficient enthusiasm was created among the people for local works and other projects and their co-operation in the form of cash or labour contributions secured, it would indirectly have the same effect as an increase in the revenues of the Government'.[22] As this incident suggests, an unrealistic reliance on building mass enthusiasm for the Plans might have led some politicians to support over-optimistic plan targets.

The degree to which the government stressed this reliance on public support even became the butt of cartoonists' jokes. *Shankar's Weekly* carried a cartoon by the noted Malayali cartoonist Abu Abraham titled 'Sun-Cooking Era'. In it, manpower was symbolized as the Sun whose rays cook a dish of plan projects. The Minister of Planning is depicted gesturing towards this scene of solar cooking with evident pride, as a pleased Nehru looks on. The description below the cartoon read, 'The Planning Commission has urged the need to harness the nation's manpower for the economic development of the country.'[23] Another cartoon, years later and in a different publication, compared the Plans to a donkey. R. K. Laxman, the beloved visual chronicler of independent India, portrayed the Plans as an obstinate ass that would not budge in the direction of prosperity (marked by a road sign). Unmoved by pulling, pushing, and not tempted by the dangling carrot of foreign aid, the lazy donkey (or Five-Year Plan) makes progress only when people lift it over their heads and run with it.[24] In a Hindi cartoon by 'Ananth,' drawn while the Second Plan was in the doldrums, prominent members of the Planning Commission are on a small boat representing the Plan, linking arms for balance. The paddle they are using to get them through the economy's troubled waters is '*sarvajanik sahayog*' (public cooperation).[25]

The reliance on popular participation to meet Plan targets was evident even in seemingly technical papers produced by the Planning Commission. For example, in a document described by one scholar as the 'Plan Frame for the Third Plan', Pitambar Pant wrote optimistically about a 'massive mobilization of surplus manpower for carrying out projects of permanent improvement.' If this could be achieved 'on a sufficiently large scale all over the country, *in the main without recourse to normal wage-payments*, not only the main difficulty of employment but that of investable funds would be substantially eased' (emphasis mine).[26] Given the heavy industry focus of the first three Five-Year Plans and the cold shoulder to consumer goods industries, citizens were being asked to contribute despite knowing that it wasn't likely to improve their lives as consumers in the near future. '*Aj parishram, kal labh*,' Nehru said – 'toil today, benefit tomorrow'.[27] The Plans counted on citizens' capacity for delayed gratification.

The political stakes were high. Failure to accomplish this would not only result in shortfalls in Plan targets; it also potentially undermined the structure of representative government. Speaking in 1958 at an event organized by the Bangalore Y.M.C.A., Home Minister G. B. Pant cautioned that India's Plans had to succeed 'in order that democracy may be preserved here'. Unless people's 'physical needs are fulfilled, we will ever be on the brink of a precipice'.[28] Or, as the Congress Planning Sub-Committee noted a year later, a climate of consciousness about the Plans was necessary. And while this consciousness in favour of planning was growing, the 'right kind of consciousness' also implied citizens recognizing their share of responsibilities. Otherwise, 'planning will not succeed, and at any rate its democratic basis cannot last'.[29] Success, on the other hand, would justify both the Plans and the decision to combine centralized planning and liberal democracy. As Planning Minister Gulzarilal Nanda told the Lok Sabha when speaking about the Second Five-Year Plan, 'We can beat China and Russia – if we get public cooperation'.[30] Democracy could be vindicated, even on economic measures, if only citizens participated in the Plans.

Democratic planning was an article of faith for Nehru and several others in the Planning Commission and Congress Party. Educating Indians about the Five-Year Plans – their purpose, shape, and the citizen's role in them – was an end unto itself, for it was important that they knew about the nation's undertakings. The prime minister made no exception for his own cabinet, insisting that they be intimately familiar with India's exercise in planning. To the cabinet secretary fell the unenviable task of reading out loud the entire First Five-Year Plan to a captive ministerial assembly. As one might imagine, this was not a text conducive to public reading. It took 3 days and, in a reminder that nation-building was not always a stirring affair, many dozed.[31] Nevertheless, to many in that same cabinet, making the nation Plan-conscious was the necessary minimum of democratic planning and the vaunted middle way that the Indian government lost no opportunity to lecture a Cold War divided world about.

Finally, there was the psychological aspect Nehru spoke of. It was in the government's interest that the populace bought into the epic narrative it was selling. Early during the planning process, he wrote that a 'major psychological change was necessary [among Indians] and this called for a plan which offered something dramatic'.[32] The right plan could steer the national mood. The government presented citizens a sweeping story whose arc explained where they were (as citizens constitutive of a nation), how it came to be (overcoming the shackles of British rule), and the direction in which they were headed (industrial and egalitarian modernity). In it was encoded a backstory of colonialism and stagnation, a diagnosis of present troubles, and a map towards a plentiful future. It was a way for Indians to plot themselves into the saga of development. This was what Tarlok Singh, the energetic Deputy Secretary of the Planning Commission, was referring to when he wrote about the 'psychological, educational and human relations aspects of the Plan'.[33] The concept of democratic planning at once promised individual freedom (in the classic liberal sense) *and* freedom from colonization (understood as the cause of economic backwardness and poverty). Democratic planning was meant to represent political and economic democracy through a new conceptualization of the state and the relationship of citizens to it.

The effect of citizens plotting themselves into a rousing developmental narrative was compelling enough for it to enter politicians' electoral arithmetic. For instance, in summer 1966 during a Planning Commission meeting convened to discuss the upcoming Fourth Five-Year Plan, Prime Minister Indira Gandhi conveyed her opposition to the idea of a 'small Plan'. She insisted that the matter had to be 'viewed from the psychological and political aspects'. Although she was no economist, the prime minister clarified, she could claim to know something of the people of India. 'Even the poorer class of people wanted to have big projects which would bring prosperity. They were prepared to make all possible contribution[s] for something really big for their State ... This was human psychology and should not be lost sight of.'[34] The message Tarlok Singh took away from the meeting was simple: 'PM says that "A small plan will lose the election."'[35] The message a Five-Year Plan sent out could not only impact the success of economic policy, it could even shape the electoral landscape.

Let us pause over a few crucial caveats. First, Plan-publicity did not reach as many people as it hoped to, nor did it have the desired level of impact. But this does not invalidate the quest to understand the nature of this campaign because despite its shortcomings, it reached millions. Second, while the phrase 'democratic planning' was regularly bandied about in official pronouncements, little was done to actually democratize it by enabling citizens to influence real time economic decision-making. Gunnar Myrdal noted the artful and often deliberate 'fuzziness' of the phrase democratic planning, describing it as 'romantically confused verbiage'.[36] Democratic planning was less a reflection on the process of planning than about the political dispensation under which Plans were formulated. Plan-consciousness exhausted the official understanding of what democratic planning meant. It was never really the government's intention to allow policymaking to be plebiscitary; it was instead an invitation to participate in development projects without questioning its terms. Bottom-up support was sought for Plans that were decidedly top-down in their creation.

The reason the subject merits our attention and scrutiny is that the slogan nonetheless reflected the government's desire to make people Plan-conscious, and the manner in which planning was packaged in a democracy. In other words, we must distinguish between the self-serving slogan of democratic planning and the real object of this study – planning *in* a democracy. Rather than extending a vote on the Planning Commission to ordinary Indians, democratic planning signalled the salience of the Indian experiment (of Plans passed in a parliament) and the government's desire to make people Plan-conscious. To a substantial degree, then, democratic planning was simply Plan publicity, and Plan publicity merely propaganda with state legitimation as its goal. The Planning Commission was, after all, an unelected, extra-constitutional body of experts (created by a government resolution), eager to be seen as engaged in a democratic process. To the sceptic, the call for democratic planning reflects the peculiar contortions of a self-appointed technocratic elite that fundamentally believed it knew best, but needed to be viewed as channelling the people's will. Despite the posturing and rhetoric that were certainly at play in the government's attempt to convey Plans to the people, this still cannot account entirely for the sheer effort and resources the government expended in a campaign that lasted decades. It was propaganda, but the aims, content, and form of this propaganda merit inspection.

The calls to make Plans popular and people Plan-conscious drew legitimacy and force from the highest official echelon. In 1951, during an extemporaneous speech delivered one late spring morning at the Economic Planning Conference in New Delhi, Nehru explained why it mattered so much. A few days earlier, clambering up and down the construction site of the Damodar Valley dam, Nehru had encountered a few engineers at work. He asked them if they had explained the significance of this massive project to the labourers under their direction. Met with sheepish evasion, Nehru walked over to the workers, motioned them to gather, and asked, 'What are you doing?' Puzzled and probably nervous, they responded that they were digging earth. The prime minister pressed on; 'What does this lead to?' Receiving vague answers and realizing that they were thrown by this line of questioning, he launched into an explanation. Although their individual roles might be small, he pointed out, they were contributing to a feat of engineering that would bring prosperity to the countryside, offer employment to hundreds of thousands, and prevent disastrous floods. To Nehru, it was vital that they understood the scale of an enterprise in which each was but a speck. It was imperative that the worker is 'made to feel that he is engaged in some very big undertaking and is not merely working for Re. 1/- or Re 1/8/- per day ... They must know what they are doing, that they are taking part in a huge undertaking, a huge enterprise.'[37]

In December 1952, in his last fortnightly letter to chief ministers for the year, Nehru encouraged them to take the Plan to the people, believing that knowledge of, and involvement in the Plans would cement national cohesion. The Five-Year Plans embodied an India whose different geographies and sectors were all related; they were based, he asserted, on a 'conception of India's unity and of a mighty co-operative effort of all people of India'. If citizens could feel a 'sensation of partnership' in the nation's journey, and understood how it bound them to each other, they could combat 'fissiparous tendencies and parochial outlook[s]'. The Plan's theme of common purpose and interest would, according to him, even make the 'crooked paths of provincialism, communalism, casteism' less tempting.[38] The mechanics of how Plans were supposed to loosen the historical grip of region, religion, and caste did not restrain his enthusiasm. Written within 3 years of the country turning a republic, these lines reflect the wide-eyed idealism of its moment. Far-fetched, deluded even, as these claims now seem, they represented the sheer magnitude of the hopes with which democratic planning was freighted.

Bridging Plan and People

In his inaugural address to Parliament in the new republic, on 31 January 1950, President Rajendra Prasad announced the government's intention to establish a Planning Commission. He told parliamentarians that planning could only succeed with complete cooperation from the Indian people: 'It is only when Governmental agencies and popular enthusiasm and cooperation are yoked together that large scale economic and social development can take place.'[39] Two years later, when the First Five-Year Plan was published, it included a chapter entitled, 'Public Co-operation in National Development.' Its opening section, on Democratic Planning, began with the belief that 'Public co-operation and public opinion constitute the principal force and sanction behind planning'. The Plan called for the press, writers, artists, universities, professional associations, elected representatives, and public servants to join hands in carrying the Plan 'into every home in the language and symbols of the people'.[40]

The government created a cross-party National Advisory Council for Public Co-Operation, chaired by the prime minister.[41] It included

Congress members like Gulzarilal Nanda and Jagjivan Ram, representatives of opposition parties, and prominent citizens: Shyama Prasad Mookherjee of the Hindu nationalist Jana Sangh; Ashoka Mehta of the Socialist Party; industrialists G. D. Birla, Lala Shri Ram, and Kasturbhai Lalbhai; the Sikh Shiromani Akali Dal's Udham Singh Nagoke; J. B. Kripalani from the Kisan Mazdoor Praja Party; Jayaprakash Narayan of the Socialist Party; and social worker Achamma Matthai, among others.[42] It was established in order to offer advice to the Planning Commission's Public Co-Operation Division about ways to solicit popular support for the Plans. The next year, the Ministry of Information and Broadcasting established a Five-Year Plan Publicity Organisation and discussions at the Ministry of Finance yielded an Integrated Publicity Programme for the First Five-Year Plan. By the end of the decade – possibly in an effort to roll back a dizzying profusion of publicity limbs – the initiatives were consolidated into a Directorate of Field Publicity.[43]

Perhaps the earliest mass campaign to publicize the Plans was in 1954 at the *Kumbh Mela* in Allahabad. A religious pilgrimage in which the Hindu devout gather to bathe in the Ganga's holy waters, the *Kumbh Mela* is among the largest congregations of people on the planet. In the government's estimation, it was ideally suited to publicity. The idea was for the estimated five million who would attend between January and March to have a spiritual and educative experience, so that they could 'take back with them the message of the Five Year Plan'. The mela grounds were divided into seven zones, each with stalls distributing pamphlets and booths screening films. This, as we shall see later, wouldn't be the last time the secular discourse of economic planning would comingle with the religious, specifically Hindu, sphere.[44]

Headquartered in New Delhi, the Five-Year Plan Publicity Organisation oversaw a nationwide network of publicity units that pushed the Planning Commission's message. In its operations, India was divided into sevens zones, each of which functioned under a Regional Officer complemented by five or more Field Officers whose job it was to travel through the districts with their own units. Regional Officers were expected to travel for 12 days a month, while Field Officers were prescribed 20 days on the road.[45] Depending on the terrain the latter had to cover, they were either assigned a van, boat, or bullock cart. The bullock cart units were meant for areas without paved roads, or regions that were rendered unfit for motorized traffic during the monsoon.[46] Boat units plied coastal towns and villages on riverbanks. Whether on land or water, each was equipped with a film projector, a public address system, a generator, and tape recorder. The Films Division of India furnished them with films such as *Working for the Plan* or *Tomorrow is Ours* in the appropriate Indian language.

Regional officers delivered lectures and screened documentaries in schools and villages about the Plans and people's participation in them.[47] They distributed pamphlets, leaflets, and posters that exhorted onlookers to 'Help the Plan – Help Yourself', 'Invest in National Saving', and instructed them on 'Five Year Plan Projects'.[48] They also publicized the Plan at significant social and religious events; during fairs, for example, they often set up Five-Year Plan stalls. In 1963 alone, official estimates claimed that approximately 23 million people had been reached through the Directorate of Field Publicity. This included 16,000 places visited, 21,000 film shows screened, 22,000 public meetings and group discussions, and 4,000 drama and song performances by eighty-three field units overseen by fourteen regional offices.[49]

Handlers in New Delhi sometimes found it hard to keep track of what the roving publicity officers were doing. Given the size of the country, the state of communications, and the number of languages across which the message had stay to consistent, it was not surprising that there were long periods without effective oversight. That they had to send daily reports on their activities to the Regional Officer was no guarantee of supervision; after all, the latter was himself expected to be travelling for half the month. Sometimes the message packaged in Delhi lost shape or simply lost its way by the time it reached the villages. As an irate official at the Ministry of Information and Broadcasting in Delhi dryly noted, 'I have found that one of the officers in his daily reports is still talking about the National Plan Loan which was wound up about three years ago.'[50]

City dwellers could learn of the Plan through exhibitions staged by the government that showcased development as a spectacle. The biggest Plan-promoting exhibition took place in the capital and was titled 'India 1958'. It presented a country in the middle of the Second Five-Year Plan as 'an ancient nation in the throes of regeneration'.[51] Opening in October and lasting 2 months, it had been timed to capitalize on the Dussehra and Diwali holidays, and conferences of the World Bank and International Monetary Fund. Located on Mathura Road in the shadow of the Mughal fort of Purana Quila and spread over a hundred acres (in the space that would later become Pragati Maidan), the exhibition welcomed visitors through four entrances. Each had an imposing name – Gateway of Progress, Gateway of Commerce, Gateway of Science, and Gateway of Industries – and led to pavilions related to each gate's theme. For example, entering the main gate (Gateway of Progress), one walked onto a wide boulevard named Vikas Vatika (Garden of Development). On one side of this was *Yojana Path* (Plan Avenue) that

Figure 4.1. The 'India 1958' Five-Year Plan exhibition in Delhi.

led you to a Planning and Development Centre. There were more than 300 pavilions, and it was estimated that the exhibition drew over three million visitors.[52]

Such was its scale and significance to the government's publicity machinery that this exhibition became the subject of both a commemorative postage stamp and a Films Division documentary titled *Bharat ki Jhanki* (Indian Panorama). The Hindi documentary opened with a shot of people streaming towards the main entryway. The narrator declares that 'exhibitions came and went, but our country has never seen one like this'. It had such a draw, he continued, that it attracted citizens from all over the country. One such visitor was Boorey Thakur, a lean, middle-aged farmer from a village in Rajasthan who was outfitted in a white turban, light blue-and-red-embroidered *angarakha*, a large metal pendant dangling on his chest, and a sturdy walking stick in hand. The rest of the documentary took the viewer on a tour of the exhibition by following Thakur and sometimes viewing it through his eyes. With him we witness the installations that reflected the nation's success after independence. Thakur alights at unpolished metal sculptures of burly men and women wielding implements, at buildings and exhibits, murals and puppet shows, cafes and Ferris wheels. He was particularly gratified to visit the Food and Agriculture pavilion where a billboard pronounced the farmer as 'The Most Important Man in India'. A wide smile lights up Thakur's face.[53]

The next year, as part of the effort to take the Plan's message to rural areas and small towns, the government pressed mobile exhibitions into action. These vans travelled with promotional material like posters, calendars, and bookmarks, and some were outfitted with displays that could easily be set up, to showcase models, charts, and photographs.[54] A few carried film projectors to screen movies whenever possible. They followed set routes: one was based in Delhi, another in Allahabad, and one more set out from Coimbatore in the south. There was even a railway coach that was converted into a Plan exhibition that set out from Delhi and stopped at junctions and wayside stations to offer travellers on platforms a quick lesson on where their nation was headed.[55]

Through the first decade of independence, the government was concerned about its youth learning something of the elaborately hatched Plans. The government's Publications Division published a steady stream of subsidized books and pamphlets that abridged, explained, and attempted to popularize the Plans to a variety of audiences. Published in English, Hindi, and a host of regional languages, they included pamphlets with titles like For This We Plan and Prashan Aur Uttar (Question and Answer). In September 1952, Nehru wrote to the Ministry of Education and the Planning Commission about an 'excellent suggestion' he had received regarding the production of short, simple pamphlets about the Five-Year Plan that could be sent to all schools so that teachers could read them to their students. Abul Kalam Azad, the Minister of Education, responded enthusiastically saying that such pamphlets should be sent to colleges as well. The next summer, the Joint Secretary wrote to all the Directors of Education that the government was 'anxious that intelligent understanding of the Plan and intelligent cooperation of all classes of citizens in the Plan should be promoted'. This was to be carried out by incorporating lessons from the Plans into books on social studies, civics, and economics. Soon thereafter, the Planning Commission's Durgabai Deshmukh wrote to chief ministers expressing the view that introducing the Plan in middle and high school curricula would 'make our youth Plan minded and Plan conscious'. Of the twenty-one states that responded to her call, eighteen were in broad agreement with the idea; the rest – Bombay, Madras, and Bengal – made alternative suggestions. The Government of Madras, in its response, cautioned that 'direct propaganda or compulsory curriculum is not advisable'.[56]

The Planning Commission prepared booklets titled *India Has a Plan* for children in middle school and *Our Plan* for high school, and had them translated into regional languages. *India Has a Plan* began by noting, in large and bold font, that nowadays one heard a lot about planning. It was covered so often in newspapers, radio broadcasts, and in the prime minister's speeches that it seemed another of the 'dull and difficult subjects that the grown-up people like to talk about and that it doesn't concern you [children] at all'. But, as the author quickly reminds the young audience, this would be a mistake as 'The Five-Year Plan concerns all of us who consider India our home and call ourselves Indians'.[57] In 1957, the government included the study of Five-Year Plans in a draft syllabus for social studies classes and, having sent it to all state governments, encouraged them to use it with whatever modifications they saw fit. The Director of Public Instruction from Andhra wrote back saying that it had been taken into consideration while drafting syllabi for higher secondary schools in the state. 'In the "Social Studies" (History and Civics) syllabus for the Higher Secondary Schools, the topics "A Study of the Five-Year Plans of India", "Community Development Projects ... have already been included."' The University of Travancore wrote to say the 'Study of Five-Year Plans has been included as a subject in the syllabuses for Civics and Economics'. The governments of Rajasthan, Kerala, Assam, Delhi, Punjab, and Orissa also sent notes assuring the central government that planning had been incorporated into their social studies syllabi for children in middle school.[58] In 1963, during a summer meeting regarding Plan publicity at Yojana Bhavan, officials proposed that the Ministry of Education and Publications Division collaborate on directing publications relating to the Plan towards a younger generation. They felt there was need for a general book on the Plan to be introduced as a textbook in high schools, as had already been done in several states.[59] The attempt was to 'outline, in simple language, the major aspects of India's development plans, keeping facts and figures down to the minimum'. In the image-heavy *We Plan for Prosperity*, the concept of planning was explained by analogizing it to the manner in which a mother budgets household finance.[60]

The government engaged in campaigns directed at more grown-up audiences as well. Among them was one titled 'Help The Plan – Help Yourself' or '*Yojana Ki Siddhi – Aap Ki Samriddhi*' that tailored a code of action for professional groups like farmers, industrial workers, office workers, and college students. One of the posters in this campaign specifically targeted women, unambiguously relegating them to the domestic and familial realm. Under the triangular outline of a roof, it declared 'A HAPPY HOME IS PART OF THE PLAN'. At the very bottom were images of sari-wrapped women engaged in the activities the poster endorsed, namely working in the kitchen garden, readying a child for school, and operating a sewing machine. The accompanying text declared that, 'Efficient housekeeping promotes family welfare and helps national progress.' Bullet pointed in between were terse recommendations directed at the country's women: avoid waste, do not buy for the sake of buying, plan your family, train your children to be worthy citizens, invest in small savings schemes, and knit or sew during spare time.[61] The ideal woman, according to this poster, was the thrifty, nurturing, resourceful wife or mother. Serving the family and the home, it would seem, was the best way for a woman to serve the Plan.

That poster, while probably reflective of the norm, did not represent the only perspective on gender roles to be found in official publicity outlets. The magazine that featured this poster – the government-sponsored *Yojana* (The Plan) – carried more feminist pieces within weeks. In one titled 'Working Women of India', Padmini Sengupta argued that Indian women were as much workers and labourers as they were wives and mothers. They toiled alongside men in farms, factories, quarries, and public works. The essay, however, also betrayed the patronizing tone of an elite observer by romanticizing the labours of working class women. A running theme was that female workers 'always seem happy. They smile and talk and sing.'[62] The accompanying photographs were of beaming women – balancing pots and wicker baskets on their heads, a sickle in one hand, and children balancing on their hips. 'Do they not look lovely', the essayist asked, 'stooping in the golden sunshine in their bright coloured saris, amidst the green waving paddy or wheat?'[63] There were similar descriptions of happy Santali tribal women, returning from work at sunset through mustard fields, arms around each other, song and laughter on their lips. Sengupta praised the Five-Year Plans for expanding the industries in which women worked and enhancing their workplace protection while acknowledging that progress was slow and that many women were yet to join the workforce.

Presenting working women as cheery, grateful, and unthreatening Plan participants to a mostly male readership may have been calculated to be the safest way to loosen the bonds of tradition that tied women to the kitchen and cradle. An article in the next month's Hindi issue of *Yojana* hit much harder. Subhadra Devi began the essay by using Nehru's words against his government. She reminded readers that the prime minister had once said that you could measure a society's progress by its steel output and the status of its women. In the years since, Devi argued, no effort had been spared in the pursuit of steel. But the position of women? The problem, according to her, was not a lack of virtuous intent; after all,

Figure 4.2. Advertisements from the 'Help the Plan – Help Yourself' and '*Yojana ki Siddhi, Aap ki Samriddhi*' campaign (January 1959 and February 1959).

the Constitution and the Hindu Code Bill had improved the *legal* status of women. But had they made any difference to the position of women within the home, family, or in society? Devi blamed a religious society that was bound to conventions and superstitions, backed by the priestly class of 'pujaris and pandits and mullahs and maulvis and qazis'. Despite what some educated but ignorant city-dwellers may believe, she clarified, *purdah* (seclusion of women) was still practiced by Hindu and Muslim families across North India. It was a 'demonic tradition' that made women live like 'caged birds'. A country in which 'half the population is imprisoned in order to tend to the kitchen or raise children', she declared 'is a country that can never be truly free'. There was acknowledgement that the Plans, and the Social Welfare Board led by Durgabai Deshmukh, were making some efforts. But the government needed to confront the imbalance in efforts towards industrial versus social progress. No matter how industrially advanced India became, she warned, it would remain crippled if it stayed socially backward.[64] These pieces, while outliers in the larger publicity campaign, shed light on the kinds of critiques expressed even within official channels. They represent some of the different ways by which reform-minded middle-class women sought to push the government and the Indian public to come to terms with women in contexts outside the family and the home.

Occasionally, local authorities gambled with somewhat more unorthodox publicity endeavours. If you were a resident of Jaipur in January 1957 and glanced skyward on Makar Sakranti (the harvest festival), you might have caught a glimpse of government-sponsored kites soaring, dipping, and jostling with hundreds of other colourful kites piloted by child and adult alike, each trying to cut others down for sport. Publicity personnel for the Rajasthan government had arranged vans to go from door to door to distribute more than 100,000 free kites across the city. Jaipur's sky became an advertisement with each kite declaring: 'Make the Second Five-Year Plan a Success'.[65]

Every once in a while, a private citizen chimed in. The novelist and urban planner Mulk Raj Anand sounded a note of caution: the publicity campaigns, he sensed, had not instilled an ownership of the Plans among people. What India lacked was 'a *dynamic* which may give the people a will to pursue the Five-Year Plan (that will make the difference between survival and disintegration)'. The only remedy he saw was a drastic one. Nehru must renounce the prime minister's office and instead 'speak to the people directly and infuse in them the spirit of togetherness and sacrifice needed to carry out the ideals of the Second Five-Year Plan'. In Gandhi's absence, he was the only individual with the moral authority to do so. Suggesting that this was not just a personal opinion, he claimed that he was only expressing the 'secret wish' of many. 'Panditji should bring to bear all the sanctions of his personal prestige to knit this country emotionally together for the carrying out of the Plan.'[66]

Another citizen – Gujarati designer Manu Desai – offered suggestions of a more practical nature. The New York-trained, Bombay-based designer bemoaned the Indian public's ignorance of the country's Plans. He claimed that the farmer had no idea that planned river valley projects would irrigate his farm to double yield, and the villager was oblivious to how his home would light up with electricity. The challenge of enthusing this population was as ambitious as the Five-Year Plans themselves. Without wide publicity, they had no hope of succeeding. One of the questions this begged, according to Desai, was the choice of design in publicity materials. As vast numbers of Indians were illiterate, he argued, it made sense to rely on art and images more than text. But this still left open the choice of what kind of art to employ. Desai concluded that the most effective medium to popularize Five-Year Plans was folk art, the 'language of the people'. The government needed to harness India's 'rich and vital folk tradition' whose virtues were 'simplicity, refreshing colour, and direct emotional impact'.[67]

By way of demonstration, Desai presented two images. The first, subtitled 'The Wrong Way', was taken from a daily newspaper and was meant to characterize the government's dour aesthetic. Not only did it contain a realist image – a photograph of a woman carrying mud in a vessel on her head, and men digging up earth in the background – it was also text heavy and in English. 'Hard Work Is Our Motto Today – The Uttar Pradesh Five-Year Plan Must Be Implemented – Construct Good Roads', it read. The second was a poster designed by Desai himself and subtitled 'Suggested Way'. It was composed of a Hindu swastika at the top and two artistically rendered feet within an archway in the centre. Written below was, '*Lakshmiji padharengey – panchvarshiya yojana mey haath batao*' (Goddess Lakshmi Will Enter – Lend a Hand to the Five-Year Plan).[68] In the bottom left-hand corner, in appreciably smaller font, was the suggested brand logo for plan publicity – a lotus with the word *Panchvarshiya* (Five-Year) above and *Yojana* (Plan) below.

The swastika and feet would be immediately recognizable and resonant to most observing Hindus as a reference to the practice of drawing or painting these symbols on the thresholds of houses (toes pointed towards the house) to welcome Lakshmi, goddess of wealth and fortune, into homes on such auspicious occasions as Diwali and Lakshmi Puja. The lotus, chosen as the insignia, also carries hefty symbolic weight in Hindu and other Indian traditions. A symbol of divine beauty and purity associated with several deities, the lotus is Lakshmi's pedestal and the flower she bears in her hands. The unmentioned, yet obvious, distinction between the two images was of course that the image Desai proposed involved religion. Manu Desai's recommendation of Indian folk art was a call to overcome the secular state's bashfulness over the use of overtly religious language and motifs in its propaganda. By passing it over, Desai implicitly suggested, government officials were foregoing a vast resource that held deep and powerful meaning for Indians. As we shall see in this chapter and the next, the government was not unaware of this. While there is no evidence that the government consciously adopted Manu Desai's suggestions, it does point us towards one direction that plan publicity would take over the next few years – towards Hindu cultural and religious themes. Manu Desai had put his finger on a tension that would persist between secular and religious messaging throughout the government's Plan-publicity campaigns.

Song and Dance

Realizing that Plans were inherently dreary, the government of India decided to wrap them in the attractive packaging of song, dance, and drama. The experiment began in Punjab where local authorities had some success in recruiting musicians and poets to publicize Plans.[69] In 1954, a Song and Drama Division was established under the energetic leadership of Colonel Hemachandra Gupte, who ran it for many years. Initially nestled under All India Radio (AIR), it would find more permanent lodging within the Plan Publicity section of the Ministry of Information and Broadcasting within a few years. According to the colonel, he had been inspired to follow the lead of parties like the Communist Party of India and the southern Indian *Dravida Munnetra Kazhagam* that had woven their agendas into traditional art forms. Many initially derided his project, and he had trouble recruiting actors and dramatic troupes in the cities. He faced difficulties of a different kind with rural troupes since many of these performers were illiterate. To even begin, plays had to be penned by scriptwriters and then repeated word for word, over and over until the troupes could memorize them.[70]

The first performance was of a play named *Hamara Gaon* (Our Village) in March 1954 in Bahadurgarh, a short distance from Delhi.[71] The Ministry had asked the Delhi-based Three Arts Club to stage a production based on Ramesh Mehta's script. Mehta was one of India's pioneering post-independence playwrights and a leading light of the Three Arts Club, one of India's most prominent theatre companies. *Hamara Gaon* was about life in an Indian village during the First Five-Year Plan. By staging this the government hoped to convey to 'rural audiences the significance of the great projects undertaken and achieved under the First Five-Year Plan'. Within a year, the Three Arts Club alone performed this play thirty-six times to gatherings that included the president, members of parliament, foreign dignitaries, and thousands of ordinary Indians. They also performed it on the lawns of the prime minister's residence at Teen Murti Bhavan. Once included in the Song and Drama Division's roster, it was translated and performed across the country more than two thousand times to spectators totalling millions within three years.[72] AIR even requested a performance of *Hamara Gaon* in its studio so that listeners across the country could tune in to hear it.

Set in a village named Barakpur, the play opens with a family awaiting the arrival of a relative from the city. Jugal Kishore, a handsome 18-year-old city boy, is visiting his aunt and her family and looking forward to some rejuvenation in the countryside. By the time he arrives at their door, however, he is covered in dirt having lost his footing in the dark and fallen into one of the village's many open gutters. He had not been met at the train station because his illiterate relatives could not read the letter he had sent in advance. Jugal has entered a village where barely anyone can read, the roads are unpaved and unlit, and filth lies strewn everywhere. Although the village is named Barakpur, he remarks, in reality it is more like Narakpur (a play on 'hell').[73] Throughout the rest of the play, the young Jugal echoes the logic and language of planning, holding up a developmental mirror to this backwards village. When one of the village elders asks him why the government has done so little, Jugal responds by saying that this popularly elected government, unlike the erstwhile white colonial masters, is doing the best it can for the people. He then lists what the new democratic government has done since independence: it has provided shelter to tens of millions, created cities, erected millions of buildings, and opened businesses. Most importantly, it had not let anyone die of hunger. But, he asks, what stops the villagers from joining hands with the government and helping themselves?[74] '*Ab aap ki baari hai. Panchvarshiya yojana aap hi ke liye banayi hai*' (Now it is your turn. The Five-Year Plan has been made for you, after all).[75] With the support of his uncle and the village elder, Jugal decides to spend time in the village in order to set it on the path to progress.

The play touches on a variety of socio-economic issues that most villages grappled with: questions of caste conflict, the acceptability of widow remarriage, the need for land reform, the importance of voting, and corruption. Through Jugal's influence and the newly converted – his aunt, uncle, the village elders, and a like-minded village youth – all of these questions are addressed, even if they are not completely resolved. The Indian government's position is made clear by Jugal, its steadfast ally and advocate. When asked about what millions of unemployed country-men will do for sustenance, Jugal responds: 'This is exactly why a Five-Year Plan has been made ... Jungles will be cut down to give land to the landless ... Roads are being built. So are canals. Through these, people will get jobs and two meals a day.'[76] As another inspired youth explains to fellow villagers, 'If we do not support the government with the Five-Year Plan our situation will never improve'.[77]

Five months later, on the eve of Jugal's return to the city, much has changed. It is apparent that most villagers have rallied around Jugal and taken his message of self-help to heart. Barakpur is on the move; it now has a school, clean paved roads, a panchayat, and a hospital is on the way. These have led to other happy changes, such as the opening of a bookstore and the presence of a tailor. People have also changed: two landlords have donated small parcels of their land to deserving landless labourers, the once lazy uncle is hard at work all day, the elderly Anaro Tai now spends her time spinning thread on the charkha rather than on idle chatter, the dairy farmer who used to dilute milk with water has been shamed into honesty, and the low caste barber now has the confidence to confront the casteist village doctor. Bidding adieu to many grateful villagers, Jugal reminds them that although his time at the village is over, the work must go on. Barakpur, once accused of being like Narakpur (hell), is now on its way to being Swargpur (heaven).[78]

This simple drama provides an insight into the planner's gaze as it pertained to the rural countryside. Standing in for India's villages, Barakpur is portrayed as pitifully backward – intellectually, socially, and economically. The redeeming features of this village are its inhabitants, who are mostly sympathetic. As a character in the play points out, con-trary to urban perception, villagers are not simpletons. Furthermore, they are more honest and not duplicitous like city-dwellers. The shortcomings, then, were not in their mental faculties or moral fibre. What they lacked really was a spark and a road map. The Five-Year Plan, through the character of Jugal Kishore, plays that part, ushering them towards village self-improvement along the lines of the Community Development pro-gramme begun in 1952.[79] Betraying a prevailing concern about rural-urban migration and suspicion about the possibility (and desirability) of whole scale urbanization, Jugal points out that progress does mean vil-lages must become cities. If they worked at it, 'everything that the city has, will be in the village'. The play's bubbly optimism masked a wilful blind-ness about the deep hold of social practices such as caste. Left unclear was how exactly Jugal, and the Five-Year Plan, would address this centuries-old mechanism of prejudice.

Beginning with 300 performances in its first year, the Song and Drama Division's productions played in front of audiences numbering an estimated 3.5 million within its first two years.[80] Soon it would count the new Director of the National School of Drama, Ebrahim Alkazi, among its advisory council members. By the early 1960s, the Song and Drama Division was co-ordinating more than 3,000 Plan-related dramatic and musical perfor-mances annually across the nation.[81] Subsidizing the stage performances of private musical and dramatic troupes, they supported a wide range of formats including drama, dance-drama, ballet, folk dances, operas, puppet shows, poetic symposia (kavi sammelans, mushaira), extempore recitals (harikatha, burrakatha, kathaprasangam), Jatra, and 'Ras, Tamasha, Bhawai, Nautanki, Maach, Dodatta'.[82]

The Division paid them to perform pieces that conveyed development goals and Plan achievements, and they ensured artists stayed on message by distributing scripts for plays, skits, and songs that were collated and vetted by Regional Scripts Committees and a Headquarters Scripts Committee at the Ministry.[83] It seems safe to assume that the performers were motivated as much (or more) by state patronage and funding as by any ideological commitment to planned development or nation-building. There were also instances of politicians hectoring artistes. According to *The Deccan Herald*, a prominent politician inaugurating a kavi sammelan (poet's gathering) in Mysore in October 1957 'told poets and authors that it was time for them to fall in line with current changes in the country and to inspire the public with the correct notions about the Plan.'[84]

The plays that were actually popular with audiences included *Aur Bhagwan Dekta Raha* (And God Looked On), *Hamara Gaon, Gaon Ka Savera* (The Village's Dawn), and *Man Bhang* (The Mind Dissolved). Operas or dance-dramas that found favour included *Indra Puja* which depicted the Five-Year Plan and *Gangavataran*, on dam building.[85] These scripts, sadly untraceable at the archives, were made available in the regional language to the Regional and Field Offices and from there, they were sent to the registered artists in their districts. Once in the field, they gained further circulation if they were used in performances by independent private troupes.

In order to maintain standards in productions that were going to be associated with the government's message the Division decided to begin a list of approved troupes instead of offering grants on an ad hoc basis. The Bir Budhalwa Dramatic Troupe was one of those chosen by the government to represent its message. Composed of 'mainly ex-criminals' from a village named Bir Budhalwa, it was organized by the Block Development Officer of Nilokheri (in present-day Haryana). It was through this officer's efforts that the troupe came to be registered, and as the review of their application observed: 'What is important in this case is that all actors belong to an ex-criminal tribe & their publicizing the plan on our behalf is in itself of publicity value.'[86]

By early 1959, the number of troupes on the rolls had shot up to nearly 300. The Division even created its own elite model troupe, called the Central Drama Troupe, to experiment with new plays and set standards. But due to the ballooning numbers, there was now only occasional work for troupes and, worse still, 'some of them were even disloyal to the cause and took liberty with approved scripts'.[87] It was decided that their numbers would have to be pared down to only four or five to a state. Those that were dropped received a letter from the Director of the Song and Drama Division. The note concluded with a polite, if overly idealistic, note thanking them for disseminating 'Plan-consciousness among the masses', adding that he hoped as 'missionaries-cum-artists' they would continue the work on their own to spread the message, 'Help the plan – Help yourself'.[88]

Yojana

Long before Khushwant Singh became one of India's best known writers, he worked to publicize the country's Five-Year Plans. He was living in Paris when the Planning Commission first approached him. Singh was the privileged beneficiary of education in Delhi, Lahore, and London, where he had been called to the bar at the Inner Temple. After a few unremarkable years lawyering at Lahore High Court, he began working for the Ministry of External Affairs in 1947 as a press officer in Britian and Canada. After returning to India to begin his career as a journalist at All India Radio he left the country again in 1954 for work at UNESCO's Department of Mass Communications in Paris. It was there that the Planning Commission's Tarlok Singh, a friend from their university spell in London, made contact to recruit him as Chief Editor of a new government-sponsored magazine. *Yojana* (The Plan) was to be a publication that would broadcast news and opinion relating to the Five-Year Plans. Tempted by the opportunity to travel across India to locations off the beaten path and edit an Indian journal, Singh looked beyond the paltry salary. The blow was softened by the keys to a car and a well-located apartment, courtesy of parental largesse. One of the job's perks was having two offices, one in the Old Secretariat Building near Metcalf House and the other, 6 miles away, at the Planning Commission in New Delhi. This, he said, had the 'great advantage of my being able to pretend that I was in the other office when I was in neither'. Khushwant Singh had quickly warmed to the privileges of government employment. Before the journal's debut, he took the advice of Tarlok Singh and set off on a month long 'Bharat Darshan tour'. On his return, he threw a champagne-soaked party to mark the magazine's launch (probably inviting charges of champagne socialism).[89]

Yojana began on Republic Day 1957 as a English and Hindi fortnightly, soon extending its scope to major regional languages.[90] The Hindi edition's editor was Manmath Nath Gupta, a man whose background was a contrast to Khushwant Singh's. A former revolutionary and associate of Chandrasekhar Azad in the Hindustan Republican Association, Gupta had spent years jailed by the colonial government for his part in the Kakori Conspiracy Case, only escaping the hangman's noose on account of his youth.

The opening page of *Yojana's* very first issue prominently displayed the iconic outline of Gandhi marching, an instrumental and even cynical use of Gandhi given how removed the centralized state and industrial economy was from Gandhi's own vision for independent India. The editorial beside Gandhi's image explained that *Yojana's* brief was to spread the message of the 'Plan and an understanding of its aims and values to villages throughout the country'.[91] Marketed as an 'intelligent man's guide' to the Plans, it carried news, stories, and opinions.[92] Interspersed between updates on the Plans, essays by social scientists, short stories, and poetry were pieces highlighting inspiring work by citizens. Tracking a nation in transition, *Yojana* featured contributions by prominent politicians and high-ranking bureaucrats alongside established writers, such as Mulk Raj Anand, Ruskin Bond, Kusum Nair, Khwaja Ahmad Abbas, and Manohar Malgonkar.

In 1959, the Minister of Information and Broadcasting directed that the English and Hindi versions of the journal target different segments of the population. The English issue, he hoped, would promote dissemination and discussion on all aspects of planning among the intelligentsia. The Hindi version was to address the masses, especially in rural areas, and was intended for wider circulation.[93] The journal's initial print run was 50,000 copies in English and 25,000 in Hindi and, by the following year, it counted 18,000 paying subscribers.[94] But *Yojana's* reach extended far beyond its paying subscriber base for it was also sent, without charge, to an array of official arms that included the Press Information Bureau, Field Publicity Units, Films Division, Plan Information Centres, the Planning Commission, Community Development Blocks, tourism offices, State Legislatures, reading rooms, trade unions, voluntary organizations, and college Planning Forums. It was also distributed abroad through the External Publicity

Division, which sent copies to India's embassies and consulates, foreign newspapers, foundations, periodicals, and universities.[95]

Yojana's inaugural issue offers a fair representation of the magazine's content and style. It contained short journalistic reports on a meeting of the National Development Council and Nehru's visits to hydroelectric power projects, opinion pieces by members of the Planning Commission, and essays with the titles 'Why We Plan' and 'History of Planning'. The editor contributed a lengthy piece on the dams in the Chambal River and the tribal Bhils who lived on its banks. The issue carried a profile on an ordinary, yet inspirational, Indian. Called 'Success Story', it was about 22 year old Dependra Bhatt from Dainthly in Madhya Pradesh, who built a bridge over the Retam, a tributary of the Chambal. There were also sections on Community Projects and Cooperation, News from the States, and a recurring section on women called The Hand that Rocks the Cradle in which Freda Bedi discussed the work of *gram sevikas* (female social workers) in Himachal Pradesh. Even the advertisements were tailored to the Plans. A Hindi advertisement for the electronics company Voltas, for example, declared: 'India's Second Five-Year Plan will require an enormous effort ... Apart from manpower, this will need a variety of heavy machinery and tools. We at Voltas are ready.'[96]

As *Yojana* strived to both edify and entertain, things were not all serious between its covers. The same issue of the journal also delivered a short dose of fiction with a story called 'Journey's End' about 'love and fulfilment in New India'. There was even a splash of history in a section titled 'Our Cultural Heritage', conveyed through verse composed by the tragic nineteenth century Mughal poet-emperor Bahadur Shah Zafar.[97] One of the comic strips was about a good-natured, responsible, and respectful young woman who – in the punch-line panel – proved herself simultaneously resourceful and kind. The next instalment of the cartoon in the following issue revealed her name to be Yojana (Plan). As the editor would explain, this woman – Yojana – was meant to embody a 'youthful Mother India'.[98]

Yojana in Hindi tried to cater to the concerns of a vaster public. It carried fewer pieces on abstract Plan goals and devoted much of its content to addressing matters of more immediate concern to a villager such as farming, education, sanitation, and caste discrimination. A single magazine issue would include broad topics like 'Co-operative Farming and National Necessity' alongside practical information such as 'Ways to Stay Safe from Rats'.[99] The Hindi issues appear to have carried more short stories and poetry than its English counterpart. The poems, with their uniformly upbeat and rousing tone, addressed the journal's well-trodden themes of hard work, sacrifice, and social reform in the task of nation-building. For example, in *Likhna Hai Itihaas Naya* (A New History Must be Written), published on the cover page, the poet wrote: 'It is not through speeches that Plans are nurtured, hands are what carry them .... We will have to drive out hunger and poverty far from our land, We will have to make successful our beloved Plan.'[100] Or in the anti-caste *Dwaar Khol Do* (Open the Doors) the author decrees, 'Open the doors of every temple in India; let them come. Let Harijans pray at the feet of the Lord, and offer flowers in worship. Open the doors.'[101]

In a section called Small Talk, Khushwant Singh, a life-long raconteur, regaled readers with brief anecdotes that not only offered a light-hearted peek into the ways in which the Plans reached far-flung areas, but also reinforced the expectations of citizens' participation. For instance, the village of Malhargarh in Madhya Pradesh was proving especially uncooperative despite the neighbouring villages making strides in building schools and dispensaries. Instead, it relied on the government doing it for them because it was the home of one of the state ministers. An exasperated Block Development Officer struck on a clever idea; using a film camera, he took footage of the progress being made in the neighbouring villages, followed by a shot of the recalcitrant village with just a donkey grazing in the fields. He then screened the film for all the surrounding villages, without comment. 'It worked. A deputation from the lazy village came and begged the donkey portion of the film to be deleted as they were becoming a laughing stock in the countryside. It was. But only after the foundations of the school and hospital had been dug by the villagers.'[102]

Motion Pictures

The Films Division of India produced the moving images that solidified postcolonial nationhood in the popular imaginary. Established in 1948 as a branch of the Ministry of Information and Broadcasting, it was an institutional holdover from the colonial Informational Films of India. Apart from promoting officially endorsed imagery of the nation, the primary effect of the Films Division's stream of frequently preachy and ponderous productions was, as Srirupa Roy argues, to present the state as signifying the nation.[103] The films, newsreels, and documentaries by the Films Division visually identified the state, allowing Indians to quite literally 'see the state' and the activities it was taking on behalf of the nation.[104] In the second half of the twentieth century, it was the largest producer of documentary films in the world, with a production catalogue of more than 8,000 short films, documentaries, and newsreels. Its audience was massive because their prints were supplied to the Department of

Field Publicity and the Ministry of Welfare for fully subsidized screenings in the countryside. And, until 1994, they were also played mandatorily in all cinema theatres across the country for up to twenty minutes before any commercial movie. It was a distribution network that reached 80 million per week.[105]

Nearly 40% of all the films produced by the Division between 1949 and 1972 were related to development and planning, the largest share by a distance.[106] As Peter Sutoris puts it, the documentary was used as 'a tool for legitimizing the development regime'.[107] During the First Plan period thirty-three documentaries related to plan themes, and that number rose over the Second Plan period to 123.[108] In fact, from late 1953 onwards the Films Division began producing films specifically to match the publicity requirements of the Five-Year Plans.[109] Within the Division, they came to be referred to as Five-Year Plan Publicity Films. The films were not only meant as updates tracking the progress of nation-building; as their audience was largely uneducated and illiterate, they endeavoured to teach as well. As Congress leader S. K. Patil explained, these documentaries had an important role to play in 'educating our masses and more particularly in inducing their voluntary cooperation for the successful implementation of our Second Five-Year Plan'.[110]

In *Sarey Jahan Sey Achcha* (Better Than All the World), a short black-and-white Hindi movie released in 1958, planning is portrayed as engineering the return of India's historic greatness. The Plans represent a phoenix-like resurrection of an ancient land's inspiring past. As the curtains part in the opening scene, an achkan-draped narrator walks on stage: 'Today we will present a glimpse of India's golden past, its present, and its hope-filled future.' The story of India then follows in a highlight reel of myth, history, and religion – its tradition of '*satyam, shivam, sundaram*' (truth, goodness, beauty). In a succession of images, we witness the legendary Raja Harishchandra handing over his crown to the sage Vishwamitra; the divine Ram and Sita with their loyal accomplice, the simian god Hanuman; a scene from the *Mahabharata* in which Vishnu's avatar Krishna blesses the warrior Arjuna; a serene Buddha meditating under a tree; Emperor Ashoka abjuring violence by dropping his sword and shield; Mughal emperor Akbar flanked by learned men of various faiths, symbolizing his attempt to 'bring together and unify all religions'; and people paying their respects to the valorous Maratha ruler Shivaji.

'India was once admired by the entire world', boasts the baritone narrator at the end of this millennia-spanning montage. 'But', he continues as violins turn plaintive and the British flag dominates the frame, we 'became slaves. Slaves for two hundred years.' However, Mahatma

Gandhi nurtured the 'flickering lamp of freedom' in the hearts of these 400 million slaves. Following the patriotic cry of 'Vande Mataram!' (Hail, the Motherland!), the chains around a map of India are sloughed off, and we watch soldiers carrying the Union Jack trooping out. In the next scene, this outline of the subcontinent turns into Bharat Mata (Mother India) represented as a crowned goddess standing at the heart of India, halo spinning behind her head, and proudly wielding the national tricolour. As devotees shower petals at her feet and garland her with flowers, the borders of the nation alight with ceremonial *diyas*, and cries of 'Jai Hind!' (Victory to India!) rent the air. But this happy scene is rudely interrupted. India's independence, the narrator gravely informs us, was attended by the problems of Partition, hunger, superstition, and poverty.

To face these grim circumstances, 'to achieve political independence along with economic freedom – we made a Plan'. As the music turns upbeat, women and men gather around and underneath a giant book titled *Bharat Ki Pehli Panchvarshiya Yojana* (India's First Five-Year Plan). The Plan document has taken the place, both literally and figuratively, of the goddess Bharat Mata and the map of India. The viewer is told that to fulfil one's duty to the nation, it is necessary to first understand the Plan. As the enormous pages are turned by citizens, we see that each page represents one of the Plan's aims: 'An India with no shortage of food', 'An India where is no trace of unemployment', 'An India where water reaches every field', 'An India where there is a dam on every river.' The future depended on this, but to fulfil 'such Plans, the enthusiasm and help of ordinary people is required'. Whatever your station and employment, everyone including children had to lend a hand. Against the backdrop of scenes of people breaking earth with hoes, clearing brush, and carrying soil, the narrator intones that by participating in such work through a platform like the *Bharat Sewak Samaj*, we can lend a hand to our poor brethren across the country and help in improving their lives. The film ends with an image of children of different faiths and geographic regions gathered around symbols of independent India – its map, the Ashokan lions, and the flag. They sing Iqbal's patriotic hymn, *Sarey Jahan Sey Achcha*: 'Better than all the world, is our Hindustan; We are its night-ingales, and this is our garden.'[111]

As its name suggests, *Sarey Jahan Sey Achcha* stokes the Indian viewers pride in their ancient and early modern past, choosing not to sift between legend and history, and taking pains to underscore its pluralist triumphs. However, within minutes, the filmmaker is unable to resist the portrayal of India as a Hindu goddess, and the film positions the viewer and citizen of independent India as a worshipful Hindu devotee. The problems attendant on independence – Partition, hunger, poverty represented as

Figure 4.3. Scene from *Sarey Jahan Sey Achcha* (1958).

smoke, lightning, and thunder – cause Bharat Mata anguish and send her children-devotee-citizens scurrying. The Five-Year Plan is presented as the solution to this elemental chaos and misery. Planning, representing economic independence, was the necessary corollary to political independence. Given the modes in which India is represented in the film – as a civilization enslaved, a Hindu goddess, and an infant nation – participating in planned development is presented as a cultural, religious, and civic duty. The English version of the movie was aptly titled *Working for the Plan*.

In *Shadow and Substance*, an animated film from 1967, an alien visits India from a faraway star and acts as an impartial observer of the progress made during the first three Five-Year Plans (1951–1966). It begins with an orange space ship, of the classic flying saucer variety, zigzagging across the stars towards Earth and heading to the subcontinent. As it hovers over an unnamed village in India, we look down at a villager trundling down a dirt path on his ox cart. Startled by the spaceship, the droopy-whiskered man in a dhoti and turban abandons his cart and runs into the nearby woods. An extraterrestrial – squat, metallic, humanoid, and friendly – emerges. Apparently experiencing only moon-gravity, the alien gently bounces over to the frightened villager who is seen peeping out from behind a tree trunk. After exchanging vigorous *namastes*, the foreigner points to the sky and reveals to the stuttering villager that he comes from 'Planet Number 7468932'. Firecrackers light up the sky and the narrator tells us that it is 26 January 1950. The Indian Republic is born. The alien turns to our villager and asks, 'Republic? You no smile?' In response, this new citizen of India shrugs and turns to the viewer: 'Have we got anything to smile about? Huh?' They then set off on a journey in the spacecraft, after the alien resorts to his extraterrestrial-to-Hindi dictionary to say 'Chalo!' (Let's go!). As they travel over the country, we see houses half submerged by torrential rains, scorched plains of drought, and bleached bovine bone. When they land, the vindicated villager asks, 'Now tell me, is there anything to smile about?'

The spaceship departs, and to the tune of upbeat music we are shown figures relating to increased fertilizer production, land under cultivation, and food production during the years of the First Five-Year Plan. When the alien returns in 1956, the sad-eyed villager tells him that there is still nothing to smile about – all they had was 'talk, talk, talk'. The unconvinced and empirically minded extraterrestrial takes the villager on another airborne tour to test this diagnosis. They pass over green fields irrigated by a large dam, red tractors ploughing farms, and trains passing under bridges bearing cargo trucks. The villager responds to the alien's chiding – 'you bluff me, its change!' – by pointing out that no progress had come to *his* life. Once again, leaning into the viewer, he asks, 'Are *you* any better off?' As we see greater numbers of automobiles on the roads, and buildings sprouting from the ground, it suddenly turns dark and, to a soundtrack of babies screaming, the screen is filled with infants multiplying alarmingly. Throwing his hands in the air, the Malthusian visitor from space makes his views on family planning known with little subtlety: 'Babies! Babies! Babies! Too much babies! It's trouble. Too much people, no food, no house. Too much babies – too little for you!' After shamefacedly admitting that he had five children, the villager then speaks with pride about them – an engineer, a carpenter, a teacher trainee, and two schoolgoers. The youngest even receives free lunch at school: 'more than

I got in my time'. Acknowledging that there had been some progress and promising not to have any more children, he bids the alien goodbye.

Returning in 1961, at the close of the Second Five-Year Plan, the extraterrestrial is greeted by the villager with a kettle of chai (the Indian slurps it from the saucer and smacks his lips, while the other deposits it into a retractable chute). They set off on their customary tour of the land, bearing witness to factories, power plants, and graphs attesting to increased steel and cement production. Our villager had also begun building a spacious house the previous year, but cannot find enough material to complete it. Reminding his friend that 'half house better than no house', the alien leaves once again. The year is now 1966, and the three-room house with a red-tiled roof has finally become a home. Named *Sukh Niwas* (Happy Home), it even has a picture-perfect picket fence around the yard. Inside, looking content, our villager lazily strolls about a drawing room that betray the marks of modern comfort – upholstered chairs, a desk, a transistor radio, bookshelves, an electric fan, and lights. A framed family portrait on the wall confirms that he kept his reproductive promise. The once crotchety man now even has time to pause and smell the red flowers in a vase on his dining table. When his non-earthling friend arrives, he takes him on a motorbike ride and plays a broadcast from AIR on his transistor. It reports, in the clipped and declarative tone of AIR newsreaders, that the Planning Commission has found that at the end of the first three Five-Year Plans, per capita income has increased by 27% industrial production has increased by 300% and production of food grain has risen from 54.9 million tons in 1950–1951 to 88.9 million tons in 1964–1965. Meanwhile, the travel companions have switched from a motorbike to a train, and are now exploring various industrial plants. At an airplane hangar, they meet the man's smartly dressed son who has grown to become an aeronautical engineer. This time, for their tour from the sky, instead of the spaceship, they board an Indian-made aircraft, and the villager finally allows himself an unreserved laugh.[112]

What the gambit of the alien achieves in *Shadow and Substance* is perspective. The rides in the space shuttle serve to expand the villager's spatial horizons. It collapses the distance between the man's seemingly unchanging village and the dramatic advances occurring in other parts of the country to present proof of the Planning Commission's assertions. But in addition to this geographic perspective, the alien's visits offer temporal insight. The extraterrestrial allows the pessimistic villager, and the jaded citizen-viewer, to look at their own life and that of the nation from an Archimedean point. Viewed from this perch, what is perceived in the moment as stagnation is revealed to be the Plan's steady accomplishments.

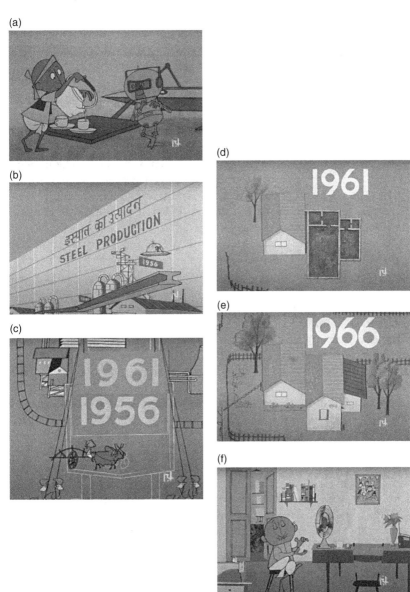

Figure 4.4. Scenes of planned progress from *Shadow and Substance* (1967).

And the 5-year intervals between the alien's visits, timed to match the completion of Five-Year Plans, only make the changes starker. This perspective, outsourced by the film to someone unaffiliated with the government (or anything earthly), is presented as objective and scientific. By having the alien speak for the state, the film is also able to indirectly scold citizens for their failings – such as with family planning – and lecture them on how that retards both individual and national economic progress. The contentment experienced by our villager towards the end of the film, in the mid-1960s, is thus both a result of the state fulfilling its 5-year promises and of the citizen aligning his personal life with that of the Plan. The implicit message is that the role average citizens played mattered to the overall success of the Five-Year Plans, in actions that extended from their professional performance in offices, factories, and fields to personal choices made in their homes, including their bedrooms.

These films shared a narrative arc in which India was portrayed as traversing a great figurative distance from colonial slavery towards greatness, or from the miseries of Partition to palpable material progress. Addressing the most common denominator through the figure of a rural peasant or urban worker, the films sought to integrate the stories of these unremarkable individuals with an authorized account of remarkable national advance of which they were a part. In some films, this was achieved through an informational barrage of facts and figures, charts and diagrams in what has been referred to as postcolonial India's 'fetishized litany of numbers'.[113] Others resorted to the trope of a sceptic whose doubts are dissolved and concerns allayed by an informed outsider or with a tour through the country with stops at sites of blossoming industrial modernity. In their message, they assembled varying combinations of publicity about the Plans and calls for the public to participate enthusiastically in them. The images employed to arouse pride and awe are revealing – soaring aircraft, colossal hydroelectric dams, coal-powered plants billowing smoke, molten metal ore flowing in steel plants, tractors and automobiles on the move, scientific laboratories with precision instruments and beakers, and modern ports with cranes and hulking ships. They display a fascination with scientific and industrial modernity, undergirded by the view that India's entry into it would dispel its many problems. As a *gram sevak* (village worker) explains to a group of villagers in *Tomorrow Is Ours*, 'the throb of the machine captures the new spirit of India'.[114]

There were some who believed that even commercial cinema owed a responsibility towards the Plans. Prominent among them was Khwaja Ahmad Abbas, the noted progressive writer-director involved with several iconic Hindi films such as *Dharti Ke Lal* (1946), *Shree 420* (1955), and

Bobby (1973), who also launched the career of megastar Amitabh Bachchan in *Saat Hindustani* (1969).[115] An admirer of Nehru from his college days, Abbas described it as 'my long love affair'.[116] He was a believer in the project of a social transformation through planned industrial modernity and the name of his production company, *Naya Sansar* (New World), reflected that conviction. Writing in the Republic Day issue of *Yojana* in 1958, Abbas began with the condescending remark that for 'millions in our country the cinema represents almost the only cultural and artistic influence to which they are exposed'. Having noted the exaggerated importance that films had acquired as the sole entertainment in the cultural desert in which India's illiterate millions supposedly lived, Abbas asked where the film industry fit into the Plans. The answer was discouraging: 'The fact is that the Planners are as ignorant of the potentialities of the cinema as the film-makers are oblivious of their duty to the Plan.' To Abbas, the short films made by the Films Division were simply not good enough to enthuse the vast movie-going public. The transformations attempted by the Five-Year Plans contained enough substance and human drama for screenwriters and directors to portray 'the most important contemporary reality in our country but also inform, inspire and enthuse our entire people with the ideals of the Plan'. Pushing for a 'happy alliance' between Plans and motion pictures, Abbas called for planners to assist filmmakers with facilities and funding, and for film-makers to respond by integrating their 'creative energies with the ideals and purposes of the Plan'. However, this was not a long-term solution. As the title of his essay screamed, to Abbas the only lasting resolution would be to 'Nationalize Motion Pictures'.[117]

Public expressions of commitment to the Plans were not limited to Abbas alone. *Yojana* carried advertisements in which Bollywood stars Meena Kumari, Manohar Desai, and Kamini Kaushal were photographed reading the magazine, and by extension, promoting the Five-Year Plans.[118] There was also the possibly apocryphal (yet revealing) anecdote about one of the reigning film stars of the era. The matinee idol and country's highest paid actor, Dilip Kumar, was supposedly once offered 5 million rupees for a role, which he declined and instead suggested that the producer invest in the Five-Year Plan.[119] Whether or not the tale is accurate, the sentiment expressed is credible given the mutual admiration the leading man and Nehru are known to have had for each other.[120]

Plans seeped into Bollywood cinema and songs. They archive a popular culture and national discourse drenched in the language of planned development. In the duet 'Kaamyab hum karke rahenge' from the 1956 Hindi movie *Kya Baat Hai*, for example, the Plans are explicitly invoked.

१२   योजना   १ फ़रवरी, १९५९

फ़िल्मी कलाकारों में योजना की लोकप्रियता

मीना कुमारी, मनहर देसाई, कामिनी कौशल
योजना पढ़ते हुए

योजना से आपको क्या प्राप्त होता है ?

योजना सम्बन्धी लेख

भाखड़ा से हम क्या सीख सकते हैं ?
तुंगभद्रा के अजीब किसान
केरल में भूमि सुधार
भिलाई—निर्माण की दिशा में एक महान कदम
मद्रास और महाबलिपुरम
मयूराक्षी   कोयना   दामोदर

कवि और कहानीकार

माखनलाल चतुर्वेदी   नागार्जुन
यशपाल   मोहनसिंह सेंगर
सुमित्रा कुमारी सिन्हा   मनमोहन
वृन्दावन लाल वर्मा   चन्द्रकिरण सोनरिक्सा
हंसराज रहबर

पेड़-पौधे और पत्ती

कटहल	राजहंस
करंज	मधु
सोहांजना	भारत पद्म पुष्प
काजू	गोरैया
बंजुका	अबाबील
बरना	अडक्क
रीठा	कोरिकीट

योजना सम्बन्धी लेखक

वी० टी० कृष्णमाचारी
अशोक मेहता
ए० सी० गुह
नौशेर भरुचा
मिन्नू मसानी
डा० वी० के० आर० वी० राव
डा० के० एन० राज

ये सब आकर्षण
ढाई रुपए वार्षिक में

पोंगापन्थ विरोधी रचनाएं

समाज सुधार के कानूनों की दुर्गत
पढ़े-लिखे भी रूढ़ियों के चक्कर में
यह कुएं का मेंढकपन कब तक चलेगा
हमारे देशों की बेड़ियाँ
भटके हुए लोग
मोच के ठेकेदारों के नाम

Figure 4.5. An advertisement for *Yojana* in the same magazine, claiming popularity among film stars and detailing its offerings. Pictured here are actors Meena Kumari, Manohar Desai, and Kamini Kaushal (February 1959).

Sung by the iconic duo of Mohammad Rafi and Late Mangeshkar, its politics are laid out in the chorus:

> *keh do ye gaun ke jaat ko aur shehar ke gentleman ko*
> *kaamyab hum karke rahenge panch saal ke plan ko*
> *haan panch saal ke plan ko*
> *ho panch saal ke plan ko*

> Tell this to the Jats of the village and the gentlemen of the city
> We will ensure the success of the Five Year Plan
> Yes, the Five Year Plan
> the Five Year Plan

In the verses that followed, the song conveyed what a successful Plan would mean. Fields would bloom and *panchayati raj* (village self-government) would reign supreme, schools would appear in every village and hospitals in slums, tractors would plough farms and every gully would be lit with electricity. But the Plan was not only about material advancement; it represented a cultural renaissance as well. The song spoke of showcasing Indian civilization to the world. Homes would buzz with cultured chatter, and the historic musical tradition of Mirabai, Tulsidas, and Tansen would be reawakened. Finally, it asked people of different castes – 'Ram babu' and 'Ramaswami', 'Ram Singh' and 'Ramu bhai' – to join forces. All of this, however, depended on citizens helping the Plan. 'Don't speak of leisure, and forget about rest', Rafi and Mangeshkar sang. 'We will ensure the success of the Five Year Plan.'

Plan-consciousness suffused *Naya Daur* (New Era), a movie directed by B. R. Chopra, whose oeuvre reflects an allegiance with the Nehruvian emphasis on democratic socialism and secularism. As his brother and fellow filmmaker Yash Chopra revealed in an interview, 'Nehru and his policies were always part of our sub-consciousness ... We had internalized his words.'[121] Released in 1957, it was dubbed into Tamil the next year and released as *Pattalayin Sabatham* (The Proletariat's Vow). *Naya Daur*'s central theme was the conflict between traditional employment and modern machinery, a debate that dogged the Second Five-Year Plan. As Dilip Kumar, the lead protagonist put it: *'jhagda toh haath aur machine ka hai bas'* (the fight is between hand and machine). It reflected the timing of the movie's release, a year after the inauguration of the Second Five-Year Plan, with its emphasis on large-scale industrialization. It was, according to Meghnad Desai, a 'quintessentially Nehruvian film'. The plot turns around the destabilization and threat of unemployment that the introduction of a bus and a mechanical sawmill bring to a bucolic village. The hero of the film, Shankar, is one of the *tongawallahs* (driver of a horse-drawn cart) whose livelihood the proposed bus threatens. But at the end of the film, despite holding his own in this competition between man and machine through ingenuity and collective action, Shankar magnanimously proposes a compromise. He tells the antagonist; 'We poor people have no hatred for machines ... Find a way for us all to coexist in the village – you, us, motorcars, and machines.' Machinery was not to be rejected outright as the villain, for it was the way of the future; what was necessary was to use it in a manner that best served the people. What this slightly awkward resolution allowed was an acknowledgement of the concerns about redundancy through mechanization while maintaining an ultimately optimistic view of where the country was headed under the strategy adopted by the Second Five-Year Plan.

One of the most popular songs from the movie, *Saathi Haath Badhaana*, provided an anthem and advertisement for democratic planning and rural community development. The flattering low-angle shots of Shankar and other villagers volunteering to build a road together might as well have come from the pages of *Yojana*. The song featured enthusiastic villagers digging earth with pickaxes, carrying loose mud to build a road, all performed with a song and smile on their lips. The lyrics, penned by Sahir Ludhianvi and sung by Mohammad Rafi and Asha Bhonsle, echoed the government's message on collective effort:

> *Saathi haath badhaana. saathi re*
> *Saathi haath badhaana, saathi re*
> *Ek akela thak jayega, milkar bhoj uththana . . . .*
> *Hum mehnat walon ne jab bhi milkar kadam badhaya,*
> *Sagar ney rasta choda, parbat ney shish jhukaya*

> Friends, join hands
> Friends, join hands
> Alone you will tire, let's carry the burden together . . . .
> Whenever workers like us have stepped forward together
> The sea has parted, the mountain has bowed down

Another commercial Hindi film that displayed Plan consciousness, and actively promoted it, was Khwaja Ahmad Abbas' *Char Dil Char Rahein* (Four Hearts Four Paths). Released in 1959, it starred box-office draws such as Meena Kumari, Raj Kapoor, and Shammi Kapoor. The movie revolves around three parallel love stories, all of which are linked to a four-way road intersection. One road led to Sultanabad, a feudal kingdom about to lose its status as a princely state; the second leads to Ram Kund, a caste-ridden village; the third to Hotel Parbat, a holiday destination for the rich; and the fourth to Nav Bharat (New India). By the end of the film, all the principal characters work on building the road to Nav Bharat. The intersection symbolizes the different paths independent India could take and the perils most of them represent.

A crucial interaction in the film is between the low-caste dark-skinned beauty, Chavli (Meena Kumari) – who has been driven from her village in Haryana and separated from her higher caste lover Govinda (Raj Kapoor) – and the *jhola* carrying trade unionist Nirmal Kumar. The socialist requests a weary Chavli, the Dalit 'Chamaran', to join him in building a new road that leads away from the retrograde destinations of Sultanabad, Ram Kund, and Hotel Parbat. He tells her that this road is their path to progress, and the only way towards what she seeks. Building the road will mean confronting some seemingly insurmountable obstacles, both material and metaphorical. The 60-mile road they are building, he continues, 'is no ordinary task. It is a part of our Five-Year Plan. It is these tiny projects that together will move the country forward, and bring us nearer socialism'. Seated under a Hindi banner about 'Moving Towards Socialism', Chavli asks what that means. 'Socialism is a kind of dynamite', he explains, 'one that will blow up backward ideas and will give birth to a new world ... where no one will be naked, hungry, or homeless'. The labour leader directly challenges assumed caste and gender hierarchies. Referring to her respectfully as Chavli Devi rather than simply Chavli, he accepts a glass of water from her hand despite her warning that she is 'achchut' (from an 'untouchable' caste). He even insists that she sit on a chair, and not on the floor, to converse with him as an equal. Surprised, and overcoming her shyness, she asks if this socialist order would go so far as to allow an 'Ahir boy to marry a Chamar's daughter?' The socialist tells her this new world will not allow such things as caste to come in the way of love. It is towards this new order that the road they are building leads. Chavli Devi ends the scene declaring with determination, 'Then I will *certainly* build this road.'

The invocation of socialism was no doubt a response to that word's wide public dispersion in the years since 1955, when the Congress Party adopted a socialistic pattern of society as its objective. By explicitly tying together Five-Year Plans and socialism with the dismantling of caste, gender, and capitalist exploitation, the filmmaker was projecting the Congress vision of planned modernity as the only road to salvation. With the state awarding the contract for the new road to the worker's committee, Abbas portrayed a government that was on the side of the people, and not allied with scheming middlemen like the feudal lords of Sultanabad, the hidebound upper caste village headmen of Ram Kund, or the craven capitalists of Hotel Parbat. Like in *Naya Daur*, Abbas' film also featured a song that pictured workers building a road while brimming with hope in a way that mirrored the stock images of plan publicity and propaganda. Sung by Lata Mangeshkar and Manna Dey, and once again written by Sahir Ludhianvi, the song's lyrics underlined the spirit of public participation and the promise of the Plans:

Saathi re, Bhai re
Utha liya hai ab samajvaad ka nishaan, samajvaad ka nishaan
Alag alag na hogi ab hamari khetiyan, yeh hamari khetiyan
Chalegi sabke vaste milon ki charkhiyna

O comrades, O brothers
We hold aloft the symbol of socialism
Our fields will no longer be broken up
The mills will work for us all

The next year, 1960, the movie *Hum Hindustani* (We Indians) opened with a song that has been described as a candidate for the 'theme song of Nehru's vision'.[122] *Chhodo Kal Ki Baatein* channelled the still young nation's patriotism, postcolonial optimism, and Plan-consciousness. An upbeat tune accompanied stills that conveyed the country's march towards planned modernity through images of Nehru at a Congress session, the construction of hydroelectric dams, modern roads and cities, soaring fighter jets, trains forging ahead, and factories with tall chimneys billowing smoke. Once again, the song beseeched its listener to both take pride and take part in independent India's economic progress. In this new India, work was worship:

Chhodo kal ki baatein, kal ki baat purani
Naye daur mein likhenge milkar nayi kahaani
. . .
Aao mehnat ko apna iman banayein
Apney haathon ko apna bhagwan banayein

Let's leave talk of yesterday, it is old
In the new era, together, we will write a new story
. . .
Come make toiling our faith
Make our hands our God.

In November 1958, the Hindi issue of *Yojana* carried responses by readers to the question, 'Can Films Contribute to National Building?' They provide a glimpse of what some ordinary Indians made of the relationship between planned development and cinema. Most respondents, like Shyam Bihari Bansal from Jaipur, had been disappointed by recent experience but remained hopeful. Lakhan Vyas from Madhya Pradesh wrote to say that both filmmakers and audiences shared the blame for this. In order to incentivize the production of Plan-related films, he proposed that the government institute major cash awards that would soften the blow for exceptional movies that suffered losses. Ratankumari Porbal took a brighter view. Writing from the Ajmer Soap Factory in New Delhi's Karol Bagh, she believed Hindi movies had played an important role in bringing a 'new awakening' in India. While they may be few and far between, films such as *Hum Log* (Us People) and *Do Bigha Zameen* (Two Bighas of Land) had, in her view, explained the merits of a socialist life. The government's efforts with documentaries, she added, were admirable though insufficient. Surendra Kumar Puthiya from Moradabad was excited to share how impressed he was by the Films Division's Hindi production *Hum Par Bhi Daya Kijiye* (Take Pity on Us as Well). Jagdish Chandra from Ghaziabad pointed out that, in reality, the most influential aspect of commercial films was their songs; these had a deep impact on people. The songs he listed included the now-iconic patriotic lament, *Jinhe naaz hai Hind par, woh kaahan hai?* (Where are those who take pride in India?).

There were others who were altogether more pessimistic about the role movies played in society. Govind Narayan Tripathi narrated an incident he had witnessed one evening. Three men – a lawyer, a schoolteacher, and an office worker – were strolling past a group of young women, when they began harassing them by shouting sexist lines from movie songs. Tripathi was so angered he wanted to slap them. If the movies fed us obscene songs, he asked, were they likely to contribute to 'national progress or ruin?' Even progressive movies such as *Naya Daur* were often lost on their audiences. He recounted the time he watched it in a slum, seated beside a '*dehaati*' (rustic). He was sure that this man was not following the finer points of the film. When he asked, 'Did you understand anything?' The man laughed and lasciviously added, '*Saali – sab matak matak kar naach rahi hain!*' (Look at how all those women are cavorting!).[123]

Decades later, describing the impact of films and their songs, the literary critic Rakshanda Jalil, a self-described child of the 1960s, spoke of being 'infected by the spirit' of its progressive idealism. The radio, she recalls, 'blaring from every panwadi and kirana store, played songs from the popular cinema eulogizing all that was best about a sovereign, socialist, secular republic'. The Films Division's documentaries 'portrayed the nation's history-in-the-making in drab monochrome through de rigeur screenings in every big and small cinema hall in every big and small Indian town'.[124]

The male lead in numerous Hindi films from the 1950s to the mid-1960s embodied the broad spirit of postcolonial national economic development. According to sociologist Sanjay Srivastava, for the middle classes in early independent India, masculinity was signified on screen by rationality and a scientific worldview. This led to a masculine type that he refers to as the 'Five-Year Plan Hero' to whom a scientific temper was the 'fundamental attitude'. This cultural archetype took inspiration from the figures such as Mahalanobis, whom Srivastava refers to as its quintessential figure.[125] The Professor was likely viewed through this lens because he was seen as a powerful planner and patriotic technocrat whose achievements included the National Sample Survey, directing computers to India, and delivering the Second Plan. The pantheon of Plan heroes would have included others cut from similar cloth; institution-building scientists like Homi Bhabha, Meghnad Saha, and Vikram Sarabhai. The masculinity of the 'Five-Year Plan Hero' was exhibited not through brawn or aggression, but rather by being scientific and modern. This middle class 'science-based masculinity' was often expressed in the hero's profession – an engineer, doctor, scientist, or bureaucrat. The hero was an agent of modernity, catalysing the transition of the 'the irrational native into the modern citizen'.[126] In a similar vein, historian Dilip Menon observed that while the national movement elevated the 'disciplined *Satyagrahi*' to heroic proportions, the postcolonial discourse of development 'offered the engineer and the scientist as the objects of devotion'.[127]

The Five-Year Plan Hero showed up even in literature. Yashpal's *Jhoota Sach* (False Truth) is one of the iconic Hindi novels of the era. The author's guarded optimism about the project of democratic planning probably owed something to his own past as a revolutionary socialist. In his youth, Yashpal had been a leader of the Hindustan Republican Socialist Association, and waged armed rebellion against British rule alongside Sukhdev, Chandrasekhar 'Azad', and Bhagat Singh. Arrested in 1932 for crimes including detonating a bomb on the Viceroy's train, Yashpal was defended in court by Nehru's niece, the lawyer Shyam Kumari Nehru. He would spend 6 years in prison, and after his release he turned to the pen. While disillusioned by the reality of postcolonial India, he retained an admiration for Nehru, even dedicating his 1956 novel, *Amita*, to him.[128]

Yashpal's two-volume magnum opus, *Jhoota Sach*, was published in 1958 and 1960. It follows individuals and families in colonial north India whose lives are transformed by Partition and who make new lives in independent India. The character of Professor Pran Nath – an acclaimed economist with an Oxford doctorate who has published pieces in *The Economist* – typifies the Five-Year Plan Hero. On his return to India, Nath becomes a professor of economics at Punjab University and, after World War II, he is an economic advisor to Punjab's governor. By the mid-1950s, Professor Nath is employed in New Delhi as an advisor to the Planning Commission, with an office at Yojana Bhavan. He is described as 'helping to launch the First Five-Year Plan' and drafting the Second Five-Year Plan as well.[129] Significantly, he is also one of the few good men in the novel. Nath helps Tara (the novel's real hero and emotional core) pay for her undergraduate degree and keeps her terrible secret (of abduction and rape during Partition). It is at the Planning Commission's offices that Professor Nath and Tara meet once again after a decade, in a chance encounter that kindles a romance. In one of the few lasting glimmers of hope in the novel, Tara and the planner eventually marry. It suggests, perhaps, that the scars of Partition and the strife of the early republic could only be overcome through planned development.

It is no surprise, of course, that the sociocultural icon of postcolonial nationalism would be the 'man of science' or the 'Five-Year Plan Hero'. D. P. Mukerji, one of the founders of Indian sociology, observed a transformation in the nature of national heroes in a series of essays in 1953 titled 'Man and Plan in India'. He suggested that 'the new man' during Gandhian anti-colonialism had been a moral one. This figure valorised discipline, sacrifice, honesty, and spiritual devotion. Under Nehru in independent India, he wrote with foreboding, there was a 'transference of allegiance from Ram-rajya to a planned social order . . . from sacrifice to planned endeavor'. As someone who believed in fusing Indian tradition with Western modernity, religious ethics with scientific advance, he likely had mixed feelings about this new India that venerated engineers and technocrats, whom he called the 'middle-class know-how type'. The technocrat – as Mukerji speculated, and preceding chapters confirm – was the 'future leader'.[130]

Despite the heroic framing of the scientific and development expert, it is worth mentioning that Mahalanobis and the Institute did not feature with any prominence in the democratic planning publicity campaigns, and nor did any other famous technocrat. This is due to a dissonance that ran through Indian planning – seeking to be simultaneously technocratic and democratic at once, or technocratic in operation and democratic in projection. Elite and exceptional figures like the Professor, so central to how the Plans were formulated, were incompatible to how the Nehruvian government sold 'democratic planning'. The campaigns to build Plan-consciousness and Plan-participation addressed the average citizen, telling them that their priorities were reflected in the Plans, that they were ultimately responsible for it, and that they alone could ensure its fulfilment. Drawing attention to a singular, technocratic Plan Hero like the Professor would undercut the message that ordinary Indians were, or could be, Plan Heroes.

***

In early independent India, the Congress government often defended its policies by pointing to the electoral mandate it had secured in the world's largest elections. When forced to answer questions about the Five-Year Plans, representatives of the Nehru government frequently resorted to using electoral popularity as a shield. This was a disingenuous argument that continues to be employed both in India and beyond. Its hollowness was apparent to frustrated contemporaries such as Minoo Masani. Responding in March 1958 to the claim that Indians broadly approved of the Second Five-Year Plan, Masani asked in Parliament: 'Do they really?' Citizens, he argued, did not just vote once every 5 years; they also 'from time to time vote outside the ballot boxes'. The shortfall in the small savings campaign was a case in point. Was not every Indian who had savings but did not invest in the government scheme, really voting *against* the Second Five-Year Plan? Every peasant who has to hoard, he argued, and every businessman who abandons a business idea has essentially voted against the Plan. The Congress may win elections by using the flag, 'the mantle of Mahatma Gandhi ... the great personality of the Prime Minister ... all kinds of sentimental and extraneous issues'. But to use that to assume that Indians approved of the Second Five-Year Plan was to 'miscalculate the real feelings of the people'.[131]

A year later, an article in the *Hindustan Times* warned that there was a danger that the government's expectations regarding public participation was losing a 'sense of proportion'. 'Its prophets are at the moment inclined to claim for it almost miraculous powers.'[132] While carping about the effectiveness of these Plan publicity campaigns was common, it is notable that criticism of the aims and methods seem much less so (though they probably existed), possibly indicative of the popular sanction and desirability of the *idea* of democratic planning.

After more than a decade of Plan publicity, the Government of India decided that it was time to assess the levels of Plan-consciousness in the nation. Appointed in March 1963, the Study Team on Five-Year Plan Publicity (also known as the Vidyalankar Committee) visited nine states and covered eighty-nine districts in addition to conducting sample surveys, meetings, and inviting memoranda.[133] Their report painted a dismal picture, confirming many of the government's fears. The publicity apparatus had 'fallen short of expectations in enlisting public cooperation and canvassing public opinion which constitute the principal force behind planning'. The average citizen, it found, lacked 'an intelligent understanding of the essentials of planning and ... the efforts and sacrifices demanded of them'.[134] It acknowledged the scale of the challenge in a country as diverse as India, and one where, as it described, 'the tenth, fifteenth and twentieth centuries co-exist'.[135] Despite their concerns about conveying democratic socialism to villagers, the team concluded that on the whole, rural audiences were more receptive and responsive than their urban counterparts. They recommended that printed word publicity be emphasized only in city and town settings since film, radio, songs, dramas, and exhibitions were more popular and effective in the countryside.[136] Ultimately, and unmindful of the irony, the study team concluded that the signal flaw in the government's efforts was inadequate planning.[137]

Given the very uneven results, why did the government of India remain committed to these publicity campaigns? While inertia can explain some part of it, there was a logic to consciously choosing to persist as well. The idea of democratic planning was important to how the state had come to view itself, and how it was trying to define the independent Indian state. The reason they kept up with this rhetoric and these means of outreach, even when engagement fell short of expectations, was because it was a part of the Nehruvian self-definition, critical to the state's self-presentation and the legitimacy of its economic agenda.

Democratic planning, to a significant degree, remained an aspirational slogan. As we will see in the next chapter, however, there were several instances of popular enthusiasm for the Plans that kept the claim alive. It took the form of voluntary bodies with participants numbering in the tens of thousands, emerging from civil society but backed by the state. As the following pages will clarify, the activities of College Planning Forums and the development works of the Bharat Sewak Samaj kept afloat the idea of planning as a popular undertaking and national mission. These initiatives brought attention to the Plan's welfare policies and to its embrace by some citizens' groups. A contemporary foreign scholar observed that, 'compared with other non-Communist countries in Asia, India has been by far the most successful in enlisting public support for an economic development program'.[138] And while these methods may not have been successful in achieving the lofty goal of making India entirely Plan-conscious their inability to do so should not obscure the significance of what the effort represented.

Planning was not just an economic policy: it was fused to a political project and endeavoured to be a mass movement. Planning in India was distinguished by its operating in a democracy. And this was no ornamental detail; it was a fundamental feature of the Indian state, and a principle that the Nehruvian government was voluble about. To this government, the braiding of Parliament and Plans, at a time when the Cold War presented them as mutually exclusive, symbolized the distinctive path the Indian republic had chosen to tread and the example it offered to other poor, decolonizing nations. In such a context, it would not do for planning to be of concern only to the technocrats in Yojana Bhavan.

For democratic planning not to ring entirely hollow, the government believed, Indians had to be made Plan-conscious at least, if not Plan-participants. Self-interestedly, this was important for the government because it conveyed the Congress' economic vision to voters, under-lined the projects it had undertaken, and legitimized its status as the party in power. Further, appealing for citizens participation was a matter of necessity due to the inadequacy of state capacity combined with the ambitious targets set by planners. The Plans simply could not fulfil their objectives without a sympathetic, Plan-conscious populace. Plans were never meant to be drafted through plebiscite, but they could be implemented with an informed and willing citizenry. This was also based on the idea that citizens fully inhabited citizenship only when they were aware of the national narrative and their role in it. It was then that citizenship passed from formality to substance. However, this understanding of Indian citizenship did not extend to a substantive engagement with the citizenry about their priorities and aspirations for the Plans. There were very few channels through which ordinary Indians – of whom so much was being asked – could effectively com-municate their preferences and needs. It may be one of the many reasons why the planned economy did so poorly with primary educa-tion and healthcare. Planners wanted knowledgeable and consenting foot soldiers, not a citizenry empowered to share their own views on grand strategies. Instrumentally speaking, the Planning Commission was aware that even the most expertly crafted Plan was only likely to succeed if the people championed it.

Planning in India, then, was marked by the compulsion to create a productive citizenry and a commitment to educate the ordinary Indian about it. Informed, involved, and productive – that, according to the Government and Planning Commission, was what it meant to be an Indian citizen.

5   Salvation in Service

Khushwant Singh crossed paths with an American family sightseeing in Delhi in early 1958, when on their first trip to India. The Horners were peering up at Qutub Minar, a medieval tower that had pierced the sky for nearly 800 years. Striking up a conversation, Singh learned that they were about to travel to Agra to see the Taj Mahal. According to the woman, her middle-aged husband, Lee Horner, a business executive, could not wait to see the marble wonder. Mere mention of Agra apparently caused the otherwise unsentimental man to 'drool around the mouth'. When Singh met the family later, he asked how the trip was. The Taj was superb, Lee Horner said, but he had been even more impressed by something else. The American earnestly described what he had seen: 'A whole village empty – not a single person left behind. All had gone to build a road. Voluntarily! . . . this was free labour. This stumps me.'[1] The exchange would have been music to the government's ears. As editor of the government magazine in which this anecdote was printed, Khushwant Singh knew what his employers wanted to read.

Plan-consciousness was a topic elected representatives and officials frequently and wishfully spoke of throughout the 1950s. On occasion, official pronouncements suggested that one of the achievements of the First Five-Year Plan, or the early years of planning in general, was that India was becoming Plan-conscious. Plan-consciousness – rather than the class-consciousness favoured by China and the Soviet Union – was considered the appropriate mental outlook for the citizens of a nation. That way, India could commit to a 'socialistic pattern of society' but explicitly denounce communism. As the First Five-Year Plan document put it, 'the basic premise of democratic planning is that society can develop as an integral whole and that the position which particular classes occupy at any given time . . . can be altered without reliance on class hatreds or the use of violence'.[2] In choosing Plan-consciousness, the government was implicitly suggesting it was better than class-consciousness. Though never explicitly stated, doing so enabled the government to validate the state architecture it controlled and also present a model of consciousness that could accommodate all citizens and rally them under a unifying banner. Presumably, those who were Plan-conscious would believe that the interests of all Indians were both in political and economic alignment. Where class-consciousness – like other forms of identity such as caste or ethnicity – drew lines of separation within society, Plan-consciousness was meant to erase those divisions.

What was the state's measure of this Plan-consciousness? Perhaps it was the extent to which Indians not only participated in the schemes of planned development, but also *volunteered* for them. Democratic planning did not depend on such voluntary efforts, but their existence reinforced the government's most lofty claims. One might assume that, in the official mind, such supposedly unbidden contributions to the Plans reflected elevated levels of Plan-consciousness. This was what motivated the government to assist in the creation of voluntary organizations of college students, ordinary citizens, and *sadhus* (ascetics). These oxymoronic entities – government-initiated voluntary organizations – represented a different facet of the democratic planning schemes discussed earlier. What distinguishes them is their voluntary nature, underlining the participatory claims of democratic planning.

This chapter explores those experiments and demonstrate the hollowness of this discourse's assertions about an organic Plan-consciousness. Rather than trying to ascertain levels of Plan-consciousness, the chapter studies some of the ways in which the state tried to engineer a specific mentality among citizens. The instances of Plan-volunteering analysed here are not representative of the public mood; they simply are the sites that demonstrate the greatest degree of public engagement with the Plans. It is an engagement explained, in large part, by the state nudging these experiments forward.

The secular, scientific language of planning often came undone in quite dramatic ways when it had to be packaged for mass consumption in an overwhelmingly religious country. Just a short distance away from the Planning Commission's warren of offices, the Ministry of Information and Broadcasting promoted the message of planned development through means that were drastically at odds with its otherwise technocratic tone. Given the nature of its audience, the Ministry found that sometimes the modern scientific language of planning had to be both packaged in indigenous cultural forms and hybridized with religious symbols, specifically Hindu ones. Planning had to shape-shift and submit to significant cultural mediation in order for it to appeal to Indians. Plan propaganda came to involve even Hindu ascetics, or *sadhus*, as carriers of the message. It forces us to question the presumed chasm between technocracy and tradition, and recalibrate our understanding of what we refer to as 'Nehruvian'. Moreover, the alliance between the government and *sadhus* reemphasizes the deep tension between technocratic and democratic planning, and the contortions inherent in pursuing them simultaneously.

University Planning Forums

Planners wanted the country's youth on their side. When the outlines of the First Five-Year Plan were being drawn up, the Planning Commission requested university vice-chancellors to ensure the circulation and discussion of the documents, ostensibly with a view to solicit ideas and suggestions before the Plan was finalized. As the first Plan was drawing to a close, the Deputy Minister for Planning, S. N. Mishra, decided that it was time to involve the university community in a more sustained dialogue with planners. As he later wrote in the pages of *Yojana*, it was regrettable that a 'considerable section of our educated men and women still seem to think that the Plan is largely the responsibility of the Government'.[3] This was a deplorable complacency because 'planning was too important a thing to be left to planners alone'. Insufficient Plan-consciousness, according to Mishra, was the outcome of politicians and intellectuals not explaining the problems of democratic planning to the populace. The issue was compounded when even college students were unfamiliar with the Plans. In the early 1950s, he ruefully noted, it was rare to find a copy of the First Five-Year Plan in a college. This was unacceptable. 'A generation of students, and that too a generation of students passing through a revolutionary period in a country's history, could not live in isolation and be ignorant of their historic role.'[4]

The proposed solution was planning forums in campuses across India. The Planning Commission wrote to university vice chancellors in August 1955 inviting them to establish University and College Planning Forums. An attempt to generate a 'much more intimate and continuing association of teachers and students with planning', these bodies were envisioned as the nuclei of informed discussion, debate, and recommendations about the Five-Year Plans.[5] Their purpose was to discuss problems relating to planning and 'bring to bear the latent capacity of teachers and students on their solution'.[6] To Nehru, planning forums were relevant because, 'It was not for some wise man at the top to impose his ideas on the country and insist on those being carried out' – despite that being a fair description of how planning actually functioned.[7] These forums were envisaged as not simply deliberative bodies, but also as voluntary organizations that would take initiative in developmental activities themselves. Assuring them that there would be two-way traffic between the Planning Commission and forums, Mishra promised close consideration of any worthy ideas that might emerge from the students.[8] It was hoped that officially initiated voluntary participation of this kind would prove a model for how to responsibly engage with the struggle for national development, both at the level of ideas and action.

Parliament House hosted a national conference of the Representatives of the Planning Forums in April 1956. Delegates from twenty-five universities and seventy separate planning forums were invited to discuss a draft of the Second Five-Year Plan. The roster of dignitaries in attendance included, among others, the prime minister, the Deputy Chairman of the Planning Commission, the finance minister, and the Minister for Planning. During the opening speech, Mishra extolled the virtues of democratic planning and spoke of how students and teachers were uniquely capable of contributing. In between speeches by a string of official heavyweights, the delegates got down to the business of discussing the Second Five-Year Plan. After wide-ranging conversations on unemployment and deficit financing, among other themes, the delegates made their way to Rashtrapati Bhavan, the sprawling sandstone complex, where the president granted them an audience.[9]

University Planning Forums began acquiring a bureaucracy and outlining their role in the months that followed. Close on the heels of the establishment of a Central Executive Committee, State Executive Committees sprouted in nine States, and regional conferences were set up. Apart from intellectual engagement with the Plans within campuses in the form of seminars, symposia, debates, and discussion, these forums were also presented with a more far-reaching agenda. Members were now expected to take neighbouring high schools under their wing and initiate teenagers into the discourse on development. Each forum was also asked to adopt a village in their vicinity. In rural outposts, they were to instil Plan-consciousness among villagers, conduct socio-economic surveys (based on schedules sent by the Planning Commission), and help rural citizens implement development programmes.[10] The Madras Veterinary College Planning Forum, for instance, assisted five villages on the outskirts of the city, introducing them to better methods of poultry keeping, dairy farming, farm planning, and marketing. Nine hundred staff and students visited the villages in batches of fifty over 3 days for discussions. They even trained fifty 'progressive farmers' in the management of large livestock enterprises.[11]

For National Plan Day – celebrated annually on 13 September – and National Plan Week, planning forums were offered grants to organize celebrations.[12] These included exhibitions, posters, film screenings, debates, elocution contests, dramas, kavi sammelans, or mushairas on

Plan subjects.[13] In addition, if planning forums really wanted to distinguish themselves, they could organize a Plan Information Centre, an adult literacy centre, or a night shelter for children. They sometimes also ran a small library of the planning literature made available to them in which they would display charts, diagrams, and tables depicting the progress of plans in India and elsewhere in the world.

A report on the National Plan Week celebrations in 1962 by the Planning Forum at Government Post-Graduate Basic Training College in the Himalayan town of Dharamsala gives us an idea of their activities. In the span of a week in November, its members delivered a series of lectures to other students on the phases of planning, the progress achieved in different fields, small savings schemes, the welfare of Dalits, and the importance of executing Plan schemes. On the final day, the forum collected charts and pamphlets on the Five-Year Plan from the local District Public Relations Officer to display and distributed them among students. In order to make sure their message was heard further afield, the Forum also organized a trip to the village of Bagli. With the help of the *sarpanch* (village headman) and the school headmaster, they gathered an audience of villagers and students at the local high school. The Forum lectured on the village uplift, small savings, the role *panchayats* could play in village reconstruction, and development in Kangra district. Another trip soon followed, this time to the village of Bandi. There, apart from speaking at the primary school on similar subjects, forum members also helped the students and teachers of the school to clean the school grounds and the village.[14]

Planning Forums were projected as organic institutions sprouting from India's peculiar trajectory in which democracy and economic transformation were braided by planning. Mishra described it as 'India's own answer to the dictates of a planned economy ... to attain a socialist pattern of society through peaceful means.'[15] Of course, they were not entirely organic, grafted as they were onto universities through government intervention. While claiming to be innovative spaces designed to make suggestions to the Planning Commission, the Forums appear to have effectively functioned more like debating clubs with an outreach programme. And while little came of the pretensions to participative planning, Planning Forums did make some headway with their publicity purpose, keeping the Five-Year Plans front and centre in the minds of India's educated youth. Beginning with seventy-two in 1956, there were around 1,000 planning forums a decade later, involving tens of thousands of students in their work.[16] The Planning Forum at St Stephen's College in Delhi – still in operation after being founded in 1960 by Nehru – owes its existence (and continuing policy focus) to this experiment in democratic planning.

Villagers Volunteer

Rights and benefits came with duties and obligations. The tight constraints of state capacity and the manner in which Indian citizenship was being defined by the government made voluntary participation by citizens essential. A Local Development Works Programme was launched in April 1953 as a way of addressing village infrastructural concerns through the 'direct participation of the people in the Plan'. New Delhi would pay up to half the cost of a village project, with the rest supplemented by state and local bodies. Labour was to emerge voluntarily from the villagers themselves. The projects typically included repairs to the village school, maintenance of irrigation facilities, or building a new bridge. On occasion, the funds were earmarked for student camps. Lasting 3 to 4 weeks, these camps were meant to bring school children face-to-face with the problems confronting the nation and instil in them the 'dignity of manual labour' and 'condition them emotionally and intellectually for their role in national development'. In its first year, forty-three such camps were organized in which more than 11,000 students participated.[17]

One of the more publicized instances of voluntary participation through this programme came from Etah district in Uttar Pradesh. It was, as a newspaper report put it, 'one of the foremost in the saga of organized self-help in post-independent India'. A tributary of the Ganga, the Kali (named for its twisting serpentine course) cut Etah into halves but had only one bridge over it. As a result, the only other way across the Kali was on a privately operated ferry that was now in a legal dispute. The inaccessibility of the eastern half of the district had led to some part of it, such as Aliganj tehsil, becoming notorious as a 'haven for dacoits' like the feared Girand Singh and Birey. It was said that not a day went by without the civil surgeon being called upon to conduct post mortems on their victims.

Two decades earlier, in the early 1930s, a 'far-sighted and altruistic' zamindar had tried to address this riverine isolation by proposing a bridge. He put up 20,000 rupees and collected another 18,000, but with the outbreak of World War II, the project headed nowhere. But in February 1952, villagers from Dhumri decided to revisit the idea and formed a cooperative society to build a bridge. When approached, the government offered 3.5 lakh rupees on the condition that the concerned villagers raise another 1.5 lakh. When the district planning committee set about this task, not only did the coin roll in – 'most of the contributions being in 1-anna donations from low-income people' – but they also floated a proposal for building two roads as part of the project. As the government had not sanctioned funds for these roads, the committee invited *shramdan* (a donation of labour) from the public. The response was enthusiastic. More than 50,000 people including 'politicians, lawyers, teachers, businessmen, peasants, students, officials' turned up over 6 weeks to be *shramdatas* (donors of labour). They came from over 600 villages in buses, lorries, creaky bullock carts, horse-drawn carriages, and on foot. Braving the cold, they slept in tin sheds or under trees, fuelled by their own rations of wheat and gram. They brought their pick-axes and shovels, and worked with the cry of 'Mahatma Gandhiji ki jai' [Hail Mahatma Gandhi] on their lips. As a newspaper reported: 'Basket by basket, earth has been thrown over what were formerly fertile fields of wheat, mustard, gram, and millets [the cultivator's lands having been paid for by the government] and ponds which were the haunts of ducks, storks and water-fowl.'[18]

According to engineers from the Public Works Department who collaborated in this undertaking, more than 2 million tons of earth had been moved through 50,000 man-days of voluntary work, at a cost of 50,000 rupees. If a private contractor had taken up the project, estimates suggested, it would have taken a year and cost twice the sum. A charismatic District Magistrate, Rajeshwar Prasad, led the government presence on-site. The young civil servant arrived at the site on a jeep, sporting leather jacket and scarf, offering encouragement and exhorting effort. Engulfed in the puffs of dust thrown by patriotic limbs at work, he would launch into song, with volunteers joining the chorus: 'Oh spade, dig away with music and gusto, we are born to serve the country.'[19]

The Bharat Sewak Samaj, or Service to India Society, emerged out of a proposal in a draft of the First Five-Year Plan.[20] Its primary backer was the Gulzarilal Nanda, the Deputy Chairman of the Planning Commission, who believed that everyone had 'something to offer in this Yagna [lit. Hindu religious offering]'.[21] The Planning Commission released a pamphlet formally introducing the Samaj in April 1952, and a couple of months later Nehru reiterated its relationship with the government when he wrote to chief ministers that it had been 'fathered' by the Planning Commission.[22] The Samaj's constitution was drafted by Nanda, and despite being 'non-official and non-political' it opportunely named Nehru its nominal president, Nanda its vice president, and received substantial funding from the Planning Commission.[23] Another Congress worker, Indira Gandhi, soon became the president of its Delhi wing.

The claim that the Samaj was a 'non-political' body was questioned from the very beginning by Congress's opponents who saw in it a means by which to keep the party's cadre mobilized. In fact, despite its proximity to the kind of 'constructive work' Gandhi advocated, Gandhians, such as J. C. Kumarappa and Vinobha Bhave did not care much for this supposedly non-governmental organization so closely associated with the government. An article in *Harijan*, Gandhi's journal, described the Samaj as a wholly Congress body that was instituted to promote the Five-Year Plans.[24] A year after its founding, scholar D. P. Mukerji observed that 'a number of people' believed that the Samaj's 'ultimate purpose is to strengthen the party in power'.[25] The criticism provoked a curt response from the prime minister who said that membership was open to all individuals: 'anybody who wants to take a spade and dig can dig'.[26]

The Bharat Sewak Samaj was a voluntary organization, but it was the government that had volunteered to establish it. However, if the origin story supplied by Nehru is to be believed, what tilted the scales was 'a surprisingly large number of letters coming to us enquiring about it and expressing a desire to join it'. Reading into this what it wished to believe, the government concluded, 'It was not something being imposed from above ... It was something that, perhaps, was supplying a want.'[27] The claim failed to convince sceptics. As sociologist D. P. Mukerji wrote: 'It almost seems that a people's instrument had to be devised ... for expiating the original sin of formulating the Plan mainly with the help of bureaucrats and with the last-minute suggestions of a few hand-picked leaders of other parties, and presenting it to the people as an accomplished fact.'[28]

The Samaj was meant to be 'the people's sector of the plan'.[29] Nanda made clear in another pamphlet that this was evidence of India's distance from totalitarian planning. It was also why he and the government ultimately brushed aside repeated suggestions about considering labour conscription in order to ensure citizen involvement.[30] The steadfast emphasis on voluntary participation clearly appealed to Western audiences. A front-page story in the *New York Times* took a veiled swipe at China and the USSR when it complimented the Samaj for its potential as 'a fitting challenge to dictatorial governments that force regimentation on people in executing their national plans'. The attractiveness of the Bharat Sewak Samaj was made clear in the title of the piece: 'Nehru Labor Plan Stresses Freedom.' The subtitle, for good measure, added: 'Would Use India's Manpower on Local, Voluntary Basis in Contrast to Police States.'[31]

The Samaj's logo was a tautly muscled man in loincloth, hands aloft, ready to strike down forcefully with a pickaxe. The image, celebrating the heroic volunteer, reflected the organization's emphasis on action and constructive work. The Samaj's brief was to educate people about the Plans, conduct local surveys for the purposes of bottom-up planning, participate in development projects, initiate anti-corruption and anti-adulteration drives, organize youth camps, and promote national savings.[32] When inaugurating different branches of the Samaj across the country, Nehru invoked Gandhi in calling for the creation of an 'atmosphere of work' in the nation.[33] Within 4 years of its inauguration, it had approximately 50,000 members and had opened branches in a large majority of the country's districts.[34]

One of the Bharat Sewak Samaj's biggest successes was the stream of volunteers it channelled towards the Kosi between 1955 and 1959. A river that descended from Tibet into Bihar, the Kosi had wreaked havoc for years as it flooded the plains through which it flowed. In the village of Nirmali, in January 1955, Bihar's Chief Minister Krishna Sinha inaugurated the construction of a dam and embankments on the 'river of sorrow'. As saffron robed priests chanted Vedic hymns, Sinha unveiled stone tablets marking the project's beginning. Similar ceremonies were performed in other villages that lay on the river's banks. The sight earlier that morning, a newspaper reported, was of a 'stream of villagers waving flags, playing music and dancing merrily with baskets on their heads ... braving the winter wind'. They commenced work to shouts of '*Kosi Maiya Ki Jai*' (Victory to Mother Kosi) and '*Kosi Yogna Safal Ho*' (May the Kosi Plan be a Success).[35]

The Bharat Sewak Samaj was instrumental in inspiring people to surrender land to build protective embankments and in eliciting *shramdan*, a donation of work. It even acted as a low-cost contractor, organizing paid labour through *gram panchayats* (village councils). Most of the people who contributed through their unremunerated labour were middle-class peasants, social workers, and students from high schools and colleges, including Bihar University. The volunteers were ferried from the railway station to the job site; once there, they were provided tools to work and thatched sheds to rest in. Music was played at work sites to lighten the load of unpaid manual labour, while radio sets and cinema shows offered entertainment in the sheds.[36] The embankment scheme was completed two years ahead of the projected timeline and at a significantly reduced the cost, down from the initial estimate of 11.5 crore to 6.5 crore rupees.[37] The overwhelming response at Kosi led to the Samaj pursuing and being awarded government contracts for similar work in other parts of the country, including on the Jamuna Bund in Delhi, the Nagarjuna Sagar in Hyderabad State, the Mahanadi Delta in Orissa, and the Chambal Project in Rajasthan.

Participation in the Samaj's activities is not direct evidence of public enthusiasm for the Plans. The motivations behind volunteering could have been numerous. They might have included unemployment, pressure from lower-level officials, or even desperation for vital infrastructure that the government had failed to provide. Regardless of the volunteers' reasons, across the country, the Samaj played a role in digging tanks and wells, laying roads, and constructing schools and dispensaries. In 1956, it was active in health and sanitation pursuits of 'about 2,000 villages and 100 towns'. And during the Indo-China war of 1962, their construction capabilities were even enlisted in building defence works on the border.

One of the health initiatives undertaken with particular verve at the Delhi branch of the Samaj was yoga. Begun in 1952, their Yoga Health Department published a book on *yogasanas* in Hindi and Urdu, and set up fifteen centres within four years. This included two centres for members of parliament, one for ministers, and two exclusively for women. Yoga had backers within Parliament. Gulzarilal Nanda believed that the 'Yogic system has immense potentialities for the physical, moral, and spiritual generation of the people'. The Speaker of the Lower House, A. S. Ayangar, agreed that 'these exercises contribute to peace of mind and mental and physical fitness'. At a function hosted at the prime minister's residence in August 1956, Nehru – himself a daily practitioner of yoga and *siraasanas* (headstands) – awarded diplomas to Yoga teachers and recommended that simple asanas be introduced in schools and colleges.[38]

Within the Bharat Sewak Samaj, mass contact and publicity were the responsibility of the Jan Jagran Vibhag (People's Awakening Department).[39] It was through this department that the Samaj began receiving grants from the government in 1953. They circulated brochures, launched a monthly journal called Bharat Sewak in several languages, and spread their message through song, dramas, mushairas, and bhajans.[40] The nodes of this endeavour were Jan Sahyog Kendras (Public Cooperation Centres) and a cadre of volunteer *pracharaks* (messengers).

In order to direct the Samaj towards the most pressing matters, numerous Lok Karya Kshetras (People's Work Zones) were established in 1958. Focused on the successful implementation of the government's Community Development programmes, each zone was assigned two or three Samaj workers who were paid through government grants to act as 'catalytic agents'. Trained centrally by the Samaj in Delhi for three months, the *sahyogies* (helpers) were all expected to foster local leadership in the villages where they worked to build a band of voluntary workers. Each *kshetra* or zone comprised 100 villages and the *sahyogies* began by working with ten villages, gradually scaling upwards.[41] The activities in which they were engaged reflected the goals of Community Development: increasing food production, promoting health, sanitation and education, strengthening *panchayats* and community centres, encouraging maternity health and children's welfare, construction works, and even *sadachar nirman* (character building). By 1966, there were 184 Lok Karya Kshetras entirely funded by the central government, and more than 200 jointly sponsored with the states.[42]

Holy Men, Worldly Job

A temple in Delhi to the god Vishnu and goddess Lakshmi hosted an unusual meeting on 19 February 1956. Ministers, parliamentarians, and fifty holy men gathered at Birla Mandir around a curious idea.[43] They were discussing a proposal for *sadhus* – Hindu ascetics who have renounced family and materialism for austere spirituality – to offer their services to the Five-Year Plans.

It is not clear whether the suggestion germinated in government or among the holy men. According to one prominent *sadhu*, Tukdoji Maharaj, he had been present at prior conversations about this with the president, the prime minister, the Minister of Planning, and Gandhian social reformers Vinoba Bhave and Kakasaheb Kalelkar.[44] Politicians apart, even the ascetics needed to be convinced. As Tukdoji Maharaj wrote in a book addressed to other *sadhus*, 'Now that the people are ours, the government is ours, the Five Year Plan is ours ... why should we remain distant [from the work of the government]?'[45]

The Bharat Sadhu Samaj (Indian Society of Ascetics) received enthusiastic backing from religiously minded national figures such as President Rajendra Prasad and, especially, the Minister for Planning, Gulzarilal Nanda. Apart from helping establish it, Nanda would subsequently serve as chairman of its central advisory committee.[46] According to Swami Anand, the organization's first secretary, it was the planning minister who persuaded him to join the Samaj.[47] So close was Nanda to this venture that a cartoon in *Shankar's Weekly* months after the Birla Mandir meeting depicted the Minister of Planning *as* a *sadhu* – bare-chested, ribs protruding, loin-clothed, hair bound in a top-knot.[48]

Official interest in recruiting *sadhus* was predicated on the belief that unlike distant government functionaries and town-bred volunteers, these holy men – numbering in the millions according to the 1951 census – could convey the Plans to the unlettered and religious millions in familiar idioms. In his speech at the Birla temple, Nanda spoke of the influence *sadhus* wielded and asked them to create an upsurge in favour of the Second Five-Year Plan. Soon after, he recommended that *sadhus* organize themselves into a formal society, which became the *Bharat Sadhu Samaj*. The document announcing its birth decried India's drift

Figure 5.1. 'Food For Thought'. Timed to coincide with Nehru presenting the Second Five-Year Plan to Parliament, it depicts Gulzarilal Nanda as a *sadhu*. Nehru is the waiter and V. T. Krishnamachari is holding the 'Plan Menu'. On the left, lined up as chefs, are C. D. Deshmukh (bottom left) and P. C. Mahalanobis (third from left). Cartoon by Shankar in *Shankar's Weekly* (20 May 1956).

towards materialism under colonial rule, and urged the country's holy men and women to 'help a free government and a free people'.[49] Tukdoji Maharaj, the spiritual leader presiding over the meeting, implored those in attendance to blend devotional practices with national development and preach the message of work to their vast following.[50]

Following the temple gathering, the fifty ascetics representing the newly formed Bharat Sadhu Samaj paid a visit to Rashtrapati Bhavan. While the President of India is usually the person conferring distinctions on Indian citizens, the roles were reversed this time. The *sadhus* bestowed on President Rajendra Prasad the title of '*Sant*' (saint) while chanting sacred Sanskrit mantras. They sprinkled in some flattery as well, likening the President of India to King Dasharatha from the *Ramayana*, and themselves to the sages who advised the legendary royal court in Ayodhya.[51] The mutual regard was no surprise. An uncompromisingly religious man, Rajendra Prasad had only a few years earlier deferentially washed the feet of 200 Brahmin priests in Benares, anointing their foreheads with sandalwood paste, garlanding them, and handing each

11 rupees in *dakshana*.[52] He had also inaugurated the rebuilding of the Somnath temple (attacked during medieval raids by Mahmud of Ghazni and Alauddin Khilji) despite the prime minister expressing alarm about the President associating himself with a sensitive religious symbol while the wounds of Partition were still raw. Like the Planning Minister, India's first President was not bashful about appearing to be a patron of Hindu causes.

Even before Independence, the Congress Party had associated with Hindu symbols, festivals, and *sadhus* while overtly espousing secularism. For instance, hundreds of Naga (warrior) *sadhus* attended the 1920 Congress session at Nagpur, where they promised to help fulfil Gandhi's non-cooperation agenda. Gandhi personally thanked them and requested that they take the message to military bases and cantonments to convince Indian recruits in the colonial army to resign.[53] William Gould's study of the Congress Party in the United Provinces from the 1930s shows that the party's secularism was deeply ambiguous. Nehru's secularism was not always symmetrical with that of other Congress leaders in the northern Hindi belt. Several Congress leaders, such as Sampurnanand and Purushottam Das Tandon in particular, routinely employed Hindu idioms and symbolism in a manner reminiscent of the Hindu Mahasabha and Arya Samaj. This could take the form of invoking Hindu epics through public religious rituals like the Kumbh Mela, or harnessing *sadhus* to spread the Congress' anticolonial message. For instance, Sampurnananad – who would become chief minister of Uttar Pradesh in the 1950s – believed in the possibility of a Vedantic socialism. 'Socialism', he would write, 'is the logical outcome of shankara's advaita [non-dualism].'[54] To Congressmen like him, economic and scientific progress did not mean the decline of religion in public life, as it did in Europe.

In independent India, the saga of the Sadhu Samaj illustrates the lengths to which Plan publicity went, the difficulties inherent in tying together technocratic planning with its democratic imperative, and the unlikely pairings this produced. The secular logic of Five-Year Plans was dressed in spiritual robes and disseminated through a religious vehicle, driven by men and women who embodied material renuncia-tion. This episode, with its ripples through politics in the ensuing decades, offers a different vantage from which to observe the enmeshing of politics and religion in modern India. The presumed secular dis-course of planning was pried open by the Congress government to admit the participation of Hindu ascetics in the process of Plan propagation. Once granted official legitimacy, however, the Congress party would find it difficult to control the *sadhus* who had their own commitments to controversial issues like cow protection and building a Hindu temple at the site of a medieval mosque in Ayodhya. In this instance, it was the Congress Party that knotted the secular and sacred, a gamble that eventually redounded to the benefit of its biggest rival, the BJP.

The Bharat Sadhu Samaj's recipe, combining spiritual and material, proved irresistible to the American press. It played into the stereotype of India as an exotic ancient land and offered a lurid drama of a new nation scrambling to be modern when straddling several centuries simultaneously. The *New York Times'* India correspondent, A. M. Rosenthal, reported a piece titled 'India's Holy Men Get Worldly Job: Wandering Sadhus Asked to Say a Good Word for Goals of the 2nd Five-Year Plan'. The point, he reported, was to have hundreds of thousands of *sadhus* 'put in a good word wherever they go for the goals of the five year plan'.[55] Even the modest *Battle Creek Enquirer* from Michigan reported that India's Planning Minister was trying to 'shake this country's half million Hindu holy men out of their spiritual world into the material world of five-year development plans'.[56] These pieces often included detailed sketches of *sadhus'* appearance, their life, and explanations of their alleged abilities. R. K. Narayan, already a writer of international renown, explained in the pages of the *New York Times* that *sadhus* occupied an exalted position in Indian society. 'He can stand anywhere and ask for food and money: may live in the veranda of any public building or even private house without having anyone ask who he is, much less ask him to move on.' These were their privileges. But their responsibilities, he added, extended only to prayer and meditation. While the article's tone was sceptical, Narayan also wrote about the 'magical prowess' the ascetics seemed to wield. One had a grown Bengal tiger following him like a pet, without so much as a leash. When asked about the docile beast, the holy man explained that the obedient tiger was simply the reincarnation of a deceased disciple.[57]

Two months after the inaugural temple meeting, 500 holy men gathered on the banks of the Ganga, at Rishikesh, on the auspicious occasion of the Ardh Kumbh Mela. A reporter for the *Washington Post* observed that 'India's shaven-headed, saffron-robed Sadhus (Holy Men) are to help preach the virtues of the five-year plan to the people ... They have decided to leave the isolated retreats where they lead lives of renunciation and meditation to support national development.' Those pledging their support to the Plans included, 'Sadhus from the south, semi-naked saints from Himalayan caves, ash smeared wandering mendicants with their begging bowls and the heads of famous hermitages in the Himalayas'. The reporter explained to his American audience that among them were some of the brightest minds in the country – lawyers, engineers, doctors, and professors – who had renounced their families, professional lives, and the comforts of the world for a life of meditation.[58] R. K. Narayan noted that when in Benares he was occasionally taken aback by a *sadhu* addressing him in fluent English. Upon further query, 'one may find an ex-Cambridge scholar or an ex-secretary to the Government' who had now shed such worldly associations.[59]

The government's involvement with this band of holy men did not go unnoticed in Parliament. Bhakt Darshan, a writer and Congress MP, sarcastically asked the Planning Minister in Hindi if the Sadhu Samaj was an official fundraising enterprise. Was the aim 'for Indian citizens to take inspiration from these *sadhus,* adopt lives of hardship and austerity, so that they could save money and contribute to programmes of national development?' Another Congress parliamentarian, Mulla Abdullabhai, asked if there was to be a Muslim equivalent of this body. Would, for example, *maulvis* [Islamic scholars] also be asked to help through a joint 'Bharat Sadhu Maulvi Samaj?' Another member, the left-wing Hari Vishnu Kamath, raised an important concern: what assurance could the Congress Party provide that the Bharat Sadhu Samaj would not be used for partisan 'political propaganda ... especially as the vote-catching season approaches?' Each expressed worries that would be repeatedly raised about the Bharat Sadhu Samaj. How exactly were ascetics to help in the Five-Year Plans? Was not it dangerous to link economic policy with a Hindu religious organization? And, did not the close relationship between certain Congress politicians and the Samaj render it a quasi-political arm?[60]

There were 7.5-million *sadhus* in India, according to the census. Of these, a majority was widely believed to be faking it.[61] Acknowledging the problem, the Bharat Sadhu Samaj made efforts to ensure that only genuine *sadhus* could join their organization: only those known by a member of the Sadhu Samaj could be proposed for membership. Even among them, the Central Executive Committee would grant membership only after a thorough review of the *sadhu's* past beliefs and his activities from the time 'he first renounced the world'. The programme they adopted in service of the Plans involved the following: promoting education, encouraging the purchase of government bonds and savings instruments, imparting spiritual training through prayer meetings, preventing diseases through yogic exercises and Ayurveda, encouraging voluntary gifts of land, wealth, and labour (*bhoodan, sampattidan,* and *shramdan*), prohibition, preventing corruption, encouraging village industries, and caring for cattle.[62]

The president of the Bharat Sadhu Samaj told the press in late June 1956 that they had launched a mass-awakening programme for the success of the Plan. It also requested a grant of 15 crore rupees from the government to be used for constructive activities and propaganda towards the Second Plan.[63] Two months later, Gulzarilal Nanda managed to usher the Sadhu Samaj's representatives into the Prime Minister's office for a meeting.[64] That December, they convened an All-India *Sadhu Sammelan* in Rajasthan; a 1,000 holy men and women gathered in Nathdwara, an ancient town ringed by hills. Predictably, Gulzarilal Nanda opened the meeting and messages of goodwill poured in from politicians including Nehru, K. M. Munshi, and Morarji Desai. The prime minister's message expressed his happiness about the Bharat Sadhu Samaj taking part in the work of national reconstruction: 'In this way much assistance could be given for the success of the Five Year Plan.'[65]

Next winter, President Prasad addressed a 3-day conference of the Bharat Sadhu Samaj in Ahmedabad. Speaking to the 1,000 holy men who had gathered under a giant colourful tent, he expounded on the *sadhus'* capacity for setting off a countrywide moral regeneration. In keeping with India's ancient traditions, he said, spiritual advancement had to be synthesized with worldly progress as well. 'You need hardly be told that there is an intimate relationship between the world we live in and "parlok," the world we strive for', he began. 'It is not possible to achieve anything in the other world without settling things in order in this world ... our scriptures do not enjoin indifference towards this world.'[66] The president was conjuring a portal between the mortal realm and the immortal beyond, by way of participation in the Five-Year Plans.

There had been protests in the prelude to this conference in Ahmedabad. The local Harijan Social Welfare Committee had requested the Sadhu Samaj to partner in the battle against caste discrimination and the outlawed practice of untouchability. Their specific ask was for the conference of ascetics to formally include 'mixed dinners for caste Hindus and Harijans (Dalits)' on its programme. As the most respected within the Hindu fold, the *sadhus* could certainly have played a special role in dismantling caste. But it appears that the Sadhu Samaj – a body of mostly upper caste Hindu men – found the hard limits of their commitment to nation-building at this precise point. In protest, the Harijan Committee decided to employ Gandhian methods of protest by launching a *satyagraha* in which they peacefully picketed the Samaj's Ahmedabad office to 'endeavour a change of heart through continuous singing of Bhajans [Hindu devotional songs]'.[67]

When the Sadhu Samaj made plans to build their New Delhi headquarters in Chanakyapuri's Diplomatic Enclave, on government-allotted land at a projected cost of 5 lakh rupees ($100,000), both the president and vice-president of India were present to officiate over the foundation ceremonies.[68] J. B. Kripalani saw the influence of Gulzarilal Nanda behind the Samaj being granted this plot. The Praja Socialist Party leader would lament the sort of ascetics who traded their humble '*kutiyas*' (huts) in order to move into a 'palatial house' in the Delhi's 'most fashionable quarters'.[69] The link to the government and ruling party was so evident that the Hindu Mahasabha dismissively referred to those in the Bharat Sadhu Samaj as 'Congress sadhus'.[70]

Repeated cries of 'Congress sadhus' notwithstanding, the party's and government's relationship with these Hindu ascetics was complicated. While the country's religiously minded president and Minister for Planning were wholehearted believers in the *sadhus*' potential, others looked askance. Nehru's own view of them was dim at best, and his relationship with them had been testy. During independent India's first general elections, Nehru's primary opponent in his constituency was Prabhu Dutt Brahmachari, a bearded *sadhu* who had sworn a religious vow of silence years before. Though the nationalist icon triumphed handily, this silent challenger had drawn large crowds and made enough of an impression for Nehru to return to Allahabad from his national campaign for the Congress to protect his own seat in Parliament.[71] Nehru publicly upbraided sadhus as a group for including many fakes who were 'lazy rascals'. He regarded the impostors as spongers and parasites who took on the saffron robe and begging bowl merely as a costume, to avoid honest work.[72] This was not an isolated opinion. As R. K. Narayan put it, it was impossible to distinguish between *sadhus* and shams. Those calling themselves *sadhus* included 'acrobats, alchemists, fortune tellers, quacks, members of outlandish cults (who may be fit for Freudian studies), conjurors and illusionists'.[73]

Just months after the Bharat Sadhu Samaj was formed, the Sadhus Registration Bill was tabled in Parliament, in November 1956. It called for all of India's holy men and women to be registered and licensed or face the threat of going to jail for up to 2 years for impersonating real *sadhus*. It accused some *sadhus* and *sanyasis* of using the 'guise of saintly order' to indulge in 'vices, begging and other anti-social activities . . . which, if not checked, will help the crime incidence to increase unabated'. The movers of the bill included two Congressmen, including Feroze Gandhi. It required *sadhus* to write to the local magistrate to secure a license and be recorded on a national register of verified *sadhus*.[74] As the *New York Times* reported, the ascetics struggled to know from month to month whether the Government will 'scold them for laziness and begging or praise them as leaders and organize them in the name of planned economy'.[75] Though the bill did not pass the legislature (partly due to Sadhu Samaj opposition), it nonetheless attests to the antipathy felt towards *sadhus* by several members of Parliament.[76]

Fuelling this sentiment were numerous reports throughout the late 1950s about self-sanctified charlatans who donned the saffron robes of *sadhus*. These incidents included the arrest of a *sadhu* from the Aghori sect in Macchiwara (Punjab) for eating the flesh of a cremated body; the arrest of several holy men for kidnapping children; and an episode where a self-styled *sadhus* 'set himself up in a fortress castle in Eastern India with a vast collection of kidnapped women. When the police arrived, they were set upon by an army of believers trained in archery and stone-throwing. Tear gas finally broke the resistance'.[77] The Bharat Sadhu Samaj found these incidents and the pressure from civil society threatening enough to issue identity cards to all its members and other genuine *sadhus*, in order to stanch the guilt by association.

Gulzarilal Nanda took a brighter view of *sadhus*, trusting that the unsavoury individuals were wild outliers. This was a man who fondly recalled his devout grandfather's reverence for *sadhus*. As a child he had accompanied his grandfather in receiving blessings from *sadhus* who passed through the village, arranging for their food, and inviting them home for esoteric discussions on the finer aspects of Hindu spirituality.[78] Amenable to saintly persuasion, he was ripe for the Sadhu Samaj's picking. Nanda believed that *sadhus* could serve the Plan through their legitimacy in the eyes of India's overwhelmingly religious and Hindu population. The Sadhu Samaj's use of religious language, iconography, and personnel affirmed the predilections of its most powerful backer.

Tall, gaunt, moustachioed, and bespectacled in dark tortoise shell, Nanda cut an austere figure with a reputation for stern probity. The severity was evident in his diet of milk, fruit, boiled vegetables, and nuts, and the uprightness in the anecdote of him scolding a grandson for using official stationery. A satirical column in *Shankar's Weekly* described him unkindly as a prim, humourless man from whom 'Gloom drips'; someone who had led a 'hectic political life of unbrilliance'.[79] Nanda's politics was an idiosyncratic combination of a modernizing drive and traditionalist impulse. The one-time professor of economics, trade unionist, and life-long Gandhian was also an orthodox Hindu who frequently consulted an astrologer named Haveli Ram and associated himself with causes such as cow protection and an Institute of Spiritual and Psychic Research. In his parliamentary Member's Profile, Nanda listed 'Yogic culture and religious studies' under special interests.[80]

The eccentric fusion of socialist planner and *sadhu* promoter quickly became part of Nanda's public image, repeatedly referenced in political cartoons. In one, Nanda is shown on a stage wearing a loose robe and passionately preaching – hand aloft, eyes bulging, and mouth agape, reading from a Plan scroll that rolled down to the floor. Beside him, heads bowed and also enrobed, are Nehru and V. T. Krishnamachari, Chairman and Deputy Chairman of the Planning Commission. In the audience, people look up in reverence, hands joined in prayer. It was titled 'The Oracle of Delphi', but with the 'p' crossed out. The cartoonist was invoking the classical Greek shrine that the ancients believed connected the world of men to that of the gods, whose priestesses offered often cryptic answers to the questions that mortals travelled from far and wide to pose. It was no surprise that Nanda, the most high-profile backer of the Bharat Sadhu Samaj, would be likened to Pythia, Delphi's high priestess.

Figure 5.2. Gulzarilal Nanda delivers a sermon. On stage with him are Nehru and deputy chairman of the Planning Commission, V. T. Krishnamachari. Cartoon by Shankar in *Shankar's Weekly* (27 March 1960).

A believer in the occult, Nanda's private papers indicate that he was in touch with someone going by 'Gurudev' who claimed to be in communication with Nanda's deceased father through a mysterious medium based at an ashram in Ranchi. The notes are quite extraordinary. A handwritten letter in the summer 1963 began in the following manner: 'I am Gurudev. Oh my sincear devoteey Gulzari Lall. I am your life and I am of your everything. I am omnipotent. What you do I see everything ... you will feel my presence during your prayer time.' Gurudev sent messages on matters grand and granular, ranging from the Kashmir dispute to the Nanda family's health, all the while directing the minister to perform *pujas* (religious offerings).[81] In one letter, 3 weeks after Nehru's death, Gurudev wrote that the medium had not been able to get in touch with Nanda, now the prime minister of India. Bemoaning the delay, Gurudev wrote, 'Alass! Otherwise Neheru would have been saved by this sudden attack.'

If people are to be judged by the company they keep, then the *New York Times* was fair in describing Nanda as 'a socialist, a vegetarian, and a bit of a mystic'.[82] *Shankar's Weekly* explained that Nanda was 'doubly solemn' because he was 'socialist and sadhu'. The column continued sarcastically: 'Imagine the mental strain in washing the feet of a thousand Brahmins and then go on to talk of perspective planning.'[83] L. M. Singhvi, an independent parliamentarian, found Nanda to be moved by seemingly contradictory impulses. He 'has a touch both of the yogi and the commissar. He has a bit of the Sadhu Samaj and a bit of the Congress Socialist Forum: a bit of astrology and a bit of planning'.[84] To Nanda, the material could not be separated from the social and spiritual. Economic development was but a mode of national spiritual regeneration. It was a different way of abstracting the economy: while technocrats like Mahalanobis saw the economy in statistical schedules and input-output tables, Nanda and the Sadhu Samaj saw the economy as belonging on a continuum with the spiritual. It is another measure of the distance that could separate technocratic planning from democratic planning.

Nehru was not well disposed towards the Sadhu Samaj. In late 1958, he wrote to the Deputy Chairman of the Planning Commission regarding papers sent to him by the Bharat Sadhu Samaj. He expressed doubts about relying on the Sadhu Samaj for the kinds of work they suggested, and about assisting them in setting up central offices. The prime minister had misgivings about those who merely dressed as *sadhus* to cheat the public ('a very bad lot'). Large funds were also being 'misused by mahants [monks] and their maths [monasteries]'. He cautiously recommended asking Nanda for his advice and concluded that the Sadhu Samaj might serve a purpose. However, it 'would not [be] a good thing for the Sadhu Samaj to become an agent of Government'.[85]

By the next summer, however, Nehru had been convinced by Nanda to address a convention of the Bharat Sadhu Samaj. On a Sunday afternoon in May at the Ramlila grounds, following a lavishly complimentary intro-duction by Tukdoji Maharaj, the prime minister addressed a gathering of four hundred holy men. The ascetics sat cross-legged on the ground as the prime minister spoke. 'Some wore turbans and others came clean shaven. Some had covered their bodies in ashes, with marigold garlands around their necks. Some wore nothing but loin-cloths and others were in saf-fron-dyed robes'.[86] A spectacle befitting the 'sadhu tradition of rugged individualism', declared another international news report. The very existence of a professional organization for sadhus was a wonder, it continued, given that they represented the 'world's most outlandish collection of individualists'.[87]

Nehru began by asking his audience to ignore the introduction given by the Samaj's president about him: 'they get carried away by their love for me and say all sorts of exaggerated things'. He proceeded to explain why he was, and had been, hesitant to speak at this event. As a member of the government, Nehru explained, he did not know if it was appropriate to associate with a religious body. Furthermore, while there were certainly 'some great men among our *sadhus*', there were others whom 'it would be difficult to even call human beings'. This harsh judgment was based on rumours of *sadhus*, or those adopting the look of *sadhus*, 'abducting small children and whatnot'. In another prolix *ex tempore* speech, Nehru expounded to the *sadhus* on atomic energy, Five-Year Plans, inter-faith harmony, and changes in modes of transportation over centuries.[88] The prime minister's ramble received an ovation and the Samaj's president assured Nehru that his members would carry 'the new gospel of social, economic and moral reform' to every village in India.[89]

Not everyone could pretend that this *neta-baba* alliance was business as usual. As a contemporary political scientist noted, the Planning Minister's involvement in a scheme to use *sadhus* to push the Five-Year Plans in villages 'evoked much merriment among the cartoonists of the Indian press'.[90] In the *Times of India*, R. K. Laxman caricatured the minister learning complex subjects – foreign aid, inflation, deficit finan-cing – from a *sadhu*.[91] In another, Laxman portrayed an exasperated government official who had just realized after hours of discussing policy that the dishevelled, sparsely dressed, bearded man he had plied with several cups of tea was not a representative of the Sadhu Samaj. He was instead a beggar, looking for some coins.[92] O. V. Vijayan produced a cartoon that mocked Nehru for his speech at the Sadhu Samaj conference in which he said that *sadhus* had a great role to play in nation-building. The image showed Nehru looking like a *sadhu*, stripped down to only a loincloth and Gandhi cap. Imitating the feats that *sadhus* perform, this ascetic Nehru walks on a path of sharp nails while incongruently holding images of technological modernity – a satellite and the symbol of the atom – in his hands. Foreigners, dressed to the nines, watch and laugh.[93] In yet another cartoon, Shankar drew both Nehru and Nanda dressed as holy men. Wearing only loincloths, they were leading a march of ascetics. The caption read: 'Nehru has associated himself with Sadhu Samaj.' It ended with a question: 'For whose salvation?'[94]

Cartoonists apart, other citizens were also taken aback by Nehru warming to the Bharat Sadhu Samaj. To some it suggested a capitulation on the principle of state secularism. The *Times of India* editorial board bristled at the 'confused thinking' that was behind inviting *sadhus* to participate in scientific nation-building. *Sadhus* by definition, it reminded readers, were meant to be detached from the world. Asking them to help in nation-building was antithetical to their fundamental pursuit. The editorial questioned the wisdom of providing 'official blessing' to values that were 'so clearly out of tune with the spirit of the times'. It was a mistake to partner with *sadhus* in the task of development when doctors and engineers remained unemployed. The nation, it sarcastically continued, seemingly had no use for them. Not bothering to conceal its contempt, the editorial suggested that the government would be better served by focusing on aspiring professionals rather than on a 'class of people not far removed in the aggregate from positive parasitism'. The piece did not spare the Congress Party. It would only be a matter of time, it suggested, before the *sadhus* expressed their gratitude for this patronage by helping out in election campaigns. That possibility could not have escaped the government's notice.[95] R. Mani, a concerned citizen in Calcutta, wrote to his newspaper to express displeasure at the 'surprising spectacle' of the prime minister 'hobnobbing with sadhus'. Mr Mani feared that the involvement of Nehru and Nanda in the affairs of the Bharat Sadhu Samaj portended a 'reversal of the secular policy of the Government'. What were the terms of this partnership, he asked. Were *sadhus* willing to stick to the government's secularism? And, could they be trusted not to betray religious biases in their activities?[96] Questions that, perhaps, Mr Mani's government should have been asking all along.

The career of the inaugural president of the Bharat Sadhu Samaj – singer-songwriter-saint Tukdoji Maharaj – offers a telling example of the kinds of individuals whom the Indian government partnered with to promote Five-Year Plans. He was born in 1909 as Manik Ingle in the village of Yavali, in the Amravati district of Vidarbha. When barely 8 years old, Manik drew attention in his own and neighbouring villages for his ability to sing devotional songs accompanied by the *khanjiri* (tambourine). Revealing a spiritual bent at a very young age, Manik abandoned formal schooling to be a disciple of the spiritual guru Aadkoji Maharaj. He spent his days in meditation and worship of Shiva, and even left his village to meditate in forests. As word of his melodious voice and compositional ability spread, he was invited to perform *bhajans* and lead *kirtans* in villages across Vidarbha. He would stay at a temple, or on the outskirts of the village, surviving on scraps of food. This is how, according to some accounts, he earned the name 'Tukdoji' (from *tukada*, 'piece'). Another version suggests that the name cropped up earlier in boyhood, bestowed by his spiritual mentor while feeding him a piece (*tukada*) of roti. When he emerged from self-imposed forest exile, he quickly acquired a following which bestowed him with the title Sant Tukdoji Maharaj.

In his early twenties, he often interspersed spiritual hymns with nationalist songs, and in 1935, Gandhi – whose Sevagram ashram was only 100 kilometres from Tukdoji Maharaj's – asked him to visit. The association with Gandhi would lead to Tukdoji Maharaj developing a national profile. On the day they first met, Gandhi was observing one of his days of silence. However, such was the sway of Tukdoji Maharaj's voice, that Gandhi was soon requesting songs of him and breaking his silence. The *sant* stayed at Sevagram for a month, sharing a small room with the Mahatma, learning the tenets of Gandhian philosophy from the master, and treating him to *bhajans*. A few years later Tukdoji Maharaj, now a committed Gandhian, would participate in the Quit India movement of 1942, using his tunes to invigorate villagers in Vidarbha.[97] After independence, he became a vociferous ally of the Gandhian social reformer Vinoba Bhave, using his talents to advocate Bhave's message of *bhoodan* (gifts of land) and land reform. In 1949, Rajendra Prasad bestowed upon him the unofficial title of '*Rashtrasant*' or National Saint. The now walrus-moustached Sant Tukdoji Maharaj would become the first president of the Bharat Sadhu Samaj. Despite the prime minister's qualms, they met on multiple occasions and Tukdoji Maharaj performed at several functions in which Nehru was present. He supported the Five-Year Plans and its message of national development through such sermons and songs as, 'Let's go back to our villages, let's not live in the city', and 'Farmers and villagers, let's become socially educated.'[98]

In a life brimming with contradictions, Tukdoji Maharaj would become, at various points, an advocate for world peace and somehow also a supporter of using nuclear weapons in wars against China and Pakistan. It was a striking *volte face* given that the Bharat Sadhu Samaj had, under his leadership, written a letter to Nikita Khruschev, Dwight

Eisenhower, Harold MacMillan, Chou-En-Lai, and Dag Hammarskjold beseeching them to 'save humanity' by halting the manufacture of atomic weapons.[99] And, in another detail that speaks volumes about the Bharat Sadhu Samaj's ideological tendencies, Tukdoji Maharaj would become one of the founding vice-presidents of the Vishwa Hindu Parishad (World Hindu Council), a far right Hindu nationalist organization committed to strengthening Hindu society and claiming to protect the Hindu Dharma.

Just as with the Bharat Sadhu Samaj, in the course of the Bharat Sewak Samaj's *Jan Jagran* (People's Awakening) activities, planning would come to be associated with contexts and people who could not have been further from the secular high-modernist technocracy in Yojana Bhavan. There were numerous instances in which the message packaged by the Planning Commission was not the one delivered to citizens. In some cases of straightforward fraud, development was entirely jettisoned by the Samaj in favour of other, less worldly interests. A commission of enquiry found that the Samaj used most of the grants meant for publishing brochures relating to development 'for bringing out reprints of some novels and short stories from religious books'. As the commission noted, this was 'a mis-utilization of the grants given for Plan Publicity and not subserving (*sic*) the ideals of a secular State'.[100] But this wasn't by any means the sole instance of it straying from secularism. More flagrant examples were to be found in the *vyas sammelans* (gatherings of Hindu ascetics) organized by the Bharat Sewak Samaj.

The first such assembly of holy men and women was in Allahabad in January 1960 on the occasion of the Ardh Kumbh Mela.[101] Organized by the Samaj, these meetings received funds from the Ministry of Information and Broadcasting. Later that year, in December, there was another three-day *Vyas Sammelan* in Pawai (near Bombay). Inaugurated by Jaisukhlal Hathi, Deputy Union Minister for Power and Irrigation, the gathering was billed as a way to discuss the 'means of creating greater consciousness among the people in the rural areas about the various welfare schemes and the Third Five-Year Plan'. Despite both these meetings being judged failures, the Samaj convinced the government to fund a third *Vyas Sammelan*, this time coinciding with the Kumbh Mela in Haridwar between March and April 1962. In their appeal to the government, the Bharat Sewak Samaj pointed out that the Kumbh Mela was expected to attract more than 2 million Hindus, presenting a ripe opportunity for Plan publicity. They reminded the government that the 'the hold of religious preachers on the minds of the masses is still strong' and that the 'importance of utilizing Vyases to arouse among the people a feeling of self-consciousness and self-reliance has been accepted by the Planning Commission in unequivocal terms'. Holding a *sammelan* and training camp for ascetics would, therefore, serve the purpose of 'bringing in a good number of Vyases under the fold of the Bharat Sewak Samaj and utilize them for Plan publicity work'.[102]

The government granted funds for a *vyas'* training camp and a *vyas sammelan* on the condition that it was coordinated with the local Field Publicity Office and that it be 'effective from the point of view of Plan publicity'.[103] The sixty-three vyases undergoing training were 'Katha and Kirtankars' (storytellers and devotional singers), men and women hailing from different parts of northern India. Sant Panchlegaonkar Maharaj opened the training camp on 17 March, 1962 at four p.m. in the afternoon. After 2 minutes of silence followed by songs of prayer, the trainees had the purpose of the camp impressed upon them. As custodians of India's cultural heritage, Panchlegaonkar said, they could be of invaluable help in the promotion of development activities and Plan publicity. Their routine involved waking up at five, praying, doing yoga, hoisting the national flag, *shramdan* (a donation of labor), studying, *kirtan*s (religious songs), and *kathas* (religious stories). Their Ministry-approved syllabus included lectures on subjects such as '3rd Five-Year Plan and upliftment of the country through them' and 'Responsibilities of Vyases and their programme for National development activities'. Less topically, they were also lectured on 'Faith and devotion for Motherland in Vedic Age' and 'The concept of Hindu religion is based on universal laws.'[104]

The chief guest at the Third All India *Vyas Sammelan*, in 1962, was once again Gulzarilal Nanda. He gave a speech in which he hoped that the ascetics would 'effectively contribute their might for the glory of our National Development'. The session was also attended by the impressively titled Mahamandaleshwara Shri Swami Shukdevananda ji Maharaj of Hrishikesh, among 'many other saints and learned scholars of high repute'. There were daily discourses on religious epics, such as the *Ramayana*, *Bhagavad Gita*, and *Durga Saptshati* at the Samaj's stall at the Kumbh Mela. All of this was capped off with a Vishnu *yajna* (sacrificial ritual for the Hindu deity Vishnu) in which Gulzarilal Nanda participated. There were so many religious personages at the event that the government's Field Publicity Section had to borrow three *sadhus* to perform at their own camp in the Kumbh Mela for 9 days. The government officer's only instruction to these holy men was that their versions of the *Ramayan* 'highlight the achievements of the Plans' that were 'for the welfare of people who were so dear to Bhagwan Ram'.[105]

The Bharat Sadhu Samaj was grateful for the state's patronage. In fact, it is likely that they were more interested in the patronage than the Plans and probably only paid lip service to planning, while pursuing their own conservative social and religious agenda. The benefits that they derived from this association with the state came in the tangible form of government funds, and the intangible, but no less significant, form of state recognition, legitimacy, and publicity. The Sadhu Samaj lost no opportunity to advertise its association with high-ranking members of the Congress party and government. In 1966, Khushwant Singh visited their spacious, two-storey office in Diplomatic Enclave, a short walk from embassies and 'where the local millionaires reside'. Inside, he noticed a calendar with a picture of Nehru hanging on the wall beside three large Hindi posters announcing a cow protection rally for 7 November 1966. Singh was surprised to note that the image of the now deceased prime minister showed him 'wearing a caste mark' even though 'he never wore one in his life'. In the last decade of his life, Nehru had reluctantly agreed to promote his beloved Five-Year Plans through ascetics; the *sadhus*, it would appear, had returned the favour by posthumously marketing him as an observant Hindu.[106] After all, Indians referred to Nehru, by the habit of caste, as 'Panditji'.

For Gulzarilal Nanda, the Bharat Sadhu Samaj's patron-in-chief, the chickens would come home to roost in 1966. On 7 November, as the posters on the wall of the Sadhu Samaj office had warned, *sadhus* of various denominations marched from the Red Fort to Parliament. This was part of a nationwide agitation for a ban on cow slaughter, demanded by Hindu conservatives since the late nineteenth century. A crowd of nearly 125,000 was led by holy men, some of whom were 'naked and smeared with ash and mud' and brandished spears, *trishuls* (tridents), and swords. It would be a day of violence and vandalism across parts of central Delhi with the holy men-agitators laying siege to government buildings and commercial property including Irwin Hospital, two electrical substations, and Odeon and Delite Cinemas.

The scene of the worst violence was right in front of Parliament. Swami Rameshwaranand, a parliamentarian from the Hindu nationalist Jan Sangh, inflamed the crowd with a microphone. He instructed them to 'teach them [in Parliament] a lesson'. Unable to storm its premises due to a police cordon and locked gates, the *sadhus* charged at the police and pelted stones at them. Initially repulsed by the police's tear-gas shells, baton charges, and then firing, the mob hurled 'petrol soaked rags' at government buildings. By mid-afternoon, according to *The Tribune*, 'there was hardly a building in Parliament Street or Connaught Circus which did not bear evidence of vandalism'. They did not spare government or private vehicles either. The Congress President, K. Kamaraj, managed to slip sway before his house was attacked. By evening, a curfew had been declared and the army was patrolling the streets of Delhi for the first time since the cataclysmic violence of Partition. Forty people were seriously injured and eight died that day. More than 800 were arrested, mostly *sadhus*.

By the time the curfew was lifted two days later, the Jan Sangh and future Bharatiya Janata Party (BJP) leader Atal Bihari Vajpayee was defending Swami Rameshwaranand in the Rajya Sabha in a sign of things to come. Meanwhile, amidst a chorus of outrage, Gulzarilal Nanda had sent his letter of resignation to the prime minister. As Home Minister Nanda was not only responsible for law and order across the country, including in the city; crucially, he was also widely known to be a *gau rakshak* (cow protector) who was sympathetic to the *sadhus*. It effectively marked the end of Nanda's political career.[107] Speaking in the Rajya Sabha 10 days after the convulsion, Congress MP Arjun Arora attacked both Nanda and Jan Sangh sadhu-sympathizers for inviting these 'ascetics' into politics, describing it as 'criminal'. To him, like many others, the sight of *sadhus* on the rampage in the national capital, crying for cow protection, was frightening. It was, in his view, a repudiation of the scientific temper that Nehru had tried to instil. What Arora chose to ignore was that it was Nehru who – despite his instincts to the contrary – had fatefully allowed Nanda to ally his government with the Sadhu Samaj a decade earlier and in doing so, elevated their public image and emboldened them. Arun Chatterjee, a communist parliamentarian from West Bengal, went further in his denunciation. The events of 7 November were a 'naked expression of reactionary obscurantism and revivalism'. It was disingenuous, however, to rub one's eyes in surprise because, 'it is the ruling party circles who, in spite of their protestations, have been rearing this ugly monster in their laps'.[108] Fellow Bengali communist, Bhupesh Gupta, lashed out at the Rashtriya Swayamsevak Sangh and Jan Sangh for their role in promoting the *sadhu*'s rally, even darkly speculating that American intelligence agencies could have been involved. But he was most scathing about the party in power and its lukewarm commitment to secularism. 'Scratch a Congressmen, he is essentially a Hindu, scratch a reactionary Congressman, he is a communal, obscurantist Hindu.'[109]

Despite the violence unleashed by *sadhus* in 1966 within the heart of the capital, and in spite it costing the political career of Gulzarilal Nanda, Prime Minister Indira Gandhi was not entirely done with them. Unlike her firmly agnostic father who maintained scepticism of god men, Indira Gandhi had many spiritual gurus and made sure to be seen (and photographed) as worshipful of *sadhus* and *sanyasis*.[110] We know, for instance, that even a decade later she took to the dais under a ceremonial tent at a Sadhu Samaj event at the Kumbh Mela, on 23 January 1977, just days after Mrs. Gandhi signalled the end of the Emergency (a dark period of authoritarian rule when elections were indefinitely postponed and civil liberties choked).[111] It was her first public speech after making the momentous decision to reinstate elections, and the prime minister avoided any overt mention of politics when cosying up to the ascetics. She assured them that there would be no state interference in Hindu religious traditions. The *sadhus* responded by pledging their support for the Emergency-era '25 Point Programme' – a charter of economic and social goals devised by Indira Gandhi and her son, Sanjay.

The *sadhus* bestowed Vedic blessings on Indira Gandhi (*Jivema saradah satam* – may you live a hundred years), thanked her for measures towards cow protection, and had kind words to say about her policies to help the poor. The prime minister spoke of the country's distinctive tradition of veneration for ascetics and saints, requesting them to provide moral and spiritual direction to those in need. She also spoke with pride about how even foreign youths, despairing at the materialism around them, were now looking to India for spiritual sustenance (this was a few years after The Beatles did so). She wanted to make clear that her government was in no way opposed to religious practice. It was regrettable, she felt, that some people had deliberately contorted the meaning of secularism to be atheism or irreligiousness. Instead, her government's policy was one of accepting all faiths, following the Sanskrit adage of '*sarva dharma sama bhava*' (all religions lead to the same destination).[112] By this point, the Sadhu Samaj's original links with the Five-Year Plans, though always tenuous, had been buried. The prime minister's speech at the Sadhu Samaj's shamiana was a political move. Having announced that elections would be held in March 1977, the prime minister was stepping into the electoral fray once again and trying to ensure that neither she nor her party was viewed as opposed to Hinduism. The Sadhu Samaj now represented little more than a political constituency, one that periodically wafted into the electoral line of vision.

It was at yet another Kumbh Mela that the Sadhu Samaj formally began its association with the fateful Ram Janmabhoomi (birthplace of Ram) movement, led by the hardline Hindu nationalist Vishwa Hindu Parishad (VHP). According to historian William Pinch, both the Sadhu Samaj and the VHP had been prominent at the Kumbh Mela for decades. At the Allahabad Kumbh in 1989, both these organizations scheduled their conferences within days of each other. The VHP conference was angry and bellicose, ending with a resolution to 'capture' the birthplace of the Hindu god Rama – which they alleged was located at the very spot in Ayodhya where a sixteenth-century Mughal mosque, Babri Masjid, stood – and build a temple there. The Sadhu Samaj convention was to be held 3 days later. Because their more hardline leaders had felt upstaged by the VHP's aggressive 'defence of the faith' declarations, the *sadhus* decided to invite the VHP to their conference. The result was a 'VHP takeover of the BSS agenda'. The *sadhu*'s conference saw several combative speeches about 'reclaiming' Ayodhya and the birthplace of the Rama. One of the speakers is noted to have said, 'there are 6 lakh villages, and 80 crore Hindus. If every villager donates one brick and every Hindu donates just 1 rupee the battle for Ram Janam Bhoomi will be half over. This programme has to be taken from village to village'. Pinch points out that, even at the time, members of the press saw the dominance of the VHP agenda at a Sadhu Samaj conference as a 'coup'. The Sadhu Samaj had, thus far, been associated with the Congress Party, and many viewed it as part of the Congress' outreach to Hindus. One of the Samaj's long time leaders, Swami Harinarayanand for example, had been understood to be a 'mainstay of the Congress Party'. But with the drift of the Sadhu Samaj towards the VHP and, by extension, the BJP, 'the Congress government (it was argued) effectively lost control of its only means to influence religious opinion'.[113]

A glossy magazine based in Hawaii, called *Hinduism Today*, carried a piece on the Bharat Sadhu Samaj in 1994. It was titled 'Can 40,000 Holy Men Shepherd India's Future?' The author was a businessman and freelance journalist named Rajiv Malik, who was sympathetic to *sadhus*. Knowing *Hinduism Today's* audience, the piece flattered the Samaj, making questionable but revealing claims about its past influence. The Samaj's clout was such, Malik claimed, that it had managed to 'quash the Uttar Pradesh government's plan to regulate temples and ashrams some years ago'. What was the secret behind such power? 'It has more or less had the ear of India's central government to the present day, enjoying the patronage of successive prime ministers, including Pandit Nehru, Mrs. Gandhi, Morarji Desai and Rajiv Gandhi.' Despite this, Malik hastened to point out, the Samaj was somehow both 'financially and morally' independent of the government and political parties. One of the interviews in the essay was with Swami Harinarayananad, conducted in his personal quarters within the spacious Samaj building. In this air-conditioned room with a small shrine inside, the Samaj's secretary general told Malik that the organization was open to any *sadhu* who had turned eighteen. The annual membership fee was the equivalent of $4. Another representative, a 74 year old president of the Delhi State Samaj branch, explained that the Samaj's *sadhus* belonged to 'all castes and communities of India'. He was quick, though, to define their caste limits: 'let me clarify that we do not admit sudras as sadhus directly in the Samaj'. Women, Swami Harinarayananad added, were not allowed as members either. Membership may have been theoretically open to 'all castes and communities of India', but Dalits and women were where they drew the line.

Later in the essay, Swami Harinarayananad expressed his distaste at how politics was mixing with religion. He was referencing recent events. This conversation was only two years after the fateful demolition of Babri Masjid by Hindu nationalists riled up by the rhetoric of the BJP and the VHP. It was an event that would set off deadly riots across the country in the months that followed, claiming the lives of nearly 2,000 and altering the course of national politics towards religious majoritarianism. In the past, the Swami had been critical of the BJP for politicizing the issue of the birthplace of Ram. No one party, he had said, could lay claim to representing the Hindu community. This, however, did not mean that his views on the mosque were conciliatory. Even before the mosque was brought down, the swami had made clear that he sided with the Vishwa Hindu Parishad's uncompromising stance. He believed that Prime Minister Narasimha Rao, of the Congress Party, should simply hand over the site to Hindus. Unmindful of the inconsistency or the irony, he recommended that 'fundamentalist Muslims' should withdraw their claims in the interest of the nation's 'emotional integration'. He dismissed reporters' questions about the need for historical and archaeological verification of the claim that this was the site of a former temple and the birthplace of Ram. The matter was one of faith and sentiment, he said. Besides, he somewhat confusingly added, Lord Ram had lived millennia ago, so the question of evidence was absurd.[114] Looking back on the grim events of December 1992, the Swami made clear: 'Babri Masjid had to be removed .... Moreover, the temple has to be constructed at the exact birth site.' On this, he said, 'we have no difference of opinion with the Vishwa Hindu Parishad'.[115]

The Sadhu Samaj had been a creation of the Congress Party. It was what had led to the charge of them once being called 'Congress Sadhus'. Delivered into existence by the Congress, the Sadhu Samaj was sheltered and legitimized by them. The ascetics, for their part, were assiduous in highlighting its political and governmental patronage. But as the attack on Parliament made clear, the Sadhu Samaj was always a problematic client, unwilling to compromise on emotive religious issues like cow protection. Despite the shock and embarrassment of the *sadhus* violence in 1966, the Congress continued its rhetorical indulgence of the Sadhu Samaj. The party certainly did not want to be known (or remembered) as one that opened fire on Hindu ascetics in the capital. Congress governments viewed it as electorally prudent to bow before the *sadhus* at Kumbh Melas. It was endorsement by association for both. But beginning with the 1989 Kumbh Mela in Allahabad, the Bharat Sadhu Samaj – once birthed by Congress – began staking positions that perfectly aligned with the campaigns of its foremost political rival, the BJP and other Hindu nationalist outfits. The story of the Sadhu Samaj's swing from the Congress Party to the BJP is, in some ways, the history of the Congress Party's changing electoral fortunes and of the fate and meaning of secularism in India. The *sadhus* of the Samaj had first found patrons in a party that claimed to be committed to a secular 'socialistic pattern of society' and afterwards to one that endorsed market–friendly Hindutva.

***

The campaigns by government and voluntary organizations to educate citizens about the Five-Year Plans and invite voluntary participation draw attention to the mutability of planning discourse. In the hands of the Bharat Sadhu Samaj, planning could take on meanings that might appear irreconcilable with the way it is conventionally understood. The Sadhu Samaj's discourse on planning was a world away from that which the Professor and Yojana Bhavan resorted to. The partnership struck with *sadhus* is important to consider for what it says about the extremes to which the Plan publicity campaign went, the strange bedfellows that democratic planning fostered, and the tension between planning in its technocratic and democratic modes. It reveals a surprising degree of dilution in the Indian state's scientific discourse on planning and a compromise in its claims to secularism. In a country as religious as India, officials reasoned, it helped if those with religious authority translated technical Plan jargon into familiar spiritual idioms, consecrating economic policy in the process.

Using religion, specifically Hindu tropes, was deemed necessary. But at what cost to state secularism? And if harnessing religion was indeed imperative, then why not, as one Muslim parliamentarian half-seriously suggested, have a joint cross-faith 'Bharat Sadhu Maulvi Samaj'? In its partnership with the Samaj, the Indian government was willing to swallow the contradiction of promoting planning – the very symbol of secular technocracy and scientific modernity – through the language of religion and cultural particularity. A government that claimed to be secular advertised its Five-Year Plans through Hindu iconography and rhetoric. Furthermore, it even subcontracted parts of this outreach to wandering, mendicant Hindu ascetics, with little to no oversight. Given the absence of a regulatory structure, one can assume that the Sadhu Samaj's Plan propaganda projected a social vision that mirrored its Hindu, upper caste, and male demographic.

Today, the Sadhu Samaj no longer enjoys the stature it once boasted, when it was an ally of the government in planning and developmental ventures. It does, however, exist and retains offices in the Diplomatic Enclave – appropriately along Dharam Marg. The local bus station right in front of its headquarters is officially named 'Bharatiya Sadhu Samaj'. In the middle of the last century, a scholar observed that the 'saintly idiom' was conspicuous in Indian politics, gesturing to the roles played by figures like Gandhi and Vinoba Bhave.[116] The Sadhu Samaj and Vyas Sammelans were promising ventures for governments to ally with because of the vitality of this idiom. Enterprising saffron-robed ascetics could thrive at the intersection of religion, politics, and the economy. It worked during India's Congress-led socialistic era just as it has in the BJP-led capitalist context. The fortunes of the BJP-friendly 'Billionaire Yogi' Baba Ramdev, Uttar Pradesh Chief Minister Yogi Adityanath, and parliamentarian Sadhvi Pragya Thakur offer testimony that the saintly idiom retains power.[117]

Prominent in Narendra Modi's backstory, in his telling, are the 2 years he spent wandering the Himalayan mountains during his late teenage years, when he was in search of God. It was a decision prompted by conversations with *sadhus* on the railway platform in Gujrat's Vadnagar, where a young Modi helped his father sell tea. In the Himalayas, Modi says, 'The *sadhus* I lived with taught me to align myself with the rhythm of the Universe.'[118] As Prime Minister, Modi has referred to himself as a *'fakir'* (ascetic) who has undertaken *'tapasya'* (penance). The widely publicized photograph of him meditating after the 2019 general elections in a Himalayan cave, draped in a saffron shawl, suggests that he is certainly aware of the potency of this saintly idiom. Mid-twentieth century proponents of the Sadhu Samaj, like the BJP in 2019, were counting on the blend of Hindu spiritualism and development to garner mass appeal. The price paid – to the principle of secularism, and the public's perception of the state's religious bias – were deemed acceptable costs.

The activities of voluntary organizations like College Forums, the Bharat Sewak Samaj, and the Bharat Sadhu Samaj, open a window onto the ways in which Indians, across the country and spanning a wide spectrum of backgrounds, participated in the Five-Year Plans. Participants included men and women, urban and rural, rich and poor. However, while the participation may have been voluntary, the institutional vessels for them were state-sponsored, and the sphere of engagement was strictly limited to implementation. It was unidirectional and represented the state's monologue about itself. Every instance of 'volunteering' needed the state's push and purse to get them off the ground. These were not sites for criticism of the Plans or venues that allowed for a feedback loop to the government. Even the College Planning Forums, which did the most to encourage that impression, barely kept up the pretence. Even within this limited frame, expectations outpaced achievement; large-scale Plan-consciousness was certainly not achieved, however defined. What we gain from looking at these failed enterprises is some understanding of the ways in which planning in a democracy was promoted by the state as a political experiment and mass national undertaking.

Despite the Indian state's strenuous proclamations about democratic planning, ultimately planning was a top-down technocratic enterprise. This was not only because the projects of democratic planning failed to leave a dent, but more so because of how narrowly what counted as democratic was even defined. The 'democracy' in democratic planning was of impoverished meaning. It was mostly a formally democratic state informing citizens about economic policies that had been determined by technocrats and politicians, who reached out to the populace to ensure compliance. By asserting democratic planning as a national narrative and an example of India's unique global role, the state sought a swell of enthusiasm to offset weak state capacity. Ordinary citizens could support in implementing the Plans, but could not participate in their design. The gleaming vision of democratic planning that figures like Nehru and Nanda sold was naive and unrealistic at best, and at worst a cynical means to cloak technocracy in the rhetorical attire of democracy. Either way, planning was better at building data capacities than at improving the quality of Indian democracy. The history of Indian planning teaches us how different it looked in its technocratic and democratic realms, their dissonance running like a fracture through the project of planned modernity in a democracy.

Epilogue

The Planning Commission was consigned to history in Narendra Modi's first term as prime minister. *Yojana*, the Plan magazine, however, still survives as a stale official publication. Sold on footpaths outside Metro stations in central Delhi, it now seemingly caters to the hopeful thousands preparing to take the notoriously competitive civil services examinations. Once boasting advertising from the nation's leading business houses, its pages now mostly attract advertisements from coaching centres. It lives as a relic of a bygone era.

'India grows cool to five year plans', the *New York Times* observed from afar in 1967.[1] A decade and half later, the editor of the *Economic and Political Weekly* noted the 'fairly widespread conviction' that the Plans pronouncements 'do not mean a thing'.[2] What caused this change in fortune? While the Planning Commission and the Five-Year Plans had faced setbacks during the ascendant 1950s as well, the challenges in the mid-to-late 1960s were more numerous and of a different order. When Jawaharlal Nehru died in May 1964, shortly after writing the prologue to a book on planning, it lost its most powerful champion. The deceased prime minister had made planning central to the vision of an independent India from the 1930s, and done much to institutionalize it in the new republic. But planning in India had become far too embedded in the machinery of government for it to wobble merely because of the loss of an individual, however significant. There were structural factors at play.

When foreign exchange became scarce in 1956–1957, parts of the Second Five-Year Plan had to be scrapped and the entire thing had to be scaled back considerably.[3] The crisis opened the door to sharp criticism of the Planning Commission and power began gradually shifting to the Ministry of Finance. The attacks began with the T. T. Krishnamachari-led Finance Ministry, but soon extended to the press and Parliament, even leading to calls for members of the Planning Commission to resign. As a near contemporary observer remarked, this phase marked the 'nadir' of the Planning Commission's reputation in Parliament, and its 'darkest hour' up to that point.[4] Pitambar Pant wrote of how people at the Planning

Commission 'were seen in groups talking in hushed tones about the future of the Planning Commission'.[5] According to scholars Vivek Chibber and Medha Kudaisya, although it was the Planning Commission that faced the music for the foreign exchange debacle (due to an over-optimistic Second Plan), the hidden culprit was Krishnamachari himself. 'TTK', as he was known, had been the Minister of Commerce and Industry when that ministry liberalized private sector imports in early 1956, resulting in depleted foreign exchange reserves.[6]

Over the following years, criticisms of the Plans mounted among economists, the press, bureaucrats, and politicians.[7] While there was broad support for the essentials of the Mahalanobis model – emphasizing capital good industries and self-reliance through import substitution – a whole host of other concerns were aired.[8] Along with the Five-Year Plans, the Planning Commission was also assailed. It was accused of being staffed with too many civil servants and politicians, lacking sufficient technical expertise, and stepping on the toes of the Finance Commission in determining the disbursement of central revenues to the states. Parties ranging from the liberal Swatantra Party to the Praja Socialist Party to the religiously conservative Jana Sangh all chimed in with their displeasure. Leading businessmen and merchant chambers added to the growing chorus of denunciation. In 1967, G. D. Birla, who had risen on the floor of the Federation of Indian Chambers of Commerce and Industry three decades earlier to make a case for 'National Economic Planning', now judged both planning and the Planning Commission to be 'total failures'.[9]

The proximate cause for this intemperate outpouring was the shambles in which the Third Five-Year Plan (1961–1966) found itself. It had grossly underperformed, resulting in national income growth that barely matched population increases. Armed conflicts with China in 1962 on the northeastern border, and with Pakistan in 1965 on the northern front had strained public finances. The battle with Pakistan had also caused the United States to withdraw aid from India, adding to the squeeze. The 2 years of drought that followed were cruel blows to a nation already reeling from wars. In 1966, the government devalued the rupee by nearly 60% in order to salvage an increasingly perilous trade deficit. As the shortage of food grains, rising inflation, and increased unemployment made clear, the Indian economy was in trouble.

How did the Professor fare? According to his biographer, Mahalanobis' involvement in planning diminished over the course of the Second Plan due to differences with Nehru over the Planning Commission.[10] While the nature of these differences remains vague, we do know that the Professor was closely associated with the Planning Commission for an entire decade longer, as a Member until late 1967. It seems probable that the foreign exchange crunch's damage to the Plan and the ensuing blow-back side-lined Mahalanobis. Further, with the resignation of Deshmukh and the appointment of 'TTK' as finance minister in 1956, Mahalanobis had at once lost a partner and acquired an opponent. The businessman-turned-minister from Madras, a backer of the private sector, was soon butting heads with the Professor and the Planning Commission.

Months after the Second Five-Year Plan was launched, Mahalanobis wrote to a friend that he did not even know whether he would have 'any connection with either the planning work or the Institute after a few months'. He was uncharacteristically deflated. 'All I want is that Government & Panditji [Nehru] should make final decisions one way or the other.'[11] According to Mahalanobis, TTK even issued him an ultimatum: make peace or look on as grants dried up.[12] Exhausted and struggling to sleep, the Professor tentatively decided that he would quit on 1 April 1957, unless the 'Finance Minister himself desires that I should continue my work in Delhi'. Meanwhile, ironically, the minister was also offering to resign. Nehru managed to broker an uneasy peace and these threats never came to pass. The next year, Krishnamachari would find himself accused of corruption in Parliament in what would come to be known as the Mundhra scandal, leading to his resignation under a cloud of perceived impropriety. The replacement, Morarji Desai, was yet another market-oriented finance minister who was critical of Mahalanobis and happy to trim his sails.

Still, the Professor continued juggling positions in New Delhi and Calcutta as a member of the Planning Commission and head of the Institute. He was picked to lead a panel to study the effects of planning on income distribution and inequality – the Mahalanobis Committee, as it came to be known.[13] And since the Third Plan was derivative of its predecessor, Mahalanobis' fingerprints were detectable in national economic policy well into the 1960s.[14] However, even in the context of the Planning Commission's waning powers vis-a-vis the Ministry of Finance, the Professor was losing ground within the Commission. He was never again nearly as influential as he had been in the previous decade. At Yojana Bhavan, his orbit shrunk from formulating plan models and writing plan frames to supervising perspective planning (long-term planning), a pet project under his charge. Along with Pitambar Pant, he coordinated research on this, both at the Planning Commission's Perspective Planning Department and at the Institute's Delhi-based Planning Unit. The calculations they produced were used right until the Fifth Plan (1974–1979).[15]

Mahalanobis retired from the Planning Commission in 1967, now well into his seventies; just 3 days after the Professor stepped down, his acolyte

Pant was elevated to the position of a Member.[16] The next year, in his retirement from planning activities, the Professor was awarded the prestigious Padma Vibhushan, the nation's second highest civilian honour. In 1970, Indira Gandhi thanked him for his contributions and relieved him of some of his supervisory power as Statistical Adviser, modifying the position such that his opinion would not be sought as a matter of course, but only when deemed necessary.[17] The Professor remained, until his death in 1972, both the Director of the Institute, and the Honorary Statistical Adviser to the Government of India.

Since the early 1960s, the Planning Commission had seen its powers eroded from inside. The chisel and hammer were wielded by those Nehru had favoured – Deputy Chairman Ashok Mehta who was appointed by Nehru in 1963, and Prime Minister Lal Bahadur Shastri. Until recently the president of the Praja Socialist Party, Ashok Mehta was known as a critic of some of the Commission's informal powers. He recommended that the new prime minister prune the Commission's authority. The indefinite tenures planners had enjoyed were now replaced with fixed term contracts. The secretarial link between the Commission and the Union Cabinet was severed. Under Nehru, the Cabinet Secretary (the topmost bureaucrat to whom all others reported) had also functioned as the Planning Commission's secretary, putting the Commission in a privileged position. Much to the displeasure of other Planning Commission members, this cord was cut. Prime Minister Shastri further circumscribed the Planning Commission's influence by creating a National Planning Council and expanding the role of the Prime Minister's Secretariat to include a team of experts on the economy.

Things did not look up for the Planning Commission when Nehru's daughter Indira Gandhi became prime minister, after Shastri's sudden death in January 1966. Deputy Chairman Ashok Mehta made it clear to other members of the Planning Commission that their sway stopped at the Cabinet's door. Without mincing words, he said they 'had no right to enter into the picture so far as Cabinet decisions on vital economic questions were concerned'.[18] Indira Gandhi's political opponent within the Congress Party – Morarji Desai, who was appointed deputy prime minister and finance minister – was also not a fan of the Planning Commission's loosely defined and sprawling powers. He insisted that he, and by extension the Finance Ministry, would have the last word on economic matters. In 1967, the Administrative Reforms Committee published a scathing indictment of the Planning Commission. The report recommended that the Commission shed its de facto executive authority and political nature to become a purely expert body that interfered less in centre-state relations. While the government ultimately decided to ignore the majority of these suggestions, the report rode a rising tide of official antipathy.

The next Deputy Chairman of the Planning Commission, Dhananjay Gadgil, was in the mould of Asoka Mehta and Morarji Desai, and shared their desire to restrain the Planning Commission. As fellow fiscal conservatives, both Gadgil and Desai opposed the hitherto mainstream commitment to ever-larger Five-Year Plans. This 'bold approach' was what Nehru and Mahalanobis had endorsed, and it continued to have backing from the Perspective Planning Division (headed by Pitambar Pant) and Prime Minister Indira Gandhi. But eventually, the conservatives prevailed and not only were targets trimmed and expectations adjusted, but the Fourth Five-Year Plan was also postponed. This 3-year gap of annual plans, from 1966 to 1969, came to be known as the period of the Plan Holiday.

Desai and Gadgil were also of similar mind regarding decentralizing the Planning Commission, particularly with reference to the Commission's discretionary role in doling out central government grants-in-aid and loans for development expenditure and Plan outlays. Despite being a non-statutory body, over the years the Planning Commission had side-lined the Finance Commission, a statutory body whose role it was to define the division of revenues in India's federal structure. In what was to be called the 'Gadgil formula', the Deputy Chairman devised a ratio which defined a standardized criterion based on which the Centre would transfer funds every year to the states.

The Planning Commission's hold over the purse strings was being questioned in a new political context for the Congress party. The Gadgil formula, which improved the position of the states vis-a-vis the Centre, was proposed soon after the 1967 general elections in which the Congress suffered historic losses. The party ceded several states and their seat count in the Lok Sabha dropped to unprecedented lows. The Congress government in Delhi now faced emboldened opposition parties in several state capitals. It is not surprising then that the Gadgil formula, passed in July 1968, was welcomed by states. Gadgil took a scalpel to other aspects of the Planning Commission as well. He cut down the number of working groups operating at Yojana Bhavan and its direct involvement in a range of activities including public cooperation. Desai also promoted another move aimed at decentralizing planning: he backed the consolidation of 'multi-level planning' – which entailed setting up planning boards and organizations at the state, district, and *taluka* levels.

The gradual downsizing of the Planning Commission's influence seemed to be where Indian planning was headed. It had been the trend in the years since Nehru died. But this was to change quite dramatically beginning in the summer of 1969, courtesy of Nehru's daughter. Prime Minister Indira Gandhi's decision to nationalize all banks reflected her resolve to cast aside those members of her cabinet who were not sufficiently deferential. The day before bank nationalization was announced, she relieved Morarji Desai of his posts as Deputy Prime Minister and Minister of Finance, claiming that his opposition to the policy made these roles untenable. With Morarji Desai no longer a roadblock, and Gadgil enfeebled by the loss of a like-minded finance minister, the prime minister revived the 'bold' approach to plan formulation. The Fourth Five-Year Plan's expenditure targets were raised along with a renewed emphasis on the public sectors. Workarounds were devised to dilute the Gadgil formula.

In 1971, on the back of the heady success in the general elections, Indira Gandhi went about reconstituting the Planning Commission to suit her purposes. Gadgil was summarily asked to leave and he died the next day on a train back home to Pune. The rest of the Commission's members were asked to step down as well, thus beginning the process of making the Planning Commission a thoroughly political body. It was described at the time as, the 'ministerialization of planning'.[19] The idea of the Commission as a semi-independent body of experts had fallen victim to Mrs. Gandhi's centralizing drive. It was now staffed with political appointees who made clear that the 'political agenda would define planning'.[20] Taking stock many years later, the editor of the *Economic and Political Weekly* would write that the Planning Commission – like other institutions – had withered under Indira Gandhi's watch. By this point, he wrote in late 1984, pronouncements made in the Five-Year Plan documents 'do not mean a thing'.[21]

According to at least one observer of planning, Indira Gandhi's buttressing of the Planning Commission in the early 1970s had only been an aberration. After Nehru's death, the 'concern with planning objectives, the importance of the planning process, and the Commission's influence over the Governmental system tended to decline. The public esteem in which the Commission was held diminished in part because of some visible failures of planning, but also because Nehru's successors were less concerned with the planning system'.[22] Even Indira Gandhi, in the latter years of her tenure as prime minister, began to look beyond the Planning Commission for advice on the economy.

In 1985, a grieving pilot named Rajiv Gandhi took on the role of prime minister, following the assassination of his mother. The youthful modernizer knew little about the Planning Commission. As the probably apocryphal joke goes, Prime Minister Rajiv Gandhi once asked for Mahalanobis to be summoned to his office, unaware that the Professor had died more than a decade ago. By the time he referred to the Manmohan Singh-led Planning Commission as a 'bunch of jokers', the writing was on the wall. As an institution, the Planning Commission would survive for nearly three more decades. It served Congress and BJP governments, and even weathered the transformation of India's economy in the era of market reforms, albeit with many scars.

With the election of Narendra Modi as prime minister in 2014, it was clear that the Planning Commission was near the end of the line. Given Modi's penchant for marking his distance from the Congress Party's policies, and Nehru's legacy in particular, it was evident that the Planning Commission was on the chopping block. Modi's own frustrations with this body while he was chief minister of Gujarat could only have hastened the end. As a powerful and popular regional leader between 2001 and 2014, Modi chafed at having to negotiate and plead with the Planning Commission every year for his state's allocation of federal funds. Like the chief ministers of many other states, Modi did not care for this Delhi-based body of elites controlling his purse and pronouncing judgment on his performance.

When Prime Minister Narendra Modi finally scrapped the Planning Commission entirely in 2014 – to replace it with a new think tank, the NITI Aayog – few lamented its passing. However, its ghost was feebly revived by the Congress dynast Rahul Gandhi on the ill-fated 2019 general election campaign trail. If voted to power, he tweeted, a 'lean Planning Commission' would return. The chief minister of West Bengal, Mamata Banerjee, used this strategy as well. Pointing to Subhas Chandra Bose's role in establishing the National Planning Committee and criticizing Modi for disbanding the Planning Commission, she declared in January 2021 that she will establish a Planning Commission for Bengal, one she claimed will utilize the talents of Nobel winners Amartya Sen and Abhijit Banerjee along with that of Harvard historian Sugata Bose, 'Netaji's' grandnephew. It is revealing of the legitimacy that the idea of planning and the institution of the Planning Commission continued to hold in some quarters.

From the late 1960s, planning had lost the cachet and independence it once enjoyed in the Nehruvian state. As I. G. Patel put it, 'Truth to tell, enthusiasm for planning and bold plans which abated then never really caught a second breath in India.'[23] Moreover, in the national discourse, planning no longer signified the unifying national project that it once did. It ceased to be the generative force it once was, either in the economy or in shaping Indian statehood and citizenship. Tarnished by the experience of the 1960s, it ceased to hold the same promise as an economic policy, as a mobilizing ideology, or as the political instrument of a middle way between communism and capitalism. Democratic planning progressively diminished as the master narrative of the postcolonial state.

While the Planning Commission would be anachronistic in India's increasingly capitalistic society, the data capacities that planning launched in the 1950s remain relevant as ever to the contemporary state. It is information harvested from national sample surveys and the work of national statistical bodies, for example, that tells us about the levels of poverty and unemployment in the country. Unfortunately, over recent decades, India's national statistical infrastructure has suffered decay from a combination of neglect and understaffing. The regular and embarrassing reminder of this, as economists have noted, comes when the NSS Organization and CSO 'tell entirely different stories' about the GDP. The economists Abhijit Banerjee, Rohini Somanathan, Pranab Bardhan, and T.N. Srinivasan co-wrote in the pages of the *Economic Times* in April 2017: 'From being the world leader in surveys, we are now one of the countries with a serious data problem'.[24] The financial daily, *Mint*, ran an editorial the next month titled, 'Repairing the House that Mahalanobis Built'.[25]

Since the 1970s, beginning under Indira Gandhi's government, there have been signs that neglect has occasionally turned to something more calculated.[26] Good data, unfortunately, can be bad politics. In the past few years, as the sky has darkened over the Indian economy – with growth slowing and unemployment rising – the country's national statistics has been the subject of repeated controversy. While Indian institutions have sadly never been completely immune from political interference, Indian statistical bodies had remained relatively uncorrupted. In fact, as we have seen, they had cultivated a global reputation for innovation and excellence in the 1950s and 1960s. When Mahalanobis died, the UN Statistical Office adopted a resolution that noted his 'tremendous contribution to the Commission and the statistical community at large', his 'pioneering efforts on behalf of social statistics', and recognized him as a 'champion of the statistical needs of developing countries'. It concluded by remembering the 'outstanding stimulus he gave to statistical development throughout the world'.[27] On the importance of the NSS' household surveys, the Nobel winning economist Angus Deaton and Valerie Kozel observed in 2005: 'Where Mahalanobis and India led, the rest of the world has followed, so that today, most countries have a recent household income or expenditure survey from which it is possible to make a direct assessment of the living standards of the population.' They added, 'Most countries can only envy India its statistical capacity and the central part that poverty and poverty measurement play in Indian public life.'[28]

With India's economy involuntarily braking, the BJP-led government appears to have determined that it is best to protect citizens from some kinds of information. In January 2019, the financial newspaper *Business Standard* published leaked findings from a report of the NSS Office. The document was supposed to have been made public a month earlier, but the government sat on it. The alarming report revealed that unemployment in India had touched a 45 year high in 2017 – an uncomfortable revelation in the months leading up to a general election. It struck at the heart of the Modi-led BJP government's claims regarding its economic record. A few days earlier, two members of the National Statistical Commission (a body that reviewed the report) resigned to protest the report's suppression.[29] Kaushik Basu, former Chief Economist of the World Bank, surmised that India was in a 'job crisis' that 'the government would rather you didn't notice'.[30] Two months later, prompted by these worrying signs, over a 100 economists and social scientists from India and the United States published a statement that noted the weakening institutional independence of the country's statistical system. India's statistics, they wrote, have 'come under a cloud for being influenced and indeed even controlled by political considerations ... Any statistics that cast an iota of doubt on the achievement of the government seem to get revised or suppressed on the basis of some questionable methodology.'[31] The signatories included economists ranging from MIT to Jawaharlal Nehru University, from former Planning Commission member Abhijit Sen, to the soon-to-be recipients of the Nobel Prize in Economics, Esther Duflo and Abhijit Banerjee.

It was not just academics who noted the fall in data quality. Several banks, think tanks, and foreign funds admitted that they were moving towards 'alternative data sources, or at least official data of a different kind'.[32] Before the end of the year, the now re-elected BJP government was again accused of a self-interested lack of transparency in its handling of official data. After a newspaper reported that household consumer spending had dropped for the first time in more than four decades in 2017–2018, the government decided to scrap the official survey on which it was based, citing issues of 'data quality'. According to the article, this was 'the first time the government decided not to release a survey conducted by the NSO, formerly known as the National Sample Survey Office, a statistical body set up in 1950'.[33] It led, once again, to an appeal by nearly 200 academics in India and abroad – including Angus Deaton and French economist Thomas Piketty – appealing to the government to reconsider its decision. National statistics, they argued, should not fall prey to politics. The BJP government's record on this score, they stated, 'has been very poor'. India's statistical system and sample surveys had, until recently, been 'a shining example and a model to the rest of the world'. The government had damaged that credibility through its repeated 'disinclination to make public any information that may show its own performance in a poor light'.[34] By early 2020, with an economic downturn having taken firm hold, even the recent Chief Economic Advisor to the government, Arvind Subramanian, was writing in the pages of the *Financial Times* about the damage unreliable statistics had caused. One of the essential ingredients in arresting the decline, he wrote, was 'instituting reliable data systems'.[35] Perhaps he meant *re*-instituting. The plunge has since continued: in the summer of 2021, economist Jean Dreze and researcher Anmol Somanchi began their op-ed in the *Economic Times* stating what was increasingly obvious, 'India's statistical system is in bad shape.'[36] Sharing the article on Twitter, Thomas Piketty lamented that, 'We are supposed to live in an age of big data, but this looks more like big opacity.'[37]

The Indian present echoes its past. Industrial policy, self-reliance, and protectionism – all features of the Nehruvian economy – appear to be back in fashion with Modi's *Atmanirbhar Bharat* and Make in India campaigns, despite the government's protests to the contrary. This is not peculiar to India. World over, from New Delhi to Washington and Beijing to London, governments are falling in love once again with economic self-sufficiency and state intervention.[38] It is part of a broader backlash against free trade, globalization, and the Great Recession, along-side renewed popularity of the view that national security depends to some degree on economic self-reliance. Concern about national resilience during the devastating coronavirus pandemic has only entrenched this perspective. What distinguishes the present moment in India from the initial postcolonial decades – despite some similarities in policy emphases – is an official anti-intellectualism that manifests in the short shrift given to expertise.

Like in the early years of the republic, the public still yearns for a technocrat who can deliver economic bounty. It was a role the Professor played in the popular imagination during the 1950s, and subsequently by Manmohan Singh in the era of market reforms in the last decade of the previous millennium. As Sunil Khilnani put it, Manmohan Singh – the finance minister who would go on to be a two-term prime minister – was a 'Mahalanobis for the 1990s'.[39] Now, as before, civil society seeks a technocratic saviour. It perhaps explains the national celebrity of economist Raghuram Rajan while he was Governor of the Reserve Bank of India (2013–2016). During Modi's tenure as prime minister, analysts have wondered who he takes economic advice from, especially after the rollout of policies such as the 2016 'demonetization'

that left most experts scratching their heads. The question, in one colum-
nist's framing, was: 'Who will be BJP's Mahalanobis?'[40]

* * *

India's experience with economic planning has to be understood through
the frame of technocracy, social science, and technology on the one hand,
and the political projects of democratic planning on the other.
Establishing a planned economy required instituting certain social-
scientific capacities such as national sample surveys, national income
accounts, and a centralized statistical body, alongside new technologies
like the digital computer. The adoption of centralized economic planning
also led to far-reaching changes in the ways in which the national economy was defined and enumerated. It elevated the discipline of statistics to
a status rivalling economics in its usefulness to the nation's economic
management. As the transformations in statistics and computing make
clear, planning set off a boom in the Indian state's quantitative capacities
and scientific infrastructure. This historical moment highlights both the
expansive license that technocrats were granted in early independent
India, and how the country's quantitative expansion entrenched them
deeper within the state. The lasting effects of this dedication to planning
at the outset of independent India were a significant expansion in the
state's data capacities, an intensifying of state centralization, and a greater
reliance on expertise.

Planning in a democracy, however, also necessitated governmental efforts
to draw the citizenry into the project. Democratic planning sought popular
participation and a mobilized citizenry due to the limited capacities of the
postcolonial state, and because key figures in the government believed in
generating mass support for planned development. Mobilizing citizens for
developmental ends without using totalitarian means was also integral to the
Nehruvian state's self-definition as a country representing a possible middle
path during the Cold War. To this government, what distinguished its
citizens from those of capitalist democracies was that Indians did not have
a narrowly atomized sense of economic purpose and self-interest, divorced
from wider national objectives. And what set Indians apart from the inhabitants of communist regimes was that this shared vision and mobilization was
not enforced by the threat of punishment or violence by the state. The
government of independent India used a panoply of means to educate its
citizenry on planning and elicit support. But, as the rhetoric used by the
Bharat Sewak Samaj and the Bharat Sadhu Samaj reveals, the terms of this
publicity and outreach was often at odds with the high modernist technocracy we have come to associate with economic planning. The vaunted

Nehruvian 'scientific outlook' was careful to accommodate local cultural idioms and court religious sensibilities.

Along with democracy and secularism, planning was one of the defining features of independent India. To the Nehruvian government, planning referred not only to economic policy making; planning also referred to the political practice of democratic planning. The term invoked a constellation of ideas that combined expert-led economic decision-making aimed at rapid development, the citizenry's consent and participation in such a path, and India's uniqueness on the world stage (through the combination of Parliament and Plans during the Cold War). Democratic planning claimed to represent a new kind of state; one in which centralized planning could coexist with democratic participation. This was an experiment that fused Western parliamentary democracy and Soviet-style centralized economic planning at a time when the Cold War portrayed them as antithetical to one another. Planning produced new kinds of knowledge about the economy and sought to mould a new citizenry. The rhetoric of planning contributed to how democracy and citizenship were defined in India – participatory and ground-up in theory, but predictably paternalist and top-down in reality. Planning was simultaneously a technocratic exercise in directing the economy, a means of modern state building, and a state-directed social movement. When viewed in this expansive sense, planning was fundamental to independent India, revealing the far-reaching ambitions of the state, its promise, and failures.

Notes

Introduction

1. Narendra Modi, 'PM on Independence Day: Planning Commission to be Replaced' (19 August 2014), YouTube Video, 3:31, www.youtube.com/wa tch?v=P0c6FCi-FRg&ab_channel=NarendraModi (translation mine).
2. 'Revised Draft of President's Speech on January 31, 1950', F. No. 35, Jawaharlal Nehru Papers (henceforth JN Papers) (post 1947), Nehru Memorial Museum and Library (henceforth NMML).
3. Speech by Dr. B. R. Ambedkar, Friday, 25 November 1949, Constituent Assembly of India – Volume XI, http://parliamentofindia.nic.in/ls/debates/v ol11p11.htm, accessed on 25 March 2017.
4. Government of India, *First Five Year Plan*, https://niti.gov.in/planningcommis sion.gov.in/docs/plans/planrel/fiveyr/1st/1planch8.html, accessed on 15 January 2020.
5. Lionel Fielden, 'Which Way Will India Turn?', *New York Times* (henceforth *NYT*) (16 July 1950), SM8; Chester Bowles, 'Asia Challenges Us through India: Our Aid Is Needed to Keep Democracy as a Bastion against Communism', *NYT* (23 March 1952), SM7; 'State Department Pamphlet Praises India as Best Hope of Democracy in the Far East', *NYT* (21 August 1953); Barbara Ward, 'Fateful Race between China and India: Their Programs for Economic Modernization are Watched by Asians as a Test of Communist Dictatorship versus Democratic Freedom', *NYT* (20 September 1953), SM9; 'An Ideological Contest for Asia between India and China is Seen', *NYT* (17 May 1954); James Cameron, 'Nehru vs. Mao – A Key Contest in Asia', *NYT* (7 August 1955), SM13.
6. Martin Luther King Jr, 'My Trip to the Land of Gandhi', *Ebony* (July 1959), 92.
7. Douglas Ensminger, *The Ford Foundation Overseas Development Self-Study of the India Program*, 1966, Report 002348, Unpublished Reports, Ford Foundation Papers, Rockefeller Archive Center, New York (henceforth RAC).
8. Thomas Balogh, 'India's Experiment', *The Observer* (13 March 1955), 6.
9. Jawaharlal Nehru, *The Discovery of India* (New Delhi: Oxford University Press, 1985), 400.
10. For the 'capabilities approach', see Amartya Sen, *Development as Freedom* (New York: Anchor Books, 1999).

11. James Scott defines high-modernism as a strong 'version of the self-confidence about scientific and technical progress, the expansion of production, the growing satisfaction of human needs, the mastery of nature (including human nature), and, above all, the rational design of social order'. This was not the same as trusting science. High-modernism was 'unscientifically optimistic about the possibilities for the comprehensive planning of human settlement and production'. James C. Scott, *Seeing Like a State* (New Haven: Yale University Press, 1998), 4.

12. See, for instance, Gyan Prakash, *Emergency Chronicles: Indira Gandhi and Democracy's Turning Point* (Princeton: Princeton University Press, 2018).

13. See, Bipan Chandra, *The Rise and Growth of Economic Nationalism in India: Economic Policies of Indian National Leadership, 1880–1905* (New Delhi: People's Publishing House, 1966); Manu Goswami, *Producing India: From Colonial Economy to National Space* (Chicago: Chicago University Press, 2004); C. A. Bayly, *Recovering Liberties: Indian Thought in the Age of Liberalism and Empire* (Cambridge: Cambridge University Press, 2011).

14. Partha Chatterjee, *The Nation and Its Fragments: Colonial and Postcolonial Histories* (Princeton: Princeton University Press, 1993), 203.

15. Quinn Slobodian, *Globalists: The End of Empire and the Birth of Neoliberalism* (Cambridge, MA: Harvard University Press, 2018), 99.

16. Ibid., 97.

17. For two brief surveys that locate pre-independence Indian planning in late nineteenth and twentieth century economic thought, see Niranjan Rajadhyaksha, 'The Long Road to Indian Economic Planning (until 1950)', and Shruti Rajagopalan, 'Ideas and Origins of the Planning Commission in India', in *Planning in the 20th Century and Beyond: India's Planning Commission and the NITI Aayog*, ed. Santosh Mehrotra and Sylvie Guichard (Cambridge: Cambridge University Press, 2020), 43–88.

18. Benjamin Zachariah, 'India: The Road to the First Five-Year Plan', in *Decolonization and the Politics of Transition in South Asia*, ed. Sekhar Bandyopadhyay (New Delhi: Orient BlackSwan, 2016), 199–227.

19. M. Visvesvaraya, *Planned Economy for India* (Bangalore: Bangalore Press, 1934), 145, 146.

20. Parasnath Sinha, ed., *The Path to Prosperity: A Collection of the Speeches and Writings of G.D. Birla* (Allahabad: The Leader Press, 1950), 1–26.

21. The Haripura posters, as they have come to be known, were created by Santiniketan artist Nandalal Bose who spent weeks in rural Gujarat observing everyday life. Bose would later illustrate the Indian Constitution.

22. Subhas Chandra Bose, 'The Haripura Address', 'Science and Politics', 'Letter to Jawaharlal Nehru', and 'The National Planning Committee', reproduced in *Subhas Chandra Bose: Pioneer of Indian Planning* (New Delhi: Planning Commission, 1997), 23–61, 70–91.

23. Gandhi to Nehru, 11 August 1939 (date unclear), Vol. 25, Part 1 (Correspondence), JN Papers, NMML.

24. Nehru, *The Discovery of India*, 340–341.

25. Rabindranath Tagore to Nehru, 19 November 1938, Vol. 48, Part 1 (Correspondence), JN Papers, NMML.

26. A. K. Chanda to Nehru, 28 November 1938, Vol. 11, Part 1 (Correspondence), JN Papers, NMML.
27. K. T. Shah, ed., *Report: National Planning Committee* (Bombay: Vora, 1949).
28. Nehru to Krishna Menon, 11 June 1939, Vol. 47, Part 1 (Correspondence), JN Papers, NMML.
29. On the colonial state's expansion during World War II, see Indivar Kamtekar, 'The End of the Colonial State in India, 1942–47', unpublished PhD thesis (1988), University of Cambridge; Yasmin Khan, *India at War: The Subcontinent and the Second World War* (Oxford: Oxford University Press, 2015).
30. Zachariah, 'India: The Road to the First Five-Year Plan'.
31. Titled the *Second Report on Reconstruction Planning*.
32. David Lockwood, 'Was the Bombay Plan a Capitalist Plot?', *Studies in History*, Vol. 28, No. 1 (2012), 106.
33. In-depth studies of pre-independence planning include Raghabendra Chattopadhyay, 'The Idea of Planning in India 1931–1951', unpublished PhD thesis (1985), Australian National University, and Benjamin Zachariah, *Developing India: An Intellectual and Social History, c. 1930–50* (Oxford: Oxford University Press, 2005).
34. The others included A. D. Shroff, Sir Ardeshir Dalal, and Kasturbhai Lalbhai.
35. For the former position, see Aditya Mukherjee, *Imperialism, Nationalism and the Making of the Indian Capitalist Class, 1920–1947* (New Delhi: Sage, 2002); Lockwood, 'Was the Bombay Plan a Capitalist Plot?'; Medha Kudaisya, '"The Promise of Partnership": Indian Business, the State, and the Bombay Plan of 1944', *Business History Review*, Vol. 88, No. 1 (Spring 2014), 97–131. On the latter, see Vivek Chibber, *Locked in Place: State-Building and Late Industrialization in India* (Princeton: Princeton University Press, 2003) and Zachariah, *Developing India*.
36. Chatterjee, *The Nation and Its Fragments*, 202.
37. Dipesh Chakrabarty, 'In the Name of Politics', *Economic and Political Weekly* (henceforth EPW), Vol. 40, No. 30 (23 July 2005), 3293–3301.
38. Chairman's speech, 19 March 1960, *Summary Record of Discussion of the National Development Council (NDC) Meetings, Vol. 1: 1st to 14th Meetings*, Planning Commission, Government of India, New Delhi, 2005, 512.
39. 'Programme of Planning Body', *Times of India* (henceforth *TOI*) (6 March 1950), 1.
40. Chibber, *Locked in Place*, 148–151; Letter from Jawaharlal Nehru to Vallabhbhai Patel, 25 May 1950, File No. 45, Part 1 (Correspondence), JN Papers, NMML.
41. The letters exchanged between Matthai and Nehru, and the press coverage, reveal that Matthai was upset about matters other than the role of the Planning Commission as well – government expenditures, and the Nehru–Liaquat Pact. File No. 46, Parts 1 and 2 (Correspondence), JN Papers, NMML.
42. 'Pandit Nehru Refutes Charges of Authoritarianism', *TOI* (2 June 1950), 1, 7.
43. Tarlok Singh, 'C.D. Deshmukh and the First Phase in Planning', *India International Centre Quarterly*, Vol. 22, No. 4 (1995), 294–295.

44. This consequential secretarial connection was severed in 1964, when Lal Bahadur Shastri was prime minister. It was re-introduced in 1973.
45. K. Shankara Pillai, 'Plan or Perish', *Shankar's Weekly* (7 May 1950), reproduced in *Don't Spare Me Shankar* (New Delhi: Children's Book Trust, 1983), 39.
46. The postcolonial fear of neocolonialism was perhaps most explicitly articulated by Ghanaian freedom fighter and leader, Kwame Nkrumah, who wrote a book with that title. Nkurmah saw the economic experience of Latin America after decolonization as a form of neocolonialism (underdevelopment through material dependence on Europe) and a cautionary tale for decolonizing African states. See Adom Getachew, *Worldmaking after Empire: The Rise and Fall of Self Determination* (Princeton: Princeton University Press, 2019), 23, 149–151.
47. Slobodian, *Globalists*, 99.
48. Reginald H. Green, 'Four African Development Plans: Ghana, Kenya, Nigeria, and Tanzania', *Journal of Modern African Studies*, Vol. 3, No. 2 (1965), 249.
49. Tony Killick, 'Development Planning in Africa: Experiences, Weaknesses, and Prescriptions', *Development Policy Review*, Vol. 1 (1983), 47.
50. Sara Lorenzini, *Global Development: A Cold War History* (Princeton: Princeton University Press, 2019), 5.
51. The private papers of Jawaharlal Nehru, stored at the NMML, are divided into pre-1946 and post-1946 periods. Both are the legal property of the Jawaharlal Nehru Memorial Fund. Up to and including when much of the archival research for this book was done (2012–2014), the latter collection was closed to the public and scholars. Exceptions were made if one secured permission from the Jawaharlal Nehru Memorial Fund and the Prime Minister's Office (since the prime minister is ex-officio chairperson of the NMML Society). As a member of the Nehru–Gandhi family usually chairs the Fund, scholars have to petition a legal heir of Nehru (since 1998, Mrs Sonia Gandhi) and the Prime Minister of India. Prime Minister Indira Gandhi put these rules in place after Nehru's death. Since November 2014, the rules have changed such that scholars now *only* need permission from the prime minister's office. Recently, the subject of whether the Nehru papers belongs to the Jawaharlal Nehru Memorial Fund or the NMML has become controversial, making research even harder for scholars. Chibber, *Locked in Place*, xi, xii; Seema Chishti, 'Sonia Gandhi Hands Over Key to Nehru Papers, Access Now Controlled Only by PMO', *The Indian Express* (16 November 2014), https://goo.gl/QrYtdt, accessed on 28 March 2017; 'Breaking Norms: Sonia Gandhi Permits Access to Nehru's Private Papers', *Firstpost* (16 November 2014), https://rb.gy/8koixl, accessed on 15 February 2020; Jyoti Malhotra, 'Modi Govt Wants to Evict Sonia Gandhi-led Jawaharlal Nehru Fund from Teen Murti', *The Print* (24 September 2018), https://bit.ly/2Z6kixM, accessed on 15 June 2020).
52. Chibber, *Locked in Place*, xi–xiii.
53. Recent works on the Partition and the manifold ways it shaped Indian state and society include, Vazira Fazilah-Yacoobali Zamindar, *The Long Partition and the Making of Modern South Asia: Refugees, Boundaries, Histories*

(New York: Columbia University Press, 2007); Yasmin Khan, *The Great Partition: The Making of India and Pakistan* (New Haven: Yale University Press, 2007); Joya Chatterjee, *The Spoils of Partition: Bengal and India, 1947–1967* (Cambridge: Cambridge University Press, 2007); Neeti Nair, *Changing Homelands: Hindu Politics and Partition of India* (Cambridge, MA: Harvard University Press, 2011); and Uditi Sen, *Citizen Refugee: Forging the Indian Nation after Partition* (Cambridge: Cambridge University Press, 2018).

54. Though the terrain has improved considerably since Ramachandra Guha's call to action (for evidence, see endnotes 55 and 56), there is yet vast room to grow. Ramachandra Guha, 'The Challenge of Contemporary History', *EPW*, Vol. 43 (2008), 192–200.

55. Sunil Khilnani, *The Idea of India* (New York: Farrar, Straus and Giroux, 1999); Bipan Chandra, Aditya Mukherjee, and Mridula Mukherjee, *India since Independence* (New Delhi: Penguin, 1999); Ramachandra Guha, *India after Gandhi: The History of the World's Largest Democracy* (New York: Harper Collins, 2008); Gyanesh Kudaisya, *A Republic in the Making: India in the 1950s* (New Delhi: Oxford University Press, 2017). There has also been a spate of multi-author volumes: Dipesh Chakrabarty, Rochona Majumdar, and Andrew Sartori, eds., *From the Colonial to the Postcolonial: India and Pakistan in Transition* (New Delhi: Oxford University Press, 2007); Taylor C. Sherman, William Gould, and Sarah Ansari, eds., *From Subjects to Citizens: Society and the Everyday State in India and Pakistan, 1947–1970* (Cambridge: Cambridge University Press, 2014); Sujit Choudhry, Madhav Khosla, and Pratap Bhanu Mehta, eds., *The Oxford Handbook of the Indian Constitution* (Oxford: Oxford University Press, 2016); Gyan Prakash, Michael Laffan, and Nikhil Menon, eds., *The Postcolonial Moment in South and Southeast Asia* (London: Bloomsbury, 2018).

56. Recent historical works on the Nehruvian state includes, for example, Eleanor Newbigin, *The Hindu Family and the Emergence of Modern India* (Cambridge: Cambridge University Press, 2013); Jahnavi Phalkey, *Atomic State: Big Science in Twentieth Century India* (Ranikhet: Permanent Black, 2013); Ornit Shani, *How India Became Democratic: Citizenship and the Making of Universal Franchise* (Cambridge: Cambridge University Press, 2017); Benjamin R. Siegel, *Hungry Nation: Food, Famine, and the Making of Modern India* (Cambridge: Cambridge University Press, 2018); Rohit De, *The People's Constitution: The Everyday Life of Law in the Indian Republic* (Princeton: Princeton University Press, 2018); Anjali Bhardwaj Datta, Uditi Sen, and Mytheli Sreenivas, eds., 'A Country of Her Making: Women's Negotiations of Society and Politics in Post-Colonial India', Special Section in *South Asia: Journal of South Asian Studies*, Vol. 44, No. 2 (2021), doi: 10.1080/00856401.2021.1899170.

57. V. T. Krishnamachari, *Planning in India* (Bombay: Orient Longman, 1961); The standard account of the first three Five-Year Plans is A. H. Hanson, *The Process of Planning: A Study of India's Five-Year Plans, 1950–1964* (London: Oxford University Press, 1966); Tarlok Singh, *India's Development Experience* (New Delhi: Macmillan India, 1974); Sukhamoy Chakravarty, *Development Planning: The Indian Experience* (Oxford: Clarendon Press, 1987);

K. L. Datta, *Growth and Development Planning in India* (New Delhi: Oxford University Press, 2021).

58. Among political scientists, a landmark contribution was Francine Frankel's book, first published in 1978. Francine Frankel, *India's Political Economy: The Gradual Revolution (1947–2004)*, 2nd ed. (New Delhi: Oxford University Press, 2005). Other works include Lloyd I. Rudolph and Susanne Rudolph, *In Pursuit of Lakshmi: The Political Economy of the Indian State* (Hyderabad: Orient Longman, 1987), and Atul Kohli, *State Directed Development: Political Power and Industrialization in the Global Periphery* (Cambridge: Cambridge University Press, 2004). For economic studies, see for example, Jagdish Bhagwati, *India in Transition: Freeing the Economy* (London: Clarendon Paperback, 1993); T. J. Byres, ed., *The Indian Economy: Major Debates since Independence* (Oxford: Oxford University Press, 1998); Isher Judge Ahluwalia and I. M. D. Little, eds., *India's Economic Reforms and Development: Essays for Manmohan Singh*, 2nd ed. (New Delhi: Oxford University Press, 2012); Chirashree Das Gupta, *State and Capital in Independent India Institutions and Accumulation* (Cambridge: Cambridge University Press, 2016). For a brief survey of studies on the Planning Commission, see Sylvie Guichard, 'From Economists to Historians: Studying the Planning Commission, 1950–2014', in *Planning in the 20th Century and Beyond*, ed. Mehrotra and Guichard.

59. For a survey of scholarly literature on economic development in Nehruvian India, see Nikhil Menon, "Developing Histories of Indian Development," *History Compass*, Vol. 19, No. 10, October 2021, 1–14.

60. Medha Kudaisya, '"A Mighty Adventure": Institutionalising the Idea of Planning in India', *Modern Asian Studies*, Vol. 43, No. 4 (July 2009), 960–965; Medha M. Kudaisya, *Tryst with Prosperity: Indian Business and the Bombay Plan of 1944* (New Delhi: Penguin Random House, 2018); Zachariah, *Developing India*; Zachariah, 'India: The Road to the First Five-Year Plan'. Others include David Washbrook, 'The Rhetoric of Democracy and Development in Late Colonial India', in *Nationalism, Democracy, and Development: State and Politics in India*, ed. Sugata Bose and Ayesha Jalal (New Delhi: Oxford University Press, 1997), 36–49; and Chattopadhyay, 'The Idea of Planning in India 1931–1951'.

61. Chibber, *Locked in Place*; Nasir Tyabji, *Forging Capitalism in Nehru's India: Neocolonialism and the State, c. 1940–1970* (New Delhi: Oxford University Press, 2015).

62. David C. Engerman, *The Price of Aid: The Economic Cold War in India* (Cambridge, MA: Harvard University Press, 2018).

63. Others include David Ludden, 'India's Development Regime', in *Colonialism and Culture*, ed. Nicholas Dirks (Ann Arbor: University of Michigan Press, 1992), 247–87; and Sugata Bose, 'Instruments and Idioms of Colonial and National Development: India's Historical Experience in Comparative Perspective', in *International Development and the Social Sciences: Essays on the History and Politics of Knowledge*, ed. Frederick Cooper and Randall Packard (Berkeley: University of California Press, 1998), 45–63.

64. Partha Chatterjee's article on planning has been published, with minor modifications, in multiple venues. Chatterjee, *The Nation and Its Fragments*, 200–219; Partha Chatterjee, 'Development Planning and the Indian State', in *The State and Development Planning in India*, ed. T. J. Byres (Oxford: Oxford University Press, 1994), 82–103, and Partha Chatterjee, 'Development Planning and the Indian State', in *Politics and the State in India*, ed. Zoya Hasan (New Delhi: Sage, 2000), 115–141.
65. The literature on the history of development in the 'Third World' (a phrase and typology itself a creation of this era) is rich and longstanding. Recent works linking South Asia in global histories of development and the Cold War include, for example, Daniel Immerwahr, *Thinking Small: The United States and the Lure of Community Development* (Cambridge, MA: Harvard University Press, 2015); Corinna Unger, 'Toward Global Equilibrium: American Foundations and Indian Modernization, 1950s to 1970s', *Journal of Global History*, Vol. 6, No. 1 (2011), 121–142; Nick Cullather, *Hungry World: America's Cold War Battle against Poverty in Asia* (Cambridge, MA: Harvard University Press, 2010); Matthew Connelly, *Fatal Misconception: The Struggle to Control World Population* (Cambridge, MA: Harvard University Press, 2010). On India's role in the Cold War more broadly, see Paul McGarr, *The Cold War in South Asia: Britain, the United States and the Indian Subcontinent, 1945–1965* (Cambridge: Cambridge University Press, 2013), and Manu Bhagavan, ed., *India and the Cold War* (Chapel Hill: University of North Carolina Press, 2019).
66. Angus S. Deaton and Valerie Kozel, 'Data and Dogma: The Great Indian Poverty Debate', *The World Bank Research Observer*, Vol. 20, No. 2 (2005), 177–200;
67. Michael Mann, 'The Autonomous Power of the State: Its Origins, Mechanisms and Results', *European Journal of Sociology*, Vol. 25, No. 2 (1984), 185–213.
68. I am drawing on James Scott's discussion of twentieth century high-modernist states and their conscious simplifications of complexity in nature and society in order to make it legible and manipulable. James C. Scott, *Seeing Like a State* (New Haven: Yale University Press, 1998) 2–5, 11–52.

1   A Nation in Numbers

1. Abhindranath Mahalanobis, *Prasanta Chandra Mahalanobis* (New Delhi: National Book Trust, 1983).
2. On the role of quantification in colonial India, see Arjun Appadurai, 'Number in the Colonial Imagination', in *Orientalism and the Post-Colonial Predicament*, ed. C. A. Breckenridge and P. Van der Veer (Philadelphia: University of Pennsylvania Press, 1993), 314–339. For studies of the rise of statistics as a discipline and as a tool of administration, see Theodore Porter, *The Rise of Statistical Thinking* (Princeton: Princeton University Press, 1988); Theodore Porter, *Trust in Numbers: The Pursuit of Objectivity in Science and Public Life* (Princeton: Princeton University Press, 1996); Adam Tooze, *Statistics and the German State, 1900–1945: The Making of*

Modern Economic Knowledge (Cambridge: Cambridge University Press, 2007).

3. Timothy Mitchell has argued that the meaning we attach to 'the economy' as a concept today dates back only to the mid-twentieth century, assuming a fixed meaning by around the mid-1950s. 'Fixing the Economy', *Cultural Studies*, Vol. 12, No. 1 (1998), 82–101.

4. Jawaharlal Nehru, 'The Human Aspect in Statistics and Planning', in *Selected Works of Jawaharlal Nehru* (henceforth *SWJN*), Second Series (henceforth SS), Vol. 17, ed. S. Gopal (New Delhi: Jawaharlal Nehru Memorial Fund, 1995), 288.

5. While the popular view is certainly much less nuanced than that of writers who have addressed this question, the latter have nonetheless confirmed its broad outlines. See Shashi Tharoor, *Nehru: The Invention of India* (New York: Arcade, 2003), 244; Gurcharan Das, *India Unbound: The Social and Economic Revolution from Independence to the Information Age* (New York: Anchor, 2002). Among historian's accounts, see Kudaisya, '"A Mighty Adventure"'; Khilnani, *The Idea of India*, 82–85; Guha, *India After Gandhi*, 206–207.

6. James Scott argues that one of the primary impulses of high modernist states is to seek to 'make a society legible'. Scott, *Seeing Like a State*, 2.

7. Sophia Rosenfeld, *Democracy and Truth: A Short History* (Philadelphia: University of Pennsylvania Press, 2019), 65–69.

8. Appadurai, 'Number in the Colonial Imagination', 314–339; Goswami, *Producing India*, 73–85.

9. Bernard S. Cohn, *Colonialism and Its Forms of Knowledge: The British in India* (Princeton: Princeton University Press, 1996), 8; David Ludden, 'Orientalist Empiricism and Transformations of Colonial Knowledge', in *Orientalism and the Post-Colonial Predicament*, 250–278; Nicholas Dirks, 'The Ethnographic State', in *The State in India: Past and Present*, ed. Masaaki Kimura and Akio Tanabe (New York: Oxford University Press, 2006), 229–254.

10. As Partha Chatterjee has noted, the census and the survey (along with land revenue histories and the museum) comprised the pillars of colonial knowledge production and organization. Much of modern Indian social science traces back to them. Partha Chatterjee, 'The Social Sciences in India', in *The Cambridge History of Science Vol. 7: The Modern Social Sciences*, ed. Theodore M. Porter and Dorothy Ross (Cambridge: Cambridge University Press, 2003), 482–497.

11. Josiah Charles Stamp, *Some Economic Factors in Modern Life* (London: King and Son, 1929), 258.

12. Goswami, *Producing India*, 224–227.

13. Bayly, *Recovering Liberties*, 174.

14. Gyan Prakash, *Another Reason: Science and the Imagination of Modern India* (Princeton: Princeton University Press, 1999), 178–187; Goswami, *Producing India*, 209–276.

15. The Economic Enquiry Committee, led by M. Visvesvaraya, made its recommendations in 1925. The Bowley-Robertson Committee followed

in 1934. The recommendations of these bodies were supported by those of an Inter-Departmental Committee assembled in 1942.

16. J. K. Ghosh, P. Maiti, T. J. Rao, and B. K. Sinha, 'Evolution of Statistics in India', *International Statistical Review/Revue Internationale de Statistique*, Vol. 67, No. 1 (April 1999), 13–34.

17. W. Edwards Deming, 'P. C. Mahalanobis 1893–1972', *The American Statistician*, Vol. 26, No. 4 (October 1972), 50; Rabindranath Tagore to Mrs. Mahalanobis, quoted in Alladi Sitaram, 'Editorial', *Resonance* (June 1999), 1–2.

18. C. D. Deshmukh, 'Prasanta Chandra Mahalanobis as I Knew Him', in *Papers on Planning*, ed. P. C. Mahalanobis (Calcutta: Statistical Publishing Society, 1985), xiv; Ashok Rudra, *Prasanta Chandra Mahalanobis: A Biography* (New Delhi: Oxford University Press, 1996), 411–413.

19. C. R. Rao, 'Prasanta Chandra Mahalanobis 1893–1972', *Biographical Memoirs of Fellows of the Royal Society*, Vol. 19 (December 1973), 455.

20. 'He prided himself in sometimes not taking the help of any architect or any engineer in the construction of buildings. The results were, of course, disastrous but he was quite blind to this'. Rudra, *Prasanta Chandra Mahalanobis*, 353.

21. Andre Beteille, *Sunlight on My Garden: A Story of Childhood and Youth* (New Delhi: Penguin, 2012), 270.

22. P. C. Mahalanobis, 'Anthropological Observations of the Anglo-Indians of Calcutta: Part I – Analysis of Male Stature', *Records of the Indian Museum*, Vol. 23 (1922), 1–96; On Mahalanobis' early anthropometric studies, see Projit Bihari Mukharji, 'Profiling the Profiloscope: Facialization of Race Technologies and the Rise of Biometric Nationalism in Inter-War British India', *History and Technology*, Vol. 31, No. 4 (2015), 376–396.

23. Rudra, *Prasanta Chandra Mahalanobis*, 167.

24. P. C. Mahalanobis, 'Editorial', *Sankhyā*, Vol. 1, No. 1 (June 1933), 1–4.

25. Rabindranath Tagore, 'Sankhyā', *Sankhyā*, Vol. 2, No. 1 (1935), 1.

26. P. C. Mahalanobis, 'Why Statistics?', *Sankhyā*, Vol. 10, No. 3 (September 1950), 195.

27. The letter was addressed to G. M. Morant of University College London in 1934. Quoted in Benjamin Zachariah, 'Development of Professor Mahalanobis', *Economy and Society*, Vol. 26, No. 3 (August 1997), 438.

28. Angus Deaton, 'Data and Econometric Tools for Development Analysis', in *Handbook of Development Economics Vol. III*, ed. J. Behrman and T. N. Srinivasan (Amsterdam: North Holland, 1998), 1799.

29. Mahalanobis, 'Why Statistics?', 212.

30. Ibid., 213.

31. Quoted in Chatterjee, *The Nation and Its Fragments*, 200.

32. Nehru, 'The Human Aspect in Statistics and Planning', 287.

33. 'Minutes Dated 17 June 1939', in J. C. Kumarappa Papers, NMML, 11. Cited in Raghabendra Chattopadhyay, 'The Idea of Planning in India 1931–1951', unpublished PhD thesis (1985), Australian National University, 113.

34. Ibid., 118.

35. Tagore encouraged Mahalanobis' interest in statistics. Mahalanobis, in turn, was secretary of Tagore's Viswa-Bharati University in Santiniketan, and a travel companion to the poet on his tour of Europe.
36. Jayanta Ghosh, Pulakesh Maiti, and Anil K. Bera, 'Indian Statistical Institute: Number and Beyond, 1931–47', in *Science and Modern India*, ed. Uma Dasgupta (New Delhi: Pearson India, 2011), 1013–1056.
37. Zachariah, 'Development of Professor Mahalanobis', 438; Shah, ed., *Report: National Planning Committee*, Appendix VII, 112, 118, 119.
38. Shah, ed., *Report: National Planning* Committee, Appendix VII, 118–119.
39. Radhakamal Mukherjee, 'Statistics in the Service of Planning', *Sankhyā*, Vol. 7, No. 2 (November 1945), 173.
40. Durgabai Deshmukh, *Chintaman and I* (New Delhi: Allied, 1980), x, 39, 75; 'Delhi in Doldrums', *The Economic Weekly* (2 April 1955), 418.
41. C. D. Deshmukh, *The Course of My Life* (New Delhi: Orient Longman, 1974), 59.
42. C. D. Deshmukh, 'Foreword', in *Contributions to Statistics*, ed. C. R. Rao (Calcutta: Statistical Publishing Society, 1963), 2.
43. On the role played by Deshmukh and the rest of the Indian delegation at Bretton Woods, see Aditya Balasubramanian and Srinath Raghavan, 'Present at the Creation: India, the Global Economy, and the Bretton Woods Conference', *Journal of World History*, Vol. 29, No. 1 (2018), 65–94.
44. Ashok Mitra, 'A Rare Man', *EPW*, Vol. 31, No. 41/42 (12–19 October 1996), 2789, and Peter Coleman, Selwyn Cornish, and Peter Drake, *Arndt's Story: The Life of an Australian Economist* (Canberra: Asia Pacific Press, 2007), 227.
45. Rao, 'Prasanta Chandra Mahalanobis 1893 – 1972', 465.
46. Mahalanobis, 'Why Statistics?', 195.
47. In 1950, Mahalanobis would be appointed President of the Indian Science Congress.
48. 'National Planning Committee', *TOI*, Bombay (18 September 1945). Cited in Chattopadhyay 'The Idea of Planning', 256.
49. Mahalanobis, *Prasanta Chandra Mahalanobis*, 49.
50. Jawaharlal Nehru to Pitambar Pant, 7 May 1946, Installment 2, Correspondence, Pitambar Pant Papers (henceforth Pant Papers), NMML.
51. Pant became the secretary to the Chairman of the Planning Commission in 1952. Four years later, he joined the commission as head of the new Manpower Division. In 1958, he took charge of its new Perspective Planning Division. Pant was inducted as a member of the Planning Commission in 1967, a position he held till 1971. Although never a formal employee of ISI, he held the honorary positions of Joint Secretary and Vice-President, and led the activities of its Delhi branch.
52. A. M., 'Calcutta Diary', *EPW*, Vol. 35, No. 40 (30 September–6 October 2000), 3547.
53. Statistics Division, Department of Economic and Social Affairs of the United Nations Secretariat, *United Nations Statistical Commission 1947–2007*, http://unstats.un.org/unsd/statcom/doc07/UN_Stat_Commission_1947-2007_bookmarks.pdf, accessed on 16 June 2015.

54. 'Report of the Statistical Commission to the Economic and Social Council', *Journal of the Economic and Social Council* (31 May 1946), 238.
55. The others on the committee were W. E. Deming, Frank Yates, G. Darmois, and R. A. Fischer, 'United Nations Sub-Commission on Statistical Sampling', *The American Statistician*, Vol. 2, No. 4 (August 1948), 10–12, 19.
56. Frank Yates, 'The Work of the United Nations Sub-Commission on Statistical Sampling', *Sankhyā*, Vol. 12, No. 3 (June 1953), 15–16.
57. UN Statistical Commission, 'The Preparation of Sampling Survey Reports', Statistical Papers, Series C, No. 1, Lake Success, New York, 1950.
58. Jelke Bethlehem, 'The Rise of Survey Sampling', Discussion Paper 09015, The Hague: Statistics, Netherland, 2009, 16.
59. Deming, 'P. C. Mahalanobis 1893–1972', 49.
60. Quoted in C. R. Rao, 'Statistics Must Have a Purpose: The Mahalanobis Dictum', *Sankhyā*, Vol. 55, No. 3 (October 1993), 335.
61. P. C. Mahalanobis, 'Statistics Must Have a Purpose: Presidential Address at the Third Pakistan Statistical Conference Held in Lahore, Feb 1956', *Samvadadhvam*, Vol. 1, No. 1, 1956, 4.
62. Rao, 'Statistics Must Have a Purpose', 331; Mahalanobis, *Papers on Planning*, 53.
63. Khilnani, *The Idea of India*, 62.
64. P. C. Mahalanobis, 'Statistics as a Key Technology', *The American Statistician*, Vol. 19, No. 2 (1965), 43.
65. Arunabh Ghosh, *Making it Count: Statistics and Statecraft in the Early People's Republic of China* (Princeton: Princeton University Press, 2020), 13–14, 59.
66. Mahalanobis, 'Statistics Must Have a Purpose', 4.
67. Mahalanobis, *Papers on Planning*, xiiv.
68. Government of India, *Report of the Advisory Planning Board* (New Delhi: Government of India Press, 1947), 25.
69. K. V. Rao, 'Indian Affairs', *Triveni* (July 1955), http://trivenijournalindia.com/indianaffairsapr55.htm, accessed on 1 July 2016.
70. Jawaharlal Nehru, 'On Expansion of the Cabinet and Reconstitution of the Planning Department', *SWJN*, SS, Vol. 5, 488.
71. Nehru, 'A Central Statistical Organisation', in *SWJN*, SS, Vol. 7, 476–477.
72. Nehru, 'Statistical Organisation', in *SWJN*, SS, Vol. 8, 30.
73. Nehru, 'Statistical Methods in Administration', in *SWJN*, SS, Vol. 9, 47.
74. Extracts from 'The Role of the Central Statistical Organization in the Indian Statistical System', reproduced in Rudra, *Prasanta Chandra Mahalanobis*, 218.
75. *Indian Statistical Institute: History and Activities 1931–1957* (Calcutta: Statistical Publishing Society, 1965), 15.
76. Colin Clark, *The Conditions of Economic Progress* (London: Macmillan, 1940) cited in Daniel Spiech, 'The Uses of Global Abstraction: National Income Accounting in the Period of Imperial Decline', *Journal of Global History*, Vol. 6, Issue 1, (2011) 6, 7.
77. Earlier studies of national wealth, national income, and taxable capacity included those by Dadabhai Naoroji, George Findlay Shirras, K. T. Shah,

K. J. Khambata, and A. Heston, 'National Income', in *The Cambridge Economic History of India, Vol. 2*, ed. Dharma Kumar and Meghnad Desai (Cambridge: Cambridge University Press, 1983), 376–462; Eleanor Newbigin, 'Accounting for the Nation, Marginalising the Empire: Taxable Capacity and Colonial Rule in the early Twentieth-Century', *History of Political Economy* (May 2020), 455–472.

78. Government of India Resolution No. 15(33) P-49, as quoted in Government of India, *First Report of the National Income Committee April 1951* (Calcutta: Eka Press, 1951), 1, 8.

79. On the early years of national income accounts globally, see Spiech, 'The Uses of Global Abstraction', 6, 7–28.

80. Government of India, *First Report of the National Income Committee*, 1, 4.

81. 'Need of National Planning: Statistician's Role', *Amrita Bazaar Patrika* (3 January 1950), reproduced in 'Planning Commission-Press Cuttings', File No. 21/5/50 – RE, Ministry of Home Affairs, NAI.

82. 'Proceedings of a Press Conference on 6th January 1950', File No. 34, Part 1 (Correspondence), JN Papers, NMML.

83. In a letter to Home Minister Vallabhbhai Patel (stamped 'Top Secret and Personal'), the Prime Minister admitted to having nearly proposed the Professor's name for membership in the inaugural Planning Commission, before deciding against it.

84. 'Revised Draft of President's Speech on January 31, 1950', File No. 35, Part 1 (Correspondence), JN Papers, NMML.

85. Prime Minister of India to Chief Ministers, 2 February 1950, File No. 36, Part 1 (Correspondence), JN Papers, NMML.

86. Nehru to Prime Minister's Secretariat, 12 March 1950, File No. 38, Part 1 (Correspondence), JN Papers, NMML; and Nehru to Prime Minister's Secretariat, 20 April 1950, File No. 42, Part 1 (Correspondence), JN Papers, NMML.

87. Planning Commission Meetings on 28 March 1950, 20 April 1950, and 21 April 1950. Record Notes of the Meetings of the Planning Commission, Planning Commission, P.C. Department, 1950, F. No. 2(2)-ECC/50, NAI.

88. Hanson, *The Process of Planning*, 59.

89. Nehru to Maulana Abul Kalam Azad, 20 April 1950, File No. 42, Part 1 (Correspondence), JN Papers, NMML.

90. Nehru, 'The Human Aspect in Statistics and Planning', 290.

91. Y. D. Gundevia, *Outside the Archives* (Hyderabad: Sangam Books, 1987), 199.

92. Note prepared by PCM and 'handed over to the Prime Minister for his information', 4 March 1959, Record No. 119, Mahalanobis Papers, Prasanta Chandra Mahalanobis Memorial Museum and Archives, Kolkata (henceforth PCMMMA).

93. David Vere-Jones, 'The Coming of Age of Statistical Education', *International Statistical Review*, Vol. 63, No. 1 (1995), 7.

94. Mahalanobis to Pant, 17 July 1954, Pant Papers, NMML.

95. This was the biennial Conference of the International Statistical Institute. Nehru, 'The Human Aspect in Statistics and Planning', 287.

96. By 1960, the Institute was offering courses of varying levels and differing durations in Calcutta, Delhi, and Bombay.

97. Ghosh, *Making it Count*, 228.

98. Ibid.

99. 'Plan Activities Need More Statisticians', *Yojana*, Vol. 3, No. 16, (23 August 1959), 13.

100. On the crisis of food and its political salience in early independent India see Sunil Amrith, 'Food and Welfare in India, c. 1900–1950', *Comparative Studies in Society and History*, Vol. 50, No. 4 (October 2008), 1010–1035; Siegel, *Hungry Nation*. For a survey of scholarship on food, hunger, and famine in modern South Asia, see Rachel Berger, 'Alimentary Affairs: Historicizing Food in Modern India', *History Compass*, Vol. 16, No. 2 (February 2018) https://doi.org/10.1111/hic3.12438.

101. Nehru, 'A Central Statistical Organisation', 477.

102. 'Collecting Economic Data for Long-Term Economic Planning: National Sample Survey', *TOI* (1 September 1953), 5.

103. 'The National Sample Survey: General Report No. 1. First Round: October 1950–March 1951', *Sankhyā*, Vol. 13, No. 1/2 (December 1953), 52.

104. For a detailed explanation of the NSS operation, see M. N. Murthy and A. S. Roy, 'The Development of the Sample Design of the Indian National Sample Survey during Its First 25 Rounds', in *Social Research in Developing Countries: Surveys and Censuses in the Third World*, ed. Martin Bulmer and Donald P. Warwick (London: Routledge, 1993), 111–125.

105. 'Professor P. C. Mahalanobis', Dispatch Number 192, American Embassy (New Delhi to Department of State, Washington DC), 30 July 1953, U.S. State Department Files, India 1950–54, Internal Affairs, RG 59, General Records of the Department of State.

106. Mahalanobis to Pitambar Pant, 12 July 1950, File No. 49, Part 2 (Correspondence), JN Papers Installment 1, NMML.

107. Except for West Bengal and thirteen districts in Bombay, where the field-work was done by the Institute and the Gokhale Institute of Politics and Economics, respectively.

108. 'The Biggest Sampling Inquiry in the World', *Hindustan Times* (30 August 1953).

109. Deming, 'P. C. Mahalanobis 1893–1972', 49.

110. Deaton and Kozel, 'Data and Dogma', 178.

111. Rudra, *Prasanta Chandra Mahalanobis*, 214–216.

112. The National Sample Survey: General Report No. 1. First Round: October 1950 – March 1951, *Sankhyā*, Vol. 13, No. 1/2 (December 1953), 51–59.

113. Rudra, *Prasanta Chandra Mahalanobis*, 205–206.

114. The National Sample Survey: General Report No. 1. First Round: October 1950–March 1951, *Sankhyā*, Vol. 13, No. 1/2 (December 1953), 138–139.

115. P. C. Mahalanobis, 'The National Sample Survey. Number 2. Tables with Notes on the Second Round April–June 1951', *Sankhyā*, Vol. 13, No. 3 (March 1954), 269–271, 317–324.

116. The April–June 1951 NSS survey covered a population of 360 million people.

117. Ludden, 'India's Development Regime', 251.

118. Scott, *Seeing Like a State*, 4.

119. Ghosh, *Making It Count*, 59.

120. Ibid., 13–14.

121. Adam Tooze, 'Imagining National Economies: National and International Economics Statistics 1900–1950', in *Imagining Nations*, ed. G. Cubitt (Manchester: Manchester University Press, 1998), 213–214.

122. Cathryn Johnston has argued that the NSS also contributed to 'population' being conceived as a national problem enmeshed with issues relating to the economy and development, and amenable to national planned solutions. The NSS represented new methods by which to generate the data that would become the ground on which demographers debated population policy. Cathryn Anne Johnston, 'Demography and the Population Problem in India: Data, Research and Policy, 1938–1974', PhD thesis (2016), King's College London, 59–89.

123. Ibid., 214.

124. Michelle Murphy, *The Economization of Life* (Durham: Duke University Press, 2017), 1–34.

125. Deming, 'P. C. Mahalanobis 1893–1972', 49.

126. For an excellent study of Chinese statistics in the early PRC, see Ghosh, *Making It Count*. Y. P. Seng quoted in D. B. Lahiri, 'Prasanta Chandra Mahalanobis and Large Scale Sample Surveys', *Sankhyā*, Vol. 35, Supplement: Prasanta Chandra Mahalanobis (December 1973), 32.

127. Frank Yates, 'Review of the Work of the Indian National Sample Survey', submitted to the Technical Assistance Administration, reproduced in 120B, Mahalanobis Papers, PCMMMA.

128. Vidura, 'Outside-Inside India: An Indian View', *NYT* (1 May 1960), 26. Reproduced in the *NYT* after original publication in *Shankar's Weekly*.

129. 'Minutes of the Third Meeting of the National Development Council Held on 9th November 1954', in *Summary Record of Discussions of the National Development Council Meetings, Vol. 1 (1st to 14th Meetings)*, Government of India, Planning Commission, 2005, 22.

130. Abhijit Banerjee, 'Draw the Right Line', *Hindustan Times* (24 October 2011).

131. Abhijit Banerjee, Pranab Bardhan, Rohini Somanathan, and T. N. Srinivasan, 'From Being World Leader in Surveys, India is Now Facing a Serious Data Problem', *Economic Times Blogs* (4 April 2017).

132. A. B. Atkinson and E. Marlier, *Analysing and Measuring Social Inclusion in a Global Context* (New York: UN Department of Economic and Social Affairs, 2010), 21.

133. Banerjee, Bardhan, Somanathan, and Srinivasan, 'From Being World Leader in Surveys, India is Now Facing a Serious Data Problem'.

134. Jairaj Devadiga, 'A Dearth of Data Helped Hong Kong Succeed: Without Statistics, You Can't Prepare a Five-Year Plan – And That's Good News for Prosperity', *Wall Street Journal* (7 June 2019), www.wsj.com/articles/a-dearth-of-data-helped-hong-kong-succeed-11559944078, accessed on 20 February 2020.

135. Mahalanobis, *Papers on Planning*, 52.

2   Calcutta Conquers Delhi

1. Deming, 'P. C. Mahalanobis 1893–1972', 50.
2. Cited in Krishna R. Dronamraju, *Popularizing Science: The Life and Work of JBS Haldane* (New York: Oxford University Press, 2017), 289.
3. Mahalanobis to Pant, 12 April 1954, Pant Papers, NMML.
4. Mahalanobis to Pant, 20 June 1954, Pant Papers, NMML.
5. Mahalanobis to Pant, 23 June 1954, Pant Papers, NMML.
6. Mahalanobis to Pant, 24 June 1954, Pant Papers, NMML.
7. Rudra, *Prasanta Chandra Mahalanobis*, 433–434.
8. 'Professor P. C. Mahalanobis', 30 July 1953, Desp. No. 192, Confidential U.S. State Department Files, India 1950–54, Internal Affairs, RG 59, General Records of the Department of State.
9. The prediction never came to pass, despite *Business Week* magazine reporting in 1975 that Robinson was 'on everyone's list for this year's Nobel Prize in Economics'. She was likely passed over due to her admiration for Mao and defence of his policies, including the Great Leap Forward and Cultural Revolution. Julian Gewirtz, 'How Mao Cost a Cambridge Economist the Nobel Prize' (Los Angeles Review of Books: China Channel, 13 December 2017) https://chinachannel.org/2017/12/13/fellow-travellers-tale/, accessed on 30 October 2019.
10. Amartya Sen, 'Biographical', *The Nobel Prize* (1998) www.nobelprize.org/prizes/economic-sciences/1998/sen/biographical/, accessed on 30 October 2019.
11. Mahalanobis to Pant, 24 June 1954, Pant Papers, NMML; For more on Joan Robinson's relationship with India, see Ashwani Saith, 'Joan Robinson and Indian Planning: An Awkward Relationship', *Development and Change*, Vol. 39, No. 6 (2008), 1115–1134.
12. Mahalanobis to Pant, 24 June 1954, Pant Papers, NMML.
13. Mahalanobis to Pant, 4 July 1954, Pant Papers, NMML.
14. Mahalanobis to Pant, 7 July 1954, Pant Papers, NMML.
15. Mahalanobis to Pant, 17 July 1954, Pant Papers, NMML.
16. Mahalanobis to Pant, 7 July 1954, Pant Papers, NMML.
17. Mahalanobis to Pant, 17 July 1954, Pant Papers, NMML.
18. Letter from K. A. Abbas to K. G. Saiyidian, 4 December 1954, reproduced in Iffat Fatima and Syeda Hameed, eds., *Bread, Beauty, Revolution: Khwaja Ahmad Abbas, 1914–1987* (New Delhi: Tulika, 2015), 104.
19. This was the explanation Mahalanobis received from Oskar Lange.
20. The gathering included A. N. Nesmeyanaov (president of the official journal of the USSR Academy of Sciences, *Doklady Akademii Nauk*), Topchiev (chief executive of the Academy) and his wife, and Academician Vladimir Engelhardt and spouse Militza Lyubimova (both biochemist winners of the Stalin Prize for scientific distinction).
21. Mahalanobis to Pant, 17 July 1954, Pant Papers, NMML.
22. Mahalanobis to Pant, 16 July 1954, Pant Papers, NMML.
23. Mahalanobis to Pant, 17 July 1954, Pant Papers, NMML.
24. Ibid.
25. Ibid.

26. D.O. No. 11533-P/54 (Ministry of Finance, Dept. of Economic Affairs), C. S. Krishnamoorthi to P. C. Mahalanobis, 25 January 1954, reproduced in Record No. 44, P. C. Mahalanobis Papers, PCMMMA; Mahalanobis, *Papers on Planning*, 54.

27. Bettelheim returned the favour by inviting Mani Mukherjee to spend a fortnight with his research group in Paris acquiring information about technological coefficients for planning. Another of Mukherjee's visits was to Oslo, where he spent a few weeks working with the pioneering Norwegian econometrician Ragnar Frisch and his team on questions relating to physical planning. The Planning Division at the Institute also sent workers abroad for training in subjects that were of particular significance to planning. Dr Ajit Biswas, for example, did a stint at MIT in 1956 training, in input–output analysis and linear programming. C. S. Krishnamoorthi to P. C. Mahalanobis, 25 January 1954, Record No. 44, P. C. Mahalanobis Papers, PCMMMA; ' Operational Research Relating to Planning (Planning Division)', *Samvadadhvam*, Vol. 1, No. 1 (1956), 49.

28. C. Rajagopalachari to Jawaharlal Nehru, 6 March 1954, File No. 239, Part 1 (Correspondence), JN Papers Installment 1, 102, NMML.

29. Mahalanobis, *Papers on Planning*, 55.

30. Indian Statistical Institute: Studies Relating to Planning for National Development, Inaugural Speech by Jawaharlal Nehru, 3 November 1954, Record No. 1010 (B), P. C. Mahalanobis Papers, PCMMMA.

31. P. Chakraborty, 'The I.S.I. and Planning', *Samvadadhvam*, Vol. 1, No. 1 (1956), 12.

32. Third National Development Council Meeting, 10 November 1954, *Summary Record of Discussion of the National Development Council (NDC) Meetings*, Vol. 1, 39, http://planningcommission.nic.in/reports/genrep/50N DCs/vol1_1to14.pdf, accessed on 29 June 2016.

33. Record No. 74, P. C. Mahalanobis Papers, PCMMMA.

34. P. C. Mahalanobis, 'The Approach of Operations Research to Planning in India', *Sankhya*, Vol. 16, No. 1/2 (December 1955), 7.

35. Taylor C. Sherman, '"A New Type of Revolution": Socialist Thought in India, 1940s–1960s', *Postcolonial Studies*, Vol. 21, No. 4 (2018), 485–504; Daniel Kent-Carrasco, 'A Battle Over Meanings: Jayaprakash Narayan, Rammanohar Lohia and the Trajectories of Socialism in Early Independent India', *Global Intellectual History*, Vol. 2, No. 3 (2017), 370–388.

36. Sudipta Kaviraj, 'Democracy and Development in India', in *Democracy and Development*, ed. Amiya Kumar Bagchi (New York: St. Martin's Press, 1995), 103–104.

37. Nehru to V. T. Krishnamachari, 8 January 1955, Subject File No. 23, Installment I, C. D. Deshmukh Papers, NMML.

38. In February 1957, the Planning Cell was renamed the Statistics and Surveys Division of the Planning Commission. Record No. 42, P. C. Mahalanobis Papers, PCMMMA.

39. Following criticism from chief ministers that they weren't sufficiently kept abreast of developments in planning, a Standing Committee of the National Development Council was created on 10 November 1954. It was to be kept

appraised of planning activities and discussions on a more regular basis than the NDC as a whole. It comprised the Chief Ministers of Bombay, Hyderabad, Madras, Rajasthan, Punjab, Travancore-Cochin, West Bengal, and Uttar Pradesh.

40. Nehru to V. T. Krishnamachari, 8 January 1955, *SWJN*, SS, Vol. 30, 384–385.
41. Mahalanobis accepted formal membership in the Planning Commission in 1959, and he remained in this position till 1967. Nehru to V. T. Krishnamachari, 8 January 1955, *SWJN*, SS, Vol. 30, 384–385; Mahalanobis to Nehru, 31 May 1955, Record No. 120 (A), P. C. Mahalanobis Papers, PCMMMA; *SWJN*, SS, Vol. 29, 88.
42. I. G. Patel also happened to be Prime Minister Narasimha Rao's first choice for Finance Minister in 1991. When Patel turned it down, the position went to Manmohan Singh, who soon began India's market reforms.
43. I. G. Patel, *Glimpses of Indian Economic Policy* (New Delhi: Oxford University Press, 2002), 45.
44. The Institute's Delhi Centre moved into its current campus in Qutb Institutional Area, South Delhi, in 1974.
45. Indian Statistical Institute, 'Twenty-Fourth Annual Report: April 1955 to March 1956', *Sankhyā*, Vol. 17, No. 3 (1956), 279.
46. Though Mahalanobis is usually credited (or blamed) for the second Five-Year Plan, I. G. Patel maintained that he was its original author, along with Anjaria. In this telling, Mahalanobis rewrote their Draft Plan Frame without changing much of substance. Patel, however, does not make any claim to the two-sector and subsequent four-sector models that expressed the strategy mathematically and provided much of its intellectual heft. Patel, *Glimpses of Indian Economic Policy*, 46–47; and V. N. Balasubramanyam, *Conversations with Indian Economists* (New York: Palgrave Macmillan, 2001), 46–47. The Draft Plan Frame is reproduced in P. C. Mahalanobis, *Talks on Planning* (Calcutta: Statistical Publishing Society, 1961), 19–27.
47. Mahalanobis, *Papers on Planning*, 47.
48. Onlooker, 'Through Indian Eyes: The Ethics of Economic Planning', *TOI* (23 June 1955), 6; Chakravarty, *Development Planning*, 3.
49. Patel, *Glimpses of Indian Economic Policy*, 47.
50. Aye-a-Sigh, 'The Pity of it, Iago', *The Economic Weekly* (18 June 1955), 727.
51. On the Mont Pelerin Society, see Angus Burgin, *The Great Persuasion: Reinventing Free Markets since the Depression* (Cambridge, MA: Harvard University Press, 2015).
52. Surprisingly, Brahmananda does not appear to bear any ill will towards Mahalanobis, whom he described as a 'brilliant man with fresh ideas'. He remembers the Professor as 'non-ideological' and open-minded enough to write to him after reading *Planning in an Expanding Economy* (written by Vakil and Brahmananda in 1956). Responding to the criticism of his capital-goods model, Mahalanobis wrote, 'I am not an economist, but I want the quantitative details of the wage goods model worked out'. P. R. Brahmananda in Balasubramanyam, *Conversations with Indian Economists*, 33–34.

53. For debates over the Second Five-Year Plan, see Terence J. Byres, 'From Ivory Tower to the Belly of the Beast: The Academy, the State and Economic Debate in Post-Independence India', in *The Indian Economy: Major Debates since Independence*, ed. Terence J. Byres (New Delhi: Oxford University Press, 1998), 74–115.

54. Record No. 119, P. C. Mahalanobis Papers, PCMMMA.

55. Tarlok Singh had been Nehru's private secretary from late 1946 onwards and took on secretarial duties at the Planning Commission once it was formed in 1950. He ascended from secretarial functions in the Planning Commission to becoming a member of the Planning Commission in 1962. He remained a member till 1967. Inder Malhotra, 'Once Upon a Plan: Looking Back at the Early Years of the Planning Commission', *The Indian Express* (26 September 2014), http://indianexpress.com/article/opinion/col umns/once-upon-a-plan/, accessed on 1 April 2017.

56. Mahalanobis to Pant, written from 8 King George Avenue, 3 May 1955, Correspondence, Installment 2, Pant Papers, NMML.

57. Mahalanobis, 'The Approach of Operations Research to Planning in India', 7–8; Record No. 119, P. C. Mahalanobis Papers, PCMMMA.

58. Balasubramanyam, *Conversations with Indian Economists*, 31.

59. 'East Wind, West Wind', Delhi Letter, *The Economic Weekly* (4 June 1955), 651.

60. 'Economists, Political Economy and Government', *The Economic Weekly* (26 January 1955), 143.

61. 'Vrindaban without Krishna', *The Economic Weekly* (23 April 1955), 490.

62. Aye-a-Sigh, 'The Pity of it, Iago', 727.

63. 'Planning Technique and the Second Plan', *The Economic Weekly* (18 June 1955), 731, 733.

64. A. M., 'Ideology and Friendship: Early Days of Planning', *The Telegraph* (Sunday 19 May 2013), http://goo.gl/4ZSSj9, accessed on 24 June 2016.

65. Meghnad Desai, *The Raisina Model* (New Delhi: Penguin, 2017), excerpted in *Scroll.in*, https://scroll.in/article/861901/the-nehruvian-approach-groun d-the-economy-down-to-a-low-growth-path-meghnad-desai-in-his-new-b ook, accessed on 8 May 2018.

66. Byres, 'From Ivory Tower to the Belly of the Beast', 91.

67. A. M., 'Calcutta Diary', 3547.

68. Onlooker, 'Through Indian Eyes', 6.

69. Thomas Balogh, 'Why Nehru Needs Our Help', *The Observer* (18 August 1957), 3.

70. Onlooker, 'Through Indian Eyes', 6.

71. Rao, 'Indian Affairs'.

72. To be clear, this was before it became widely known that Stalin was a murderous tyrant. Even Western journalists based in Moscow were not aware of Stalin's bloody excesses until Khrushchev's 'secret speech' in early 1956. P. C. Mahalanobis to Oskar Lange, 18 March 1953, cited in David C. Engerman, 'The Professor Goes to Moscow', *EPW*, Vol. 53, No. 7 (February 2018), 29.

73. A. M., 'Ideology and Friendship'.

74. Mahalanobis to Pant, 12 August 1955, Record No. 90, P. C. Mahalanobis Papers, PCMMMA.

75. Sanjay Srivastava, 'Voice, Gender and Space in Time of Five-Year Plans: The Idea of Lata Mangeshkar', *EPW*, Vol. 39, No. 20 (15 May 2004), 2025.

76. 'Physical Planning', *The Economic Weekly* (3 September 1955), 1055.

77. Mahalanobis to Pant, 23 October 1955, Correspondence, Installment 2, Pant Papers, NMML.

78. Quoted in Das, *India Unbound*, 89.

79. Pant to Mahalanobis, 26 November 1955, Record No. 90, P. C. Mahalanobis Archives, PCMMMA.

80. Prime Minister's Speech at the Meeting of the National Development Council on 20 January 1950, File No. 822, Part 1 (Correspondence), JN Papers, NMML.

81. Nehru, *SWJN*, SS, Vol. 33, 336.

82. The First Five-Year Plan – buoyed by favourable monsoons, high crop yields and brimming foreign exchange reserves – exceeded the targeted growth of 2.1% to achieve 3.6%. Planning Commission, Government of India, *Second Five Year Plan 1956–61*, http://planningcommission.nic.in/plans/planrel/fiveyr/6th/6planch1.html, accessed on 18 June 2015; Patel, *Glimpses of Indian Economic Policy*, 47.

83. Rudra, *Prasanta Chandra Mahalanobis*, 432.

84. For the context surrounding the First Five-Year Plan, see V. K. R. V. Rao, 'India's First Five Year Plan – A Descriptive Analysis', *Pacific Affairs*, Vol. 25, No. 1 (March 1952), 3–23. For India's food situation in these years see Taylor C. Sherman, 'From "Grow More Food" to "Miss a Meal": Hunger, Development and the Limits of Post-Colonial Nationalism in India, 1947–1957', *South Asia: Journal of South Asian Studies*, Vol. 36, No. 4 (2013), 571–588; and Siegel, *Hungry Nation*.

85. The basis for the Third Five-Year Plan, in A. H. Hanson's account, were three papers: two by J. J. Anjaria and one by Pant. The latter's paper is described as 'Essentially ... the Plan Frame for the Third Plan.' Hanson, *The Process of Planning*, 174.

86. A. M. Rosenthal, 'New 5-Year Plan Offered By India', *NYT* (16 May 1956).

87. Peter Bauer, *From Subsistence to Exchange and Other Essays* (Princeton: Princeton University Press, 2000), 121–122.

88. Soviet economist G. A. Feldman had produced a nearly identical two-sector model in 1928. However, there is no evidence that Mahalanobis was aware of it. Planning Commission, Government of India, *Second Five Year Plan 1956–61*, http://planningcommission.gov.in/plans/planrel/fiveyr/index2.html, accessed on 18 June 2015.

89. Prime Minister's Speech at the Meeting of the National Development Council on 20 January 1956, reproduced in File No. 822 (Press Clippings), Part 1, Subject Files, JN Papers, NMML.

90. Speech by Nehru to the Rajya Sabha, September 1961. Quoted in 'Central Challenge of Our Lives', *Yojana* (17 September 1961), 19.

91. See Cullather, *Hungry World*.

92. Engerman, *The Price of Aid*; Nicole Sackley, 'The Village as Cold War Site: Experts, Development, and the History of Rural Reconstruction', *Journal of Global History*, Vol. 6, No. 3 (November 2011), 481–504.
93. H. Chandra, 'Pancha-Varshiya-Yojana Tantra: A Fable for Planners', *Yojana*, Vol. 4, No. 14 (24 July 1960), 35.
94. For a brief intellectual history of import substitution, see Douglas A. Irwin, 'The Rise and Fall of Import Substitution', Working Paper 20–10, Peterson Institute for International Economics, July 2020, 1–24.
95. Contemporary scholars of varying disciplinary backgrounds and political persuasions identify import-substitution industrialization as a flaw in the Indian growth strategy. Export led economies, such as Japan, Taiwan, and South Korea, performed much better during this same period. Today, pro-market economists Jagdish Bhagwati and Arvind Panagriya make this argument, as does Marxist sociologist Vivek Chibber. The case for paying greater attention to exports had also been made by a young economist named Manmohan Singh in 1963, in a paper titled 'Export Strategy for the Take-Off' for *The Economic Weekly*.
96. Based on a cross-country comparative study, political scientist Atul Kohli has argued that state intervention and import substitution was effective in promoting industrialization in developing nations from the mid-twentieth century onwards. What distinguished the contrasting trajectories of India, South Korea, Brazil, and Nigeria – all of whom pursued this strategy – was the nature of the state and its effectiveness in economic intervention. Kohli, *State Directed Development*.
97. I. G. Patel, 'The Landscape of Economics', *The Indian Economic Journal*, Vol. 45, No. 1 (1997), 30.
98. Balasubramanyam, *Conversations with Indian Economists*, 46–47.
99. Lorenzini, *Global Development*, 98–99; Kathryn Sikkink, 'Development Ideas in Latin America: Paradigm Shift and Economic Commission for Latin America', in *International Development and the Social Sciences*, ed. Cooper and Packard, 228–256.
100. Bauer, *From Subsistence to Exchange*, 117–118.
101. Chibber, *Locked in Place*, 39–43.
102. P. R. Brahmananda in Balasubramanyam, *Conversations with Indian Economists*, 33.
103. Prabhat Patnaik, 'Amartya Sen and the Theory of Public Action', *EPW*, Vol. 33, No. 45 (7–13 November 1998), 2855; Amartya Sen, 'A Note on the Mahalanobis Model of Sectoral Planning', *Arthaniti*, (May 1958), Vol. 1, No. 2, 26–33; Amartya Kumar Sen, 'Why Planning', 'Freedom and Planning', *Seminar*, Vol. 3 (November 1959), 15–17.
104. Balasubramanyam, *Conversations with Indian Economists*, 144–145.
105. Ibid., 91.
106. Among India's economists, it was Manmohan Singh who first seriously questioned India's export pessimism in his 1961 Oxford D. Phil.
107. Bhagwati, *India in Transition*, 54–55.
108. Once import-substitution has been set in motion, Chibber argues, 'it has the dynamic effect of eroding the export capacity domestic firms over time, as

the guarantee of domestic profits reduced the pressure to innovate. This is the basic dilemma of ISI [import-substitution industrialization]'. Indian firms underwent a long-term decline in both efficiency and marketing ability, making a potential turn towards entering foreign markets even harder. Chibber, *Locked in Place*, 200–201.

109. P. N. Rosenstein Rodan, *Notes on the Theory of the Big Push* (Cambridge, MA: Center for International Studies, Massachusetts Institute of Technology, 1957), 1.

110. From Mahalanobis' review of Gunnar Myrdal's *Asian Drama*, quoted in Rudra, *Prasanta Chandra Mahalanobis*, 226.

111. Milton Friedman and Rose. D Friedman, *Two Lucky People: Memoirs* (Chicago: University of Chicago Press, 1998), 262–263.

112. Hanson, *The Process of Planning*, 152.

113. Ibid., 136.

114. Lok Sabha Debates, 8 September 1956, Vol. 6I, No. 40, 6281–6295.

115. Neville Maxwell, *India's China War* (Dehradun: Nataraj, 1997), 112.

116. For an intellectual history of the Swatantra Party and its founders (Masani, C. Rajagopalachari, and B. R. Shenoy), see Aditya Balasubramanian, 'Contesting "Permit-and-Licence Raj": Economic Conservatism and the Idea of Democracy in 1950s India', *Past and Present*, Vol. 251, No. 1 (May 2021), 189–227; and his forthcoming *Partisans of the Free Economy* (Princeton: Princeton University Press).

117. Lok Sabha Debates, 20 November 1957, Vol. 8, No. 8, 1474–1484.

118. Lok Sabha Debates, 11 March 1958, Vol. 8, No. 21, 4402.

119. Lok Sabha Debates, 20 November 1957, Vol. 8, No. 8, 1474–1484. On the postcolonial fascination with steel, Srirupa Roy notes that it was of 'national symbolic importance ... steel was more than a mere industrial substance'. Srirupa Roy, *Beyond Belief: India and the Politics of Postcolonial Nationalism* (Durham: Duke University Press, 2007), 138.

120. Record No. 119, P. C. Mahalanobis Papers, PCMMMA; F. No. 87/19/CF-61, Cabinet Secretariat Papers, NAI.

121. Planning Commission, Government of India, 'Chapter 12: Research and Statistics for Planning', *Second Five Year Plan 1956–61*, http://planningcommission.gov.in/plans/planrel/fiveyr/2nd/2planch12.html, accessed on 18 June 2015.

122. In January 1960, Mahalanobis proposed changing his status from de facto to *ex-officio* member of the Planning Commission. V. T. Krishnamachari protested that it would 'imply an unintended nexus between the post of the Honorary Statistical Adviser and membership of the Planning Commission'. Though agreeing with this assessment, Nehru felt Mahalanobis could still be inducted – by conferring membership on him as an individual, and not the office of Statistical Adviser. As member of the Planning Commission, Mahalanobis was now placed in charge of the Perspective Planning Division. Nehru to V. T. Krishnamachari, 8 January 1955, *SWJN*, SS, Vol. 30, 384–385; Mahalanobis to Jawaharlal Nehru, 31 May 1955, Record No. 120 (A), P. C. Mahalanobis Papers, PCMMMA; *SWJN*, SS, Vol. 29, 88; *SWJN*, SS, Vol. 57, 183.

123. Mahalanobis to P. A. Gopalakrishnan (Joint Secretary, Cabinet Secretariat) 18 October 1956, Record No. 119, P. C. Mahalanobis Papers, PCMMMA.

124. The creation of a separate cell for perspective planning was likely inspired by the splitting of current and long-term planning within the Soviet Gosplan, File No. 823 (Speeches delivered in Prague, Moscow), Subject Files, Installment 1, JN Papers, NMML.

125. Record Nos. 65, 90, 124, P. C. Mahalanobis Papers, PCMMMA.

126. Interview with Jagdish Bhagwati, Balasubramanyam, *Conversations with Indian Economists*, 140.

127. Jagdish Bhagwati and Altaf Gauhar, 'Jagdish Bhagwati', *Third World Quarterly*, Vol. 2, No. 2 (April 1980), 211.

128. Balasubramanyam, *Conversations with Indian Economists*, 140.

129. Mahalanobis to Pitambar Pant, 8 February 1956, Record No. 90, P. C. Mahalanobis Papers, PCMMMA; Mahalanobis to Bhanu Pant, 29 June 1956, Installment 2, Correspondence, Pant Papers, NMML, 72–74.

130. Amartya Sen acknowledges Pant's influence on his early research on poverty in the 1970's: 'my interest in these problems was much stimulated by conversations with Pitambar Pant'. Jagdish Bhagwati also recalls working on poverty and income distribution during his time with the Institute and the Perspective Planning Division in the early 1960s. Byres, 'From Ivory Tower to the Belly of the Beast', 81–82; Bhagwati in Balasubramanyam, *Conversations with Indian Economists*, 140; T. N. Srinivasan, 'Minimum Standard of Living for all Indians', *Livemint* (12 October 2016), www.live mint.com/Opinion/Lcyz2vC1qSJJOGtHM0HVWN/Minimum-standard-of-living-for-all-Indians.html, accessed on 9 July 2019.

131. Mahalanobis, *Talks on Planning*, 130.

132. Ibid., 144.

133. Note prepared by Pant on 'Planning Commission: Perspective Planning Division', 9–6–1959, Record No. 119, P. C. Mahalanobis Papers, PCMMMA; Coleman, Cornish, and Drake, *Arndt's Story*, 228; George Rosen, *Globalization and Some of Its Discontents: The Autobiography of a Russian Immigrant* (Bloomington: Xlibris, 2005), 58–59; H. W. Arndt, *Economic Development: The History of an Idea* (Chicago: University of Chicago, 1989), 67.

134. Mahalanobis to Pant, 8 February 1956, Record No. 90, P. C. Mahalanobis Papers, PCMMMA.

135. 'Kalyanasree: A New Experiment', *Samvadadhvam*, Vol. 1, No. 1 (1956) 26–27. Mahalanobis to Pant, 8 February 1956, Record No. 90, P. C. Mahalanobis Papers, PCMMMA; Indian Statistical Institute, 'Twenty-Fourth Annual Report', 251; Indian Statistical Institute, 'Twenty-Fifth Annual Report: April 1956 to March 1957', *Sankhyā*, Vol. 20, No. 1/2 (September 1958), 126; 'Kalyanashree', www .isical.ac.in/~repro/history/public/notepage/Kalyanasree-F.html, accessed on 3 October 2019.

136. On the role of big dams in the Indian development imagination, see Daniel Klingensmith, *'One Valley and a Thousand': Dams, Nationalism,*

and Development (Oxford: Oxford University Press, 2007); and Sunil Amrith, *Unruly Waters: How Rains, Rivers, Coasts, and Seas Have Shaped Asia's History* (New York: Basic Books, 2018).

137. P. C. Mahalanobis address to the Standing Committee of the National Development Council, 5 May 1955. Cited in Hanson, *The Process of Planning*, 130.

138. Indian Statistical Institute, 'Twenty-Fourth Annual Report', 270.

139. On the feminization of crafts (especially textiles) in independent India, and its opportunities and limitations, see Abigail McGowan, 'Mothers and Godmothers of Crafts: Female Leadership and the Imagination of India as a Crafts Nation, 1947–67', *South Asia: Journal of South Asian Studies*, Vol. 44, No. 2 (April 2021), doi: 10.1080/00856401.2021.1876589.

140. 'Kalyanashree'.

141. Indian Statistical Institute, 'Twenty-Fifth Annual Report', 126.

142. Indian Statistical Institute, 'Annual Report: April 1959–March 1960, 22, http://library.isical.ac.in:8080/xmlui/bitstream/handle/10263/1900/ISIAR-1959-60-A.pdf?sequence=3&isAllowed=y; Indian Statistical Institute, 'Twenty-Fifth Annual Report', 126.

143. 'A Cottage Industry Research Project: Report from Three Bengal Villages', *Samvadadhvam*, Vol. 2, No. 2 (January–March 1958), 41.

144. Pant to Mahalanobis, 10 June 1956, P. C. Mahalanobis Papers, PCMMMA.

145. *Kalyanashree* was shuttered in 1967.

146. Nirmala Banerjee, 'Whatever Happened to the Dreams of Modernity? The Nehruvian Era and Woman's Position', *EPW*, Vol. 33, No. 17 (25 April–1 May 1998), WS2.

147. Shah, ed., *Report: National Planning Committee*, 218.

148. K. T. Shah, ed., *Woman's Role in Planned Economy*, National Planning Committee Series (Bombay: Vora, 1947); Durgabai Deshmukh, 'Women in Planning', in *Women in India*, ed. Tara Ali Beg (New Delhi: Government of India, 1958), 261–268.

149. Banerjee, 'Whatever Happened to the Dreams of Modernity?', WS2–WS7.

150. Complicating earlier narratives of the state's co-option of the women's movement in the 1950s, recent scholarship asserts the role played by women in shaping parts of the Nehruvian state. The limitations of the state's policies in certain fields like social welfare and family planning, in this view, reflects to some extent the ideologies and class backgrounds of the women involved in policymaking. See essays in Bhardwaj Datta, Sen, and Sreenivas, eds., 'A Country of Her Making'.

151. For more on her fascinating life, see Deshmukh, *Chintaman and I*.

152. On the possibilities opened to some women by the Central Social Welfare Board and state feminism more generally (despite its limitations), see Taylor C. Sherman, 'Not Part of the Plan? Women, State Feminism and Indian Socialism in the Nehru Years', *South Asia: Journal of South Asian Studies*, Vol. 44, No. 2 (April 2021), doi: 10.1080/00856401.2021.1884790. Social welfare apart, family planning was another realm of policymaking in which women were prominent in the Nehruvian period. Feminist organizations and organized women played a key role in

promoting family planning 'as a form of national planning' for and by women. They lobbied the government to include family planning in the Plan documents. Mytheli Sreenivas, 'Feminism, Family Planning and National Planning', *South Asia: Journal of South Asian Studies*, Vol. 44, No. 2 (April 2021), 3, doi: 10.1080/00856401.2021.1886731.

153. David C. Engerman, 'Learning from the East: Soviet Experts and India in the Era of Competitive Coexistence', *Comparative Studies of South Asia, Africa and the Middle East*, Vol. 33, No. 2 (2013), 230.

154. Gerald M. Meirs and Dudley Seers, eds., *Pioneers in Development* (Oxford: Oxford University Press, 1984), 277.

155. Engerman, 'Learning from the East', 230.

156. Alluding to this in his own memoirs, Friedman sportingly took credit for Galbraith's eventual appointment as the American Ambassador to India. J. K. Galbraith, *A Life in Our Times: Memoirs* (New York: Balantine Books, 1981), 324, 328; Friedman and Friedman, *Two Lucky People*, 269.

157. Andre Beteille, *Sunlight on the Garden: A Story of Childhood and Youth* (London: Penguin, 2012), 283–284.

158. See Engerman, 'Learning from the East'; and David C. Engerman, 'Mission from Moscow: Soviet Advisers and the Second Indian Five-Year Plan', *NCEEER Working Paper* (30 September 2014), 1–20.

159. Jerzy Neyman, '"Impressions from a Trip to India," December 15, 1956 to February 5, 1957: A Tribute to the Memory of Professor P. C. Mahalanobis', *Sankhyā: Indian Journal of Statistics*, Vol. 35, Supplement: Prasanta Chandra Mahalanobis (December 1973), 73; Coleman, Cornish, and Drake, *Arndt's Story*, 231.

160. Coleman, Cornish, and Drake, *Arndt's Story*, 231.

161. I. A. Ershova, Report on travel to India, November–December 1954, Archive of the Russian Academy of Sciences, 579/3/536/1–19, cited in Engerman, 'The Professor Goes to Moscow', 32.

162. I owe the discovery of this letter to Mirceau Raianu, who I am grateful to. D. D. Kosambi to Homi Bhabha, 23 September 1946, D-2004–00387–8 (1–2), Homi Bhabha Papers, TIFR Archives, Mumbai.

163. Mahalanobis to Pitambar Pant, 16 December 1956, Record No. 90, P. C. Mahalanobis Papers, PCMMMA.

164. Ghosh, *Making It Count*, 71–73.

165. I draw these insights from Arunabh Ghosh, 'Accepting Difference, Seeking Common Ground: Sino-Indian statistical Exchanges, 1951–1959', *British Journal for the History of Science*, Vol. 1 (2016), 61–82.

166. Engerman, 'Learning from the East', 231.

167. Aye-a-Sigh, 'The Pity of it, Iago', 727.

168. For details of the 1956–1957 foreign exchange crisis, its causes, and impact on the course of the Second Five-Year Plan, see Chibber, *Locked in Place*, 196–221; Kudaisya, 'A Mighty Adventure', 968–974; and Hanson, *The Process of Planning*, 136–170.

169. Kingsley Martin, 'India Revisited: A Decade of Change', *TOI* (15 April 1958), 6. And Chibber, *Locked in Place*, 196–198; Kudaisya, 'A Mighty Adventure', 968–975.

170. Quoted in Dasgupta, ed., *Science and Modern India*, 1050.
171. Tenth National Development Council Meeting, 3 May 1958, Morning Session, *Summary Record of the Discussions of the National Development Council Meeting Vol. I (1st to 14th Meetings)*, 242, http://planningcommission .gov.in/reports/genrep/50NDCs/vol1_1to14.pdf, accessed on 7 January 2016.
172. Hanson, *The Process of Planning*, 174.
173. C. R. Rao, ed., *Essays on Econometrics and Planning*: Presented to P. C. Mahalanobis on the Occasion of his 70th Birthday (New York: Pergamon Press, 1963), 155.
174. Patel, *Glimpses of Indian Economic Policy*, 35.

3   Chasing Computers

1. A version of this chapter was earlier published as '"Fancy Calculating Machine": Computers and Planning in Independent India', *Modern Asian Studies*, Vol. 52, No. 2 (March 2018), 421–457. Copyright © Cambridge University Press 2017. Reprinted with permission.
2. Morton Nadler, *No Regrets* (2008), chapter 26, http://goo.gl/y6sRUK, accessed on 15 November 2014.
3. F. A. Hayek, ed., *Collectivist Economic Planning* (London: Routledge and Kegan Paul, 1963); Paul Erikson, Judy L. Klein, Lorraine Daston, Rebecca Lemov, Thomas Sturm, and Michael D. Gordin, *How Reason Almost Lost Its Mind* (Chicago: University of Chicago Press, 2013), 70–71; Tadeusz Kowalik, ed., *Economic Theory and Market Socialism: Selected Essays of Oskar Lange* (Brookfield: Edward Elgar, 1994), 252–300, 361–365.
4. In Britain, the Colossus was used in code breaking during World War II. In the United States, the Army Ordnance Department sponsored the development of ENIAC to facilitate the calculation of artillery firing tables. The first digital computer in the USSR, or in continental Europe, the MESM, was used for calculations relating to rocketry and atomic bombs.
5. The scarcity is particularly acute with regard to histories of India's earliest computers. R. K. Shyamsundar and M. A. Pai, eds., *Homi Bhabha and the Computer Revolution* (New Delhi: Oxford University Press, 2011); Ross Bassett, 'Aligning India in the Cold War Era: Indian Technical Elites, the Indian Institute of Technology at Kanpur, and Computing in India and the United States', *Technology and Culture*, Vol. 50, No. 4 (October 2009), 783–810; Dinesh C. Sharma, *The Long Revolution: The Birth and Growth of India's IT Industry* (Noida: Harper Collins India, 2009); V. Rajaraman *History of Computing in India (1955–2010)* (Bangalore: IEEE Computer Society, 2012), accessed on 30 November 2014. Notable studies of the history of computers outside the United States, western Europe, and the USSR include Eden Medina, *Cybernetic Revolutionaries: Technology and Politics in Allende's Chile* (Cambridge: MIT Press, 2011); Honghong Tinn, 'Modeling Computers and Computer Models: Manufacturing Economic-Planning Projects in Cold War Taiwan, 1959–1968', *Technology and Culture*, Vol. 59, No. 4, Supplement (October 2018),

66–99; Victor Petrov, 'The Rose and the Lotus: Bulgarian Electronic Entanglements in India 1967–1989', *Journal of Contemporary History*, Vol. 54, No. 3 (2018), 666–687.

6. The account of Nadler's life is based primarily on his unpublished memoirs. Nadler, *No Regrets*, chapter 17.
7. Ibid., chapter 18.
8. Ibid., chapter 19.
9. Ibid., chapter 21.
10. Ibid., chapter 22.
11. Nadler's renunciation of American citizenship was reported in the *New York Times*. 'Citizenship Renounced: American in Prague Says He Seeks Czech Nationality', *NYT* (4 November 1950), 34. Ibid., chapter 21.
12. Nadler, *No Regrets*, chapter 25.
13. Ibid.
14. The Walter-McCarran Act deemed ineligible for an entry visa 'anybody who is or has ever been' a member of a long list of subversive groups. Nadler had been a member of at least eight. Ibid., chapter 24.
15. Ibid., chapter 25.
16. Nadler would only learn about his mother's contact with the FBI years later when sifting through documents in his Freedom of Information file. Ibid.
17. Ibid., chapter 24.
18. Ibid., chapter 25.
19. British biologist J. B. S. Haldane relocated to India in 1956 under similar circumstances – disillusioned with communism and the Party, searching for inspiration and professional opportunity in a democracy pursuing 'socialistic' ideals. Haldane responded to an invitation from Mahalanobis and spent the rest of his career in Calcutta at the Institute. On Haldane's fascinating life, see Samanth Subramaniam, *A Dominant Character: The Radical Science and Restless Politics of J. B. S. Haldane* (Noida: Simon and Schuster, 2019).
20. Nadler, *No Regrets*, chapter 25; Record No. 74, Mahalanobis Papers, PCMMMA.
21. A. M. Rosenthal, 'U.S. Exiles Merge Into Prague Life', *NYT* (30 August 1959), 20.
22. Nadler's unpublished memoir ends with his arrival in Calcutta. We know he spent 1959 at the Institute in Calcutta as Electronic Data Processing Machine consultant, working at the Computer Laboratory. Beginning in 1960, he was a scientific adviser for French computation firms until 1983. Nadler would become a pioneer in pattern recognition, especially optical character recognition (OCR), founding North American Digital Logic Inc. in 1985 (a company that, post renaming and acquisition, would deliver the CIA a multilingual OCR system). He also became a professor of electrical engineering at Virginia Tech in 1984, serving on its faculty till 1991. Nadler was computer-savvy till the end of his life (he had an active Facebook profile). He died at the age of ninety-two on 13 November 2013. 'Morton Nadler', *IEEE Transactions on Electronic Computers* (1963), 927, http://goo.gl/6U5DGT, accessed on 3 January 2015; Morton Nadler, *Topics in Engineering Logic* (New York: Pergamon Press, 1962); Morton Nadler, 'Some Notes on

Computer Research in Eastern Europe', *Communications of the ACM*, Vol. 2, No. 12 (December 1959), 1–2; 'In Memoriam: Morton Nadler, Professor', News/Events: Bradley Department of Electrical Engineering, Virginia Tech, http://goo.gl/QSIZ0U, accessed on 20 December 2014.

23. Mahalanobis to Maurice F. Ronanyne, 12 February 1960, Record No. 74, Mahalanobis Papers, PCMMMA.

24. Mahalanobis to William Deming, 25 March 1946, Record No. 26, Mahalanobis Papers, PCMMMA.

25. Record No. 74, Mahalanobis Papers, PCMMMA.

26. Mahalanobis was attending this event as a representative of the National Institute of Sciences of India.

27. It appears nothing came of this exchange between Mahalanobis and Von Neumann. P. C. Mahalanobis, 'Report on Tour of Canada, U.S.A. and U.K. October 15 to December 15, 1946', *Sankhya*, Vol. 8, No. 4 (June 1948), 404.

28. Ibid., 405, 409–410.

29. 'Tour Report: 26 January–15 April 1947', F. No. 17 (10) 48-PMS, PMO, NAI.

30. Karen R. Polenske, 'Leontief's "Magnificent Machine" and Other Contributions to Applied Economics', in *Wassily Leontief and Input-Output Economics*, ed. Erik Dietzenbacher and Michael L. Lahr (Cambridge: Cambridge University Press, 2004), 12.

31. The workshop also manufactured, maintained, and repaired desk calculators, punched card machines, precision measuring instruments, and machine tools. Indian Statistical Institute, 'Twenty-Second Annual Report: 1953–54', *Sankhyā*, Vol. 14, No. 4 (February 1955), 395.

32. Samar Mitra, 'A Child Grown Into Manhood', *Samvadadhvam*, Vol. 1, No. 3 (March 1957), 10–11.

33. Though the computer was not christened, it is referred to in one Institute annual report as the Analogue Linear Equation Solving Machine. Record No. 74, Mahalanobis Papers, PCMMMA; and Devaprasanna Sinha, 'Glimpsing Through Early Days of Computers in Kolkata', *CSI Communications*, Vol. 36, No. 5 (2012), 5.

34. Sharma, *The Long Revolution*, 7.

35. Speech by Mahalanobis quoted in Indian Statistical Institute, 'Twenty-Second Annual Report', 406.

36. Note made by Mahalanobis on 9 June 1957, Record No. 72, Mahalanobis Papers, PCMMMA.

37. Announced by President Harry S. Truman in 1949, the Point Four program provided technical assistance to developing countries.

38. The Professor wanted another Institute employee who worked in the Electronics Division, Mani Mukherjee, to join him in the search, but it was too expensive for the Institute to afford. Mahalanobis to Pant, 12 April 1954, Pant Papers, NMML.

39. Mahalanobis to Pant, 23 June 1954, Pant Papers, NMML.

40. Mahalanobis to Pant, 20 June 1954, Pant Papers, NMML.

41. Mahalanobis to Pant, 24 June 1954, Pant Papers, NMML

42. At the time $200,000 was roughly equivalent to ten lakh Indian rupees.
43. Mahalanobis to Pant, 24 June 1954, Pant Papers, NMML; Mahalanobis to C. S. Krishna Moorthi, Deputy Secretary, Ministry of Finance, 16 September 1954, Mahalanobis Papers, PCMMMA.
44. The US FOA was a governmental international aid organization that was instituted in 1953 to provide economic and military aid. President Eisenhower shut it in 1955 and its functions were transferred to the Department of State.
45. Mahalanobis to Pant, 23 June 1954, Pant Papers, NMML.
46. Ibid.
47. Mahalanobis to Pant, 27 June 1954, Pant Papers, NMML.
48. Ibid.
49. Note prepared by Mahalanobis and 'handed over to the Prime Minister for his information', 4 March 1959, Record No. 119, Mahalanobis Papers, PCMMMA; *Life Magazine*, No. 46 (31 March 1958).
50. Note prepared by Mahalanobis, 4 March 1959, Record No. 119, Mahalanobis Papers, PCMMMA.
51. Slava Gerovitch, '"Mathematical Machines" of the Cold War: Soviet Computing, American Cybernetics and Ideological Disputes in the Early 1950s', *Social Studies of Science*, Vol. 31, No.2, Science in the Cold War (April 2001), 272–276.
52. Note prepared by Mahalanobis, 4 March 1959, Record No. 119, Mahalanobis Papers, PCMMMA.
53. Ibid.; and Iqbal Singh, *Between Two Fires: Towards an Understanding Jawaharlal Nehru's Foreign Policy – Volume 2* (New Delhi: Orient Blackman, 1998), 264–265.
54. Ibid.; Mahalanobis to Pant, 16 July 1954, Pant Papers, NMML.
55. Indian Statistical Institute, 'Twenty-Third Annual Report: April 1954– March 1955', *Sankhyā*, Vol. 16, No. 1/2 (December 1955), 18–19.
56. BESM stood for *Bystrodeystvuyushchaya Elektronnaya Schetnaya Mashina* or 'High-Speed Electronic Calculating Machine'.
57. The parameters of the BESM would be formally disclosed to other nations more than a year later at the Conference on Electronic Digital Computers and Electronic Processing in Darmstadt, West Germany, in October 1955. Gerovitch, 'Mathematical Machines', 274–275.
58. 'Soviet Experts to Visit India', *Hindustan Standard* (19 July 1954) as reproduced in, Desp. No. 536, Confidential US State Department Files, India 1950–1954, Internal Affairs, RG 59, General Records of the Department of State.
59. Mahalanobis to Pant, Moscow, 7 July 1954, Pant Papers, NMML.
60. Ibid.
61. Note prepared by Mahalanobis, 4 March 1959, Record No. 119, Mahalanobis Papers, PCMMMA.
62. Ibid.
63. Mahalanobis to Pant, 16 July 1954, Pant Papers, NMML.
64. Mahalanobis to Pant, 2 October 1954, Record No. 90, Mahalanobis Papers, PCMMMA.

65. Mohi Mukherjee, 'The First Computer in India', in *Computer Education in India*, ed. Utpal K. Banerjee (New Delhi: Concept, 1996), 13.
66. Indian Statistical Institute, 'Twenty-Fourth Annual Report', 265.
67. Makarand Bhonsle, 'Computer Technology in India', Vigyan Prasar Radio Serials, http://goo.gl/KnKDHI, accessed on 1 October 2014; and Indian Statistical Institute, 'Twenty-Fourth Annual Report', 265.
68. Sharma, *The Long Revolution*, 10.
69. Mukherjee, 'The First Computer in India', 13–15.
70. Dwijesh Dutta Majumder, 'Foundation of Information and Computer Technology (ICT) in India and the Indian Statistical Institute (ISI)', 8, http://goo.gl/8lTLwo, accessed on 17 November 2014.
71. These included the Indian Institute of Technology (Kharagpur), Indian Institute of Science, Indian Association for the Cultivation of Science, Physical Research Laboratory, TIFR, and Andhra University.
72. ' Electronic Computer Laboratory', *Samvadadhvam*, Vol. 1, No. 2 (October 1956), 32.
73. Mukherjee, 'The First Computer in India', 15.
74. 'Indian Statistical Institute: Electronics Computer Division', 29 January 1960, Record No. 74, Mahalanobis Papers, PCMMMA.
75. ISI Council Meeting, 29 May 1964: Supplementary Agenda, Record No. 74, Mahalanobis Papers, PCMMMA
76. Indian Statistical Institute, 'Twenty-Fourth Annual Report', 266.
77. 'Indian Statistical Institute: Electronics Computer Division', 29 January 1960, Record No. 74, Mahalanobis Papers, PCMMMA.
78. The Ural was UN property until its title was formally transferred to the Government of India. It was loaned to the Institute, but the government continued to 'retain complete freedom to utilize the equipment at their discretion'. Note prepared by Mahalanobis and 'handed over to the Prime Minister for his information', 4 March 1959, Record No. 119, Mahalanobis Papers, PCMMMA.
79. 'Quality Control Talks Begin in Calcutta', *TOI* (21 December 1958), 7.
80. 'Soviet Electronic Computer – URAL', *Samvadadhvam*, Vol. 2, No. 4 (July–September 1958), 22.
81. Rajaraman, *History of Computing*, 16.
82. 'The First Computer Comes to India', *Dataquest* (30 December 2006), www.dqindia.com/the-first-computer-comes-to-india/, accessed on 11 April 2017.
83. 'Indian Statistical Institute: Electronics Computer Division', 29 January 1960, Record No. 74, Mahalanobis Papers, PCMMMA.
84. 'Superman's Girlfriend Lois Lane, Comic Featuring UNIVAC on the Cover', Object ID 500004046, Computer History Museum, http://goo.gl/K 3gcdx, accessed on 1 December 2014; Steve Henn, 'The Night a Computer Predicted the Next President', *NPR* (31 October 2012), http://goo.gl/NmW Yf, accessed on 2 December 2014.
85. Note made by Mahalanobis on 9 June 1957, Record No. 72, Mahalanobis Papers, PCMMMA.

86. Stuart Rice's conversation with Mahalanobis, 17 February 1953, SDDF, USNA, 891.00TA/201753, cited in Engerman, 'The Professor Goes to Moscow', 31.

87. 'Professor P. C. Mahalanobis', 30 July 1953, Desp. No. 192, Confidential US State Department Files, India 1950–1954, Internal Affairs, RG 59, General Records of the Department of State.

88. 'Professor P. C. Mahalanobis, Chief of the Indian Statistical Institute', 7 August 1953, Desp. No. 115, Confidential US State Department Files, India 1950–1954, Internal Affairs, RG 59, General Records of the Department of State.

89. 'United States and USSR Economic Interests in India', 12 November 1954, Desp. No. 536, 2, Confidential US State Department Files, India 1950–1954, Internal Affairs, RG 59, General Records of the Department of State.

90. Note by Mahalanobis on 'Electronic Processing Facilities', 19 March 1957, Record No. 72, Mahalanobis Papers, PCMMMA.

91. The ICA was a successor to the US FOA. John Hollister was Eisenhower's conservative pick for the Directorship of the ICA. It was viewed in America as a blow to those in favor of greater aid.

92. Ambassador in India (Bunker) to Frederic P. Bartlett, at London. Foreign Relations of the United States, 1955–1957, Volume VIII, South Asia, Document 167, https://history.state.gov/historicaldocuments/frus1955-57 v08/d167, accessed on 30 November 2014.

93. Mahalanobis to Dr. Douglas Ensminger, 5 December 1957, Record No. 72, Mahalanobis Papers, PCMMMA.

94. Copy of a letter sent from Morris H. Hansen, Samuel N. Alexander, and Russell L. Ackoff to Dr. Henry Heald (President, The Ford Foundation), 26 November 1957, Record No. 72, Mahalanobis Papers, PCMMMA.

95. Mahalanobis to S. K. Bose (Cabinet Secretary), 6 February 1958, Record No. 72, Mahalanobis Papers, PCMMMA; Mahalanobis to S. K. Bose, 14 February 1958, Record No. 72, Mahalanobis Papers, PCMMMA.

96. Mahalanobis to S. K. Bose, 14 February 1958, Record No. 72, Mahalanobis Papers, PCMMMA.

97. Shyamsundar and Pai, eds., *Homi Bhabha*, xxv.

98. Work on the TIFR's analog machine, EC-602, began in 1958.

99. Shyamsundar and Pai, eds., *Homi Bhabha*, xxv.

100. William George Penney, 'Homi Jehangir Bhabha, 1909–1966', *Biographical Memoirs of Fellows of the Royal Society*, Vol. 13 (November 1967), 35–55.

101. Bhabha to Mahalanobis, 22 August 1961, Record No. 72, Mahalanobis Papers, PCMMMA.

102. Mahalanobis to Bhabha, 25 August 1961, Record No. 72, Mahalanobis Papers, PCMMMA.

103. 'Studies in Long-term Economic Development – Tentative Scheme of Work', note prepared by Tarlok Singh, 27 April 1962, Record No. 73, Mahalanobis Papers, PCMMMA.

104. Minutes of the meeting held on 7 June 1962 in Room No. 126, Yojana Bhavan, New Delhi. Record No. 73, Mahalanobis Papers, PCMMMA.

105. 'Computers', *TOI* (10 September 1962), 6.
106. It is possible that the large computer of a UNIVAC-type was not sanctioned because the Institute had in 1962 already begun collaborating with Jadavpur University to build a second-generation digital computer. This computer, named ISI-JU, was completed in 1966. Rajaraman, *History of Computing*, 16–17.
107. The transition from punched card data processors to computers in the tabulation of NSS data began in 1965 at the Institute with the IBM 1401. 'Information Technology in the Indian Statistical System', *Ministry of Statistics and Programme Implementation, Government of India*, www.mospi.gov.in/147-information-technology-indian-statistical-system, accessed on 5 April 2017.
108. The CDC 600 (manufactured by Control Data Corporation) was installed at TIFR in May 1964. It was acquired at the cost of $1.5 million and was financed through a loan to the Government of India by the US Agency for International Development (AID). Rajaraman, *History of Computing*, 17; 'Bombay's Versatile Computer', *TOI* (7 February 1965), 6.
109. 'Computer: Magic Tool of Future', *TOI* (3 September 1964), 6.
110. Dr. Forrest E. Linder and Dr. Conrad Tauber to Dr. Douglas Ensminger, 21 January 1963, Record No. 73, Mahalanobis Papers, PCMMMA.
111. '1620 Computer Installations for New Delhi Area', Record No. 017762, Unpublished Reports, Ford Foundation Papers, RAC.
112. 'Computer Centre is Opened', *TOI* (24 September 1965), 5.
113. Ibid.; F. No. 9/51/71 RSR, Planning Commission, NAI.
114. John Thornhill, 'The Big Data Revolution Can Revive the Planned Economy', *Financial Times* (5 September 2017), 9.
115. Andrew Browne, 'China Uses "Digital-Leninism" to Manage Economy and Monitor Citizens', *The Wall Street Journal* (17 October 2017), www.wsj.com/articles/xi-jinping-leads-china-into-big-data-dictatorship-1508237820, accessed on 13 September 2018.
116. Thornhill, 'The Big Data Revolution Can Revive the Planned Economy', 9.
117. 'Backwards and Forwards: The Process of Planning in Indian Democracy', *The Economic Weekly* (January 1956), Annual Issue, 77.

4   Help the Plan – Help Yourself

1. A preliminary version of this chapter was published as '"Help the Plan – Help Yourself": Making India Plan-Conscious', in *The Postcolonial Moment in South and Southeast Asia*, ed. Gyan Prakash, Michael Laffan, and Nikhil Menon (London: Bloomsbury Academic, 2018), 221–242.
2. City Clerk, 'The Common Man and the Plan', *The Economic Weekly* (January 1956), 75.
3. Vidura, 'Outside-Inside India', 26. This article was reproduced in the *NYT* after original publication in *Shankar's Weekly*.
4. Nehru, *SWJN*, SS, Vol. 33, 92.
5. Rough Notes on National Planning Committee, June 1939, File No. 406, Part 3 (Diaries and Notebooks), JN Papers, NMML, 12.

6. 'Plan-consciousness' and 'Plan-conscious' were terms that were regularly used. See, for example, Sadath Ali Khan, 'Plan Consciousness: What It Should Really Mean', *Yojana*, Vol. 3, No. 26 (10 January 1960), 3, or in the following issue of the same journal, A. D. Mani, 'Plan Consciousness on Higher Key', *Yojana*, Vol. 4, No. 1, Republic Day Number (26 January 1960), 20.

7. Chatterjee, *The Nation and Its Fragments*, 202. James Ferguson similarly argued that the 'hegemonic problematic of "development" is the principal means through which the question of poverty is de-politicised in the world today'. James Ferguson, *The Anti-Politics Machine: 'Development,' Depoliticization, and Bureaucratic Power in Lesotho* (Cambridge: Cambridge University Press, 1990), 256.

8. See Kudaisya, '"A Mighty Adventure"', 960–965; Chatterjee, 'Development Planning and the Indian State', in *The State and Development Planning in India*; Chibber, *Locked in Place*.

9. Sumit Sarkar, 'Nationalism and Poverty: Discourses of Development and Culture in 20th Century India', *Third World Quarterly*, Vol. 29, No. 3 (2008), 432.

10. C. A. Bayly, 'Development and Sentiment: The Political Thought of Nehru's India', The First Sarvepalli Gopal Memorial Lecture, King's College London, 26 April 2012, www.kcl.ac.uk/sspp/departments/kii/documents/Bayly-lecture.pdf.

11. On Nehru's redefinition of what politics should constitute in the post-colony, see Dipesh Chakrabarty, '"In the Name of Politics": Democracy and the Power of the Multitude in India', *Public Culture*, Vol. 19, No. 1 (2006), 35–57. On 'postcolonial nationalism' see Roy, *Beyond Belief*.

12. Gunnar Myrdal, *Asian Drama: An Inquiry into the Poverty of Nations*, Vol. 2 (New York: Twentieth Century Fund, 1968), 850–851.

13. The song's lyricist, Shailendra, had been a member of the leftist Indian People's Theatre Association (IPTA).

14. Siegel, *Hungry Nation*, 88. See also Upendra Baxi, 'The Justice of Human Rights in Indian Constitutionalism', in *Political Ideas in Modern India: Thematic Explorations*, ed. V. R. Mehta and Thomas Pantham (New York: Sage, 2006), 263–284; Jayal, *Citizenship and its Discontents: An Indian History* (Cambridge: Harvard University Press, 2013), 109–135.

15. Government of India, *First Five Year Plan*, https://niti.gov.in/planningcommission.gov.in/docs/plans/planrel/fiveyr/index1.html, accessed on 15 January 2020.

16. Shah, ed., *Report: National Planning Committee*, 109, 111, 127.

17. Nehru's statement to the Press, 15 May 1940, cited in Zachariah, *Developing India*, 224.

18. Speech by prime minister at meeting of the Federation of Indian Chambers of Commerce and Industry at Imperial Hotel, 10 a.m. Saturday, 11 March 1950, File No. 38, Part 1 (Correspondence), JN Papers, NMML.

19. On the state promoted ethic of sacrifice, self-help, and voluntary participation in national development, see Siegel, *Hungry Nation*, 86–118 and Sherman, from "Grow More Food" to "Miss a Meal".

20. Congress Party resolution on the objectives of planning, April 1950. Cited in Chattopadhyay, 'The Idea of Planning in India 1931–1951', 326–327.
21. Record Notes of the Meetings of the Planning Commission, Planning Commission, P.C. Department, 1950, F. No. 2(2)-ECC/50, NAI.
22. Hanson, *The Process of Planning*, 129–130.
23. Abu Abraham, 'Sun-Cooking Era', *Shankar's Weekly* (29 June 1952).
24. R. K. Laxman, 'Carrying it Over', *Yojana*, Vol. 1, No. 1 (January 1957), 4.
25. Ananth, *Yojana*, Vol. 1 (April 1957), 1.
26. Pant's paper was presented on 21 December 1958. Hanson, *The Process of Planning*, 174, 176.
27. 'What They Said of Plan and Country', *Yojana*, Vol. 4, No. 13 (10 July 1960), 12.
28. 'Need to Fulfill India's Plan Target Urged: Vital for Survival of Democracy Says Mr. Pant', *TOI* (22 December 1958), 9.
29. *Report of the Congress Planning Sub-Committee* (All India Congress Committee, 1959), 12, 61.
30. 'First Priority Given to Output and Jobs: Mr. Nanda's Appeal for Public Co-operation', *TOI* (9 September 1956), 10.
31. A. M., 'Thirty Pandara Road: An Address Touched by the Dynamism of History', *The Telegraph* (3 April 2013), www.telegraphindia.com/1130403/j sp/opinion/story_16716679.jsp#.V3KgSJMrJE5, accessed on 29 June 2016.
32. Record Notes of the Meetings of the Planning Commission, Planning Commission, P.C. Department, 1950, F. No. 2(2)-ECC/50, NAI.
33. Tarlok Singh, 'Can We Get More Out of the Plan?', *Yojana*, Vol. 2, No. 1 (26 January 1958), 7.
34. Summary record of the meeting of Planning Commission held on 24–25 July1966, reproduced in Box 19, Tarlok Singh Papers – Installment 2, NMML.
35. Ibid.
36. Myrdal, *Asian Drama*, 895.
37. Prime minister's speech at the Economic Planning Conference of the Indian National Congress, held in New Delhi, on 25 April 1950, File No. 43, Part 1, JN Papers, NMML.
38. G. Parthasarathi, ed., *Jawaharlal Nehru: Letters to Chief Ministers, 1947–64*, Vol. 3 (New Delhi: Oxford University Press, 1987), 203–206.
39. 'Revised Procedure for Selection of Troupes and Allotment of Performers', F. No. 20(1)/59, Plan Publicity, Ministry of Information and Broadcasting, NAI.
40. Government of India, *First Five-Year Plan*, http://planningcommission.nic.in /plans/planrel/fiveyr/1st/1planch8.html, accessed on 28 September 2015.
41. *SWJN*, SS, Vol. 19, 89.
42. 'Bharat Sewak Samaj', *The Hindu* (14 August 1952), 6; 'Bharat Sewak Samaj', *The Hindu* (9 July 1952), 6.
43. 'Directorate of Field Publicity-Creation of,' F. No. 12(3)/59-PP, 11, Plan Publicity, Ministry of Information and Broadcasting, NAI.
44. 'Villagers to be Educated about Five Year Plans', *TOI* (1 January 1954), 3.
45. F. No. 12(5)/59-PP, Plan Publicity, Ministry of Information and Broadcasting, NAI.

46. The cart units were abandoned in 1957–1958, within a year of having been established, as it was realized that the jeep or van units could do the job.
47. F. No. 12/7A/59-PP, Plan Publicity, Ministry of Information and Broadcasting, NAI.
48. F. No. 4/53/57-FYPPII, Plan Publicity, Ministry of Information and Broadcasting, National Archives of India (NAI).
49. Government of India, *Report of the Study Team on Five Year Plan Publicity* (New Delhi: Ministry of Information and Broadcasting, 1964), 67.
50. 'Directorate of Field Publicity-Creation of,' F. No. 12(3)/59-PP, 1, Plan Publicity, Ministry of Information and Broadcasting, NAI.
51. K. B. Lall, 'Renewing Faith in Nation's Economic Progress', *TOI* (17 October 1958), 1.
52. This account of India 1958 is drawn from the following sources: ' India 1958', *March of India*, Vol. 10, No. 8 (August 1958), 19–20; Ibid.; Bharat Ki Jhanki (English title Indian Panorama), directed by Krishna Kapil (Bombay: Films Division of India, 1958).
53. Bharat Ki Jhanki, directed by Kapil.
54. F. No. 23/9/59-PP (Part 1), 68, Ministry of Information and Broadcasting, NAI.
55. 'Exhibitions on Wheels Soon: Message to Rural Areas on Plan', *TOI* (11 July 1959), 5.
56. Introduction of Standard Versions of the Five-Year Plans for Study in the College, Ministry of Education, 1953, D1_1953_NA_F-30–13_53, NAI.
57. *India Has a Plan* (New Delhi: Publications Division, Ministry of Information and Broadcasting, 1953), 7.
58. Introduction of Standard Versions of the Five-Year Plans for Study in the College, Ministry of Education, 1953, D1_1953_NA_F-30–13_53, NAI.
59. File. No. 10/6/61 – Pub., Publication, Ministry of Information & Broadcasting, NAI.
60. *We Plan for Prosperity* (New Delhi: Publications Division, Ministry of Information and Broadcasting, Revised Reprint, 1963), Preface.
61. The 'Help the Plan – Help Yourself' campaign began in 1958. *Yojana*, Vol. 2, No. 26 (11 January 1959), 7.
62. Padmini Sen Gupta, 'Working Women of India', *Yojana*, Vol. 3, No. 1 (26 January 1959), 15.
63. Ibid., 18.
64. Subhadra Devi, 'Nari Swatantrata Key Bina Pragati Adhuri', *Yojana* (Hindi), Vol. 3, No. 1 (15 February 1959), 15.
65. 'Kites Carry Plan's Message', *TOI* (15 January 1957), 5.
66. Mulk Raj Anand, 'Arousing Interest in the Plan', Letter to the Editor, *TOI* (15 August 1957), 12.
67. Manu Desai, 'Publicity and Five Year Plan', *The Economic Weekly* (18 July 1953), 799.
68. Ibid., 800.
69. 'Plan Publicity Through Music: Punjab Scheme', *TOI* (18 September 1955), 10.

70. Farley Richmond, 'The Political Role of Theatre in India', *Education Theatre Journal*, Vol. 25, No. 3 (October 1973), 331.
71. Ramesh Mehta was awarded the Sangeet Natak Akademi Puraskar for Theatre by the Sangeet Natak Akademi in 2007.
72. R. M. Kaul, 'The Three Arts Club: About Us', in Three Arts Club brochure promoting 'Zamaana' (1955), 7–8; R. M. Kaul, 'The Three Arts Club', *Lok Kalyan Samiti* (October 1957), 37.
73. Ramesh Mehta, 'Hamara Gaon', in *Natakkar Ramesh Mehta Rang Samagra*, ed. Ravindranath Bahore (New Delhi: Sanjay Prakashan, 2013), 242. I am grateful to Anuradha Dar of the Three Arts Club for providing me the script.
74. Ibid., 245.
75. Ibid., 247.
76. Ibid., 258.
77. Ibid., 261.
78. Ibid., 259.
79. Inaugurated on 2 October 1952, on Gandhi's fourth birth anniversary, the Community Development Program represented the Nehruvian vision for the Indian countryside – a wide ranging modernization drive that sought to transform rural society and the agrarian economy. For more, see Subir Sinha, 'Lineages of the Developmentalist State: Transnationality and Village India, 1900–1965', *Comparative Studies in Society and History*, Vol. 50, No. 1 (2008), 57–90; Sackley, 'The Village as Cold War Site', 481–504; and Immerwahr, *Thinking Small*.
80. F. No. 23/9/59-PP (Part 1), 238–245, Ministry of Information and Broadcasting, NAI.
81. Government of India, Report of the Study Team on Five Year Plan Publicity, 80.
82. 'Song and Drama Division-Selection of Troupes', F. No. 20(1)/59, Plan Publicity, Ministry of Information and Broadcasting, NAI.
83. Occasionally they were borrowed from AIR programs. 'Study Team-Information and Community Centre', F. No. 16(12)/59-PP, Vol. 1, Plan Publicity, Ministry of Information and Broadcasting, NAI.
84. Sophia Wadia, "The Role of Non-Governmental Cultural Organizations in the Promotion of International Understanding," *The Indo-Asian Culture*, Vol. VII, No. 1, July 1958, 46-47.
85. 'Popularising Plan Projects', *TOI* (15 August 1959), 27.
86. Ibid.
87. 'Song and Drama Division-Selection of Troupes', F. No. 20(1)/59, Plan Publicity, Ministry of Information and Broadcasting, NAI.
88. Ibid.
89. Khushwant Singh, *Truth, Love, and a Little Malice: An Autobiography* (New Delhi: Penguin, 2002), 192–193.
90. The magazine would later be published in thirteen languages – English, Hindi, Urdu, Punjabi, Marathi, Gujarati, Bengali, Assamese, Telugu, Tamil, Kannada, Malayalam, and Oriya.
91. 'What is Yojana?', *Yojana*, Vol. 1, No. 1 (26 January 1957), 1.
92. *The March of India*, Vol. 9, No. 10 (October 1957).

93. F. No. 10/6/61 – Pub., Publication, Ministry of Information and Broadcasting, NAI.
94. 'Reader's Forum: Republic Day Number', *Yojana*, Vol. 2, No. 2 (9 February
1958), 6.
95. F. No. 10/6/61 – Pub., Publication, Ministry of Information and Broadcasting, NAI.
96. Advertisement, *Yojana* (Hindi), Vol. 1, No. 1 (26 January 1957), 1.
97. 'Our Cultural Heritage', *Yojana*, Vol. 1, No. 1 (26 January 1957), 17.
98. Khushwant Singh, *Yojana*, 26 January 1956, as reproduced in 'Looking
Back', *Yojana* (26 January 1967), 15.
99. *Yojana* (Hindi), Vol. 3, No. 7 (April 1959).
100. Devraj Dinesh, 'Likhna Hai Itihas Naya', *Yojana* (Hindi), Vol. 3, No. 6
(April 1959), 1.
101. Saraswati Kumar Deepak, 'Open the Doors', *Yojana* (Hindi), Vol. 3, No. 5
(March 1959), 1.
102. Khushwant Singh, 'Donkey to the Rescue', *Yojana*, Vol. 1, No. 1
(26 January 1957), 6.
103. Roy, *Beyond Belief*, 34.
104. On the Films Division, see Anuja Jain, 'The Curious Case of the Films
Division: Some Annotations on the Beginnings of Indian Documentary
Cinema in Postindependence India, 1940s–1960s', *The Velvet Light Trap*,
Vol. 71 (Spring 2013), 15–26; and Peter Sutoris, *Visions of Development:
Films Division of India and the Imagination of Progress, 1948–75* (Oxford:
Oxford University Press, 2016).
105. Roy, *Beyond Belief*, 34.
106. Ibid., 42–43.
107. Sutoris, *Visions of Development*, 132.
108. Government of India, Report of the Study Team on Five-Year Plan
Publicity, 59.
109. 'Editorial', *Indian Documentary*, Vol. 3, No. 1 (1956), 5, cited in
Judith Pernin, Evey Shen, and Swati Maheshwari, Camille Deprez compiled report *The Documentary Film in India (1948–1975)*, Hong Kong
Baptist University, March 2016, http://digital.lib.hkbu.edu.hk/documen
tary-film/india.php#footnote, accessed on 14 May 2018.
110. Pernin, Shen, and Maheshwari, The Documentary Film in India (1948–1975).
111. *Sarey Jahan Sey Achcha* (English title *Working for the Plan*), directed by
Kumar Chandrasekhar (Bombay: Films Division of India, 1958).
112. *Shadow and Substance*, directed by G. K. Gokhale (Bombay: Films Division
of India, 1967).
113. Dilip M. Menon, 'The Idea of Development as Governance: India in the
First Decade of Independence', in *Governance, Conflict, and Development in
South Asia: Perspectives from India, Nepal, and Sri Lanka*, ed. Siri Hettige and
Eva Gerharz (New Delhi: Sage, 2015), 51.
114. *Tomorrow Is Ours*, directed by T. A. Abraham (Bombay: Films Division of
India, 1955).
115. Khwaja Ahmad Abbas (1914–1987) was a left-wing screenwriter and/or
director of films such as *Naya Sansar* (1941), *Dharti Ke Lal* (1946), *Awara*

(1951), *Shree 420* (1955), *Shehar Aur Sapna* (1964), *Saat Hindustani* (1969), *Mera Naam Joker* (1970), and *Bobby* (1973) among others.

116. Fatima and Hameed, eds., *Bread, Beauty, Revolution*, 85–88.

117. K. A. Abbas, 'Nationalize Motion Pictures', *Yojana*, Vol. 2, No. 1 (26 January 1958), 19–20.

118. '*Filmi Kalakaron Mein Yojana Ki Lokpriyata*',*Yojana* (Hindi), Vol. 3, No. 2 (February 1959), 32.

119. Dinesh Bhugra, *Mad Tales from Bollywood: Portrayal of Mental Illness in Conventional Hindi Cinema* (New York: Psychology Press, 2006).

120. Meghnad Desai, *Nehru's Hero: Dilip Kumar in the Life of India* (New Delhi: Roli, 2004).

121. Avjit Ghosh, 'Nehru's Vision Shaped Many Golden Oldies', *TOI* (16 November 2009), https://timesofindia.indiatimes.com/city/delhi/Nehrus-visio n-shaped-many-Bollywood-golden-oldies/articleshow/5233286.cms, accessed on 20 May 2018.

122. Anand Vardhan, 'Hindi Cinema: Being Political in the Nehruvian Era', *Newslaundry.com* (4 August 2017), www.newslaundry.com/2017/08/04/ hindi-cinema-nehruvian-era-political-awareness, accessed on 5 May 2018.

123. '*Kya Filmein Rashtra Nirman Mein Yog De Sakti Hain?*'*Yojana* (Hindi), Vol. 3, No. 21 (8 November 1959), 13.

124. Rakshanda Jalil, 'Self and Sovereignty', *The Friday Times*, Vol. 23, No. 26 (12–18 August 2011), www.thefridaytimes.com/beta3/tft/article.php?issu e=20110812&page=24, accessed on 28 May 2018. For more on radio programming in Nehruvian India, particularly the contests between classical and popular music, see Isabel Huacuja Alonso, 'Radio, Citizenship, and the "Sound Standards" of a Newly Independent India', *Public Culture*, Vol. 31, No. 1 (2019), 117–144.

125. Srivastava, 'Voice, Gender and Space in Time of Five-Year Plans', 2025.

126. Sanjay Srivastava, '"Sane Sex," the Five-Year Plan Hero and Men on Footpaths and in Gated Communities: On the Cultures of Twentieth-Century Masculinity', in *Masculinity and its Challenges in India*, ed. Rohit K. Dasgupta and K. Moti Gokulsing (Jefferson: MacFarland, 2014), 39.

127. Menon, 'The Idea of Development as Governance', 60.

128. On Yashpal's life, see Corinne Friend, 'Yashpal: Fighter for Freedom – Writer for Justice', *Journal of South Asian Literature*, Vol. 13, No. 1/4 (1977–78), 65–90.

129. Yashpal, *This is Not That Dawn*, translated from Hindi by Anand (New Delhi: Penguin, 2010), 888; Rotem Geva, '"False Truth": Disillusionment and Hope in the Decade after Independence', in *The Postcolonial Moment*, ed. Prakash, Laffan, and Menon, 15.

130. D. P. Mukherji, 'Man and Plan in India: The Background', *The Economic Weekly* (15 August 1953), 898–900. On Mukerji see, T. N. Madan, 'The Dialectic of Tradition and Modernity in the Sociology of D. P. Mukerji', *Social Science Information*, Vol. 17, No. 6 (1978), 777–799.

131. Lok Sabha Debates, 11 March 1958, Vol. 8, No. 21, 4406–4407.

132. Cited in *Yojana*, Vol. 3, No. 7 (19 April 1959), 3.

133. Government of India, Report of the Study Team on Five-Year Plan Publicity, ii.
134. Ibid., 3.
135. Ibid., 10.
136. Ibid., 16–17.
137. Ibid., 18–20.
138. Edward S. Mason, *Economic Planning in Underdeveloped Areas: Government and Business* (New York: Fordham University Press, 1958), 71, quoted in Myrdal, *Asian Drama*, 851.

5   **Salvation in Service**

1. Khushwant Singh, 'Mr. Tourist on Men and Monument', *Yojana*, Vol. 2, No. 5 (23 March 1958), 7, 12.
2. Government of India, *First Five Year Plan*, https://niti.gov.in/planningcom mission.gov.in/docs/plans/planrel/fiveyr/index1.html, accessed on 15 January 2020.
3. S. N. Mishra, 'What Students Can Do for the Plan: The Role of Planning Forums', *Yojana*, Vol. 1, No. 19 (6 October 1957), 3.
4. S. N. Mishra, 'New Horizons for Universities', *Yojana*, Vol. 1, No. 1 (26 January 1957), 4.
5. Government of India (Planning Commission), *University Planning Forums: Summary Record of Meetings, April 1956–September 1957* (New Delhi: Publications Division, 1957), 2.
6. Mishra, 'What Students Can Do for the Plan', 3.
7. Nehru, *SWJN*, SS, Vol. 32, 30.
8. Government of India, *University Planning Forums: Summary*, 2.
9. Government of India (Planning Commission), *University Planning Forums: A Review* (New Delhi: Publications Division, December 1958), 2–3.
10. Ibid., 2–6.
11. 'Current Topics', *TOI* (3 February 1967), 8.
12. National Plan Day celebrations began in 1957, and National Plan Week began with the Third Five-Year Plan.
13. Ibid., 4–6; 'Grant-in-Aid', F. No. 1(27) 62-PP Vol. 1, Plan Publicity, Ministry of Information and Broadcasting, NAI.
14. Ibid.
15. Mishra, 'New Horizons for Universities', 15.
16. Government of India, University Planning Forums: A Review, 2; Asoka Mehta, *Towards a Better Planning Forum* (New Delhi: Central Institute of Research and Training in Public Cooperation, 1967), 1; 'Students Find Out How Life in Villages Changes or Does Not Change: Story of College Planning Forums', *Yojana* (26 January 1967), 49.
17. *Public Participation in National Development*, Publications Division, Ministry of Information and Broadcasting, April 1954, 13–14.
18. '2,000,000 Tons of Earth Piled up in Six Weeks: Saga of Planned Self-Help by 50,000 People', *TOI* (7 January 1955), 1.
19. Ibid.

20. In this early iteration it was referred to as the *Bharat Seva Sangh* (India Service Association), www.bssve.in/know-about-bss.pdf and www .bharatsevaksamaj.org/BSSConstitution.html, accessed on 22 September 2015.

21. 'Bharat Sewak Samaj' pamphlet published by Planning Commission (May 1952), reproduced on page 25 of F. No. 33(28)-Econ, 52 (Secret), Economic, Ministry of States, NAI.

22. Nehru, *SWJN*, SS, Vol. 18, 631–642.

23. *Report of the Commission of Inquiry into the Affairs of the Bharat Sevak Samaj, 1969,* reproduced in G. L. Nanda Papers, Acc. No. 2511, Reel 21, NAI.

24. Carey A. Watt, 'Philanthorpy and Civilizing Missions in India c. 1820–1960: States, NGO's and Development', in *Civilizing Missions in Colonial and Postcolonial South Asia: From Improvement to Development*, ed. Carey A. Watt and Michael Mann (New York: Anthem, 2011), 297.

25. D. P. Mukerji, 'Man and Plan in India II', *The Economic Weekly* (26 September 1953), 1059.

26. 'Bharat Sewak Samaj: Not Connected with Govt.', *The Hindu* (6 July 1952), 7.

27. 'Work Among the Masses', *The Hindu* (11 October 1952), 4.

28. Mukerji, 'Man and Plan in India II', 1060.

29. Government of India, *Bharat Sewak Samaj: What It Represents, What It Does* (New Delhi: Publications Department, undated).

30. It was, however, considered. When addressing a press conference soon after launching the Bharat Sewak Samaj in 1952, Nanda said that conscription of labor for fulfilling Five-Year Plans was 'not ruled out'. 'Labour Conscription for Five-Year Plan', *TOI* (24 December 1952), 1.

31. 'Nehru Labor Plan Stresses Freedom', *NYT* (23 June 1952), 1.

32. 'Launching Bharat Sevak Samaj Activities', *TOI* (11 May 1953), 7.

33. Nehru, *SWJN*, SS, Vol. 19, 95.

34. Government of India, *Bharat Sewak Samaj.*

35. '5000 Volunteers at Work on Kosi Embankments: Unique Experiment Underway in Bihar', *TOI* (15 January 1955), 1.

36. Kanwar Sain, 'People's Co-operation in the Kosi Project', *The Indian Journal of Public Administration*, Vol. 1, No.2 (1955), 130–136.

37. Government of India, *Third Five Year Plan*, http://planningcommission .nic.in/plans/planrel/fiveyr/3rd/3planch18.html, accessed on 2 October 2015. Though the government and the BSS touted Kosi as an unprecedented success, independent observers expressed serious doubts. See, for example, 'People's Participation in Kosi Project', *The Economic Weekly* (4 June 1955).

38. Government of India, *Bharat Sewak Samaj.*

39. The *Jan Jagran Vibhag* began receiving funds from the Ministry of Information and Broadcasting in 1953. 'Grant-in-Aid to Bharat Sewak Samaj', F. No. 1/19/62-PP, Policy Planning, Ministry of Information and Broadcasting, NAI.

40. Government of India, *Bharat Sewak Samaj.*

41. *Report of the Commission of Inquiry into the Affairs of the Bharat Sevak Samaj, 1969*, reproduced in G. L. Nanda Papers, Acc. No. 2511, Reel 21, NAI.

42. *Evaluation Report on Lok Karya Kshetras [Public Co-operation Centres]*, Programme Evaluation Organisation, Planning Commission, P.E.O. Publication No. 54, Government of India, New Delhi, October 1967.

43. Those present included Gulzarilal Nanda, S. N. Mishra (Deputy Union Minister for Planning), J. L. Hathi (Deputy Union Minister), and parliamentarians Shriman Narayan and Kakasaheb Kalelkar. 'Sadhus Form Sewak Samaj', *The Sunday Standard* (19 February 1956), 7.

44. Tukdya Das, *Bharat Sadhusamaj Ki Seva Sadhan: Bharat Sadhusamaj Kya Karega?* (Amravati: Gurudev Prakashan, 1956). Tukdya Das was Sant Tukdoji Maharaj's poetic signature.

45. Ibid., 197.

46. Donald E. Smith, *India as a Secular State* (Princeton: Princeton University Press, 1963), 260.

47. Khushwant Singh, 'Holy Men of India: In Search of the Seekers of Truth', *NYT* (8 January 1967), 268.

48. K. Shankar Pillai, 'Food for Thought', 20 May 1956, reproduced in 'Don't Spare Me Shankar.'

49. A. M. Rosenthal, 'India's Holy Men Get Worldly Job', *NYT* (19 February 1956), 13.

50. '500,000 Sadhus to Help Build Up New Nation', *TOI* (19 February 1956), 9.

51. 'Title of "Sant" for President', *TOI* (20 February 1956), 1.

52. 'Ram Rajya At Last!', *Film India* (December 1952).

53. William R. Pinch, 'Soldier Monks and Militant Hindus', in *Contesting the Nation: Religion, Community, and the Politics of Democracy in India*, ed. David Ludden (Philadelphia: University of Pennsylvania Press, 1996), 147.

54. William Gould, *Hindu Nationalism and the Language of Politics in Late Colonial India* (Cambridge: Cambridge University Press, 2004), 487–490.

55. Rosenthal, 'India's Holy Men Get Worldly Job', 13.

56. 'Reform of Holy Men', *Battle Creek Enquirer* (14 April 1956), 12.

57. R. K. Narayan, 'New Role for India's Holy Men', *NYT* (6 September 1959), 9, 21, 23.

58. V. M. Nair, 'Indian Sadhus, Holy Men to Help Sell 5-Year Plans', *Washington Post* (19 June 1956), 46.

59. Narayan, 'New Role for India's Holy Men', 23.

60. Lok Sabha Debates, 30 May 1956, Vol. 4, No. 70, 4617.

61. 'Idlers, Not Sadhus', *TOI* (3 November 1955), 1.

62. Nair, 'Indian Sadhus, Holy Men to Help Sell 5-Year Plans', 46.

63. 'Mass Awakening Programme', *TOI* (26 June 1956), 7.

64. 'Sadhus Meet Prime Minister', *TOI* (2 August 1956), 11.

65. 'Creating Atmosphere Free of Social Evils', *TOI* (18 December 1956), 11.

66. 'Sadhus Urged to Work for Uplift of Society', *TOI* (3 November 1957), 1.

67. 'Novel Form of Satyagraha', *TOI* (26 October 1957), 11.

68. The government allotted the Bharat Sadhu Samaj a plot of 12,384 square feet in Malcha Marg on 26 June 1961. Narayan, 'New Role for India's Holy Men', 9, 21, 22; Smith, *India as a Secular State*, 260.
69. Lok Sabha Debates, 23 April 1965, Vol. 38, No. 1, 10803.
70. Smith, *India as a Secular State*, 260.
71. 'Nehru Takes to Rostrum to Balk Silent Opponent', *NYT* (31 January 1952), 2; 'Nehru Beats Silent Foe', *NYT* (14 February 1952), 6.
72. 'India's New Leader: Gulzarilal Nanda', *NYT* (11 January 1966), 14; Nair, 'Indian Sadhus, Holy Men to Help Sell 5-Year Plans', 46.
73. Narayan, 'New Role for India's Holy Men', 21.
74. Smith, *India as a Secular State*, 260.
75. 'India's Holy Men May be Licensed', *NYT* (25 November 1956), 7.
76. Smith, *India as a Secular State*, 260.
77. P. K. Padmanabhan, 'Plague of Holy Men', *Los Angeles Times* (21 November 1958), B. 5.
78. Gulzarilal Nanda, Oral History Transcript, File No. 695, NMML, 4.
79. 'The Man of the Week', 20 March 1966, *Shankar's Weekly*, reproduced in *Shankar's Weekly Souvenir Number*, September 1975, 227.
80. 'Nanda, Shri Gulzarilal', Fifth *Lok Sabha* Member's Profile, http://loksabhaph.nic.in/writereaddata/biodata_1_12/886.htm.
81. I found at least three such letters from 'Gurudev' in Nanda's private papers. Accession No. 2495, Microform Reel No. 5, Gulzarilal Nanda Papers, NAI.
82. 'India's New Leader', 14.
83. 'The Man of the Week', *Shankar's Weekly Souvenir Number*, 227.
84. Lok Sabha Debates, 23 April 1965, Vol. 38, No. 1, 10901.
85. Nehru to V. T. Krishnamachari, 9 October 1958, *SWJN*, SS, Vol. 44, 349.
86. Elie Abel, 'India's Holy Men Hear Nehru's Plea', *NYT* (4 May 1959), 3.
87. P. K. Padmanabhan, 'India's 10,000 Holy Men Rally to Aid of Nehru', *Los Angeles Times* (26 May 1959), 17.
88. Nehru's address at the third annual conference of the Bharat Sadhu Samaj, 3 May 1959. Reproduced in *SWJN*, SS, Vol. 49, 23–38.
89. Rosenthal, 'India's Holy Men Get Worldly Job', 13; Nair, 'Indian Sadhus, Holy Men to Help Sell 5-Year Plans', 46; Narayan, 'New Role for India's Holy Men', 9, 21, 22; Abel, 'India's Holy Men Hear Nehru's Plea', 3; 'India's Holy Men May be Licensed', 7.
90. Smith, *India as a Secular State*, 261.
91. R. K. Laxman, 'Untitled', *TOI* (15 January 1956), 1.
92. R. K. Laxman, 'Untitled', *TOI* (22 July 1964), 1.
93. O. V. Vijayan, 'The Synthesis', *Shankar's Weekly*, 10 May 1959, reproduced in *Shankar's Weekly Souvenir Number*, 106.
94. K. Shankara Pillai, *Shankar's Weekly*, 17 May 1959, reproduced in Don't Spare Me Shankar.
95. 'In Whose Aid?', *TOI* (7 November 1957), 6.
96. R. Mani, 'Renouncing the World', *TOI* (12 May 1959), 8.
97. These passages on the life of Tukdoji Maharaj draw on Anna Christine Schultz, 'Translated Fronts: Songs of Socialist Cosmopolitanism

in Cold War India', *History and Anthropology*, Vol. 28, No. 1 (2017), 1–22; and 'Tukdoji Maharaj Passes Away', *TOI* (12 October 1968), 1.

98. Schultz, 'Translated Fronts', 12.
99. 'Bharat Sadhu Samaj', *TOI* (22 June 1959), 5.
100. *Report of the Commission of Inquiry into the Affairs of the Bharat Sevak Samaj, 1969*, reproduced in G. L. Nanda Papers, Acc. No. 2511, Reel 21, NAI.
101. F. No. 1(34)/62-PP Vol. 1, Plan Publicity, 1962, Ministry of Information and Broadcasting, NAI.
102. F. No. 1/64/61-PP, Policy Planning, Ministry of Information and Broadcasting, NAI.
103. The amount they spent in total was Rs. 16,694.81. 'Bharat Sewak Samaj-Plan Publicity Programme', F. No. 1(64)/61-PP, Policy Planning, Ministry of Information and Broadcasting, NAI.
104. Ibid.
105. Ibid.
106. Khushwant Singh, *Not a Nice Man to Know: The Best of Khushwant Singh* (New Delhi: Penguin India, 2011).
107. Inder Malhotra, 'Holy Men Stir Up Riots in Delhi', *The Guardian* (8 November 1966), www.theguardian.com/world/2016/nov/08/india-holy-men-sacred-cows-riots-delhi, accessed on 20 February 2017; Ishan Marvel, 'Fifty Years Ago, Hindutva Groups Led the First Attack on the Indian Parliament', *The Caravan* (7 November 2016), www.caravanmagazine.in/va ntage/hindutva-groups-first-attack-indian-parliament-50-years, accessed on 20 February 2017.
108. Rajya Sabha Debates, 17 November 1966, 1697–1699.
109. Ibid., 1657.
110. Indira Gandhi's *gurus* included Ma Anand Moyi, J. Krishnamurti, Vinoba Bhave, Devraha Baba, and Dhirendra Brahmachari. Christophe Jaffrelot, 'The Political Guru', in *The Guru in South Asia: New Interdisciplinary Perspectives*, ed. Jacob Copeman and Aya Ikegame (Routledge: New York, 2012), 80–96.
111. On the Emergency, see Prakash, *Emergency Chronicles*.
112. K. K. Sastry, 'PM, Sadhus Exchange Pledges to Strive for Progress', *TOI* (23 January 1977), 9.
113. Pinch, 'Soldier Monks and Militant Hindus', 142–143.
114. 'Muslims Asked to Give Up Babri', *TOI* (25 December 1990), 5.
115. Rajiv Malik, 'Can 40,000 Holy Men Shepherd India's Future?', *Hinduism Today* (October 1994), www.hinduismtoday.com/modules/smartsection/it em.php?itemid=3168, accessed on 10 October 2019.
116. William Morris-Jones, 'India's Political Idioms', in *Politics and Society in India*, ed. C. H. Philips (London: Allen & Unwin, 1962), 133–154.
117. Robert F. Worth, 'The Billionaire Yogi Behind Modi's Rise', *NYT* (26 July 2018), www.nytimes.com/2018/07/26/magazine/the-billionaire-yogi-behind-modis-rise.html, accessed on 28 July 2018.
118. Narendra Modi's interview with *Humans of Bombay*, Part 2 (9 January 2019), www.facebook.com/photo?fbid=1023811227854& set=a.188058468069805, accessed on 28 May 2020.

Epilogue

1. Cited in Medha Kudaisya, 'Retreat, Developmental Planning in "Retreat": Ideas, Instruments, and Contestations of Planning in India, 1967–1971', *Modern Asian Studies*, Vol. 49, No.3 (May 2015), 728.
2. Krishna Raj, 'Indira Gandhi's Bequest', *EPW* Vol. 19, No. 44 (3 November 1984), 1949.
3. See Hanson, *The Process of Planning*, 136–170; Chibber, *Locked in Place*, 196–221; Kudaisya, 'A Mighty Adventure', 968–974.
4. Hanson, *The Process of Planning*, 159, 161.
5. Letter from Pant to Mahalanobis, 9 May 1958, Mahalanobis Papers, PCMMMA, RC 90.
6. Chibber, *Locked in Place*, 196–198; Kudaisya, 'A Mighty Adventure', 968–975.
7. The description of the fate of planning in the late 1960s is drawn from Frankel, *India's Political Economy*, 246–340, and Kudaisya, 'Developmental Planning in "Retreat"', 711–752.
8. The exceptions to this were the 'Bombay economists', – C. N. Vakil, P. R. Brahmananda, B. R. Shenoy, and Hannan Ezekiel – who advocated prioritizing consumer goods, agriculture, and exports. The next significant critique of the Mahalanobis model came from Jagdish Bhagwati, Padma Desai, and others from around the late 1960s. See interview with Jagdish Bhagwati, in Balasubramanyam, *Conversations with Indian Economists*, 138–154.
9. Sinha, ed., *The Path to Prosperity*, 1–26; Kudaisya, 'Developmental Planning in "Retreat"', 716–717.
10. Rudra, *Prasanta Chandra Mahalanobis*, 433.
11. Mahalanobis to Bhanu Pant, 24 August 1956, Installment 2, Correspondence, Pant Papers, NMML, 117.
12. Mahalanobis to Bhanu Pant, 7 November 1956, Installment 2, Correspondence, Pant Papers, NMML, 113.
13. Poornima Paidipaty, 'Testing Measures: Decolonization and Economic Power in 1960s India', *History of Political Economy*, Vol. 52, No. 3 (2020), 473–497.
14. Hanson, *The Process of Planning*, 171–176.
15. T. Krishna Kumar, 'An Unfinished Biography: Prasanta Chandra Mahalanobis', *EPW* Vol. 32, No.23 (7–13 June 1997), 1329–1330.
16. 'List Showing Names of Members of Planning Commission', https://niti.gov.in/planningcommission.gov.in/docs/aboutus/history/past_memb.pdf, accessed on 4 July 2020.
17. F. No. 17/45/1970-PMS, PMO, NAI.
18. 'Return of Planning Commission', *Link* (21 May 1967), 23–24, cited in Kudaisya, 'Developmental Planning in "Retreat"', 718.
19. *Hindustan Times* editorial, 27 May 1971, cited in Kudaisya, 'Developmental Planning in "Retreat"', 750.
20. Ibid., 751.
21. Raj, 'Indira Gandhi's Bequest', 1849.

22. Ajit Mozoomdar, 'The Rise and Decline of Development Planning in India', in *The State and Development Planning in India*, ed. Byres, 83.
23. Patel, *Glimpses of Indian Economic Policy*, 84.
24. Banerjee, Bardhan, Somanathan, and Srinivasan, 'From Being World Leader in Surveys, India is Now Facing a Serious Data Problem'.
25. 'Repairing the House that Mahalanobis Built', *Livemint* (15 May 2017), www.livemint.com/Opinion/Cp0sGLCIQr6o3asJUg9XnN/Repairing-the-house-t hat-Mahalanobis-built.html, accessed on 24 November 2019.
26. Bernard Weinraub, 'Planning Controversy in India Intensifies as Economist Quits', *NYT* (10 December 1973), 10; Ankush Agrawal and Vikas Kumar, 'Politics Should Not Meddle with Our Official Statistics', *Livemint* (19 November 2019).
27. 'Some Condolence Messages', *Sankhyā*, Vol. 35, Supplement: Prasanta Chandra Mahalanobis (December 1973), 75.
28. Deaton and Kozel, 'Data and Dogma'.
29. Rajesh Roy, 'India Beats Back Accusations It Cooked the Books to Boost Election Prospects', *Wall Street Journal* (1 February 2019), www.wsj.com/articles/india-beats-back-accusations-it-cooked-the-books-t o-boost-election-prospects-11549025136, accessed on 24 November 2019; Jeffrey Gettlemen and Hari Kumar, 'India's Leader Is Accused of Hiding Unemployment Data Before Vote', *NYT* (31 January 2019), www.nytimes.com/2019/01/31/world/asia/india-unemployment-rate.html, accessed on 24 November 2019.
30. Kaushik Basu, 'India Can Hide Unemployment Data, But Not on the Truth', *NYT* (1 February 2019), www.nytimes.com/2019/02/01/opinion/india-unemployment-jobs-blackout.html, accessed on 24 November 2019.
31. Amy Kazmin, 'Economists Condemn Politicisation of Modi Government Data', *Financial Times* (15 March 2019), www.ft.com/content/38b9d94c-4 6d4-11e9-b168-96a37d002cd3, accessed on 24 November 2019.
32. Manoj Kumar, 'India's Incredulous Data: Economists Create Own Benchmarks', *Reuters* (9 May 2019) www.reuters.com/article/us-india-econ omy-data-insight/indias-incredulous-data-economists-create-own-bench marks-idUSKCN1SF0L6, accessed on 24 November 2019.
33. Somesh Jha, 'Govt Scraps NSO's Consumer Expenditure Survey Over "Data quality"', *Business Standard* (16 November 2019), www.business-standard.co m/article/economy-policy/govt-scraps-nso-s-consumer-expenditure-survey-ov er-data-quality-119111501838_1.html, accessed on 24 November 2019; Somesh Jha, 'Over 200 Global Economists Seek Junked NSO Report Details from Govt', *Business Standard* (22 November 2019) https://wap.business-sta ndard.com/article-amp/economy-policy/over-200-global-economists-seek-ju nked-nso-report-details-from-govt-119112101222_1.html, accessed on 24 November 2019.
34. Quartz Staff, 'Global Economists, Political Scientists Ask India to Release withheld Economic Data', *Quartz India* (21 November 2019), https://qz.co m/india/1753234/piketty-jaffrelot-others-want-withheld-indian-economy-d ata-out/, accessed on 24 November 2019.

35. Arvind Subramanian, 'India's Economy Faces Severe Challenges: Unreliable Growth Statistics Have Disguised the Depth of the Problem', *Financial Times* (14 January 2020), www.ft.com/content/25b0b690-360c-11ea-ac3c-f68c10993b04, accessed on 13 May 2021.

36. Jean Dreze and Anmol Somanchi, 'New Barometer of India's Economy Fails to Reflect Deprivations of Poor Households', *The Economic Times* (21 June 2021), https://economictimes.indiatimes.com/opinion/et-commentary/view-the-new-barometer-of-indias-economy-fails-to-reflect-the-deprivations-of-poor-households/articleshow/83696115.cms, accessed on 22 June 2021.

37. Thomas Piketty, Twitter post, 21 June 2021, 3:30 a.m.

38. Gideon Rachman, 'US-China Rivalry Drives the Retreat of Market Economics: Industrial Policy is Back in Fashion as Geopolitical Tensions Increase', *Financial Times* (10 May 2021), www.ft.com/content/1e749857-3cd6-453d-8cee-2c501cbfd53b, accessed on 13 May 2021.

39. Khilnani, *The Idea of India*, 95.

40. T. C. A. Srinivasa-Raghavan, 'Who Will be BJP's Mahalanobis?', *Business Standard* (10 October 2019), www.business-standard.com/article/opinion/who-will-be-bjp-s-mahalanobis-119080300060_1.html, accessed on 28 January 2020.

Select Bibliography

Archives and Libraries

India

Central Secretariat Library, New Delhi
Films Division of India, Mumbai
National Archives of India (NAI), New Delhi
Nehru Memorial Museum and Library (NMML), New Delhi
P. C. Mahalanobis Memorial Museum and Archives (PCMMMA),
    Kolkata
Planning Commission Library, New Delhi

United Kingdom

British Library, London
Centre of South Asian Studies, Cambridge
National Archives, Kew

United States of America

National Archives of the United States, College Park, Maryland
Rockefeller Archive Center, Sleepy Hollow, New York

Newspapers and Journals

Hindustan Times
Indian Statistical Institute – Annual Report(s)
Life Magazine
Los Angeles Times
March of India
New York Times
Outlook
Samvadadhvam
Sankhya

Shankar's Weekly
The Economic Weekly (from 1966, the Economic and Political Weekly)
The Hindu
The Indian Express
The Observer
The Telegraph (Calcutta)
Times of India
Triveni
Washington Post
Yojana

Books and Articles

Amrith, Sunil. 'Food and Welfare in India, c. 1900–1950'. *Comparative Studies in Society and History* 50, no. 4 (October 2008): 1010–1035.

Amrith, Sunil. *Unruly Waters: How Rains, Rivers, Coasts, and Seas Have Shaped Asia's History*. New York: Basic Books, 2018.

Arndt, H. W. *Economic Development: The History of an Idea*. Chicago: University of Chicago Press, 1989.

Bahore, Ravindranath, ed. *Natakkar Ramesh Mehta Rang Samagra*. New Delhi: Sanjay Prakashan, 2013.

Balasubramanian, Aditya. 'Contesting "Permit-And-Licence *Raj*": Economic Conservatism and the Idea of Democracy in 1950s India'. *Past & Present* 251, no. 1 (May 2021): 189–227.

Balasubramanyam, V. N. *Conversations with Indian Economists*. Basingstoke: Palgrave, 2001.

Banerjee, Nirmala. 'Whatever Happened to the Dreams of Modernity? The Nehruvian Era and Woman's Position'. *Economic and Political Weekly* 33, no. 17 (25 April–1 May 1998): WS2–WS7.

Banerjee, Utpal K. *Computer Education in India*. New Delhi: Concept, 1996.

Bassett, Ross. 'Aligning India in the Cold War Era: Indian Technical Elites, the Indian Institute of Technology at Kanpur, and Computing in India and the United States'. *Technology and Culture* 50, no. 4 (2009): 783–810.

Bauer, P. T. *Indian Economic Policy and Development*. New York: Routledge, 2011.

Bayly, C. A. *Recovering Liberties: Indian Thought in the Age of Liberalism and Empire*. Cambridge: Cambridge University Press, 2011.

Bayly, C. A. 'The Ends of Liberalism and the Political Thought of Nehru's India'. *Modern Intellectual History* 12, no. 3 (2015): 605–626.

Beg, Tara Ali, ed. *Women in India*. New Delhi: Government of India, 1958.

Behrman, Jere, Hollis Chenery, and T. N. Srinivasan, eds., *Handbook of Development Economics*. Vol. 3. Amsterdam: Elsevier, 1998.

Berger, Rachel. 'Alimentary Affairs: Historicizing Food in Modern India'. *History Compass* 16, no. 2 (February 2018), https://doi.org/10.1111/hic3.12438.

Bhagwati, Jagdish. *India in Transition: Freeing the Economy*. Oxford: Clarendon Press, 1993.

Bharat Sewak Samaj. *Bharat Sewak Samaj: What It Represents, What It Does*. New Delhi: Publications Department, undated.

Bose, Sugata. 'Idioms and Instruments of Colonial and National Development',
in Frederick Cooper and Randall Packard, eds., *International Development and
the Social Sciences*. Berkeley: University of California Press, 1997: 45–63.

Brecekendringe, Carol and Peter Van Der Veer, eds., *Orientalism and the Post-
Colonial Predicament*. Philadelphia: University of Pennsylvania Press, 1993.

Byres, T. J., ed. *The State and Development Planning in India*. New Delhi: Oxford
University Press, 1994.

Byres, T. J., ed. *The Indian Economy: Major Debates since Independence*. New Delhi:
Oxford University Press, 1998.

Byres, T. J., ed. *The State, Development Planning and Liberalisation in India*. New
Delhi: Oxford University Press, 1998.

Cave, Martin. *Computers and Economic Planning: The Soviet Experience*.
Cambridge: Cambridge University Press, 1980.

Ceruzzi, Paul Edward. *A History of Modern Computing*. Cambridge, MA: MIT
Press, 2003.

Chakrabarty, Bidyut. 'Jawaharlal Nehru and Planning, 1938–41: India at the
Crossroads'. *Modern Asian Studies* 26, no. 2 (1992): 275–287.

Chakrabarty, Dipesh. '"In the Name of Politics": Democracy and the Power of
the Multitude in India'. *Public Culture* 19, no. 1 (2006): 35–57.

Chakrabarty, Dipesh, Rochona Majumdar, and Andrew Sartori, eds. *From the
Colonial to the Postcolonial: India and Pakistan in Transition*. New Delhi: Oxford
University Press, 2007.

Chakravarty, Sukhamoy. *Development Planning: The Indian Experience*. New
Delhi: Oxford University Press, 1998.

Chandra, Bipan. *The Rise and Growth of Economic Nationalism in India: Economic
Policies of Indian National Leadership, 1880–1905*. New Delhi: People's
Publishing House, 1966.

Chandra, Bipan, Aditya Mukherjee, and Mridula Mukherjee. *India since
Independence*. New Delhi: Penguin Books, 1999.

Chatterjee, Partha. *The Nation and Its Fragments: Colonial and Postcolonial
Histories*. Princeton: Princeton University Press, 1993.

Chattopadhyay, Raghabendra. 'The Idea of Planning in India 1931–1951'. PhD
diss. Australian National University, 1985.

Chattopadhyay, Raghabendra. 'An Early British Government Initiative in the
Genesis of Indian Planning'. *Economic and Political Weekly* 22, no. 5
(31 January 1987): 19–29.

Chibber, Vivek. *Locked in Place: State-Building and Late Industrialization in India*.
Princeton: Princeton University Press, 2003.

Connelly, Matthew James. *Fatal Misconception: The Struggle to Control World
Population*. Cambridge, MA: Harvard University Press, 2008.

Cooper, Frederick and Randall Packard, eds., *International Development and the
Social Sciences: Essays on the History and Politics of Knowledge*. Berkeley:
University of California Press, 1998.

Cullather, Nick. *The Hungry World: America's Cold War Battle against Poverty in
Asia*. Cambridge, MA: Harvard University Press, 2013.

Das, Tukdya. *Bharat Sadhusamaj Ki Seva Sadhan: Bharat Sadhusamaj Kya
Karega?* Amravati: Gurudev Prakashan, 1956.

Dasgupta, Rohit K. and K. Moti Gokulsing, eds., *Masculinity and Its Challenges in India: Essays on Changing Perceptions.* Jefferson: McFarland, 2014.

Dasgupta, Uma. *Science and Modern India: An Institutional History, c. 1784–1947.* New Delhi: Pearson Longman, Pearson Education, 2010.

Datta, Anjali Bhardwaj, Uditi Sen, and Mytheli Sreenivas, eds., 'A Country of Her Making: Women's Negotiations of Society and Politics in Post-Colonial India'. Special Section in *South Asia: Journal of South Asian Studies* 44, no. 2 (2021): 218–397.

De, Rohit. *A People's Constitution: The Everyday Life of Law in the Indian Republic.* Princeton: Princeton University Press, 2018.

Deming, W. Edwards. 'In Memoriam: P. C. Mahalanobis (1893–1972)'. *The American Statistician* 26, no. 4 (1972): 49–50.

Deshmukh, C. D. *The Course of My Life.* New Delhi: Orient Longman, 1974.

Deshmukh, Durgabai. *Chintaman and I.* New Delhi: Allied, 1980.

Desrosières, Alain. *The Politics of Large Numbers: A History of Statistical Reasoning.* Cambridge, MA: Harvard University Press, 2011.

Dietzenbacher, Erik and Michael L. Lahr, eds., *Wassily Leontief and Input-Output Economics.* Cambridge: Cambridge University Press, 2004.

Dirks, Nicholas B., ed. *Colonialism and Culture.* Ann Arbor: University of Michigan Press, 2001.

Drèze, Jean and Amartya Sen. *An Uncertain Glory: India and its Contradictions.* Princeton: Princeton University Press, 2013.

Dronamraju, Krishna R. *Popularizing Science: The Life and Work of JBS Haldane.* New York: Oxford University Press, 2017.

Engerman, David C. 'Learning from the East: Soviet Experts and India in the Era of Competitive Coexistence'. *Comparative Studies of South Asia, Africa and the Middle East* 33, no. 2 (2013): 227–238.

Engerman, David C. 'Mission from Moscow: Soviet Advisers and the Second Indian Five-Year Plan'. *NCEEER Working Paper*, 30 September 2014.

Engerman, David C. *The Price of Aid: The Economic Cold War in India.* Cambridge, MA: Harvard University Press, 2018.

Engerman, David C. and Corinna R. Unger. 'Introduction: Towards a Global History of Modernization'. *Diplomatic History* 33, no. 3 (2009): 375–385.

Erickson, Paul, Judy L. Klein, Lorraine Daston, Rebecca M. Lemov, Thomas Sturm, and Michael D. Gordin. *How Reason Almost Lost its Mind: The Strange Career of Cold War Rationality.* Chicago: University of Chicago Press, 2013.

Fatima, Iffat and Syeda Hameed, eds., *Bread, Beauty, Revolution: Khwaja Ahmad Abbas, 1914–1987.* New Delhi: Tulika, 2015.

Frankel, Francine. *India's Political Economy: The Gradual Revolution (1947–2004).* 2nd ed. New Delhi: Oxford University Press, 2005.

Friedman, Milton and Rose Friedman. *Two Lucky People: Memoirs.* Chicago: University of Chicago Press, 1999.

Galbraith, John Kenneth. *A Life in Our Times: Memoirs.* New York: Ballantine Books, 1981.

Gerovitch, Slava. 'InterNyet: Why the Soviet Union Did Not Build a Nationwide Computer Network'. *History and Technology* 24, no. 4 (2008): 335–350.

Gerovitch, Slava. '"Mathematical Machines" of the Cold War: Soviet Computing, American Cybernetics and Ideological Disputes in the Early 1950s'. *Social Studies of Science* 31, no. 2 (2001): 253–287.

Getachew, Adom. *Worldmaking after Empire: The Rise and Fall of Self Determination.* Princeton: Princeton University Press, 2019.

Ghosh, Arunabh. 'Accepting Difference, Seeking Common Ground: Sino-Indian Statistical Exchanges 1951–1959'. *BJHS Themes* 1 (2016): 61–82.

Ghosh, Arunabh. *Making It Count: Statistics and Statecraft in the Early People's Republic of China.* Princeton: Princeton University Press, 2020.

Ghosh, J. K., P. Maiti, T. J. Rao, and B. K. Sinha. 'Evolution of Statistics in India'. *International Statistical Review / Revue Internationale de Statistique* 67, no. 1 (1999): 13–34.

Gilmartin, David. 'The Historiography of India's Partition: Between Civilization and Modernity'. *The Journal of Asian Studies* 74, no. 1 (2015): 23–41.

Gopal, Sarvepalli, ed. *Selected Works of Jawaharlal Nehru.* Vol. 5. Second Series. New Delhi: Jawaharlal Nehru Memorial Fund, 1988.

Gopal, Sarvepalli, ed. *Selected Works of Jawaharlal Nehru.* Vol. 7. Second Series. New Delhi: Jawaharlal Nehru Memorial Fund, 1988.

Gopal, Sarvepalli, ed. *Selected Works of Jawaharlal Nehru.* Vol. 17. Second Series. New Delhi: Jawaharlal Nehru Memorial Fund, 1995.

Gopal, Sarvepalli, ed. *Selected Works of Jawaharlal Nehru.* Vol. 18. Second Series. New Delhi: Jawaharlal Nehru Memorial Fund, 1996.

Gopal, Sarvepalli, ed. *Selected Works of Jawaharlal Nehru.* Vol. 19. Second Series. New Delhi: Jawaharlal Nehru Memorial Fund, 1996.

Goswami, Manu. *Producing India: From Colonial Economy to National Space.* Chicago: University of Chicago Press, 2004.

Gould, William. *Hindu Nationalism and the Language of Politics in Late Colonial India.* Cambridge: Cambridge University Press, 2004.

Guha, Ramachandra. *India after Gandhi.* New York: Harper Collins, 2008.

Gundevia, Y. D. *Outside the Archives.* Hyderabad: Sangam Books, 1987.

Hajari, Nisid. *Midnight's Furies: The Deadly Legacy of India's Partition.* New York: Mariner Books, 2016.

Hanson, A. H. *The Process of Planning: A Study of India's Five-Year Plans 1950–1964.* London: Oxford University Press, 1966.

Hayek, Friedrich, ed. *Collectivist Economic Planning.* London: Routledge and Kegan Paul, 1966.

Immerwahr, Daniel. *Thinking Small: The United States and the Lure of Community Development.* Cambridge, MA: Harvard University Press, 2015.

Jain, Anuja. 'The Curious Case of the Films Division: Some Annotations on the Beginnings of Indian Documentary Cinema in Postindependence India, 1940s–1960s'. *The Velvet Light Trap* 71 (2013): 15–26.

Jalal, Ayesha. 'Secularists, Subalterns and the Stigma of "Communalism": Partition Historiography Revisited'. *Modern Asian Studies* 30, no. 3 (1996): 681–689.

Jayal, Niraja Gopal. *Citizenship and Its Discontents: An Indian History.* Cambridge, MA: Harvard University Press, 2013.

Johnston, Cathryn Anne. 'Demography and the Population Problem in India: Data, Research and Policy, 1938–1974'. PhD diss. King's College London, 2016.

Kamtekar, Indivar. 'The End of the Colonial State in India, 1942–47'. PhD diss. University of Cambridge, 1988.

Khan, Yasmin. *The Great Partition: The Making of India and Pakistan*. New Haven: Yale University Press, 2007.

Khan, Yasmin. *India at War: The Subcontinent and the Second World War*. Oxford: Oxford University Press, 2015.

Khilnani, Sunil. *The Idea of India*. London: Farrar, Straus and Giroux, 1999.

Klingensmith, Daniel. *'One Valley and a Thousand:' Dams, Nationalism, and Development*. New Delhi: Oxford University Press, 2007.

Kohli, Atul. *Poverty Amid Plenty in the New India*. New York: Cambridge University Press, 2012.

Kohli, Atul. *State Directed Development: Political Power and Industrialization in the Global Periphery*. Cambridge: Cambridge University Press, 2004.

Krishnamachari, V. T. *Planning in India*. Bombay: Orient Longman, 1961.

Kudaisya, Gyanesh. *A Republic in the Making: India in the 1950s*. New Delhi: Oxford University Press, 2017.

Kudaisya, Medha. '"Reforms by Stealth:" Indian Economic Policy, Big Business and the Promise of the Shastri Years, 1964–1966'. *South Asia: Journal of South Asian Studies* 25, no. 2 (2002): 205–229.

Kudaisya, Medha. '"A Mighty Adventure": Institutionalising the Idea of Planning in Post-colonial India, 1947–60'. *Modern Asian Studies* 43, no. 4 (2009): 939–978.

Kudaisya, Medha. '"The Promise of Partnership": Indian Business, the State, and the Bombay Plan of 1944'. *Business History Review* 88, no. 1 (2014): 97–131.

Kudaisya, Medha. 'Developmental Planning in "Retreat": Ideas, Instruments, and Contestations of Planning in India, 1967–1971'. *Modern Asian Studies* 49, no. 3 (2014): 711–752.

Kumar, Dharma and Meghnad Desai, eds. *The Cambridge Economic History of India*. Vol. 2. Cambridge: Cambridge University Press, 1983.

Lok Sabha Secretariat, Government of India. *Lok Sabha Debates*. New Delhi: Government of India, 1954–1965.

Lorenzini, Sara. *Global Development: A Cold War History*. Princeton: Princeton University Press, 2019.

Ludden, David, ed. *Contesting the Nation: Religion, Community, and the Politics of Democracy in India*. Philadelphia: University of Pennsylvania Press, 1996.

Ludden, David. 'India's Development Regime', in Nicholas Dirks, ed., *Colonialism and Culture*. Ann Arbor: University of Michigan Press, 1992, 247–287.

Mahalanobis, Abhindranath. *Prasanta Chandra Mahalanobis*. New Delhi: National Book Trust, 1987.

Mahalanobis, P. C. *Talks on Planning*. Calcutta: Statistical Publishing Society, 1961.

Mahalanobis, P. C., P. K. Bose, and Moni Mukherjee. *Papers on Planning*. Calcutta: Statistical Publishing Society, 1985.

Mann, Michael. 'The Autonomous Power of the State: Its Origins, Mechanisms and Results'. *European Journal of Sociology* 25, no. 2 (1984): 185–213.

Medina, Eden. *Cybernetic Revolutionaries: Technology and Politics in Allende's Chile*. Cambridge, MA: The MIT Press, 2014.

Mehrotra, Santosh and Sylvie Guichard, eds. *Planning in the 20th Century and Beyond: India's Planning Commission and the NITI Aayog*. Cambridge: Cambridge University Press, 2020.

Mehta, Asoka. *Towards a Better Planning Forum*. New Delhi: Central Institute of Research and Training in Public Cooperation, 1967.

Menon, Nikhil. '"Fancy Calculating Machine": Computers and Planning in Independent India'. *Modern Asian Studies* 52, no. 2 (2018): 421–457.

Ministry of Information and Broadcasting, Government of India. *India Has a Plan*. New Delhi: Publications Division, 1953.

Ministry of Information and Broadcasting, Government of India. *Public Participation in National Development*. New Delhi: Publications Division, April 1954.

Ministry of Information and Broadcasting, Government of India. *Report of the Study Team on Five Year Plan Publicity*. New Delhi: Publications Division, 1964.

Ministry of Information and Broadcasting, Government of India. *We Plan For Prosperity*. New Delhi: Publications Division, 1963.

Mitchell, Timothy. 'Fixing the Economy'. *Cultural Studies* 12, no. 1 (1998): 82–101.

Mukherjee, Radhakamal. 'Statistics in the Service of Planning'. *Sankhyā: The Indian Journal of Statistics* 7, no. 2 (November 1945): 173–175.

Myrdal, Gunnar. *Asian Drama: An Inquiry Into the Poverty of Nations*. Vol. 2. New York: The Twentieth Century Fund, 1968.

Nehru, Jawaharlal. *Selected Works of Jawaharlal Nehru*. 70 vols. Second Series. New Delhi: Jawaharlal Nehru Memorial Fund, 1984–2017.

Nehru, Jawaharlal. *The Discovery of India*. New Delhi: Oxford University Press, 1985.

Newbigin, Eleanor. *The Hindu Family and the Emergence of Modern India*. Cambridge: Cambridge University Press, 2013.

Newbigin, Eleanor. 'Accounting for the Nation, Marginalising the Empire: Taxable Capacity and Colonial Rule in the early Twentieth-Century'. *History of Political Economy* 52, no. 3 (May 2020): 455–472.

Palat, Madhavan K., ed. *Selected Works of Jawaharlal Nehru*. Vol. 53. Second Series. New Delhi: Jawaharlal Nehru Memorial Fund, 2014.

Palat, Madhavan K., ed. *Selected Works of Jawaharlal Nehru*. Vol. 57. Second Series. New Delhi: Jawaharlal Nehru Memorial Fund, 2014.

Parthasarathi, G., ed. *Jawaharlal Nehru: Letters to Chief Ministers, 1947–64*. Vol. 3. New Delhi: Oxford University Press, 1987.

Patel, I. G. *Glimpses of Indian Economic Policy: An Insider's View*. New Delhi: Oxford University Press, 2002.

Phalkey, Jahnavi. *Atomic State: Big Science in Twentieth-Century India*. Ranikhet: Permanent Black, 2013.

Planning Commission, Government of India. *University Planning Forums: Summary Record of Meetings, April 1956–September 1957*. New Delhi: Publications Division, 1957.

Planning Commission, Government of India. *University Planning Forums: A Review*. New Delhi: Publications Division, December 1958.

Planning Commission, Government of India. *Subhas Chandra Bose: Pioneer of Indian Planning.* New Delhi: Publications Division, 1997.

Planning Commission, Government of India. *Summary Record of Discussion of the National Development Council (NDC) Meetings, Vol. 1: 1st to 14th Meetings.* New Delhi: Publications Division, 2005.

Porter, Theodore M. *The Rise of Statistical Thinking: 1820–1900.* Princeton: Princeton University Press, 1988.

Porter, Theodore M. *Trust in Numbers: The Pursuit of Objectivity in Science and Public Life.* Princeton: Princeton University Press, 1996.

Prakash, Gyan. *Another Reason: Science and the Imagination of Modern India.* New Delhi: Oxford University Press, 2000.

Prakash, Gyan. *Emergency Chronicles: Indira Gandhi and Democracy's Turning Point.* Princeton: Princeton University Press, 2018.

Prakash, Gyan, Michael Laffan, and Nikhil Menon, eds., *The Postcolonial Moment in South and Southeast Asia.* London: Bloomsbury, 2018.

Rajaraman, V. *History of Computing in India (1955–2000).* Bangalore: IEEE Computer Society, 2012.

Rao, C. Radhakrishna, ed. *Essays on Econometrics and Planning: Presented to Professor P.C. Mahalanobis on the Occasion of His 70th Birthday.* New York: Pergamon Press, 1963.

Rao, C. Radhakrishna, ed. *Contributions to Statistics. Presented to P.C. Mahalanobis on the Occasion of His 70th Birthday.* Calcutta: Statistical Publishing Society, 1965.

Rao, C. Radhakrishna. 'Prasanta Chandra Mahalanobis 1893–1972'. *Biographical Memoirs of Fellows of the Royal Society* 19 (December 1973): 455.

Rao, C. Radhakrishna. 'Statistics Must Have a Purpose: The Mahalanobis Dictum'. *Sankhyā: Indian Journal of Statistics* 55, no. 3 (October 1993): 331–349.

Rao, C. Radhakrishna and P. C. Mahalanobis. *Contributions to Statistics. Presented to P.C. Mahalanobis on the Occasion of His 70th Birthday.* Oxford: Pergamon Press, 1965.

Rosen, George. *Globalization and Some of Its Discontents: The Autobiography of a Russian Immigrant.* Bloomington: Xlibris, 2005.

Roy, Asim. 'The High Politics of India's Partition: The Revisionist Perspective the High Politics of India's Partition: The Revisionist Perspective'. *Modern Asian Studies* 24, no. 2 (May 1990): 385–408.

Roy, Srirupa. *Beyond Belief: India and the Politics of Postcolonial Nationalism.* Ranikhet: Permanent Black, 2007.

Rudolph, Lloyd I. and Susanne Hoeber Rudolph. *In Pursuit of Lakshmi: The Political Economy of the Indian State.* Hyderabad: Orient Longman, 1998.

Rudra, Ashok. *Prasanta Chandra Mahalanobis: A Biography.* New Delhi: Oxford University Press, 1996.

Sackley, Nicole. 'Passage to Modernity: American Social Scientists, India, and the Pursuit of Development, 1945–1961'. PhD diss. Princeton University, 2004.

Sackley, Nicole. 'The Village as Cold War Site: Experts, Development, and the History of Rural Reconstruction'. *Journal of Global History* 6, no. 3 (November 2011): 481–504.

Sackley, Nicole. 'Village Models: Etawah, India, and the Making and Remaking of Development in the Early Cold War'. *Diplomatic History* 37, no. 4 (2013): 749–778.

Sanyal, H. 'Prasantachandra Mahalanobis: A Biographical Sketch'. *Sankhyā: Indian Journal of Statistics* 35 (December 1973): 3–11.

Sarkar, Sumit. 'Nationalism and Poverty: Discourses of Development and Culture in 20th Century India'. *Third World Quarterly* 29, no. 3 (2008): 429–445.

Schabas, Margaret. *The Natural Origins of Economics*. Chicago: University of Chicago Press, 2005.

Schultz, Anna Christine. 'Translated Fronts: Songs of Socialist Cosmopolitanism in Cold War India'. *History and Anthropology* 28, no. 1 (2017): 1–22.

Scott, James C. *Seeing Like a State: How Certain Schemes to Improve the Human Condition Have Failed*. New Haven: Yale University Press, 1998.

Sen, Amartya Kumar. *Development as Freedom*. New York: Anchor Books, 1999.

Shah, K. T., ed. *Woman's Role in Planned Economy*. National Planning Committee Series. Bombay: Vora, 1947.

Shah, K. T., ed. *Report: National Planning Committee*. Bombay: Vora, 1949.

Shani, Ornit. *How India Became Democratic: Citizenship and the Making of Universal Franchise*. Cambridge: Cambridge University Press, 2017.

Shankar Pillai, K. *Don't Spare Me Shankar*. New Delhi: Children's Book Trust, 1983.

Sharma, Dinesh C. *The Long Revolution: The Birth and Growth of India's IT Industry*. Noida: Harper Collins India, 2009.

Sherman, Taylor C. '"A New Type of Revolution": Socialist Thought in India, 1940s–1960s'. *Postcolonial Studies* 21, no. 4 (2018): 485–504.

Sherman, Taylor C. 'From "Grow More Food" to "Miss a Meal": Hunger, Development and the Limits of Post-Colonial Nationalism in India, 1947–1957'. *South Asia: Journal of South Asian Studies* 36, no. 4 (2013): 571–588.

Sherman, Taylor C., William Gould, and Sarah Ansari, eds., *From Subjects to Citizens: Society and the Everyday State in India and Pakistan, 1947–1970*. New Delhi: Cambridge University Press, 2014.

Sherman, Taylor C. 'Not Part of the Plan? Women, State Feminism and Indian Socialism in the Nehru Years'. *South Asia: Journal of South Asian Studies* 44, no. 2 (2021): 298–312.

Shyamasundar, R. K. and M. A. Pai, eds., *Homi Bhabha and the Computer Revolution*. New Delhi: Oxford University Press, 2011.

Siegel, Benjamin Robert. *Hungry Nation: Food, Famine, and the Making of Modern India*. Cambridge: Cambridge University Press, 2018.

Singh, Iqbal. *Between Two Fires: Towards an Understanding of Jawaharlal Nehru's Foreign Policy*. New Delhi: Orient Blackman, 1998.

Singh, Khushwant. *Truth, Love and a Little Malice: An Autobiography*. New Delhi: Penguin, 2002.

Singh, Tarlok. *India's Development Experience*. New Delhi: Macmillan India, 1974.

Sinha, Parasnath, ed. *The Path to Prosperity: A Collection of the Speeches and Writings of G.D. Birla*. Allahabad: The Leader Press, 1950.

Sinha, Subir. 'Lineages of the Developmentalist State: Transnationality and Village India, 1900–1965'. *Comparative Studies in Society and History* 50, no. 1 (2008): 57–90.

Slobodian, Quinn. *Globalists: The End of Empire and the Birth of Neoliberalism.* Cambridge, MA: Harvard University Press, 2018.

Smith, Donald E. *India as a Secular State.* Princeton: Princeton University Press, 1963.

Spiech, Daniel. 'The Uses of Global Abstraction: National Income Accounting in the Period of Imperial Decline'. *Journal of Global History* 6, no. 1 (2011): 7–28.

Srivastava, Sanjay. 'Voice, Gender and Space in Time of Five-Year Plans: The Idea of Lata Mangeshkar'. *Economic and Political Weekly* 39, no. 20 (15 May 2004): 2019–2028.

Sutoris, Peter. *Visions of Development: Films Division of India and the Imagination of Progress, 1948–75.* Oxford: Oxford University Press, 2016.

Tharoor, Shashi. *Nehru: The Invention of India.* New York: Arcade, 2003.

Tyabji, Nasir. *Forging Capitalism in Nehru's India: Neocolonialism and the State, c. 1940–1970.* Oxford: Oxford University Press, 2015.

Unger, Corinna R. 'Towards Global Equilibrium: American Foundations and Indian Modernization, 1950s to 1970s'. *Journal of Global History* 6, no. 1 (2011): 121–142.

Yashpal. *This is Not That Dawn* (translated from Hindi by Anand). New Delhi: Penguin, 2010.

Yates, Frank. 'The Work of the United Nations Sub-Commission on Statistical Sampling'. *Sankhyā: Indian Journal of Statistics* 12, no. 3 (June 1953): 15–16.

Zachariah, Benjamin. 'The Development of Professor Mahalanobis'. *Economy and Society* 26, no. 3 (1997): 434–444.

Zachariah, Benjamin. *Developing India: An Intellectual and Social History, c. 1930–50.* New Delhi: Oxford University Press, 2005.

Zamindar, Vazira Fazila-Yacoobali. *The Long Partition and the Making of Modern South Asia: Refugees, Boundaries, Histories.* New York: Columbia University Press, 2007.

Index

CPSIA information can be obtained
at www.ICGtesting.com
Printed in the USA
LVHW080035240322
714113LV00015B/516